WHAT DO WE WANT THE OTHER TO TEACH ABOUT US?

Edited by
David L. Coppola

CENTER FOR CHRISTIAN-JEWISH UNDERSTANDING OF
SACRED HEART UNIVERSITY PRESS
FAIRFIELD, CONNECTICUT

Production services: Miccinello Associates
Typesetting and design: Hill Lake Consortium
Cover design: Roberta Reynolds

Library of Congress Cataloging-in-Publication Data

Center for Christian-Jewish Understanding. Jewish, Christian, and Muslim education; interreligious dialogue
Conferences in Jerusalem; Edmonton, Canada; Rome, Italy; Bamberg, Germany; and Fairfield, Connecticut.
    What do we want the other to teach about us? Essays from
    The Center for Christian-Jewish Understanding in Fairfield, Connecticut,
    2000–2003. Edited by David L. Coppola.
        p. cm.
    Includes bibliographical references and index.
    ISBN 0-9675719-5-0
    1. 2. I. Coppola, David L., 1959- II. Title.

BL65.V55 C46 2006
291.1'7873—dc21

CONTENTS

PART III
What Do We Want the Other to Teach About Our Historical Traditions?

PREFACE

Thirteen years ago, Sacred Heart University embarked on a program to establish a Center that would seek to bring about greater theological understanding and dialogue between Christianity and Judaism. Our Center for Christian-Jewish Understanding now holds a place of respect in the American Catholic and Jewish communities for its efforts in this regard. As time has passed, we have been able to foster collaboration and friendships with Muslims who seek God's will and greater understanding among religions.

Several years ago, when we were discussing ways to improve and strengthen dialogue, we recognized that there were not available—at least not in English—any books that would assist religious leaders and educators at the local church, synagogue, congregation, or school and to have resources available to help them ask and frame the simple question, "What do we want the other to teach about us?" So, beginning in Jerusalem and then moving on to Edmonton, Canada; Rome; Germany; and concluding at Sacred Heart University, we sponsored a number of international conferences on this theme. Selected papers from these conferences have been gathered into this volume and we hope this initial effort will contribute greatly to the efforts of interreligious dialogue and peace.

On behalf of the entire Sacred Heart University community, I thank all who were part of this dialogue—this search for better understanding—in a world that is so desperately in need of such efforts. By reading and teaching the ideas contained in this volume, all of us are privileged to participate as God's partners in repairing the world in our time.

Anthony J. Cernera
President, Sacred Heart University
Fairfield, Connecticut

ACKNOWLEDGEMENTS

The five conferences, "What Do We Want the Other to Teach About Us," held in Jerusalem; Edmonton, Canada; Rome, Italy; Bamberg, Germany; and Fairfield, Connecticut, from 2000 to 2003 were sponsored by the Center for Christian-Jewish Understanding of Sacred Heart University, Fairfield, Connecticut, in collaboration with the Elijah Interfaith Institute, Jerusalem; the Edmonton Interfaith Centre for Education and Action, Canada; the University of Bamberg, Germany; and Sacred Heart University. All of us at the Center remain deeply grateful for the warm hospitality and support we enjoyed with the communities of each of these countries.

These conferences and this volume were made possible in part by the generous support of the Ridgefield Foundation, Connecticut; Mrs. Louella Lieberman, Connecticut; B.L. Manger Foundation, Connecticut; Mr. and Mrs. Gregory Milbank, New Jersey; Rich Foundation, Israel; Mr. and Mrs. Joseph Roxe, Connecticut; Mr. and Mrs. Barry Sternlicht, Connecticut; and Mr. and Mrs. Leo Van Munching, Connecticut.

We are especially grateful to the hundreds of people who encourage the Center's work and have helped to bring this important effort to completion so that we can now begin the vital work of teaching its hopeful message. In particular, we are thankful to the late Pope John Paul II; Cardinal Walter Kasper, president for the Pontifical Commission for Religious Relations with the Jews, and his esteemed predecessor, Cardinal Edward I. Cassidy; Dr. Anthony J. Cernera, president of Sacred Heart University; members of the Center for Christian-Jewish Understanding's Board of Directors: Dr. Howard Ehrenkranz, Dr. Thomas Forget, Mrs. Louella Lieberman, Dr. Laura Lustig, Mr. Gregory Millbank, Rev. Michael Moynihan, Mrs. Suzanne Newmark, Mr. Vincent Roberti, and Dr. John S. Tamerin; and to the Center's many supporters.

Finally, heartfelt thanks go out to Dr. David L. Coppola, my colleague and associate at the Center, and to all of the scholars whose preparation and participation at these conferences as well as their ongoing commitment to interreligious dialogue is a declaration of hope for the future.

Rabbi Joseph H. Ehrenkranz
Executive Director
Center for Christian-Jewish Understanding

To Teach About the Other

To those involved in religious education on the local level, a common observation is that there does not seem to be enough time to teach young or new members about the essentials of their own faith, let alone learn or teach about another person's faith. To engage in interreligious dialogue and learn about another religion and to teach about those beliefs seems to go beyond what is ordinarily required of a believer. It is no exaggeration to say that, for the first time in two millennia, Jews, Christians, and Muslims have the opportunity to put aside their divisiveness and seek reconciliation and understanding. This is an ideal time to remember the past and renew hopes for the future. An important means to pave the way for reconciliation and change is to learn and educate about the other.

As an academic and research division of Sacred Heart University, Fairfield, Connecticut, the Center for Christian-Jewish Understanding (CCJU) promotes forums for dialogue and study in order to advance greater knowledge, understanding, and harmony among religions. The Center wanted to make the most of this moment in history and proposed five conferences on the topic, "What Do We Want the Other to Teach About Us?" This four-year effort began in 2000 in Jerusalem and Edmonton, Canada, followed by conferences in Rome, Italy (2001), Bamberg, Germany (2002), and Fairfield, Connecticut (2003). These conferences are based on the mission of the CCJU, which advocates a respect for the dignity of all people, acknowledges a special relationship between Jews, Christians, and Muslims and works to further interreligious dialogue by teaching and living the principles outlined in the 1965 Vatican II document, *Nostra Aetate*, excerpted here:

In our age, when people are drawing more closely together and the bonds of friendship between different peoples are being strengthened, the Church examines with greater care the relation which she has to non-Christian religions. Ever aware of her duty to foster unity and charity among individuals, and even among nations, she reflects at the outset on what people have in common and what tends to promote unity among them. . . . Indeed, the Church reproves every form of persecution against whomsoever it may be directed. Remembering, then, her common heritage with the Jews and moved not by any political consideration, but solely by the religious motivation of Christian charity, she deplores all hatreds, persecutions, and displays of anti-Semitism leveled at any time or from any source against the Jews.

                                   –Vatican II. *Nostra Aetate* (28 October, 1965).

From this new seed of mutual respect, learning together, and teaching authentically about each other can come a living relationship to serve as a model for all who believe that God desires human beings to live together in friendship and peace. The movement from defensiveness and distrust to friendship built on security and equality is still a long way from being realized, but has its hope of success in dialogue.

A follow-up document to *Nostra Aetate*, the 1974 *Guidelines*, published by the Vatican's Commission for Religious Relations with the Jews, presents authentic dialogue as a process where each participant a) genuinely wishes to know the other; b) respects the other as the other is; c) respects the other's faith and the other's religious convictions; and d) respects the other's legitimate claim to religious liberty. In more poetic language, Ruel L. Howe writes in his 1963 work, *The Miracle of Dialogue* (Seabury Press), "Dialogue is to love, what blood is to the body. When the flow of blood stops, the body dies. When dialogue stops, love dies and resentment and hate are born" (p. 3).

As the number of people involved in interreligious dialogue continues to grow, more people need to understand accurately the "others," and they also desire to be understood and presented correctly by the others. Through these conferences and the model employed, the CCJU advocates that the process of dialogue should flow in that order—understanding others to being understood by others. After respecting the genuine needs of the others first, and attempting to understand them on their own terms, only then, as friendships and relationships mature, as each asks the other sincere questions, will it be important and appropriate to share honestly and reveal one's self and tradition.

But the sharing and teaching of knowledge must also remain faithful to the "insider's" understandings. The participants in interreligious dialogue agree to trust and respect each other enough to entrust each other with their sacred stories, experiences, historical events, interpretations, beliefs, mysteries, questions, and uncertainties. Each says to the other: "We trust you enough to share these ideas, insights, and sensibilities." "Do unto others" now means that you will teach about us how you would want us to teach about you—adequately, fairly, and respectfully. We become a mirror to each other where we can recognize our kinship with each other in the mystery of God.

When the question, "What do we want the other to teach about us?" is asked in the context of interreligious dialogue, an answer in the form of a reflection on faith or belief will be given. But that answer or reflection, *de facto*, becomes an invitation to another question, which generally implies, "Now that you have heard my response, what do you think?" And so a dialogue begins where each trusts the other enough to be honest and say what he or she does not understand. Each perceives the other's faith as a vocation, literally a calling from God who dialogues with humanity.

Jewish, Christian, and Muslim experiences of the Divine all point to God as One who teaches. It is, in turn, expected that followers will study what God has revealed and teach such revelations and commandments to future generations. Dialogue and education are tools for each to approach the other as people in relationship with God first, and not as objects spouting abstract beliefs. Happily, there is some truth to the notion that one learns something well when asked to teach it. In this sense, teaching demands more of a commitment to the other and his or her beliefs, rather than simply knowing or learning about the other. Moreover, to teach teachers is important work because, as Henry Brooks Adams (1838–1918) said so well, "A teacher affects eternity; he can never tell where his influence stops."[1] In the midst of a society that "teaches" values that are antireligious, xenophobic, hateful, immoral, and violent, the need for good teachers is, indeed, pressing. The result of the dialogue process will need to be as much a pedagogical as well as a theological process.

The topic "What Do We Want the Other to Teach About Us?" comes out of a sustained reflection on how each one of us is "other," "stranger," or "outsider" to someone else. This awareness of existential otherness gives each partner in the dialogue process the humility to proceed, in the words of Pope John Paul II, by "proposing" one's beliefs, rather than imposing them (*Veritas Splendor*, 1993, sec. 12, 35, 91, 95, 108, 110). The mutual blessing that arises out of this approach is that each understands himself or herself in a deeper and richer way by understanding and teaching about the other. Different perspectives help each partner in dialogue to clarify his or her own understandings and also help to clarify the other's without demonizing or persecuting the other.

An important feature of this process is that when one authentically teaches what the other wants to be taught, the teacher also communicates through his or her method and example, the convictions of respect, reverence, scholarship, and friendship for the other as a son or daughter of God. By influencing how other religions are taught in each religion's formal educational structures or through prayer and liturgy or by publications about the other or by the deliberate efforts made to include others at festivals or appropriate celebrations, the dignity of all can be affirmed.

This book is a collection of papers by religious leaders and scholars who are actively engaged in interreligious dialogue and are faithful believers in their own religious traditions and who participated in a CCJU-sponsored conference. These essays are meant to inspire continued dialogue and education in synagogues, churches and mosques as well as to be a resource for those who seek understanding and truth, and who work for peace through dialogue. Judaism, Christianity, and Islam teach that it is God's will that all people live in peace with each other. Peace will be advanced only when religious people and religious institutions are involved in intelligent, honest, respectful dialogue with each other and are integral to the processes of social justice in their communities. It is impossible to duplicate the living, breathing, inspiring presence of the other.

Although the papers included in this book are intended to be illustrative of some of the issues and the direction that interreligious dialogue is taking, they are not meant to be official or dogmatically authoritative teachings. Efforts were made to find presenters who could express ideas from the middle of the road in each religious tradition. However, as the conferences and discussions proceeded, the middle of the road moved with the winding and hilly terrain of different denominations and traditions of religions. Often intrareligious conversations were more challenging than interreligious ones. The ideas and approaches presented are representative and widely held, but they are not exclusively normative. The reader of this collection will most likely take issue with or can nuance at least one aspect presented by a scholar in one's own tradition. This is to be expected and welcomed so that the volume has vitality and can be used with flexibility depending upon each teacher's personal resources and background.

Further, these papers are neither equal nor parallel. It turns out that, although they are all written in or translated into English, the categories and methodologies originally assumed to be broad and inclusive for study and discussion were rightly challenged by the participants as being skewed on the side of western Christianity. The result is that the book is not completely representative (as probably any book attempting this effort would not be). Rather, it is illustrative and ends up being a volume that introduces to both scholar and student some important ideas and issues with suggested ways to wrestle with profound questions of faith and religious practice.

I have included an introduction to each section of the book to set the context of the conferences and the principal ideas discussed. Additionally, each section concludes with connections, observations, and questions meant to spur further study and conversation. The questions are posed as a way to view the papers, but also allow for tailored discussions about both theoretical and practical issues.

It is a great responsibility and a great honor to help influence how the other is taught. This book is best used and discussed in the presence of the other so that he or she can define, clarify, nuance, and situate topics and categories according to his or her natural methods and traditions, as well as his or her own unique life witness. This book is not intended to be a simplified handbook of the other or to substitute for real human interaction and dialogue between religious and ethical people. It is an initial introduction to the other into very important and strongly held beliefs and traditions. When dialoguing with and learning with others, one may also be challenged to look deeper into one's own beliefs and assumptions.

Truth can be found in the experiences of individuals in their journeys towards holiness and wisdom as well as in learned theological teachings. The more one is in the presence of other believers, the more one is invited to strengthen one's religious beliefs and come to know the deeper truths of one's own tradition. It is hoped that such conversations will help to inspire Jews to be better Jews; Christians, better Christians; Muslims, better Muslims, and all God's people to act justly, and walk humbly before their God.

Portions of these papers, as well as interpretive commentary, have been published previously in the semiannual periodical, *CCJU Perspective* and on the Center's website, www.ccju.org.

David L. Coppola, PhD
Associate Executive Director
Center for Christian-Jewish Understanding

Note

i. *The Education of Henry Adams*. (1907). Chapter 4, p. 20.

PART I

Setting a Context for Dialogue

R E M I   H O E C K M A N ,   O P

The Sacred Space of Dialogue

Religions should meet where religions take their course, in God."[1] This is the perspective of the reflections which I would like to share with you this evening. They are not meant to anticipate the theological content of this conference. They only wish to offer a theological starting point from which we might like our work to proceed.

In the Book of Genesis we read: "Then God said, 'Let us make humankind in our image, according to our likeness'. . . . So God created humankind in His image, in the image of God he created them; male and female he created them" (1:26, 27).[2] Thus the human person, created by God in His image, is created 'capable of God' (*capax Dei*), capable of living in the presence of God, capable of relationship with God and with other human beings, capable of divine revelation.

"In his goodness and wisdom, God chose to reveal Himself." These words are taken from the Second Vatican Council's Dogmatic Constitution on Divine Revelation (*Dei Verbum*) which, inspired by the Sacred Scriptures, elaborates on them saying: "Through this revelation . . . the invisible God, out of the abundance of His love, speaks to men as friends (cf. Exodus 33:11; John 15: 14–15) and lives among them."[3]

According to the Christian faith, God came to live among them in a most eminent way in His Son, the Eternal Word. This understanding is essential to our Christian identity but is not part of the religious faith of Jews or Muslims. Yet, I think that all who belong to what is called the great Abrahamic tradition, in the utmost respect of each other's different faith identities, can stand together in recognizing in the One Almighty and Merciful God, a God Who has chosen to relate to us, to speak with us, to seek us out when we hide from Him. As the Bible says, "They heard the sound of the Lord God walking in the garden at the time of the evening breeze, and the man and his wife hid themselves from the presence of the Lord God among the trees of the garden. But the Lord God called to the man, and said to him, 'Where are you?'" (Genesis 3:8–9).

God is a relating God indeed, and I believe that this is what He wants us to be too: relating people, people of dialogue with Him and with one another. Did the Lord God not ask Cain, after Cain had killed his brother Abel, "Where is your brother?" (Genesis 4:9). Are the questions that God asks Adam and Eve and Cain in the Bible not put to us as well? I believe they are. In my own life I have come to realize that I cannot truly answer God's question, "Where are you?" without answering the other question as well, "Where is your brother?" That is why interreligious dialogue, i.e., a genuine dialogue between persons of faith, seems imperative to me; it is the real reason that must underlie all other reasons (and good reasons at that) that may be linked to particular contexts, emergencies, or just good opportunities. But let me qualify this affirmation by affirming again that such a dialogue can only and truly take place between persons of informed faith, between people who know their religious tradition, are nourished by it, feel secure in it, and who, therefore, are able to respect the faith tradition, and the faith experience, of the other. The Second Vatican Council's Declaration *Nostra Aetate* aims precisely at that.

In number 3, referring to the Islamic religion, it says that "upon the Muslims, the Church looks with esteem," because "they adore God, living and enduring, merciful and all-powerful, Maker of heaven and earth and Speaker to men." It urges Muslims and Christians "to strive sincerely for mutual understanding," and "to make common cause of safeguarding and fostering social justice, moral values, peace, and freedom."

In number 4, referring to the Jews and Judaism, *Nostra Aetate* states: "Since the spiritual patrimony common to Christians and Jews is thus so great, this sacred Synod [i.e., the Second Vatican Council] wishes to foster and recommend that mutual understanding and respect which is the fruit above all of biblical and theological studies, and of brotherly dialogues."

And in number 5, *Nostra Aetate* concludes: "We cannot in truthfulness call upon that God who is the Father of all if we refuse to act in a brotherly way toward . . . men. A man's relationship with God the Father, and his relationship with his brother men, are so linked together that

Scripture says: 'He who does not love does not know God' (1 John. 4:8)." This teaching is binding for us. In a Catholic understanding, conciliar documents such as *Nostra Aetate* are held to be inspired by the Holy Spirit of God who, we believe, assists, illuminates and, if need be corrects our processes of reflection and decision-making. If, therefore, according to our Catholic faith the Holy Spirit is behind *Nostra Aetate*, the teaching of this document is part of our obedient response to God; we cannot draw back from it. As Pope John Paul II has put it at the start of the *World Day of Prayer for Peace* in Assisi in October 1986, addressing persons of other faiths: "It is, in fact, my faith conviction which has made me turn to you."

2

In November 1999, Cardinal Edward Cassidy, together with Rabbi Irving Greenberg, received the *Nostra Aetate Award* from the Center for Christian-Jewish Understanding of Sacred Heart University. On that occasion he spoke on the subject "Dialogue in Our Time"—obviously in the context of Catholic-Jewish relations—and said: "We have traveled quite a long way together since *Nostra Aetate* was promulgated in 1965. We have built a completely new relationship between our communities, a solid relationship that will last, no matter what storms may come to try us or new obstacles obstruct our path." And he quite correctly added: "Credit for this is due to members of both our communities: to the Catholic Church which in *Nostra Aetate* offered the hand of friendship, and the Jewish community, which despite its memory of past experiences, took that hand and began our common journey of reconciliation. Our success has been due to sincere dialogue."

Looking back at the thirty-five years that have gone by since that common journey began, we must admit that it has not been an easy venture at all, but then, this is perhaps a reason for believing that the results will last. Unfortunately, not all who could have made a constructive contribution to it, whose positive participation could have made a difference, have shown the respect for the other that is essential for dialogue. However, all those who did—and some of them are here with us this evening—may give thanks to God for all the good that has happened with His help, while praying for the wisdom and the courage to move forward together, step by step and in the right direction, being aware that patience with one another, and, above all, deep respect for one another, will illuminate our path, while suspicion or contempt will obscure it.

A sincere encounter between Christians and Jews, Jews and Muslims, Muslims and Christians, in fact, all of us who claim to belong to the Abrahamic tradition can be of benefit to ourselves, in the sense that it can teach us both pride in our own spiritual heritage and humility in the face of the spiritual heritage of the other. "By dialogue we let God be present in our midst; for as we open ourselves in dialogue to one another, we also open ourselves to God."[4] It can also be, and will be, of benefit to those people and societies who no longer have room for God and, therefore, for people of faith in God, people who wish to live according to God's will. In fact, the erosion or the distortion of the religious values in some of our societies today do have a destructive effect on the respect for human life and human dignity, or on the respect for creation, which our religious traditions uphold. As Cardinal Cassidy has reminded us at an important meeting of Catholic and Jewish leadership in Prague, in 1990, "Let us not forget that . . . those who created the gas chambers and the gulags were atheists who, while denying the existence of God, acted as though they themselves were God." There is no reason to trust that also today or tomorrow, men and women without faith will not consider themselves equal to the God they deny. On the other hand, in some parts of our respective religious constituencies—Jewish, Christian, Muslim—there are people who in the name of religion and faith, and indeed in the name of God himself, do act as if they were God. Those people are not with us here this evening. They are not interested in dialogue. Is it not sad that their ways often become the public trademark for what religion is not?

3

A few years ago, I heard Daniel Rossing speak in Jerusalem about "the sacred space of dialogue." He spoke of the need to cleanse our hearts and minds before entering it. That is also what Pope John Paul II had in mind when he called upon the Catholic faithful—in his Apostolic Letter *Tertio Millennio Adveniente* published on November 10, 1994—to get ready for entering the third millennium in which, he hopes, people of faith, individually and together, will show "how religious belief inspires peace, encourages solidarity, promotes justice and upholds liberty." He told the two hundred participants from some fifty countries, and representing some twenty different religious traditions, gathered in Vatican City October 25–28, 1999, "The task before us is to promote a culture of dialogue." This task will require, from those who wish to share the Holy Father's hope, a willingness to purify themselves of contempt, prejudice, perhaps of suspicion and lingering hurt. They will need to learn the respect for difference and the readiness to meet with one who might not so much be in their image, but who is, nonetheless, in the image of God. Indeed, is it not in meeting the other under the gaze of God that our perception of the other can change, thus creating within us and between us that 'sacred space' which enabled Jacob to turn to his brother Esau saying, "I have seen your face as one sees the face of God" (cf. Genesis 33:10), and felt blessed by it? Of course, such an understanding of the interfaith encounter might have theological implications which, I suspect, we have hardly begun to see. But, then, is this not part of our future agenda?

4

In this Conference we want to focus our attention specifically on the question, "What do we want the other to teach about us?" History has painfully shown how important this question is, and, I would say, how very important education is in this regard. Education is the master key which opens the door to that space in a person where the deepest aspirations and expectations move, the God-given depth which allows a person to give and to receive, to reach out and to be reached, to seek and to be found, to relate and to respond, to choose and to decide, to unify tensions, to overcome limitations, to integrate differences. It is the original space in a person which is really a religious space, tending toward self, toward another, toward one another, and ultimately toward the other. It is the space that allows me to realize that you are not me and I am not you, yet that it is in our mutual otherness that we can build relationship. Rabbi Jonathan Sacks, Chief Rabbi of Great Britain, has put it like this: "If I am I and you are you, we no longer threaten one another, for we each have our own blessing."[5]

This has not been an easy discovery, Rabbi Jonathan Sacks admits— "It took many years, it took a deep inner struggle; after it Jacob limped . . .," he said, but without the 35 years of interreligious relationships and dialogue (since the promulgation of *Nostra Aetate*) many of us may not have started the process of discovery yet.

Returning to the question, "What do we want the other to teach about us?" I think I should like to put it differently, namely, "How do we want the other to teach about us?" or, and this might even be a better way to put it, "What do we want the other to learn about us?" I know, of course, that with regard to the content, this Conference will deal with "what" each religion would like the other to teach about its key theological concepts. With regard to the "how" I would like to recall a meeting that took place in Rome in December, 1970 between our office and members of the International Jewish Committee on Interreligious Consultations. The meeting agreed on a *Memorandum* which was the first step for the creation of a kind of permanent forum for dialogue, an International Liaison Committee between the Catholic Church and the world Jewish Community. The meeting dealt with the same question we are dealing with, and the answer was: we need to present the other adequately, fairly, and respectfully, i.e., truthful to the manner in which the other understands and identifies him- or herself, "in order to further the understanding both of each other and of our common responsibility to humanity and the world."[6]

It is interesting to note that already at that early stage in Catholic-Jewish relations, the ultimate goal of the dialogue was perceived beyond the dialogue itself, namely in "a common search for a more harmonious and peaceful world."[7] And reflecting on the interreligious dialogue between Muslims and Christians, at the General Audience on May 5, 1999, Pope John Paul II pointed in the same direction: "Interreligious dialogue which leads to a deeper knowledge and esteem for others is a great sign of hope" for the people in our secular societies, he said, concluding: "By walking together on the path of reconciliation . . . the two religions [Christianity and Islam] will be able to offer a sign of hope, radiating in the world the wisdom and mercy of that one God who created and governs the human family."

In fact, "let us not forget," Cardinal Francis Arinze told the representatives of the world's religions gathered in the Vatican in October of last year, "that religion is the soul of society; it is like leaven that can transform humanity."[8] Rabbi Jonathan Sacks has put it even more strongly: [In today's society, and for its sake] "we must begin to restate the interreligious imperative in more forceful terms. We must see it not simply as a gesture of good will, undertaken by men and women of exceptional liberalism and vision; but as a set of religious axioms that must be confronted by all believers. . . . What impels me to enter into the conversation with men and women of other faiths? If I can answer that question then I have provided an impetus to the interfaith encounter which goes beyond the mood of the moment, and reaches into the roots of faith."[9] Such an approach which is a religious approach to interreligious dialogue (however strange the emphasis might sound!), will help to prevent it from becoming "interreligious opportunism," or from being hijacked by agendas that have little to do with religion and faith. Yet, that risk is real; we must look out for it.

This is why, in my opinion, point number one on the interreligious agenda must be the interreligious dialogue itself, namely the care and the concern for a respectful encounter between persons of faith, who, without blurring the differences between their respective religious faith experiences, and, indeed, their respective faith expectations, nevertheless are willing and able to relate their own faith experience to the faith experience of the other, willing to learn about it and, eventually, also from it. This first asks of them "patient listening, mutual trust, and honest sharing."[10] It also asks of them their prayer.

Point number two on the interreligious agenda would then be the effort to seek together the common ground that people of faith have, the common values they share, enabling them to stand together against the evils of a godless world. As the participants of the Vatican 1999 Interreligious Assembly stated in their *Message:*

> We are convinced that our religious traditions have the necessary resources to overcome the fragmentations which we observe in the world, and to foster mutual friendship and respect between peoples. We are aware that many tragic conflicts around the world are the result of the pragmatic but often unjust association of religions with nationalistic, political, economic or other interest. We are aware that if we do not fulfill our obligation to live out the highest ideals of our religious traditions, then we shall be held liable for the consequences. . . . We know that the problems in the world are so great that we cannot solve them alone. Therefore there is an urgent need for interreligious collaboration. . . . We appeal to religious leaders to promote the spirit of dialogue within their respective communities, and to be ready to engage in dialogue themselves

with civil society. . . . In the spirit of the Jubilee, we appeal to each one
of us . . . to seek forgiveness for past wrongs, to promote reconciliation
where the painful experiences of the past have brought divisiveness and
hatred.

My friends, this message from the representatives of different religious
traditions (Jews, Christians, Muslims, Buddhists, Hindus and many others) from around the world is a message of hope, indeed. It corresponds to
what Pope John Paul II had shared with them: "I have always believed
that religious leaders have a vital role to play in nurturing that hope of justice and peace without which there will be no future worthy of humanity,"
he said. He added, "Our hope rises not merely from the capacities of the
human heart and mind . . . it has a divine dimension. Awareness that the
Spirit of God works where he wills (cf. John 3:8) . . . evokes appreciation
of what lies hidden in the hearts of others."[11] Our commitment must be to
approach that reality, where the divine meets the human, with reverence;
to enter that space with awe, for it is, indeed, sacred.

5

In May, 2000, a Jewish-Catholic conference will be held in London at the
initiative of the leadership of Reform Judaism/Reform Synagogues of
Great Britain. This Conference which will bring Jewish and Catholic
scholars together, intends to explore "The Theology of Partnership." Our
Commission supports the initiative, as it also supports this conference
sponsored by the Center for Christian-Jewish Understanding, because we
think that the idea of engaging in a theological dialogue at this point in
our relationship is possible and necessary and is a sign of maturity.

Referring to *Nostra Aetate*'s recommendation in this regard, Pope
John Paul II on April 19, 1985 addressed the Catholic and Jewish participants of a theological colloquium that took place at my university (the
Angelicum) in Rome. He said: "Jews and Christians must get to know
each other better. Not just superficially as people of different religions,
merely coexisting in the same place, but as members of such religions
which are so closely linked to one another. This implies that Christians
try to know as exactly as possible the distinctive beliefs, religious practices, and spirituality of Jews, and conversely that Jews try to know the
beliefs and practices and spirituality of Christians."

The pope further developed this thought one year later when he received the participants of the second Angelicum Colloquium, on November 6, 1986. Although the specific context in which he spoke was again a gathering of Catholic and Jewish theologians, I believe that the development of his thought makes provision for including the three Abrahamic faith traditions:

> Theological reflection is part of the proper response of human intelligence and so gives witness to our conscious acceptance of God's will. At the same time, the other human sciences, such as history, philosophy, and art, also offer their own contribution to an organic deepening of our faith. This is why . . . [our] traditions have always had such high appreciation for religious study. Honoring our respective traditions, theological dialogue based on sincere esteem can contribute greatly to mutual knowledge of our respective patrimonies of faith and can help us to be more aware of our links with one another in terms of our understanding of salvation. . . .
>
> Your colloquium can help to avoid the misunderstanding of syncretism, the confusion of one another's identities as believers, the shadow and suspicion of proselytism. This mutual effort will certainly deepen our common commitment to the building of justice and peace among all people, children of the one heavenly Father."

The Pope speaks about "mutual knowledge of our respective patrimonies of faith" and "our conscious acceptance of God's will." Is that mutual knowledge not a part of God's gift? I believe it is. I believe that it will help us to become witnesses to that gift in a secular world, as I also believe that "the strength of witness lies in the fact that it is shared."[12]

Notes

1. Marcus Braybrooke, *Time to Meet—Towards a Deeper Relationship Between Jews and Christians*, London/Philadelphia 1990, p.152.

2. The New Revised Standard Version–Catholic Edition.

3. n. 2

4. Pope John Paul II, addressing member of other religions in Madras, India, on 5 February 1986. *Cf. L'Osservatore Romano,* English edition, 10 February 1986, p. 14. *Cf.* also Jonathan SACKS, *Living Together: The Interfaith Imperative,* in *United Religions,* issue 5, p. 2.

5. In an address to a conference of the International Council of Christians and Jews, Rocca di Papa/Rome, in September 1997.

6. Cf. the document *Guidelines and Suggestions for Implementing the Conciliar Declaration Nostra Aetate,* published by the Holy See Commission for Religious Relations with the Jews on 1 December 1974.

7. Cardinal Francis Arinze in his Opening Address to the World Assembly of Religions, Vatican City, 25 October 1999.

8. *Ibid.*

9. In *Living Together,* cf. above, p. 4.

10. *Idem.*

11. In his address delivered in St. Peter's Square on the evening of 28 October 1999.

12. Pope John Paul II to the Interreligious Assembly in Vatican City, on 28 October 1999.

Tsvi Blanchard

Is There a Moral Imperative to Engage in Interfaith Dialogue?

Moving Away from Competition, Zero Sum Games, and Fear

We know that people come from multiple faiths. Historically, it was rarely the case that people spoke to each other in anything that could be termed "dialogue." Of course, sometimes they did not speak to each other at all. They engaged in hostile actions across borders, especially where religious ideology was partnered with the exercise of political or economic power. At other times there were verbal exchanges, but they were often hostile. Someone always seemed to be on the defensive—more disputation than dialogue.

The Enlightenment brought with it a critique of the role of religion and its supposed dangers and abuses of power. Although this critique was extreme at first, over the course of time it became a central way to understand the West, especially with the rise of increasingly secular economic, social, and political spheres. As a result, people are no longer beholden to triumphal views about their relationship with the world or with God. This has not been true for most of human history. Religious faith was very closely connected to economic power, ideological power, to political power and its control over territory. In fact, I believe it was too connected, and the stakes were too high. Some religious people may wish for the "good old days," but for most of us, the lowering of the stakes has freed us from a paradigm of fear. We were terrified to talk to each other because there was too much at stake.

The reasons for fear disappear when within the sphere of human life, one can actually have a conversation about important things without fear of reprisal. As this kind of dialogue takes place, it is much easier to put behind us a paradigm of fear. Additionally, if we do not need to be afraid of talking to each other, then we can also interact without fear of losing adherents to another religious or political group, and we do not have to fear that the entire community will unravel because people will come to believe things that they are not supposed to believe. Moving away from fear allows us to also move away from notions of competition where religious faith is a matter of a zero sum game—if they get someone, we lose; if they change their minds, we win.

After the Enlightenment, it is possible to engage in genuine interreligious dialogue. We now ask: is there a moral imperative to engage in such interreligious dialogue? Until now, it was not a viable possibility. There was too much fear and there was too much negative competition. Of course, we have to be sympathetic, I think, to the realities of what life was like then. But now that those realities have shifted, the question emerges whether or not one should engage in this kind of dialogue. The question has moved from the possibility of dialogue, to the degree—if any—of moral necessity or obligation. If so, what kind might that be and if not, why not?

Why are we asking this question? One of the forces fueling our interest in this question is that there has been much intellectual and social fluidity in religious matters, especially in the United States of America. People move in and out of their religious views quickly. As a result, many people with religious convictions sense that it is good to be talking to each other, if only to create some depth of conviction and stability of commitment. Many people rightly question the direction and integrity of religious faith when someone can get up on any given morning and say to himself or herself, "This Saturday or Sunday I think I'll try a new denomination, and if I don't like it, next week I'll try something else." Faith has a way of asking, where is the place of integrity in so fluid an approach? And so, if we are to talk together about important matters of faith, it has to be in a situation where the integrity of the participants and the dialogue is preserved.

I am not interesting in examining the moral imperative to get together and "make nice," although I suppose that there is such a moral imperative. Granted, if we live in the same place with other people, then we ought to get together and be civil and not hurt other people or persecute them. We all know this. But, let us examine a deeper question, one that has to do with more than self-preservation. This kind of dialogue would leave the integrity of faith positions intact and would not require them to be altered or neatly fit into categories or expressions simply because other people would be comfortable with them. We want to talk about dialogue as something which, in and of itself, shares in the Enlightenment tradition of tolerance, of accepting different positions, and of a recognizing the value of the other. I am proposing such a direction and journey. Allow me to offer a brief picture of the itinerary.

First, what are the typical reasons offered for participating in interfaith dialogue? I will group them generally and then, focus more specifically on the scope an imperative could take. Second, what is the scope of the dialogue itself and how far ranging is it? Third, what are the paradigm positions and what do the arguments then look like?

If the question is asked, "Is there a moral imperative to do something?" the mere mention of the word "imperative" would make some people uncomfortable and question whether these interfaith issues comprise a discussion about morality. But our discussion must be broad enough so that it opens plenty of doors for the reader or for the listener to go through. In this sense, any imperative for dialogue must rely on choice and must be free. Once positions are laid out, what do the terms of the conversation look like? What kind of forces or agents should initiate this kind of dialogue? What pushes a moral imperative from theory into acted-upon reality? What would make such dialogue really work? I believe that if one discusses matters of moral obligation, there ought to be some discussion of what the institutionalization of those obligations would look like. That will, I suppose, bring us then to discuss what kinds of discourse or languages this kind of morally driven dialogue would employ.

There are many ways to come to interfaith dialogue in addition to the one I am proposing here. This particular direction is steered by the question, "is there a moral imperative?" Should more people engage in interfaith dialogue? There certainly are dialogues without an imperative. For example, is there a moral imperative to agree and engage in dialogue about the meaning of popular movies? I probably would lean more in the direction of no. Certainly, there is no moral imperative to discuss differences in food tastes. But, our topic seems to be of a different order of things. I am asking whether or not interfaith dialogue is something one and all must do as part of one's religious practice.

Amicable Relationships

In order to answer our question, allow me to summarize the kinds of rationales that have been suggested as reasons to engage in such dialogue. First, some say we engage in interfaith dialogue because we want to promote amicable relationships among groups. We want to avoid social hatred or doing damage to others and we want to promote forms of "social love," mutual support, solidarity, a sense of mutual connection with citizens, and our joint responsibility toward each other. On this view, one might have a moral responsibility to engage in interreligious dialogue because it accomplishes something that other methods cannot accomplish. This reason or cluster of reasons would call for the kind of dialogue that has, as its end, a realized sense that we were in the same boat, that we were citizens, and as such, we could not divorce our religious identities from our citizenship and from our participation in civil society. And, since we can not separate our religious faith identities from our participation and also because it is a fundamental value of ours to have a civil society in which we are amicable toward each other and we do not hate each other, then at the very least, one could argue that we ought to be engaged in interfaith dialogue to make sure that we get along with each other, especially in contexts where coercion is inappropriate.

This is a minimalist perspective. It is similar to the dynamic that occurs when couples, after verbally or physically beating the daylights out of each other, show up in a therapist's office and have conversations that help them resolve problems and deal with things. Afterwards, they have more amicable relations. I do not wish to make light of such situations, but this seems to be the minimum two people could expect from a marriage. Of course, this reason for interreligious dialogue is based on the premise that our faith commitments can not be put on the side when we enter into civic society or a political society. Since such beliefs can not simply be pushed aside, we are obligated to do something to see to it that our social and political relationships connect our religious and faith identities in ways that are positive, amicable, and avoid hatred. In the end, if I understand you better, I am probably less likely to spread nasty rumors about you and burn down your house.

As an argument for interreligious dialogue, this first reason presents a thin case. I do not mean it is a poor case. It just does not get one very far. We could spend the whole evening talking to people and not understand them very well and not be able to report back anything we heard in any detail. But so what? We liked them because they were funny and interesting and they nodded when we spoke. At least at the end of our shared time we thought, "I could not possibly hurt a nice guy like that or his family and friends." Again I am not making light of this because social solidarity is a very important starting point.

A Second Reason: Learning About Others

Sometimes we engage in dialogue because it helps us to learn about others, promotes mutual understanding and helps us to see others more accurately, thus avoiding damaging stereotypes leading again to violence. This is our second group of arguments for an imperative to engage in dialogue. For some people, it would be enough to say that understanding the other better is a positive good in itself. Understanding can be seen as a manifestation of intellectual virtue, which we are morally obliged to cultivate.

Some may counter, "So what if I misunderstand you? I do not understand a lot of people and I do not understand everything. What do we really know anyway?" I suggest that the abdication of a responsibility to understand other people can lead to the dissolution of social responsibility. Ignorance is devastating in its ability to impel people to act violently. People react and respond in damaging ways when they do not understand the other. If a person is convinced that you believe in a strange and terrible doctrine, then you will be perceived as a danger to society and he or she is going to do something to prevent you from acting on such a belief. On the other hand, if dialogue occurs, false and pernicious stereotypes no longer satisfy the participants. In sum, there are really two reasons. Either one thinks that understanding others is in and of itself intrinsically good, and therefore, something that one is morally obligated to pursue in some way; or one thinks that even if it is not intrinsically good, it is instrumental as in the first view, that people have to get along with each other in a secure and free society. I am not providing evidence for this second view for the moment; I am only suggesting that many thinkers would not attempt to separate knowledge or understanding from ethical behavior. One cannot exist without the other.

A Third Reason: Learning from Others

A third set of arguments encourages not only learning about others, but learning *from* others. This set of arguments says that we are engaged as human beings in a mutual search for truth and wisdom. That is what it means to be a human: to come to understand the world and how we are to live in it together. Humans want to gain new knowledge, especially in areas where we have shared language, desires, and life. In particular, we want to share enough to have serious conversations in the search for understanding and wisdom. There is a kind of synergy that results from alternative and parallel views being presented and discussed. This is true as a basic view, and I do not think many would dispute this.

If a person wants to learn about something, he or she would not put everyone who agrees and is of the same mind in the same room. He or she would try to include some people who disagree or have different perspectives. And one would expect that, at the end of the day, if they disagreed with each other, both would likely finish knowing more than when they began their search for knowledge. The entire academic enterprise, for example, is based on the notion that if people who do not share the same views are engaged in a conversation with each other, they will probably generate new possibilities and ideas. It is essential for the process of scientific investigation, for example, that one's view be tested against other views and that one is open to criticism for the improvement of all. This is true of the social sciences and the natural sciences. In my case, I would say that there is not a greater repository of human wisdom than what faith traditions bring to the table. If we bring them together and people have a conversation, they will learn not only about each other, they will learn from each other.

I take this argument seriously because I am trying to understand the world and I am obligated to do so. In turn, my morality will have to follow my understanding of the world. That is why I would include intellectual virtues on the list of moral virtues. That is, if it is important morally to know more, rather than less, about the world, then there are certain habits of mind that need to be developed in order to fulfill this obligation.

Living Together

A student once asked me what was wrong with sloppy thinking. Falsehood has emerged from sloppy thinking and careful thinking alike, he contended. I told him that I think that to prefer sloppy thinking is a way of being in the world that stakes out a moral position—the position that it does not matter how carefully one thinks, nor what one concludes. The process and purpose of seeking answers are both denigrated. And a question about practical reason then arises: what governs how we ought to think about doing something? If it does not matter what we believe, then there does not have to be evidence for our beliefs. I do not share this view. I believe that interreligious dialogue would help us to discover important things together, that people are motivated by the mutual search for wisdom. If we live together, then there are areas of policy which we cannot avoid making decisions about together. I believe that how we make decisions is important. We do not want to make important social decisions by drawing balls from an urn. We should make those decisions about social welfare, war, or ethical relations within society, by discussing them together, and that means including religious and spiritual insights in those conversations. In present-day America, to prefer ignorance is to submit to a comfortable, but lazy and fallacious individualism.

What about believers? People from a faith tradition are going to have a difficult time saying that they belong to a faith tradition, that it has great wisdom, and yet, that faith tradition is irrelevant to the most important events of the day. If so, then either we do not have a very deep faith, or we are afraid to bring it up. We need to design a dialogue so that one can speak unafraid. If I am correct, that there must or at least will be a religious or faith dimension to dimension in public square discussions, then there would be a strong argument for doing so in a free dialogue rather than an atmosphere of hostility or coercion. If our goal is to meaningfully engage people about important social concerns, dialogue will accomplish this better than force. We share our lives and world together. We are connected to other people and we can not stop being connected to them. Language is one of the essential dimensions that connects us. Careful interreligious dialogue requires reasoned language, allows us to talk honestly to each other, to agree on rhetorical moves, to understand what is persuasive and what is not, and to lend legitimacy to all parties involved. We want to do things together. What should we do about the fact that people are going to go to bed tonight without any place to sleep? No one from a faith community can disinterestedly say, "So what?"

Some 20 years ago, I was asked by the American Jewish Committee to write a paper discussing whether or not there was an obligation to engage in interfaith dialogue in order to come to greater understanding of God. As an Orthodox rabbi, they expected I would oppose it. I did and God humbled me because within three years I had changed my mind. Why? At that time in Chicago, the late Cardinal Joseph Bernardin was the archbishop of Chicago. He had a very sophisticated mind and way of doing theology. He helped his people to develop a way of speaking about the issues of the day which could be shared by others besides those who were Roman Catholic. He was not put off by detractors and proposed morality as a "seamless garment of life" that draws many issues together. These discussions had a terrific impact upon those of us who were involved. We felt that we were in a conversation in which we could talk about our human, spiritual, and wisdom convictions and how these beliefs holistically informed discussions about poverty, homelessness, injustice, abortion and war. We saw these discussions as a way to improve society and keep us from social hatred. We were brought closer together by learning from and about each other, and we could do things together to learn about wisdom or find a way to promote equitable social policy. It would be difficult to work to achieve a tax rate to feed the poor if the only reason for feeding the poor is the avoidance of class warfare. On the other hand, when there are deep spiritual reasons for taking care of those who are vulnerable, then people will make sacrifices and be motivated to make a positive change. In short, I learned that we must have some kind of interfaith dialogue so that we can promote a social policy that actually reflects our genuine passions and ideals.

The Scope of Moral Imperatives

As I have presented these different reasons and hence differing moral imperatives for interreligious dialogue, it is clear that the obligations supported by such imperatives do not fall on every member of society at the same time. We need to remember that there are imperatives that belong to us as individuals. There are moral obligations, for example, to pay the debts that one incurs. Everyone who incurs a debt has a moral obligation to do so. Do we have a moral obligation to refrain from verbally or physically abusing our neighbor? Yes. It is not just my obligation or your obligation. It belongs to all of us as individuals.

However, there are other obligations that are appropriate to specific groups in society. For example, we have a moral obligation to provide for the vulnerable among us. If someone is sick and ill and cannot afford to take care of himself, then there is a moral obligation on the part of society to see to it that such a person is helped. But is that for all of us to do right now? No. There are some people who will be assigned one task, and others another task. Some people will not participate directly at all. If a person lives below the poverty level income, he or she will pay no taxes and will not even contribute by having a percentage go to social welfare payments. Not every imperative implies that each and every person must oblige always and everywhere. There is a communal imperative, and then the community has to figure out how to get the job done. But, such responsibility does not stipulate that any specific one of us must assume this kind of imperative. Additionally, these obligations would make no sense unless done in a conscious, articulated, public way so that people say as a community there is an imperative to participate in some form of interreligious dialogue. To the extent to which interreligious dialogue has to be public, then the dialogue is going to deal with areas of shared concern.

The scope of this kind of dialogue has to be wide. If it is going to be public and communal, then we are going to have to meet the mutually-agreed-upon criterion of fairness. There must be some ground rules for how dialogue takes place so that everyone has his or her rights and dignity protected. We have to meet in a language that all participants understand. If I began speaking in Hebrew, that would be a performance, not a dialogue. It may be valuable at times, but not in a dialogue because it does not achieve any of the goals of amicable relations, understanding each other, learning from each other, or growing closer together in concerns for social justice.

In a democratic society, if we are going to argue for a moral imperative, then there must be appropriate procedures. Also, the scope of the dialogue would have to be open to the substantive issues of the good life. If we are going to really discuss matters of serious faith, then the issues are going to be more than just procedural. They are going to be substantive agreements and disagreements. Many American policy decisions are about what procedures to employ. Given a moral imperative to dialogue, then there will have to be questions about what constitutes the good life: justice, marriage, family, sexuality, the availability of knowledge and the increase of capacity, etc. These are substantive questions. We have never stopped arguing about them and it is difficult for us to come to agreement. Happily, dialogue does not always require agreement even on substantive issues of the good life. Sometimes we agree to disagree. Nonetheless, all of us are better off settling our differences in a dialogue process rather than settling them in some other way. Dialogue is the best alternative to other means of resolving real differences in perspective among members of a society.

I spent eight years involved in Catholic-Jewish dialogue in Chicago, and my colleagues and I used to have a joke that said, someday we are going to talk about something that really divides us. It was so interesting to discover that as fast as I could think that we were divided on something, I would discover there was just too much about Roman Catholicism that I did not know. I do not think we should underplay how important it is for the voices of interfaith dialogue to be heard by all members of civil society. People get a sense of what is at stake as we share what we take to be profound insights. We do not think, for example, that the idea of a Creator who orders the structures of the universe is of no consequence to what it means to live as a human being. All the Abrahamic traditions take this conviction as a central doctrine that has important ethical implications.

Additional Benefits of Dialogue:
Powerful Images of Universal Redemption

Most religions contain striking, imaginative language to describe an eschatological period, some period of time in which the world is perfected. Sometimes the description is conservative and describes a going back to say, the Garden of Eden. Other times it is a progressive and revolutionary language where adherents are going to transform the world and fix it. Thus, *tikkun olam* is an invitation to fix the world to make it whole and bring it together now. This is not within the Abrahamic traditions alone. Buddhism also speaks of the time when the Buddha will return at the end and will take away the suffering of all sentient beings. Both of these are a vision, and the imaginative language is powerful. Anyone who reads the Hebrew prophets sees this immediately—descriptions of what it will be like when the salvific moment will occur, when the redemption will occur. This moment is not portrayed in private terms. The world as a whole will be affected by this. The images provided by Prophets are so powerful that even people who do not believe the author is a true prophet can read it and be moved.

The founding texts of Judaism, Christianity and Islam invite myriads of people who are not adherents to any of those religions but who find the texts and the visions presented therein compelling. One advantage of this universal vision being articulated in terms of faith traditions is that, although they have a rational understanding or basis, the language and the imagination of them is powerful and speaks to people. As such, we have religious faiths that articulate universally, often redemptive, world-transforming visions in a way that includes moral responsibility. We would therefore conclude that such a universal religious vision assumes the capacity of human beings to speak reasonably to each other about moral matters. Whatever the source of that universality, be it human nature or another reality, the vision that is articulated is one of humanity talking to each other.

This suggests that there is an imperative to engage in dialogue that involves working toward the common good. Even Immanuel Kant articulates the kingdom of ends where all of us treat each other as ends rather than means. But what is the essence of the obligation? The obligation pushes to action and lives in the details. If we are obligated as a society to heal the sick, then we are obviously obligated to work to heal the sick. If one is obligated to pay individual debts, then one must pay them. If one has a moral obligation to pay the rent, then one must write the check. Being obligated also means that one must articulate the kingdom of ends—not perfectly—but we articulate it, argue about it, and discuss it. The assumption is that, as human beings, we can create visions of ideal worlds.

In this section, I have suggested that the meaning of faith is not exhausted by ethics. Beliefs can have an enormous set of ethical implications about the kind of world for which we are willing to work and for the conditions under which we should work for them. Again, I am referring to Cardinal Bernardin. He articulated a vision of how society can work together, grounded in a single value, trying to connect and champion the value of life. That places Cardinal Bernardin's thoughts together with Rabbi Irving Greenberg's notion of the triumph of life. This vision imagines a society which uses the value of life to consistently reflect and critique itself. How should we behave, settle disputes, handle difficulties about child rearing, for example? All of these life-oriented questions would come up and we would agree to work toward articulating ways to making society move in that life-affirming direction, toward a universal vision that would include discussions of life-affirming religious faith. Of course, any shared moral discussion would have to strive as far as possible to allow people to speak openly about their own views, and not have them officially interpreted or presented by others.

I have argued that, indeed, there is a moral imperative to engage in noncoercive, open and honest interfaith dialogue. Perhaps, if religion had nothing to do with life, then there would not be such a moral imperative. Further, if the vision of life were not universal, there would be no moral imperative. If there were no way to talk to each other or if we did not have a common nature or way of practicing morality which generated imperatives for us all, then there might be no moral imperative. I have argued that the human race as a whole is engaged in the enormous enterprise of seeking to create a world which has profound moral value; and that is the part of the religious imperative to be part of those moral conversations and part of the imperatives of moral conversation to involve religious people. I am aware that this view is not shared by all. I realize that for some people, morality automatically moves them into the personal, private sphere. For others, morality has almost nothing to do with the give-and-take of argument or discussion. And still others hold that morality has nothing to do with the insights and wisdom that are drawn from forces other than reason. I am not going in these directions.

Do we really expect interreligious dialogue to discover a single vision for society? I think not. In probability theory we get nuanced answers that aren't absolute. Place 100 balls into an urn and begin to randomly draw them out. We draw 3 black balls and 10 white balls. We surmise that there are probably more white balls than black balls in the urn, although there could be 90 black balls and only 10 white. Probability theory is a way in which we suggest things that may not describe the entire answer. But, in the case of probability experiments, there is a correct answer because the balls in the urn can be definitely counted. The difficulty with life is one cannot count the events of human history. As soon as we are through counting, there has already been another event added to the urn of understanding.

In principle, one can imagine an end of history and how it should be and how one should act. In principle, we can imagine that there will be only one theory of religious wisdom, and there will be only one language in which it is expressed to the rest, and that somehow all of us would sign on for that. We could believe that. That position is based on the notion that we are aiming for one and only one ideal goal.

As an alternative, imagine that even in the ideal situation there would be multiple religious discourses and theories. Imagine that it is always better to have more than one theory because any one religious theory will always leave out an aspect of reality that others have reflected on differently. Whether or not these are multiple religious languages or multiple theories, and whether or not they are mutually compatible, remains to be discovered through dialogue. One could argue they are, in principle, mutually compatible but not always completely mutually comprehensible. Cardinal Carlo Maria Martini, the archbishop of Milan, reminded me at a talk that the Center for Christian-Jewish Understanding of Sacred Heart University sponsored in Rome in 2002, that there are some areas where if one is not part of the faith community, then he or she will not be able to understand those areas. It is not that, in principle, one could not get it, but in practice one would have to be part of the particular group to understand the doctrine or experience. He gave the

Eucharist as an example. He said it is probably not extremely helpful for us to sit and discuss the depth of meanings of the Eucharist. Agreed, but that does not mean there is nothing else to discuss. There are some areas where multiple languages can be helpful and other areas where they are not as helpful. Short of coming to the end of human history, there will always be a continuous search for wisdom and we are advantaged by multiple positions.

My suggestion, then, is that if religious life includes moral inquiry, and if that inquiry has to extend to conclusions that have implications for all members of society or for humanity as a whole, then we will be advantaged in that conversation by multiple languages and multiple bodies of belief. This is important and unavoidable because it is impossible to live together as a serious and responsible society without articulating a moral code which includes the kinds of insights that are found in wisdom traditions, whatever the language in which they are articulated. In doing so, we are acknowledging the power of alternative ways of expressing or understanding the world. We are acknowledging that the power to transform our society is real when we are free to share our visions through discussions and by challenging each other.

Looking Forward

Genuine interreligious dialogue will not, almost by definition, end in an increase in animosity. The conditions have to exist for the possibility of genuine participation in safety, which was not the case a few hundred years ago. For example, in business mediation, people come in, and the two sides are not in agreement. They want to be on the same page, because a good deal is a good deal. They are going to pay money to get on the same page. Financially, one gets rewarded for agreeing. To the extent to which people are able to articulate a willingness to listen to others, in which they are willing to adopt a vocabulary which shows respect for others and stop saying that the other's ideas are ridiculous and imbecilic, then these people are able to engage in dialogue. A big footnote needs to be added that says there is no imperative to engage in mutual recrimination. There is no imperative to engage in threats or intimidation and call it dialogue.

If we cannot imagine any real interfaith dialogues that could be held without an explosion, then we need more facilitators. I have never been in such an interreligious dialogue, even the difficult ones that had political freight attached to them to the point where I was nervous of being physically harmed. I have never been in a single case where it seemed anywhere near as difficult as the worst business mediation, nor did it ever get close to what I have experienced when facilitating a session with people going through a messy divorce. It was not even in the same category. Of course, there are always people who stake out turf and who do not want a dialogue. They only want to tell you what the real truth is. In those instances, no one is going to go anywhere. The imperative is not that everyone should be having dialogues all the time. The imperative is governed by the proper conditions, such that where it is possible to have such an interfaith dialogue, one is morally obligated to do so.

I have lived among some relatively monolithic societies for a while. The question is, do most of us actually live any longer in such a society, or if we think we do, are we merely creating the appearance of a monolithic religious society? Seemingly monolithic societies can go to enormous efforts to hide from outsiders that there are real social tensions and disagreements. The insiders can tell you they are not monolithic and they do not perceive themselves as being on the same page. They have long-standing differences that, in their mind, are enormous.

In the end, there are real costs to avoiding interreligious dialogue. Others cannot be ignored. If you will not talk to me on the street, so it goes. If you do not want to vote and you are not interested in changing policy, then you choose to be in your small enclave. But the day you walk into a government office, the day you are a candidate, the day you put out a pamphlet that tries to get us to change the town line, the day you build anything that affects others, on that day, we are in dialogue. There are less desirable ways of settling such issues. You have a choice. One could say either move the town line or you will not be mayor next year. Or, we could talk about it. But, the minute you want the town line moved, the minute you want anything, the minute you want protection from the police department, the minute you want doctors to treat you, the minute you want me to smile at you on the street as we go by, rather than glare and throw rocks, the minute you want any common life together, then I am recommending to you dialogue over fighting about it or ignoring it. Our individual integrity and our shared life in society depend upon it.

It is better to settle an argument by looking for a better logical argument, than for a gun. Abuse is not as effective as an attempt to understand. These are moral categories as well as religious ones, and it belongs to all people to articulate and live this essential side of our nature by promoting visions of social love and processes that cultivate mutual understanding and a common search for truth.

M ICHAEL   F ITZGERALD ,   M A FR

The Witness of the Monotheistic Religions

On the eve of a symposium which brings together scholars from three traditions, Judaism, Christianity and Islam, it is good to talk about monotheism. Yet it might be well to remember that these three are not the only monotheistic religions. One should not forget the Sikh dharma, which is definitely monotheistic in its teachings. If a link is sought between the three religions that concern us here, it is certainly better to use the term Abrahamic religions as has been done in the title of the conference. Each of the traditions takes pride in connecting itself with Abraham, and although there are significant variations, Abraham is presented as a model of faith and of witness to the one God.

Divine Unicity

Let us dwell for a moment on this concept of divine unicity. Some people tend to assert that Jews, Christians and Muslims do not adore the same God. This is certainly not the teaching of the Catholic Church. The Second Vatican Council, in its central document, the Dogmatic Constitution on the Church (*Lumen Gentium*), stated clearly: "But the plan of salvation also includes those who acknowledge the Creator, in the first place among whom are the Muslims; these profess to hold the faith of Abraham, and together with us they adore the one, merciful God, mankind's judge on the last day" (LG, 16). This did not even have to be stated with regard to Judaism, for God's dealings with the chosen people form, as it were, the prehistory of Christianity and "the Church cannot forget that she received the revelation of the Old Testament by way of the people with whom God, in his inexpressible mercy, established the ancient covenant" (*Nostra Aetate*, 4).

Each tradition has a liturgical expression of this primary article of faith. Judaism makes use of the *Shema*: "Listen, Israel . . . I am the Lord, your God, who brought you out of the land of Egypt, out of the house of slavery. You shall have no gods except me" (Deuteronomy 5:1, 6–7). Christians proclaim, *Credo in unum Deum*, I believe in one God. Muslims, at every ritual prayer (*salât*), recite the *shahâda: Lâ ilâha illâ Llâh:* There is no divinity except God.

There are, of course, differences in the way of understanding this God. For the first of these religions, God has chosen one single people to bear witness before the world. For Christians, God has become incarnate, and in so doing has shown his solidarity with the whole of the human race that he has created. It is through the incarnate Son of God that the Trinitarian nature of God comes to be known. For Muslims, such a Trinitarian concept would seem to destroy the essential unicity of God. Moreover God's transcendence would exclude the possibility of incarnation. But God has raised up within each people a prophet to remind them of their primordial covenant with him. He has finally sent Muhammad to be the Seal of Prophecy and a mercy (*rahma*) for the whole of humanity.

We are dealing then with three distinct religions, and indeed the differences are to be found at the very heart of that which unites them, faith in the one God. Moreover these three traditions have seen their boundaries defined through historical development. Christianity did not set out to be a distinct religion, but it separated itself from Judaism, perhaps not without anguish. Islam discovered that Jews and Christians did not accept its message, and had to come to terms with the continued existence of their communities. So the three traditions have to coexist, leaving it to God to resolve their differences in his own good time.

Despite the differences in understanding, the common faith in the unicity of God remains. This means a refusal of any sort of dualistic vision of the world. Good and Evil do certainly exist, but they are not two coequal principles that are eternally struggling one with the other. We know too that we cannot really divide good and evil into two distinct camps. We are conscious that in each one of us these two forces exist. Saint Paul has described in vivid terms this inward conflict: "I cannot understand my own behavior. I fail to carry out the things I want to do, and I find myself doing the very things I hate. . . . The fact is, I know of nothing good living in me—living, that is, in my unspiritual self—for though the will to do good is in me, the performance is not, with the result that instead of doing the good things I want to do, I carry out the sinful things I do not want. . . . In fact, this seems to be the rule, that every single time I want to do good it is something evil that comes to hand" (Romans 7:15, 18–19, 21). Yet Paul is also certain that there is a way out of this predicament. His cry is well known: "What a wretched man I am! Who will rescue me from this body doomed to death? Thanks be to God through Jesus Christ our Lord!" (Romans 7:24–25). Faith in the One Almighty God includes belief that, whatever appearances might suggest, the forces of evil will be overcome. Good will have the final word.

A further dimension of monotheism is naturally a refusal of polytheism where God would have to share his prerogatives with other divinities, and where indeed there could arise a certain rivalry between divinities jealous of their own spheres of influence. Our traditions are full of satirical arguments against such a conception of God. Yet there are other forms of polytheism, or at least of associating something with God, which can insidiously creep into religion. Like the Little Prince who had to be vigilant lest baobabs should take root on his asteroid and completely take it over, so the one devoted to God has to beware lest the relationship become corrupted. It is necessary to act for God alone and, in seeking to do his will, to be careful not to associate with this worship our own desires and ambitions. Islamic spirituality has developed the idea of this fight against *shirk*, associating something with God, in ways that certainly have a resonance with Christians, and I presume also with Jews in the First Commandment.

Witness

Jews, Christians, and Muslims, we are called to give witness to God in the world. Witness is a key concept in these three traditions and is worth examining more closely.

The Law which God gives to his people, as an expression of his divine will, is inscribed on two tables. When Moses is instructed on how to build the sanctuary, he is told: "Inside the ark you will place the Testimony that I shall give you" (Exodus 25:16). This is understood as a reference to the two tablets on which the Decalogue was written. It is there as a constant reminder to the people of their obligations. Now if the law is not observed, if the people abandon their God, then God will bear witness against his people. The prophet Micah presents God as if he were conducting a trial: "Listen, you peoples, all of you. Attend, earth, and everything in it. The Lord is going to give evidence against you" (Micah 1:2). This witnessing *against* is always, however, in view of conversion and a return to God, for the prophet Ezekiel conveys the word of the Lord: "As I live—it is the Lord who speaks—I take pleasure not in the death of a wicked man, but in the turning back of a wicked man who changes his ways to win life" (Ezekiel 33:11).

In the Christian tradition, the Good News of the Kingdom, preached by Jesus, is destined to be "proclaimed to the whole world as a witness to all the nations" (Matthew 24:14). This is why Jesus sends his disciples to be his witnesses "not only in Jerusalem but throughout Judea and Samaria, and indeed to the ends of the earth" (Acts 1:8).

In Islam the profession of faith takes the form of witness, but the witness of human beings is founded on divine witness: *lâkin Allâhu yashhadu bi-mâ anzala ilay-ka anzalahu bi-'ilmi-hi wa-l-malâ'ikatu yashhadûna wa-kafâ bi-Llâhi shahîdan:* "God testifies concerning that which he has revealed to you [Muhammad]; in His knowledge He has revealed it, and the angels also testify. And God is sufficient as a witness" (*Qur'an* 4:166). Also in Islam this witness has a communal dimension: *wa-kadhâlika ja'alnâ-kum ummatan wasatan li-takûnû shuhadâ' 'alâ l-nâs wa-yakûna l-rasûl 'alay-kum shahîdan:* "Thus We have appointed you a middle nation, that you may be witnesses against mankind, and that the messenger may be a witness against you" (*Qur'an* 2:143).

This theme could be further developed, but I would like to suggest some ways in which a common witness can be given in the world today. Three points will be touched upon:
- The primacy of God
- The responsibility of human beings
- Service to humanity

The Primacy of God

Are we not called, as believers in God, to that Truth which surpasses us? Is it not our duty to remind this modern society of ours that the human being cannot be its own measure? Human dignity has its source in the creative act of God, whether or not we would wish to go on and affirm that God has created the human person in his own image and likeness. This last-mentioned belief does in fact reinforce the requirement of respect for each human being. It is perhaps good to recall here the teaching of the final section of the Declaration, *Nostra Aetate:*

> We cannot truly pray to God, the Father of all, if we treat any people in other than brotherly fashion, for all men are created in God's image. Man's relation to God the Father and man's relation to his fellowmen are so dependent on each other that the Scripture says: "He who does not love, does not know God" (I John 4:8). There is no basis, therefore, for any discrimination between individual and individual, or between people, arising either from human dignity or the rights which flow from it (NA, 5).

To accept the will of the Creator is not to go against the interests of humanity but rather to act to its advantage, for it helps to achieve its destiny.

As believers in God, are we not called to make our voices heard in society in this way? It is surely an obligation on our part to demand respect for the fundamental rights of human beings: the right to life, to physical integrity (which would include opposition to torture and any form of punishment that is incompatible with human dignity), the right to respect for one's reputation, the right to the means necessary for living a decent life, the right to education and of access to cultural development and to objective information, the right to freedom in the search for the truth, freedom of conscience and religious freedom which includes also the right to profess and practice one's faith not only as an individual but as a member of a community. There is a vast field here for common endeavor. We should remember that to show respect for our fellow human beings is also to show respect for God.

The Responsibility of Human Beings

To insist on the primacy of God does not mean that the human being is reduced to the status of a pawn on the divine chess board. On the contrary, faith in the Creator God leads to an acceptance of the role that he has entrusted to the human being, namely to be a "cocreator," or, in Islamic terminology, God's *khal'ifa,* his vicegerent or deputy. We are responsible for the created world and all it contains.

The very existence of evil becomes a challenge to the one whom God has placed in this world to take charge of it. As a result of sin it is said that the earth will produce brambles and thistles and that it is only at the sweat of his brow that man will be able to reap its fruits (cf. Genesis 3:18–19). Yet this has not prevented human beings from making progress in agriculture and inventing machinery that can reduce the fatigue of labor. Similarly it is said that the woman will give birth to her children in pain and that her husband will lord it over her (cf. Genesis 3:16), but this has not put the brakes on advances in gynecology nor of helping couples to live in a relationship of equality and love.

Paul, in his letter to the Romans to which reference has already been made, says: "From the beginning till now the entire creation, as we know, has been groaning in one great act of giving birth; and not only creation, but all of us who possess the firstfruits of the Spirit, we too groan inwardly as we wait for our bodies to be set free" (Romans 8:22–23). This, as we are well aware, does not imply waiting passively. It is our duty to cooperate with the Spirit of God, to work so that the Kingdom of God may come.

Service to Humanity

From what has just been said about human responsibility, it is an easy step to the idea of service to humanity. Believers in God, we are called to bear witness to our faith in God but also to our faith in the human person. Strengthened by our faith in God the Creator, the Provident Master of all, whom we like to call Father, we can bring to the world the hope it needs. We are convinced that evil, that sin, will not be victorious. We believe that God helps us and gives us the strength to continue to strive for the good of our brothers and sisters. It is these convictions of ours that sustain us, in good moments and bad, in times of distress as in times of happiness, in the midst of conflict and when there is peace, at times of failure, apparent or real, and also in times of success.

We feel the need too for common witness in today's world. In October 1999, the Pontifical Council for Interreligious Dialogue organized an interreligious assembly, held in the Vatican, in order to examine the role of religions in the Third Millennium. In the final message the participants in this assembly declared:

> We are conscious of the urgent need to confront together responsibly and courageously the problems and challenges of our modern world; to work together to affirm human dignity as the source of human rights and their corresponding duties, in the struggle for justice and peace for all; and to create a new spiritual consciousness for all humanity in accordance with the religious traditions so that the principle of respect for freedom of religion and freedom of conscience prevail. (Pontifical Council for Interreligious Dialogue, *Towards a Culture of Dialogue*, Vatican City, 2000, p.79).

They added:

> We know that the problems in the world are so great that we cannot solve them alone. Therefore there is an urgent need for interreligious collaboration. We are all aware that interreligious collaboration does not imply giving up our own religious identity but is rather a journey of discovery: we learn to respect one another as members of the one human family; we learn both to respect our differences and to appreciate the common values that bind us to one another; therefore, we are convinced that we are able to work together to strive to prevent conflict and to overcome the crises existing in different parts of the world. Collaboration among the different religions must be based on the rejection of fanaticism, extremism and mutual antagonisms which lead to violence. (*ibid.* pp.79–80).

The next passage in the message underlines the importance of education, something that is of great relevance to this institution, Sacred Heart University, in which we are gathered and which has been a pioneer in this field. There is mention of support for the family, of helping young

people to shape their own conscience, of underlining common fundamental moral and spiritual values. There is an appeal to make sure that
textbooks give objective presentations of religious traditions, and attention is called in a similar vein to the use of the mass media to impart
objective information.

Finally the message makes two final appeals. "We appeal to religious
leaders to promote the spirit of dialogue within their respective communities and to be ready to engage in dialogue themselves with civil society
at all levels. We appeal to all leaders of the world whatever their field of
influence: to refuse to allow religion to be used to incite hatred and violence; to refuse to allow religion to be used to justify discrimination; and
to respect the role of religion in society at international, national and
local levels" (*ibid.* p. 80).

Much space has been given to this message because it is possible,
probable even, that it is not widely known. Moreover, it is evident that it
has not lost any of its relevance for today's world.

In the Service of Peace

This statement underlined the need for the cooperation of people of different religions in the service of peace. It is in fact often said that there
will be no peace in the world until there is peace among the religions.
A finger is pointed to religions as being at the origin of conflicts. It
could be questioned whether this is wholly true. Of course, it must be
admitted that religion has, in the course of history, produced conflicts,
and can do so today. But such conflicts may have a multiplicity of causes, and so it is only fair to distinguish between those which are strictly
speaking religious, taking their origin from differences of belief, and
those which are based on nonreligious motivations but take on a religious coloring.

Tensions and disputes can arise within a given religious tradition
because of different ways of envisaging the faith or of understanding it.
One could cite the Christological disputes of the first centuries of
Christianity, in which the imperial power became involved. Even today,
within the various Christian confessions, there arise serious causes of
division, though these do not usually end up in armed combat. Islam too

has known in its history grave dissensions which have given rise to assassinations and conflict.

The ways of overcoming these conflicts may be different. In Christianity, Councils were convoked in order to determine correct belief and to condemn heresies (punishment for heretics often being entrusted to the secular arm). Special courts were set up, such as the Inquisition, or the *Mihna* in Islam, again to distinguish between orthodoxy and heterodoxy, and to punish those who had strayed. Even though today we would not approve of these methods, it should be recognized that the aim in all this was to keep the integrity of the respective faith and to protect society.

Very often, however, conflicts which appear to be religious are caused by nonreligious factors. These may be socioeconomic causes, such as in Northern Ireland where the social difference between Catholics and Protestants and lack of equal opportunities has consolidated the opposition between the two groups. Something similar could be said about the recent clashes in Indonesia, in Ambon and Kalimantan, where migration has brought different groups which happen to be Islamic on the one hand and Christian on the other to oppose one another. Ethnic and cultural factors also come into play, as in the struggle between Tamils and Cingalese in Sri Lanka, or Hindus and Muslims in Kashmir. And how should one categorize the conflict between Israelis and Palestinians?

Whether the causes are religious or not, the followers of different religions feel the duty to contribute to overcoming these conflicts and to work for peace. They are conscious that peace is a gift from God which has to be implored, but which also has, in a sense, to be earned. It is this conviction that has led Pope John Paul II to invite representatives of different religions to Assisi, Italy, to pray for peace. He did this in October 1986, and more recently on January 24, 2002. Let me quote some of the words John Paul II used on that occasion:

> If peace is God's gift and has its source in him, where are we to seek
> it and how can we build it, if not in a deep and intimate relationship with
> God? To build the peace of order, justice and freedom requires, therefore,
> a priority commitment to prayer, which is openness, listening, dialogue
> and finally union with God, the prime wellspring of true peace.

To pray is not to escape from history and the problems which it presents. On the contrary, it is to choose to face reality not on our own, but with the strength that comes from on high, the strength of truth and love which have their ultimate source in God. Faced with the treachery of evil, religious people can count on God, who absolutely wills what is good. They can pray to him to have the courage to face even the greatest difficulties with a sense of personal responsibility, never yielding to fatalism or impulsive reactions (cf. Pontifical Council for Interreligious Dialogue, Peace: *a Single Goal and a Shared Intention*, Vatican City, 2002, p. 91).

The representatives gathered in Assisi on that day, where representatives from the Center for Christian-Jewish Understanding of Sacred Heart University, Rabbi Joseph Ehrenkranz and Dr. David Coppola were present, made a solemn tenfold commitment to peace, each commitment being read out in a different language. Let me quote some of these which emphasize the need for dialogue among the religions.

1. We commit ourselves to proclaiming our firm conviction that violence and terrorism are incompatible with the authentic spirit of religion, and, as we condemn every recourse to violence and war in the name of God or of religion, we commit ourselves to doing everything possible to eliminate the root causes of terrorism.
2. We commit ourselves to educating people to mutual respect and esteem, in order to help bring about a peaceful and fraternal coexistence between people of different ethnic groups, cultures and religions.
3. We commit ourselves to fostering the culture of dialogue, so that there will be an increase of understanding and mutual trust between individuals and among people, for these are the premise of authentic peace.
5. We commit ourselves to frank and patient dialogue, refusing to consider our differences as an insurmountable barrier, but recognizing instead that to encounter the diversity of others can become an opportunity for greater reciprocal understanding.

The Conditions for a True Dialogue

Dialogue is never easy. It is important to recognize that there are certain conditions required for it to be successful. The first of these is an open mind and a welcoming spirit. This means that two extremes are to be avoided: on the one hand a certain ingenuity which accepts everything without further questioning, and on the other hand a hypercritical attitude which leads to suspicion. Impartiality is required. What is being sought is an equitable solution to the particular problem which is to be resolved.

Being open-minded does not imply being without personal convictions. On the contrary, rootedness in one's own convictions will allow for greater openness, for it takes away the fear of losing one's identity. It thus facilitates the understanding of the other's convictions. Such an openness leads to the admission that the whole of the truth is not just on one side. There is always a need to learn from others, to receive from them, to benefit from their values and everything that is good in their traditions. Dialogue in this spirit helps to overcome prejudices and to revise stereotypes.

Returning to the concept of monotheism, it would seem to me that we are helped in this particular aspect of dialogue by our belief in a God who is Truth. God alone is to be identified with absolute Truth. We ourselves cannot pretend to attain this level. Without falling into relativism, we can readily admit that our view of things does not really attain to ultimate Truth. For this reason in dialogue it is necessary not only to speak but also to listen to the other in order to receive the other's part of truth.

The Pillars of Peace

Truth is the first pillar of peace, according to the teaching of Pope John XXIII in his letter *Pacem in Terris*, which he wrote forty years ago. John Paul II has recalled this anniversary in his message for the Day of Peace this year, and has brought to mind the four essential requirements for peace identified by John XXIII: truth, justice, love, and freedom. Truth brings each individual to acknowledge his or her own rights, but also to recognize his or her own duties toward others. Justice leads people to respect the rights of others and also to fulfill their duties. Love goes beyond justice, for it makes people feel the needs of others as if they were their own, and this empathy leads them to share their own gifts with others, not only material goods but also the values of mind and spirit. Freedom, finally, is a factor in building peace when it allows people to act according to reason and to assume responsibility for their own actions.

John Paul II in his message for the previous year, 2002, had himself spoken of two pillars of peace, justice and forgiveness, which is a particular form of love. Human justice is always imperfect and needs to be complemented by forgiveness. It is this which allows broken relationships to be restored. It allows confidence to be regained and a new departure to take place. This holds good not only for individuals, but also for social groups, even States. It is the capacity to forgive that can create the conditions necessary to overcome the sterility of reciprocal condemnations and the spiral of increasing violence.

This teaching of the Pope is resolutely Christian, for Jesus taught that God is a Father who loves to pardon (cf. Luke 15). Yet surely this conforms to the image of God given in the First Testament. The Psalmist invites his soul to bless the Lord and to remember his kindnesses, "in forgiving all your offenses," for he is "tender and compassionate, slow to anger, most loving" (Psalm 103:3, 8). The book of Nehemiah addresses God in a similar way: "But you are a God of forgiveness, gracious and loving, slow to anger, abounding in goodness" (Nehemiah 9:17). Does not the *Qur'an* echo this? God is constantly proclaimed *al-rahmân al-rahîm*, the Beneficent, the Merciful. He is also *al-ghafûr*, the one whose very inclination is to pardon. According to Islamic spirituality believers are to "clothe" themselves with the attributes of God, so surely there is an encouragement to forgive as God is forgiving.

Let me conclude, then, on this note. The monotheistic religions, in particular the Abrahamic religions, have much to contribute to peace. They will do so by upholding the dignity of human beings, by pursuing justice, but also by practicing and appealing for the spirit of pardon. John Paul II concludes this year's peace message with these words:

The fortieth anniversary of *Pacem in Terris* is an apt occasion to return to Pope John XXIII's prophetic teaching. Catholic communities will know how to celebrate this anniversary during the year with initiatives which, I hope, will have an ecumenical and interreligious character and be open to all those who have a heartfelt desire "to break through the barriers which divide them, to strengthen the bonds of mutual love, to learn to understand one another and to pardon those who have done them wrong."

For Further Discussion and Study

How can Jews, Christians and Muslims witness to the oneness of God, while remaining faithful to their specific revelations and unique expressions?

Does interreligious dialogue necessarily lead to relativism?

Is the primacy of God and truth compromised in interreligious dialogue?

What is the role of interreligious dialogue in sharing the truth of the one God?

What are the theological reasons for engaging in interreligious dialogue? What are the barriers or obstacles to such dialogue?

Is interreligious dialogue a means to discover truth and wisdom? If so, in what contexts?

Can interreligious dialogue be the sacred space where the divine meets the human? If so, how might we properly prepare for and promote such an encounter?

For Action in the Community

What are the reasons you believe that interreligious dialogue is important? How can you teach those reasons to others of your faith?

Is interreligious dialogue practical? Does it benefit the participants or the larger community? If so, how can you bring those benefits to your neighborhood?

Should interreligious dialogue and education be sponsored or encouraged in your synagogue, parish, or mosque? If so, how? If not, what are the appropriate forums for relating with the other, and can you sponsor one?

What are the proper conditions for authentic and respectful dialogue to take place? How can you help to create those conditions in your neighborhood?

Does dialogue offer us the opportunity to better serve humanity together, especially in the areas of social justice and the work of peace? If so, what can your community do with other faiths to promote social justice and peace?

Do you think documents such as *Nostra Aetate* or *Dabru Emet* or even the 2003 Chicago summit statement, "Urgent Call for Reflection, Hope and Action," have a positive effect on bringing people together to dialogue and understanding? How can you spread the ideas advocated in these and other documents? [See www.ccju.org for the full text of these and other interreligious documents.]

PART II

---

*What Do We Want the Other to Teach
About Our Theological Traditions?*

DAVID L. COPPOLA

What Do We Want the Other to Teach About Our Theological Traditions?

On February 8–10, 2000, the Center for Christian-Jewish Understanding (CCJU) of Sacred Heart University, Fairfield, Connecticut, in cooperation with the Elijah School for the Study of Wisdom in World Religions, Jerusalem, sponsored a conference at the Ratisbonne Papal Institute, Jerusalem, entitled, "What Do We Want the Other to Teach About Our Theological Traditions?" Over 25 scholars from the Middle East, Europe, Canada and the United States were invited to participate at the proceedings with the additional attendance of graduate students from the Ratisbonne Papal Institute and Tantur Ecumenical Institute, Jerusalem, who joined as observers for each of the sessions spread over three days.

One evening of the conference featured a panel discussion on "The Significance of the Pope's Pilgrimage to the Holy Land for the Three Abrahamic Religions," followed by an interfaith concert, at the Museum of Islamic Art, Jerusalem. Participants on the panel included His Excellency, Archbishop Pietro Sambi, Apostolic Delegate to the Holy Land, Jerusalem; Rev. Dr. Remi Hoeckman, OP, executive secretary, Commission for Religious Relations with the Jews, Vatican City; Rabbi Shear-Yashuv Hacohen, Chief Rabbi of Haifa; Mr. Daniel Rossing, former director of Ministry of Religious Affairs, Israel; Mr. Ibrahim Sarsur, leader of the Islamic Movement in Israel; and Sheik Abdul Aziz Bukhari, Sheik of the Naqshabandian Religious Method, Jerusalem. Over 250 people filled the Museum of Islamic Art to capacity, and several representatives from the Israeli press attended. Most of the panel agreed that Pope John Paul II was a man of peace and his pilgrimage would be a positive sign that all people need to move beyond violence and hatred to peace, respect and prayer. Archbishop Sambi said, "The sign value of the papal pilgrimage to the Holy Land can renew our relationships with hope and healing." Several of the panel members said that the time was right to place more time and resources not only into furthering political interreligious dialogue but spiritual interreligious dialogue. One panelist suggested that all parties needed to do more listening and less speaking in order to advance the art and goal of mutual respect and love. These comments by the panelists followed less than a week after Prime Minister Yitzhak Rabin's widow, Leah Rabin, said in Rome, "When the Pope comes to Israel, we will be very enthusiastic and greatly honored. We consider him a great friend. . . . We do not want to deny anyone access to sacred places."

The format of the conference proper included presentations of papers by noted scholars with prepared responses, followed by discussion, critiques and suggestions by all of the participants. A number of themes emerged from the papers and proceedings and are presented briefly here.

LIST OF INVITED PARTICIPANTS

Dr. Asma Afsaruddin, University of Notre Dame, South Bend, Indiana

Rev. Dr. Franz Bouen, White Fathers, Jerusalem

Sheik Abdul Aziz Bukhari, Sheik of the Naqshabandian Religious Method, Jerusalem.

Dr. David Burrel, University of Notre Dame, South Bend, Indiana

His Eminence, Edward Idris Cardinal Cassidy, Pontifical Commission for Religious Relations with the Jews, Vatican City State

Dr. Anthony J. Cernera, Sacred Heart University, Fairfield, Connecticut

Dr. David L. Coppola, Center for Christian-Jewish Understanding of Sacred Heart University, Fairfield, Connecticut

Dr. Kahlid Deran, Bethesda, Maryland

Rabbi Joseph H. Ehrenkranz, Center for Christian-Jewish Understanding of Sacred Heart University, Fairfield, Connecticut

Dr. Jamal J. Elias, Amherst College, Amherst, Massachusetts

Dr. Alon Goshen-Gottstein, Elijah School, Jerusalem

Rev. Dr. Remi Hoeckman, OP, Commission of Religious Relations with the Jews, Vatican City State

Dr. Barry Levy, Professor, McGill University, Montreal

Reverend Michael McGarry, Tantur Ecumenical Institute, Jerusalem

Mr. Daniel Rossing, former director of Ministry of Religious Affairs, Israel

His Excellency, Archbishop Pietro Sambi, Apostolic Delegate to the Holy Land, Jerusalem

Mr. Ibrahim Sarsur, leader of the Islamic Movement in Israel

Reverend Thomas Stransky, Bethlehem

Mustafa Abu Sway, Al Quds University, Jerusalem

Rabbi Stanley Wagner, University of Denver, Denver, Colorado

Rabbi Shear-Yashuv Hacohen, Chief Rabbi of Haifa

What Do We Want the Other to Teach About Our Theological Traditions?

There is no single way to teach the theology of another religion, but there is a continuity of identity, religious practice, memory and history that allows for authentic dialogue. One challenge to teaching about another's theology is that religious thought is not an isolated set of abstract philosophical truth statements written by an individual. Rather, theology is based upon important, shared values, rooted in the community's ethical and liturgical relationship with God, and born of revelation and the historical lived faith experience of a community. Accordingly, there are layers of truth in theology that only an "insider" can adequately come to understand. Additionally, there are degrees of separation or otherness that are experienced in intrareligious dialogue which may be perceived as greater than in some interreligious dialogue groups.

Teaching about the other's theology requires that the teacher is attentive to the degrees of otherness and highlight the limitations as well as the possibilities to students for understanding in such a context. Further, there are several different layers of understanding, which do not require agreement or acceptance. These range from simple language or symbolic approximations, to analogy, to correspondence, to shared communal meanings, to "knowing" in an existential or intimate way—the latter meaning representing a more invested, committed understanding, tending more toward acceptance, precisely because it is only able to be consistently experienced by insiders. This consistent insider experience of faith is frequently understood on levels beyond one's theology and has characteristics that are more visceral, artistic, relational and dialogical in the contexts of familial and communal relationships or worship. The goal of interreligious dialogue is for the sake of understanding which leads to mutual respect, trust, harmony and peace.

Another consideration when teaching about the other's theological tradition is taking into account the insights and limitations of a postmodern worldview and the importance of being attentive and respectful when using analogies or translating stories and categories across religious traditions. The historical contexts and cultural lenses in which these stories are understood can vary greatly. It should be noted also that reading the Scriptures as a believer or a skeptic has direct consequences on an adequate understanding of the core of another's beliefs. Additionally, there will necessarily be ideological and theological differences, which cannot be ignored. Nonetheless, truth can be found in the midst of different and sometimes contradictory convictions and realities. A common foundational effort that all can work together toward is to restore the central place of God in the world.

Jews, Christians and Muslims enter into dialogue because God has chosen to speak with them and to be in relationship with them first. One possible interreligious theological viewpoint could be to see the Word of God from the perspective of a history of dialogue, a covenantal relationship with a God who has chosen to communicate with a receptive, historical community, and invites humans to live faithful and ethical lives in community. Subsequently, Jews, Christians and Muslims theologize because God has been revealed to them and they want to interpret and share that message of peace, justice, unity, and compassion with the present and future generations. Since God's revelation is heard in many languages, people of faith have a responsibility to share the truth, wisdom and mercy of God with each other so that all can faithfully follow God's will in all of its plurality of expression. That plurality is expressed within and between each religion in multidimensional, multicontextual, and multivocal ways due to the influences of historical circumstances.

A promising theological starting point for teaching about the other is seeing religious beliefs and teachings embodied in the lives of holy, just, wise, or righteous people. Religions can have an important role in highlighting exemplary human beings especially by celebrating the wisdom and ethical lives of believers. By remembering the sages, saints, prophets, and holy people, as well as what they said and did, the religion and theology of the other can be taught in a way that is theologically accurate and morally appropriate. In this process, opportunities for discovering parallel teachings between religions emerge as well as the implicit communication of the ongoing vitality of the other religion.

More study will need to be pursued in the areas of the intellectual traditions, scriptures, laws, ethics, and prayer and liturgy of each religion. The advantage of pursuing these areas of study together in dialogue is that each religious tradition continues to illuminate the other by its own reflections. In particular, those who are genuinely concerned with protecting the image of God and the love and wisdom of God found in the moral weave of relationships will make every effort to know and understand the other, in spite of the obstacles that normally would interfere with such a relationship.

Teaching what the other wants to be taught about him or her is a profound act of *teshuva* (an act of reconsideration and repentance for the past, and an invitation to transformation into a deeper relationship with self, others, and God). This *teshuva* can bring participants face-to-face in honor and equality into a communion (*havurah* and *koinonia*), a communion of spirit and heart. To study others with the intention of trying to teach authentically about them, is not only to understand and know them, but is also a process of self-discovery and of knowing God more intimately. One does not simply teach about the other, but specifically the other-in-faith, the other as a son or daughter of God. This joint reflection leads Jews, Christians and Muslims down God's path of healing.

A L O N   G O S H E N - G O T T S T E I N

What We Want the Other to Know About Us

In What Sense Can "We" Instruct the "Other" About Ourselves?

As the first speaker in this conference, I wish to not only address the conference topic from the Jewish perspective, but to make some general remarks about the implied assumptions of this conference, remarks which will obviously be relevant to the different perspectives represented in the conference. My own interest in our topic is twofold. On the one hand, as director of the Elijah School, Jerusalem, where world religions are taught, the question of how to teach world religions in an interfaith context is of obvious interest. The Elijah School's attempt to strike a balance between academic excellence and interfaith dialogue based on a committed faith stance presents a particular challenge. How does one represent a religion taking into account both its historical and developmental process and its faith claims? The former perspective can lead to a critical view of the religion that at times is at odds with its own self understanding, as formulated traditionally. To a large extent, we have here an expression of the insider-outsider problem in the teaching of religion.

The title of our conference assumes, to a certain degree, that the "we" who instruct the "other" how to teach about us, are in some sense in possession of a truer or better approach to the subject matter, by virtue of our being insiders. Indeed, the Elijah School's attempt to engage teachers who are insiders to teach their religions makes a similar assumption. Yet the approach at the Elijah School is not necessarily appropriate in other contexts, for one can distinguish between a context of interfaith dialogue, where one must have an "other" to engage, and other types of academic settings. Can we always claim that only the insider has access to the true way of teaching? It seems obvious that the outsider may often bring not only critical perspective that is lacking in a tradition, but also insight and a new methodology, in light of which a religious tradition can be better understood. The insider-outsider issue will continue to occupy scholarly attention for generations to come. In the context of the present discussion, one must therefore define the sense in which it is considered that there is a "we" who somehow have a say in instructing the "other" in the teaching of religion. Three senses can be suggested:

1. The outsider's perspective may seem to the insider to be grossly mistaken, bearing false witness to the religion. Such errors are usually in the nature of a judgment upon the religion, and not simply in the order of a mistaken perception. To take the case of Judaism, the claim that can still be heard in certain circles down to present times, that Judaism is legalistic, is such a judgment. Such judgments are usually accompanied by an evaluation of one's own religion as superior to the religion of the other. Judgments form attitudes, and attitudes govern our relations with concrete others. This leads to the second point.

2. Due to the modern multicultural and multireligious context, study of religions is no longer a purely academic exercise. It bears upon the lives of peoples and communities in contact with one another. There are diverse communities of faith living alongside one another in all parts of the world. There is thus a need for the study of religion in a way that resonates with the lives of the faith communities. The fact that faith communities endow academic positions in the academy, primarily in the U.S. for the teaching of their respective traditions, gives further weight to the demand that the teaching of religions should further the interfaith situation. In other words, there is no purely neutral academic ground in which religion is taught, and the teaching of religion worldwide in some way reflects the interfaith situation. Now, to suggest that because "We" exist, "We" can determine the way in which our tradition is academically represented is far from obvious. It raises a series of problems that demand further consideration. Could there be multiple readings of

a tradition, that of the outsider and that of the insider, the one serving the purely academic study of religion and the other serving the interfaith situation? Might the study of religion controlled by the religious "We" be in some way less academic? And if so, in what way? Would it draw upon different sources? Would it make more room for experience? We have hit the insider-outsider problem here head on, and beyond pointing to the questions that arise for our discussion, I do not feel I have a significant contribution to make at this point. Let me then leave further reflection upon this point for our discussions, and move on to the third dimension, which to me is the most significant.

3. The third sense in which "We" have something to say that is unique, and that can be only heard from the insider's perspective touches upon the very act of presenting a religion. At this point, I wish to introduce the second perspective, to which I alluded earlier, that informs my presentation. This is not as director of an interfaith study program, but as a teacher of Judaism. Over the past three years I have had the privilege of teaching introductory courses on Judaism to Christian students. The first such course was taught at the Bet Jalla Latin Patriarchate Seminary, and for the past two years I have been offering such a course here at the Ratisbonne Institute. Most of what I have to say in the present lecture is in the nature of both a description and a reflection upon this dimension of my work. Hence, for convenience's sake, and in order to draw upon my personal experience, I shall for the remainder of the presentation address the question of the "we" and the "other" in terms drawn from my introductory course, and hence shall discuss the parameters and boundaries of the presentation of Judaism in such an introductory course. In parentheses, I should add that for the past months two titles for our conference have been circulating. The one has been what do we want the other to teach about us, suggesting it is the other who is doing the teaching. The second is what do we want the other to know about us. The only significant difference between the two touches on the issue of who is doing the teaching—the insider or the outsider. While the issues touched upon in my presentation are relevant for both titles, they do reflect more closely the concerns of the "to know about us" version of our deliberations.

Getting back now to the third sense in which I find it meaningful to speak of a "we" who have something to say to an "other," let me begin by sharing my experience that there is no simple and straightforward presentation of a religion. The assumption that there is something somehow "objective" in the way in which a religion is presented is fraught with complications. Rather, the presentation of a religion, in my case Judaism, is a matter of construction, as much as it is one of description. It is as much a matter of theology as it is of history of religions. It is as much a matter of the faith of the presenter as it is of laying out what are considered to be the key literary or historical facts. Hence, presenting a religion and teaching about it is ultimately a matter of sharing insight. My claim is that there is a theological insight that informs the work of the insider, and that enables the "we" to present the tradition in a way that will be significantly different from the way in which the religion will be represented by the outsider.

If every act of presentation is also an act of construction, we must weigh the different kinds of construction possible. It is arguable that history of religion provides us with certain descriptive canons, certain guiding principles and questions by means of which we can describe religious traditions. If so, a Muslim scholar may be able to adequately describe Judaism using such academic descriptive canons. Presumably, were she to know all the facts concerning all world religions, our Muslim scholar should be able to proceed to equally describe all religions, completely bracketing her own personal belief. Now, while I seriously doubt that this is really how it is, and while I note that *de facto* we have fewer and fewer generalists, one must still acknowledge that scholars such as Ninian Smart and Huston Smith do seem to represent such a type of scholarship, where religions are described seriatim, with no concern for the personal belief of the describing scholar. And yet, even while acknowledging the validity of such scholarship, it is but one type of scholarship.

The alternative model, which I wish to present, is one in which theology and history of religions cannot be fully separated, and where religion is not simply presented as some objective data, but is constructed. Indeed, I would argue that there is no one presentation of a religion. There would be as many Judaisms as there would be presenters of Judaism, and as many Islams as there are presenters of Islam, perhaps for the simple reason that Judaism does not really exist. Religion is an abstraction of the scholarly or theological mind. The historical, literary, and sociological reality that is being described is always far vaster and wider than anything we describe. Any description is an attempt to give structure and coherence to a mass of data that extends far beyond the confines of our description. In presenting we limit, define, and bring within the realm of our understanding a given phenomenon. At that moment we also create the phenomenon, and call it an –ism, in this case: Judaism. Presentation is thus an act of construction, and hence a theological no less than a historical moment. It is here that "we" have something to say. Because theology is a matter for the insider, because there is an insight that will allow for the shaping of the constructed system, and because ultimately we have the right to expect something more interesting from the theologically informed, that shapes how a tradition is constructed, than from the simple historical presentation of data. All of this suggests that in the "We" there is the power to construct religious traditions in ways that are more enriching, rewarding, and illuminating. It is this third level where I think the "we's" contribution to the study of religion is most significant. What "we" want the other to know about us is thus ultimately in some sense a construction of our own identity. The presence of the other thus serves as the context for the articulation of my own identity, expressed in the construction of a particular religious system and its presentation to the other.

Introduction(s) to Judaism

Let me do some backtracking, in order to account for how I have arrived at the above suggestion. In preparing for what I thought would be a very straightforward course, introducing Judaism to the Bet Jalla seminarians, I went over some twenty introductions to Judaism. I discovered there were no two introductions that were identical. While all of them described the same phenomenon, they did so in greatly diverging manners. The choice of sources, the ideology, and ultimately the image of Judaism that emerged in these different introductions were ultimately dictated by the personal belief or understanding of the presenter. There was no objective way of approaching the subject, and each presentation was equally subjective, or relative, in the sense of making a series of choices within the tradition, choices that could have just as legitimately have been made otherwise. Ultimately, none of these introductions did the trick for me, which meant that in order to present Judaism I had to do my own presentation of the sources, and my own construction of the meaning of the system. I soon realized that in fact I am creating one more introduction to Judaism.

It is obvious that my introduction carries no greater authority than any of the other existing introductions. Indeed, the recognition that every construction is an act of subjective representation implies that all are equally valid, and that beyond the personal appeal of my subjectivity and its creative expressions there is nothing inherently more compelling about my approach, when compared to any existing approach to the subject. I did, however, note that in Israel's 50 years of existence no introduction to Judaism was written, that was geared at a non-Jewish audience. There were many introductions written outside Israel, obviously informed by local Jewish-Christian or other relations. There were also introductions to Judaism written in Hebrew for Israel's secular readers. But Israel has not produced a presentation of the Jewish religion, geared at a non-Jewish public. This is telling of the interfaith situation in Israel and of the fact that Israeli concern is largely taken up with internal Jewish affairs and with matters of Jewish physical and spiritual survival. At the same time this seemed to justify one more presentation of Judaism. For a different kind of Judaism might be constructed in independent Israel. Both the range of topics and the range of sources may differ from those featuring in "Diaspora" presentations of Judaism. To take two examples, the role of sacred space or Holy Land, and the theologies of modern Zionist religious thinkers may significantly alter how the tradition is portrayed. Thus, the debt of my own religious self to the thought of Palestine's first chief rabbi, Rabbi Abraham Isaac Kook, obviously would come through my presentation of Judaism, coloring it in a particular way. Moreover, my choice to present Judaism as a story, to which I shall refer further below, makes the vantage point from which the story is told all the more significant.

The only way to deal with the subjectivity that I see as fundamental to the project of presenting a religion is to expose one's subjectivity. Thus, the Judaism I present is very much my brand of Judaism, informed by my own personal life choices and spirituality. It is a Judaism that is at one and the same time highly dialogical and open to conversation with others from other traditions, but also drawing on the Jewish tradition's most inward resources. It is, if you will, very mystical, heavily informed by mystical thought, in its many manifestations in Kabbala, Hasidic thought, and the Zionist mystical ideology of Rav Kook. It is, to a certain degree, a unique blend, though perhaps to the same degree that every constructive act draws upon subjectivities that are equally unique.

Let me provide an example of how the subjectivity of the writer is expressed through the choices he makes in presenting his tradition. In my presentation of Judaism, I have included a discussion of the notion of the holy man in Judaism. Following a historical survey of different types of holy men in Judaism, which follows a historical survey of different types of holy men throughout the ages, I finally arrive at a discussion of the Hasidic Zaddik as a culmination of different lines of thought. Now, to feature the notion of the Hasidic Zaddik as normative and representative of Judaism is certainly unconventional. I know of no other presentation of Judaism that has done so. This is left to introductions to Hasidism, as though the Hasidic movement were something other than Judaism. And indeed, for the writers of all the introductions that I have surveyed, this is precisely the case. There is Judaism, defined through some canonical corpus, a definition of which is usually not given to the reader, and then there are other movements, which are somehow tangential to the "real" or "essential" Judaism. Now, the decision to omit reference to Hasidism, and in this case, to its notion of the holy man, and for that matter—to the very notion of holy man, in a presentation of Judaism, is as much of a choice as to include them. What is the basis for exclusion rather than inclusion? Ultimately it reverts to the writer's own sense of what is Judaism, and what is normative and representative about it. Yet, I would argue any such decision is subjective and ultimately arbitrary. It is not simply that one may represent the Hasidic movement and its ideological and social institutions as an equally legitimate part of Judaism as those parts of Judaism that are conventionally described. More significantly, one can argue that here we have a culmination of spiritual tendencies that are manifest throughout tradition, and that find their fulfillment in the Hasidic movement. The point is not which choice is proper. My point is that any decision is a choice, and any choice is ideologically, personally, and subjectively motivated. Rather than achieve the impossible task of describing a core or essential Judaism, one must present consciously and openly one's constructed Judaism, laying bare one's assumptions and presuppositions.

One of the discoveries I made along the way was that not only is the presentation of Judaism itself a subjective act, but it is created in a context of intersubjectivity. The classroom situation out of which my work grew is here significant. Here I was a Jew, talking to Christians. The presentation of Judaism grew out of the exchange of these two subjective realities. I often asked myself how my presentation might have been different if I had to make it to Muslim students. Surely other topics would have emerged as foci of discussion. Would I have spent as much time on the notion of the Zaddik in speaking to Muslims as I did in talking to Christians, and suggesting affinities between certain Jewish notions of the Zaddik and certain understandings of Christ? One of the facts I noticed about existing introductions to Judaism is that their audience is not clearly defined. Are they addressing a religious other, a secular Jew, a generic intellectual? The question has immediate ramifications. Emil Fackenheim includes in his introduction to Judaism a discussion of whether God hears prayer. I find no need to discuss this topic in my introduction. But this is precisely because I envision a different reader at the other side of the conversation. So, what emerges is that there is no defined "we," in whose name one can talk with authority. "We" has become "we," consisting of a large collection of constructors of religion, presenting their own unique and original construction of religion, while the "other" cannot be simply thought of in the broadest terms, but must be clearly defined. My presentation of Judaism to Christians will look very different from Menachem Fruman's presentation of Judaism to Muslim clergy. Both will be equally valid.

The claim that multiple presentations of Judaism may be equally valid does not rely simply on postmodern sensibilities. Indeed, if there is one message that emerges from the history of Jewish reflection, and which I believe must be incorporated into any presentation of Judaism, it is that Judaism is multivocal. From the earliest strands of biblical thought down to modern times, Judaism supports a rich discourse in which multiple opinions coexist alongside one another. This does not mean, obviously, that any topic can be the subject of unlimited opinions, or that there is lack of consensus concerning everything. Were that the case, Judaism would completely disintegrate. Yet, Judaism cannot simply be presented as a single, facile, univocal belief. Indeed, what characterizes noncritical, what we may for lack of a better term call fundamentalist, pictures of Judaism is precisely this lack of nuance, and the presentation of Judaism as a univocal message. Therefore, the constructive presentation of Judaism must also be faithful to Judaism's fundamental multivocality. Historical description tends to present the multivocality of the multiple historical Judaisms. The constructive presentation tends to a more unified presentation. A creative tension must be maintained between these two perspectives. Multiple voices must always be given expression. This expression may be in order to contextualize or to balance the dominant voice expressed in the presentation. Alternatively, the role of the presentation may be to suggest a synthesis between the multiple voices of tradition. In any event, while we cannot define a single position as definitive of Judaism, in terms of content, there is a discourse that is typical of tradition, and which must be captured in a presentation of Judaism. This discourse is itself a major factor by means of which any presentation of Judaism is authenticated. I would suggest this factor as an important complement to the awareness of one's own subjectivity, and the ways it governs one's presentation. A responsible subjectivity would be one that is articulated within the wider multivocal and multigenerational discourse of Judaism, expressing itself in dialogue with and in relation to the rich texture of earlier Jewish reflection.

On Jews and Judaism

There is a certain confusion that is characteristic of introductory works on Judaism. This confusion may be particular to Judaism, due to its fundamentally twofold nature. Judaism is both a peoplehood—an ethnic entity—and a system of religious belief and praxis, similar to the other religions discussed in our conference. Now, in the case of Judaism, beyond all the difficulties we have already discovered in our title, the definition of "us" is particularly problematic. Not simply because there are a variety of Judaisms. On a more fundamental level, does this "us" refer to a people or a religion, defined as a religious system of doctrine and action? Are we teaching about the Jewish people in their various historical manifestations, or about the Jewish religion? I take it the task at hand, and the task which I set for myself in my introduction, is an introduction to a religious system. Hence, its method is theological and draws upon insight derived from the history of religions. Were my choice different, the method might be more heavily historical, attempting a historical presentation of the history of the Jews, including a history of their beliefs and religious practices. A presentation of the Jewish people's beliefs may be more descriptive. A presentation of Judaism as a religious system is necessarily constructive.

The understanding that what I am presenting is Judaism, and not a history of the religious life of the Jews, assumes I am able to locate Judaism somewhere. In which people do I locate it? What texts do I see as representative of a Judaism worth representing? These are matters of choice that are ultimately determined only by my own religious sensibility. The choice to describe Judaism implies one is describing not only a historical reality, such as was lived by the Jews, but rather one is presenting some ideal reality, perhaps an ideal that has never existed. The project thus involves selection. Certain elements of the system will be highlighted in the construction, while other elements that may have played a historical role may be ignored. Certain texts will be featured, while others may not be integrated into an ideal representation of Judaism as a religious system.

A further implication of the presentation of Judaism, over and against a history of the Jewish people's religious life, is that such a presentation of Judaism can become the source for a critique of diverse manifestations of historical Judaisms. If one presents a history of the Jewish people and their religious life, one need not pass judgment on the diverse forms their life has taken. The facts are what they are, and the historian can expose them for what they are. That Jews may have been religious syncretists or gangsters may be historical facts. Both may captivate the historian's imagination. However, both may be irrelevant to a construction of the Jewish religion. A construction of the religion, on the other hand, necessitates taking a stand. One may have the right to pass judgment on amulets as legitimate or illegitimate forms of religious expression. Given Judaism's own declared standards of what prayer should be, one may wish to examine the historical forms of prayer in Judaism, and expose them to criticism. The act of presenting a religion leads us not only to a selection amongst multiple forms of the religion and its texts, but also leads us to an examination and evaluation of the actual forms the religious life has taken.

The Choice of Sources—Normativity and Subjectivity

Let me expound further on the problem of the selection of sources. For the historian, all forms of Jewish life may be relevant. Indeed, if our perspective was that of presenting the historical phenomenon of Judaism to Christians, we might find special interest in certain historical phenomena that may have had particular impact upon Christianity. From a Christian perspective, interest in the Qumran sectarians makes perfect sense. Indeed, any serious historical presentation of historical Judaisms—and I use the term in the plural—following the lead of Jacob Neusner, cannot overlook the community whose theology is captured in the Dead Sea Scrolls. Yet, when we speak theologically we speak of Judaism, in the singular and not in the plural. And when such a Judaism is constructed, there will probably not be room for the Dead Sea Scrolls in it. That is, unless the writer has constructed a Judaism that in some way resonates so deeply with the world view of the sectarians as to revive their world view and to span Judaism from its roots, through the works of the sectarians and down to later manifestations of Judaism that represent a related world view. And yet, if such a Judaism were constructed would it be recognized as Judaism? For that matter, Christian kabbala might also be constructed as a form of Judaism. Are there then any minimal conditions that govern what can and cannot be presented as Judaism, beyond the subjective choices of individual writers?

Two approaches may be taken to this question. One is based on self-understanding, the other is an attempt to apply notions of canonicity and normativity to the description of a religion. The first criterion is probably the ultimate factor that determines what historical Judaism fall within the scope of a theologically constructed Judaism. Ancient Christianity, no less than Qumran covenantors, considered itself to be a Jewish movement. Yet, what ultimately determines the boundaries of Jewish self-definition, as well as of Jewish continuity, is the historical memory of the community, as it carries its own self-identity through the generations. It is important to recognize the utter subjectivity of this category. Yet, at the same time there is probably no other category besides self-understanding that ultimately governs what falls within the scope of Judaism. From a purely phenomenological point of view, the Biblical origins of Judaism may be unrecognizable to present day Judaism. Yet those roots, as well as the diverse stages and forms of Judaism's Judaisms, are held together by a sense of continuity supplied by the tradition itself through memory and through the continuous recasting of past in terms of present. To take a more contemporary example, Jewish self-identity has decided that the Sabbatean movement is beyond the boundaries of Jewish self-definition, even if the historical study of Judaism is fascinated with the Sabbatean movement. Hence, Sabbateanism is one of many historical Judaisms. It should not, however, figure in a theologically constructed presentation of Judaism. Contemporary secular Zionism presents a challenge in a different direction. While historically one may make an argument that secular Zionism is not really a Jewish movement, indeed some of its own ideologues have argued in that direction, from the theological perspective one might decide to view the Zionist revival as another legitimate expression of Judaism, bearing continuity with Judaism's long story. The criteria are far from historically objective. They reflect ideological choices of a community. Yet, to the degree that the very act of presenting Judaism is itself theologically and ideologically motivated, it must rely on the self understanding of the religious community, and the way in which it shapes its memory to construct its identity.

There is, however, a second factor that lends the presentation of Judaism a dimension of objectivity. The reason the Dead Sea Scrolls should not come within the purview of a constructed Judaism is not only that the sectarians' memory did not become part of Israel's self identity. It is because their writings did not become part of Judaism's canon. Now, applying notions of canon to the diverse religious phenomena of Judaism is complicated. It is not even clear that some of the classics are canonical. I would refer to Maimonides' *Guide for the Perplexed* or the Rabbi Yehuda Halevi's *Kuzari* as classics. I would not refer to them as canonical. I would reserve the term canonical for those texts that are universally accepted by all parts of the Jewish people. In this context, it seems to me there are two literary corpora that enjoy such a status. The first is the *halacha*, from its foundational formulation in the Mishna down to its later articulation in the Shulchan Aruch and its commentaries. Hence, if we seek to portray Judaism we must take into account the place of *halacha* in its different manifestations, as these shape Jewish life. The second corpus, which for the purpose of the presentation of Judaism is more convenient than the *halacha*, is the Siddur, the Jewish prayer book. My Christian friends have taught me that *lex orandi* is *lex credendi* (literally, the law of prayer is the law of belief). The Siddur is probably the most canonical of all Jewish texts. It is significant because, unlike law codes that are read only by scholars, even if these comprise a significant portion of Jewish intelligentsia, and even if significant portions of the Jewish people are trained in reading such codes, the Siddur is read by every single member of the Jewish community without exception. Normative Jewish prayer practice mandates regular prayer, three times daily. While some women practice less than the full halachic mandate, they are nonetheless exposed to the Siddur on a daily basis. The Siddur, along with other liturgical standards, like the Passover Haggada, articulates the community's aspirations as it faces God. It is thus the single most important source for understanding the Jewish religion.

Now, obviously not everything in the Siddur necessarily measures up to the highest religious ideals of a given construction of Judaism. Maimonides' understanding of Judaism and the perfected religious state may not recognize the contents of the Siddur as the ultimate expression of the perfected philosophic-prophetic state. Nevertheless, I would argue the Siddur, along with the *halacha*, provide any construction of Judaism at the very least with checks and balances. I believe, in fact, that they provide much more. I would argue that the ultimate test for the viability of a presentation of Judaism is its ability to make sense of the liturgical heritage, to grow out of it. From the insider's perspective, the good presentation of Judaism should allow the member of the community to reidentify with greater vigor with the liturgical life. In this sense, liturgy not only provides the orienting principle for the entire constructive venture, but also the arena where the theological usefulness of a given theological construct is tested and bears fruit.

Having suggested liturgy and *halacha* as canonical cornerstones for the presentation of Judaism does not mean that all we need to do is a theology of the Siddur or a theology of the *halacha*, and this will provide us with the appropriate presentation of Judaism. Rather, these two canonical bodies provide the basic structure, upon which, historically, multiple superstructures have been created. These superstructures include philosophy, mysticism, piety, and various expressions of Jewish spirituality. Thus, one introduction to Judaism is structured around Maimonides' thirteen articles of faith. One cannot contest the legitimacy of such a presentation. However, reference to any of the superstructures is ultimately a choice, and, as such, is subjective. There is nothing inherently more compelling about a Maimonidean presentation of Judaism than a kabbalistic representation of the religion. Both are equally valid ways of making sense of the canonical texts, the law, the liturgy and the people's story. That they are radically different from one another suggests the wide range of ways in which Judaism can be constructed.

Let me spell out the implications of the above to our guiding question: what we would want the other to teach, or know, about us. In light of all the above, one can only say there is no one single way of teaching about us. Nonetheless, whatever way is chosen for the presentation of the religion, it must take into account those elements deemed fundamental to the tradition and its self-understanding. That is, it must convey continuity of identity of the different historical Judaism, presenting them as links in an ongoing chain, forming memory, giving rise to identity. It must also take into account the canonical texts of Judaism, and enable one to make sense of the two key corpora—the halachic corpus and the liturgical corpus. Beyond that, the same diversity and variety that characterize Jewish thought, it must also characterize the way it is presented to those outside Judaism.

Apologetics and Criticism

To present a religion is not a value-free activity. It is not a purely descriptive task. It involves value judgments concerning the subject matter. I originally approached the task of presenting Judaism as a purely descriptive task. As work proceeded, I discovered the work involved me in two types of activity, both of which implied value judgments that went far beyond the presumably neutral task of description. On the one hand, I became aware at certain points that what I was engaged in was a form of apologetics, which led me to reflect upon the place of apologetics in the descriptive work. On the other hand, I also found myself critical of the tradition. By critical I mean expressing a judgment on the concrete historical phenomena of Judaism and of Jewish life, in light of the wider perspective from which my view of Judaism was constructed. It is immaterial whether it is my perspective that is adopted, or some other perspective.

The significant issue, at this point in our discussion, is that the process of presentation of a religion also involves us in making value judgments upon certain historical manifestations of the religion, judgments that are unfavorable. Let me now offer some of my reflections on how I have come to understand the task of presenting my religion with regard to both the positive apologetic perspective and the negative critical perspective.

The first time I considered that what I am engaging in is apologetics rather than a scientific presentation of Judaism, I was horrified. I had, after all, entered this project assuming there was a neutral descriptive, hence scientific, way of presenting Judaism, which would be value-free. That Judaism had to be constructed rather than described meant that I had to read it, to interpret it, and to offer my interpretation as a presentation of Judaism. While engaged in interpretation, I realized it was my task to give Judaism the best possible reading. If you will, this is the famous principle of charity, as formulated in Dworkin's *Law Empire*. In reading a system we strive to give it the best possible reading. Indeed, the interfaith context may be taken as the context par excellence for apologetics in their highest form. Apologetics is the task of presenting our reality to the other. In the process, we discern, discover and present what may have been hitherto hidden from our own awareness. The apologetic context does not call for invention of false explanation, but for the uncovering of deeper structures of meaning. These become available precisely though the presence of an other who challenges us to the new insight that such a construction provides. If the fruit of the interfaith context is the highest form of apologetics, where does the academic or scientific background of our work come to play?

Two answers come to mind. The first is that in an important way my project differs from that of the uncritical introduction to Judaism. My presentation does not seek to present a truth, a complete system or something final. When Judaism is approached from a perspective that couples theological reflection carried out in an interfaith context, and historical awareness of the varieties of historical Judaisms, what ensues is not a statement of truth but a presentation of forces, movements and tensions, that have to be put together and constructed to create a whole. That constructive moment does not lose touch with its origins. It is a postcritical constructive moment that remains aware of the historical complexities that are its building blocks, rather than a precritical construction that presents Judaism in a facile and one-dimensional manner.

The second answer is a consequence of the first, and of still greater value. As a reader of Judaism, I am willing to criticize alongside the attempt to give the best possible reading. Offering the best reading does not equal condoning everything in the religion as it is. As already suggested, the formulation of the best possible reading may itself serve as the source of criticism of elements within the tradition. Hence, the presence of the other is not only occasion for uncovering and presenting the finest of the tradition. It is also a context for addressing those parts of the tradition that are problematic. The presence of an other may be necessary to bring those parts out to light in their fullness, as part of cleansing the religion. In other words, precisely because I present my religion in a context that is inescapably apologetic, I will sooner or later find myself making the distinction between positive and negative elements in the tradition, and the corresponding distinction between Judaism, viewed as a complete and ideal system, and the historical reality of the many Judaisms, lived by Jews at different times. The imperfections will be acknowledged as historical realities of the many lowercased judaisms, thus leaving my constructed uppercased Judaism free of the taint of human imperfection. Thus, the apologetic act of presenting my religion to the other provides an opportunity for self examination and for the raising of an ideal form of religion, that serves not only the outsider to whom I present, but the insider, who thereby is confronted with a new vision of his own tradition.

Let me provide two examples of apologetics, illustrating the difference between the type that is necessitated in the act of presentation of Judaism, and the kind of apologetics that is better avoided. In thinking of the Sabbath and the meaning of the commandment to refrain from labor, one is confronted with the task of introducing the outsider to a fundamental dimension of Jewish spirituality. How the Sabbath is celebrated is radically different from how a Christian or Muslim conceives of his or her own holy day. In presenting the Sabbath, one is engaged in a form of apologetics. Yet, the apologetic task is to bring forth and articulate the internal reality of the religious life in a way that can be understood by someone on the outside. The process is not one in which the reality is distorted or made to look other than what it is. The process is one of sharing and explaining, striving to capture the inner essence of a dimension of the religious life and to present it to the outsider. What is said to the outsider is, therefore, essentially what is said to the insider, and the apologetic moment is one in which one attempts to convey the inner sense and experience as lived by a member of the religion.

Let me contrast this with an example of apologetics I would wish to avoid. In discussing *mitzvot* and women's obligations to fulfill *mitzvot*, one might be tempted to offer explanations that were suggested by modern apologists, to account for women's exemption from time-bound commandments. One such explanation is that women need not observe time-bound, positive commandments, such as Sukka and Shofar, because due to their physical nature they have a different relationship to time. Men are in need of sanctification of time through ritual actions. Women have a particular relationship to time through their monthly cycles, and, therefore, do not need the time-bound commandments to shape their attitude to time and its sanctity. Now, in this case apologetics is an attempt to justify a fact of the religion, and to shelter it from criticism. Yet, there is no accompanying educational or spiritual direction that actually directs women to live their relationship to time in light of their feminine physiology. The apologetic moment here serves to justify, protect, and preserve. Beyond providing an interesting and intelligent rationale, it does not filter into education or lived spirituality. I would, therefore, claim that the kind of apologetic move that can be condoned must stem from the attempt to share the inner meaning and experiences as experienced by the practitioners of the religion with the outsider. What is difficult in the eyes of the other must be described, along with the presentation of how it is lived by the insider. Here, justification must give way to testimony. The testimony of the insider as to his or her understanding of the meaning of his/her religious life is the ultimate apologetic move. Improper apologetic seeks to demonstrate something is right or true. Proper apologetics seek to share the experience and significance of the queried fact to the life of the believer. Where such meaning cannot be found, the door is open to querying the ultimate meaning of those portions of tradition. Apologetics must seek to present religion in its best possible sense, in relation to God, while at the same time not seeking to justify all in it that is concretely present, remaining open to exposing the human frailties of the religion.

The difference between the two types of apologetics ultimately boils down to the question of whether in presenting my religion I must present it as perfect. I would argue that one of the factors that distinguishes an academically based approach to religion from a traditional one is the willingness to not view one's religion as something perfect. This is not a necessary consequence of academic training, and there may be individuals or even intellectual communities who may not draw such consequences. Yet, there is something sobering in the academic approach to religion. The historical approach brings to light portions of tradition that the traditional approach may comfortably overlook. The comparative approach suggests that much of what my religion does is claimed by other religious traditions as well. All religion, including my own, is thus recognized for its human component, alongside being a divine revelation, in some sense. The upshot of recognizing religion's humanity is the recognition that it is not perfect.

In the case of my understanding of Judaism, there is still another factor on account of which I approach its presentation without the preconceived idea that it is "perfect." This is my understanding that Judaism is a religion in process. In my presentation of Judaism, I offer the definition of Judaism as the story of Israel's life in God's presence. Story is very different than system. Systems need to be perfect. Stories are essentially in the process of striving toward perfection. Until the story is completed, one cannot speak of perfection. If Judaism is thus still in the process of becoming, I may approach it through a dual perspective. On the one hand, I seek to offer an image of its larger sense and meaning, striving to offer my best possible reading. On the other, I do not seek to justify all that is in Judaism as perfect, and as commensurate with its ultimate goals.

Let me offer some examples of this. Understanding Judaism's notion of election is one of the most difficult subjects, especially when such understanding is not articulated to an audience of insiders, but to an audience of non-Jews. Now, some ensuing attitudes of Jews to non-Jews are problematic. In reflecting upon Judaism as a whole, its larger spiritual vision, and its ultimate message for the non-Jewish world, I am led to consider to what extent some of the negative attitudes to the non-Jew are commensurate with Judaism's own higher ideals, and to what extent they should be considered products of a historical, and hence human, process. A different subject for scrutiny might be prayer. The fact that I present

Judaism to others makes me aware of how these others themselves relate to the same ideals that I present. I find it difficult to speak of Jewish prayer to a non-Jewish audience without feeling a certain embarrassment regarding the way in which prayer is experienced in the traditional Jewish service. Now, Jewish sources themselves make me aware of higher ideals than those that find expression in the concrete circumstances of history and community. In presenting Jewish prayer, do I simply limit myself to the written expressions of the spiritual aspirations of mystically minded authors, or may I also use the occasion to express my reservations concerning the concrete expressions of the communal Jewish life of prayer?

As I understand the moment of presenting a religion to the other, it is a moment of coming to terms with one's own reality, in the presence of the other. The presence of the other forces me to both present my religion in the best possible light, and also to come to terms with its problematic elements. If there are portions of my tradition of which I am ashamed, or that are problematic, how do I handle these in presenting my religion? One strategy might be to ignore them with the goal of presenting my religion in the most favorable light. I consider this to be insincere. Assuming my fundamental attitude to my religion is one of appreciation, admiration and love, these would communicate to my audience throughout my presentation. However, these will be all the more appreciated when accompanied by an open acknowledgement of the difficulties that my tradition historically presents.

At this point an important difference emerges between the insider's presentation of his own religion and the outsider's presentation of a religion. It is only the insider who, in the act of honest and open communication with an other, can question the tradition and draw attention to its imperfections. Were an outsider to do this, he would be accused of judging the other in a vein of triumphal religious polemic. Returning then to the insider-outsider issue, we emerge with one further important distinction between the teaching of the insider and the teaching of the outsider. The insider's presentation, relying, as I suggested, on theological insight in its construction of the religion, may include the type of self-examination and reflection that should be avoided by the outsider.

In thinking of what we want the other to teach about us, I, therefore, do not see the problem primarily as one of locating errors and misconceptions the other may hold, and trying to correct those. These are potentially endless, and must certainly be corrected as they arise. Yet, the ultimate significance of having an "other" in front of whom I present my religion is that it provides me an honest context for reflection and introspection, allowing me to both offer tradition's highest vision and the frailties of its historical manifestations.

The Power of Questioning

Let me return to an important implication of the notion that to speak of Judaism is to speak of a story, and not of a system. Constructing Judaism necessarily involves one also in projecting the future of the story. Now, Judaism has long envisioned the future. In fact, it has, over the ages, projected multiple images of the ideal future. As long as one is simply engaged in the act of describing historical Judaism, one can content oneself with a historical presentation of diverse messianic expectations. Presenting in a theologically constructive fashion presents challenges here. Let me illustrate one such challenge. In my presentation of Judaism, the temple plays a major role. It is the central spiritual institution through which God's presence is mediated. Its destruction engenders a series of alternatives and substitutes. One cannot understand Judaism's evolution and vision without considering the centrality of the temple. One fundamental expression of its continued relevance and centrality is the continued prayer for the rebuilding of the temple, a pivotal element in traditional prayer. And yet, what is it that one prays for? If I follow the guidelines I suggested above, then the liturgy points to an aspiration of what Gerschom Scholem has termed a "restorative nature." The future is a restoration of the past. This would include the reestablishment of animal sacrifices. Must I, in order to be faithful to Judaism, present this as part of Judaism's future vision? The question is raised in part by my own discomfort with the notion, but only in part. For there are visions of the future temple that see an ideal time in which no animal sacrifices will be offered. How do I go about presenting Judaism in a way that is both faithful to the tradition and to my own positioning or identification within the range of possibilities tradition presents? In my work I have taken the direction of posing questions. We may make proclamations about the past. Concerning the future we may raise questions and possibilities.

These will be informed by several factors: first, our understanding of the overarching concerns of the religion, the larger contours of the story; second, by the range of possibilities furnished by tradition; and third, by the personal choice of the writer, a factor I have already suggested is crucial to the entire enterprise of presenting a religion. Thus, in the example just offered, rather than assert the nature of worship in the future temple, I preferred to highlight the aspiration for the future temple in light of what seems to me to have been its primary function—mediation of divine presence. If temple is for presence, then the aspiration for a future temple is an aspiration for the full reestablishment of God's presence amidst His people. The specific forms the future will take must be left up to divine providence and direction. We can only pose the questions to which God must provide the answers.

In my work, the method of posing questions has emerged as an important element in my presentation of Judaism. To understand this, let me return to my thematic approach to Judaism. My work begins with an attempt to define Judaism. My premise is that the religion should be defined in a way that is descriptive of itself, and unique to it, rather than simply as one more instance of a wider category, not clearly defined as such, that we call religion. Hence, my definition of Judaism as the enduring story of Israel's life in the presence of God. There are several points I hope to make through this definition. The first, which I have already addressed, is that Judaism is not a system. The second is that Judaism is related to Israel, and in view of this special relationship should be seen as story. Third, this story is still incomplete and still in process of becoming. It is precisely for this reason that Judaism should not be thought of as a system or even a worldview. On the other hand, it is not simply a story of a people, a matter for folklore or ethnology. It is the story of Israel's life in the presence of God. There are thus two components to this story, Israel's life and the ways in which divine presence is mediated and anchored in and through Israel's life.

There are several implications to this working definition. The first is that in speaking of Judaism we must somehow retain the element of story. It is important to present Judaism as a continued story. The opening chapter of the story is in the book common to Jews and Christians. Its later chapters form the unique story of Judaism. Yet, those chapters should be seen as an extension and a continuation of the foundational chapter. Hence, in my presentation, which is consciously addressed to a Christian audience (indeed, it may be even inappropriate for a Muslim audience), I try to not simply present Judaism as it is, but as it grows and emerges out of its biblical roots. To tell the story is also to realize that Judaism is multilayered. The Jewish culture of study maintains vital conscious links between the different strands of Jewish tradition. Hence, entry into the story is also entry into a dialogue and conversation among the different layers of tradition, as these relate to one another. The texture of approach to Judaism is not only, as stated above, multi vocal, but also rich in stratification of the conversations of generations. To tell the story is thus to incorporate Judaism's growth and development into the story of the people and their life in God's presence.

A further implication of this definition of Judaism brings us back to posing questions. The two poles of my presentation, Israel's life and divine presence, along with the recognition that we are listening to a story, allow me to juxtapose Judaism and the Jewish people. The spiritual reality of Judaism, as expressed in the points of highest aspiration and contact with divine presence, and the concrete historical manifestations of Judaism, as expressed in the actual manifestations of historical Judaisms are connected in dynamic tension. And there is a danger in the tension that I present. By what authority do I classify certain dimensions of Judaism as belonging to its higher and ultimate essence, manifesting God's presence in Judaism, and other dimensions as "merely" the concrete historical manifestations of the history and life of the people? Indeed, I would hope I avoid the pitfall of classifying and passing judgment in such a facile manner. Nonetheless, the recognition that religion is composed of these two dimensions does allow us to reflect upon the highest ideals articulated within tradition itself, and upon their relationship to concrete historical manifestations. It is here that the method of posing questions emerges as a significant reflective tool. While it may be wrong of me to pass judgment on certain issues or phenomena, I can pose the question to what degree these phenomena accord with Judaism's own stated highest vision. Because the story is not complete, I may pose questions regarding its unfolding, questions that may themselves point to the future unfolding of the story.

To what extent does the life of the people, including spiritual, moral and religious life, accord with the higher guiding sense of divine presence?

This is a key question that informs my thinking and my presentation of Judaism. Thus, in presenting Torah study and prayer, and in juxtaposing them, I am not content to simply describe Jewish prayer alongside the practices of Torah study. Rather, I must pose the question of how these practices also mediate divine presence. In so doing, I seek to ground the historical religious manifestations in what I see as their ultimate point of reference. Yet, this attempt goes beyond the description of the phenomena, for it introduces questions, and can serve as a source of religious critique. Has the culture of Torah study affected the life of prayer adversely? How is divine presence related to these religious practices, both in theory and in practice? In what way are these practices ultimately adequate to their own stated goals, or to the perceived inner logic of Judaism? It is because I pose such questions that my presentation is not merely an uncritical praise of Judaism, but a presentation that struggles to uncover the higher sense of Judaism, while presenting its objective manifestations. It is on account of this struggle that the work is theological, not simply descriptive. And rather than the other needing me to explain Judaism to them, I believe I need the other in order to better articulate the questions, issues and struggles, in light of which and through which I can construct one specific, unique presentation of Judaism.

Presenting Judaism—Key Topics

Having presented the wider methodological issues that are implied in my presentation of Judaism, as well as the larger thematic framework from which I have described it, let me now conclude by listing the chapters that I saw fit to include in my presentation. The chapters were chosen with a specific Christian audience in mind. Once again, it is conceivable that someone writing for a Muslim audience might have chosen other subjects for his introduction. The choice of chapters also reflects the balance I found between a purely descriptive approach and a theological-constructive approach to the subject. I open my presentation with a definition of Judaism, the one I have already shared with you: how the story of the people and the divine presence unfolds is then presented through the notion of covenant, and then through other models that are relevant for later periods of Jewish thought. Similarly,

different historical and theological models of understanding are presented in the next chapter devoted to the subject of God. Covenantal, philosophical and Kabbalistic doctrines are seen in historical context and as
they apply to a contemporary Jewish attitude to God.

My next section is devoted to *mitzvah*, commandment. I chose to
focus upon *mitzvah* due to the centrality of the notion of *mitzvah* to
Jewish spirituality. I am also aware of the charge of legalism, with which
Judaism is charged, and therefore see the importance of highlighting the
role of *mitzvah* in ways that would counteract this charge. Perhaps the
most important factor to bear in mind is this section necessarily follows
the first; namely, *mitzvah* is grounded in relationship. A further approach
to the problem emerges as different senses of the term *mitzvah*, as these
unfold in different strands of Jewish thought, are brought to light. These
illustrate that the spirituality of *mitzvah* is not simply one of commandment, but one through which communion is achieved between God and
Israel. The next section focuses on one particular *mitzvah*, one that has
indelibly stamped Judaism, and which shapes its spiritual profile for the
past two millennia and longer. I refer to the study of Torah. My choice
to open with discussions of *mitzvah* and Torah reflects a choice to begin
with the particular and with that which is specific to the religion, rather
than with general categories that are universal to religions. Indeed, I
would not even title the section on Torah "Scripture," for I understand
the type of activity that is Torah study to be in some ways so specific and
unique that I wish to preserve its uniqueness by use of internal categories, rather than resorting to more conventional and general categories
of description.

This is not necessarily the case throughout my presentation. The following chapter is devoted to prayer, by all means a universal phenomenon. Of course, in the present context it is juxtaposed with Torah study,
in order to highlight its functioning within the systemic appreciation of
Judaism. Now, the tension between internal and external categories is
obvious in the next three chapters. The next three chapters are devoted
to sacred time, sacred space and holy men, in the case of Judaism conceived as indeed primarily a matter for humans. The discussion in these
chapters attempts to strike a balance between two modes of discourse.
On the one hand, there is a history of religious type presentation that
offers categories for understanding how the holy is mediated in these

three contexts. Such a discussion may indeed be relevant for students of other religions. Here, Judaism may indeed be seen as one example of the wider phenomenon of religion, and lessons may be drawn from it that are relevant to a wider appreciation of the phenomenon of religion. On the other hand, I also try to present the internal and specific logic of holiness of Judaism. Sacred time is broken down into Sabbath and Festival, following a fundamental traditional distinction in the nature of sacred time. Sacred time is discussed in relation to specifics of Israel's story, as expressed primarily in liturgy. Sacred space is presented in relation to Jewish history, and the ongoing quest for the temple and its substitutes. Reference to sacred space is significant in view of the fact that Judaism has been said to downplay sacred space in favor of sacred time. My discussion suggests that if anything, the opposite is true. The discussion is particularly relevant in the contemporary context of Israel's resettlement in their own designated homeland, God's space set apart and made holy for them to live on, in accordance with the divine code of holiness. Holy men too are presented as part of the inner, at times unconscious, quest for divine presence and its mediation through changing religious institutions.

The final two chapters are less descriptive and focus on two questions that I believe an outsider would want to understand, and at the same time are fundamental Jewish belief and identity. The first is the notion of election. Following a presentation of holy men and the various ways in which the sacred is expressed in time, space and humanity, a discussion of the holy people fits well both theologically and phenomenologically. Finally, the subject of the messianic hope and the vision of the future is discussed. While the messianic vision is no doubt central to Judaism, I am not convinced that it must find its place in any presentation. Once again, it is clear to me that my choice to conclude the presentation of Judaism with this topic stems from the fact that this issue is central to Christians, whose very name is rooted in Jewish messianic aspiration.

The list of topics covered in the introduction is the fruit of a dialectical awareness that informs my entire work. I speak as an insider, who must adopt a particular perspective in order to talk to an outsider—one specific and particular other, the Christian. In doing so, I both describe and construct. I must speak a language that is at one and the same time the external language of description and the internal language of presentation, with its indigenous categories and particular emphasis. I must at one and the same time present a history and a theology. I cannot testify to how successful or how unsuccessful my effort has been. In the very least, the significance of the work lies precisely in its conscious attempt to straddle this dual perspective. Its uniqueness is the outcome of the conscious recognition that I speak as a unique individual Jew addressing specific Christian audiences. The type of presentation that emerges in this interpersonal situation is a fruit of the two poles in the process of communication. What emerges is, therefore, necessarily unique. Its ultimate value lies in the way both my self-understanding and the other's understanding of me are formed in an interrelated moment of common understanding. It is such understanding that makes the entire enterprise worthwhile.

D A V I D   B U R R E L L ,   C S C

Teaching Christianity as an Abrahamic Faith

Each of the faiths which traces its origin to Abraham has a triadic structure which can be characterized as Revealer, Word, and Receiving Community. The one who reveals is identified with the creator of all-that-is, while the word spoken is the same word by which the universe is created. Yet in each case of explicit divine speech, that word is spoken so that human beings will receive it, and those who receive it will be formed by that same word into a distinctive community. Indeed, any Jew, Christian, or Muslim will find this description familiar, and also recognize that many failures to understand the contours of their religious faith often fail in neglecting one or another of these three realities, or in missing the creative interaction among them. So, for example, "fundamentalists" tend to focus on the word itself, abstracted from the One who speaks it as well as the community which receives it, while revisionists typically concentrate on the word-as-received, in an effort to adapt it to the culture in which they reside.

It is crucial to our thesis that these three are internally related once the Revealer has decided to reveal God's way to a people. As with creation itself, the initiative is totally with God, so the community has no claims to identity prior to its being called forth by the revealing word, nor need God speak that word. In this sense, all is *grace*. Yet once spoken, it is equally crucial that it be received freely by the intentional beings to whom it is addressed, so each of these traditions has identified that intentionality with the divine image bestowed in creation. Moreover, free reception gives the ensuing community a sense of ownership of that word, which creates a tension with the way in which it must also allow itself to be shaped and reshaped by that same revealing word. For as God's own word, this word is not itself part of creation, even though its mode of expression must be. So the revealing word will in one way stand over against the community which it shapes, yet that very community will also need to establish that word's coherence with respect to the intellectual world it inhabits, as well as employ the resources of the revealed word to illuminate the world in which it lives. Whether one calls it interpretation or theology, as "faith seeking understanding" it represents the responsible dimension of humans freely receiving the revealing word of God.

Once this scenario is in place, it becomes clear how a Christian understanding of revelation is internally tied to God's original choice of Israel. Early attempts (such as by Marcion) to sever God's revelation in Jesus from the Hebrew scriptures were deemed heretical, linked as they were to a dualistic picture of creation and redemption, as well as opposing the two covenants to one another. There is, as we shall see, a "new" element in God's revelation in Jesus, so contrasts will be in order, but never opposition. I was reminded of this forcibly when attending a celebration of 75 years of Catholic Christianity in Mbarara, Uganda, in 1975. Startled to think that 1900 had represented a clean slate for introducing this divine revelation to this people in this portion of the globe, I wondered how the original missionaries had gone about their task. Indeed, how does one begin to talk about Jesus? I was told that these French White Fathers had listened to the people's stories. That gave them two initial good marks: they had learned the language, and they had listened. When they heard these stories, they remarked that they had similar stories. So Paul's famous image of God's revelation in Jesus being grafted onto the trunk of Israel (Romans 11:17), the parent tree planted by God's original word to Abraham and fertilized by subsequent words to Moses, came to life in this account. On reflection, of course, how else could one begin to "talk about Jesus" except in terms set by the covenant under which he was born?

How, indeed, did the earliest believers in Jesus—Jews all—speak of him? By the seamless account of Luke-Acts, as one who continued to astound them with the way he taught, "as one with authority," by contrast with their own certified teachers. And then their disillusion attending his shameful demise, followed by exaltation at his presence to them risen.

Here, in Acts, begin the proto-affirmations of his unique identity before God: "there is no other name under heaven by which. . . ." (Acts 4:10–12) Invoking the name of anyone other than "the Holy One" as a way of gaining access to "salvation" would be idolatry; but not so with Jesus' name. Jesus' *name* may be invoked as God's own name is invoked because he himself is God's revelation. As has often been remarked, there is little that is novel in Jesus' words; what is striking is his presence, presented throughout the gospels as a healing presence. As the first letter of John begins: "This is what we proclaim to you: what was from the beginning, what we have heard, what we have seen with our eyes, what we have looked upon and our hands have touched—we speak of the word of life" (1 John 1:1).

Here the triadic structure shared by all the Abrahamic faiths is stretched to a limit, for the word whereby God reveals the way for rational, responsive creatures to return all that we have received is himself a person, with the result that the community shaped by that word to receive it will be constituted as children of God, brothers and sisters of Jesus. Indeed, to belong to that community is to be reborn "in Christ," as Leo the Great announces in a Christmas sermon:

> Though each and every individual occupies a definite place in this body to which he has been called, and though all the progeny of the church is differentiated and marked with the passage of time, nevertheless as the whole community of the faithful, once begotten in the baptismal font, was crucified with Christ in the passion, raised up with him in the resurrection and at the ascension placed at the right hand of the Father, so too it is born with him in this Nativity, which we are celebrating today (*Patrologia Latina* [PL] Vol. 54, pp. 213–16).

And lest that language be nothing more than a cascade of metaphors, we are reminded by Cyril of Alexandria, commenting on the Gospel of John, that this community is constituted by "the Spirit" which Jesus received at his baptism, accompanied by the divine words: "You are my Son; today I have begotten you" (Matthew 3:17). Yet, since Jesus is Son of God, in what sense do these words announce an event? Cyril explicates:

> The Father says of Christ, who was God, begotten of him before the ages, that he is 'begotten today', for the Father is to accept us in Christ,

in so far as he is man. So the Father can be said to give the Spirit again to the Son, though the Son possesses the Spirit as his own, in order that we may receive the Spirit in Christ. The only-begotten Son receives the Spirit, but not for his own advantage, for the Spirit is his, and is given in him and through him. He receives it to renew our nature in its entirety and to make it whole again, for in becoming man he took our entire nature to himself, for it is through Christ that all gifts come to us. (*Patrologia Graeca* [PG] Vol. 73, pp. 751–54).

This is overwhelmingly rich, indeed metaphysical fare, yet the predilection of Christianity for such exposition stemmed directly from the fact of God's revelation being *in* Jesus, and not simply *from* or even *through* him. That God's word is divine should go without saying, yet early Islamic thought wavered on the issue whether the *Qur'an* was created or not, anxious as it was to safeguard the distinction of creator from everything else. Not for long, however, for a creator who is mute (or uncomprehending) proved intolerable. Yet to find the word transmuted into a person suggested that what is being revealed is more than a way, but God's own self; while the personal relation with this person Jesus (which the Gospels call "faith") is one which invites us into a comparable relation of filiation with God. So this community is an ontological one, reflecting an inner transformation of human beings into children of God. Again, John:

In the beginning was the Word, and the Word was with God, and the Word was God. All things were made through him; without him was made nothing that was made. He came into his own and to those who received him, who were born not of the will of the flesh or of man, but of God, he gave the power to become children of God. And the word was made flesh, and dwelt amongst us, and we have seen his glory, as of the Father's only son, full of grace and of truth. (John 1:1, 4, 10–14)

So it was inevitable, one might say, that the identification of Jesus with God's word would take the triadic structure common to all the Abrahamic faiths, and transmute it into a trinitarian divinity with names derived from the new revelation—Father, Son, and Spirit; a divinity ready to receive into its rich inner life all those "who believe in Jesus." Yet the fact remains that it took this community four centuries to clarify the issues surrounding the affirmations of Jesus' divinity, already implicit in Acts. The explanation seems clear: nothing could contradict the defining affirmation of one God which constituted the original covenant ("Hear, O Israel, the Lord your God is one"), and would also form the clarion call of Islam. A God who is Father, Son and Spirit could not thereby be any less One! And that the controversies should turn on the ontological constitution of Jesus, rather than a direct explication of the scriptural language of "Father, Son, and Holy Spirit," incorporates the relation between creation and redemption, since the human and divine natures united in the one person of the Word (in the culminating formula of Chalcedon in 451) reflect both creature and Creator.

We have also seen, however, how the language of Father and of Son will be filled out by that of Holy Spirit, as the one incorporating all believers into the inner life of God so effectively displayed in the person of Jesus. So Trinitarian reflection has always been more than an exercise in higher ontology, for the Spirit's role has ever been one of "divinization," of effecting the transformation of believers into children of God "in the Son." Indeed, the defining characteristic of the new covenant, already implicit in the manner of revelation in the person of the Word made human in Jesus, becomes explicit in the transformed community of faithful. It is this founding fact which accounts for the ubiquity of the language of "grace" in Christianity, a term with both personal and ontological undertones. Yet I would also call attention to its presence in Islam, where the formula for the divine reality of the *Qur'an* runs parallel to that of Jesus: as Christians believe that the Word of God is made flesh in Jesus, so Muslims contend that the Word of God is made Arabic in the *Qur'an*. Indeed, Muslims attest that meditative recitation (*dhikr*) on these words can effect in Muslim believers the same quality of transformation which Christians associate with reception of the body and blood of Christ in the Eucharist. In each case, what is said to transpire is an activity of God transforming the person ("grace"), effected via the mode of revelation proper to each community: the word of God made human in Jesus, and the word of God made Arabic in the *Qur'an*.

That the revealing activity of God takes place in a person, then, calls forth all the intellectual resources of philosophy to try to express this Creator/creature relation in a way which respects the reality of both. Indeed, the relation of Creator with creature within the person of Jesus also marks that person as a sacrament: that is, one whose very mode of being reminds us how present the Creator is to all creatures, yet present here so that very relation is displayed in a person. Similarly, Islam reminds its faithful that they are only able to notice how created thing are *signs* [*ayat*] of the creator since their minds and hearts have been opened by the *verses* [*ayat*] of the *Qur'an*. So Christianity finds God's presence in bread and wine, water and salt, because these have been transformed by the very words of the Word incarnate. So two defining features of Christian life—doctrine and sacrament—both stem from the grounding fact that this Word is flesh, or human. Moreover, the third term of the triad, the living community, which we have linked with the Holy Spirit, is also referred to as the "Body of Christ." That is, an organic unity prior to the individuality of each of the faithful who make it up, rooted in this person whose divine/human constitution reminds each of us of the call to live by God's own life. So Vatican II explains the public prayer of the church:

> Every liturgical celebration, as an activity of Christ the priest and of his body, which is the church, is a sacred action of a preeminent kind. In the liturgy on earth we are given a foretaste of the liturgy of heaven, celebrated in the holy city of Jerusalem, the goal of our pilgrimage. (Constitution on Liturgy, *Sacrosanctum Concilium,* 1963, pars. 7–8.)

Jesus, as the Spirit of Christ, prays in the Christian praying.

Another term for that new life is "grace," which signifies an adoptive relation to God-the-revealer which mirrors in creatures the generative relation of God to God's own Word. As noted previously, all these features of Christian life and thought reflect an unimaginable initiative on the part of the Revealer: not just to speak the divine Word, but to become one of us without ceasing to be that Word, and to do so in such a way as to call us "not servants but friends" (John 15:15). Features like these will inevitably "give offense," as Kierkegaard remarks (in sickness unto death especially), yet that must be part of the package. Again, the pattern can be found in biblical revelation in God's choosing this people as God's very own, or in Islam in God's gifting Muhammad with the *Qur'an*. In each case—election of Israel, Word incarnate in Jesus, Word made Arabic in the *Qur'an*—the initiative is completely God's, so no reason can be forthcoming. Philosophy can discern patterns, as we have here, yet never be able to give reasons, for in each case all is gift, as each of the revelations assures us creation is as well. This is the pattern which Augustine discerned in battling Pelagius: while humans can rightly be rewarded for good actions and punished for evil ones, no one can merit the gift of new life, or election, or hearing the *Qur'an* recited. These are as gratuitous as our very lives are, and receiving them as freely given reminds us how our lives also are gift—much as refraining from labor on *Shabbat* is designed to remind us that our work of perfecting God's creation is rooted in the gift of creation itself.

Before moving from vision to practice, a word on the relative role of understanding and judgment seems in order. As one whose practice as a philosophical theologian places me at the intersection of philosophy and theology, I have become conscious of the relative weight which these disciplines place on understanding and on judgment. The mix is never clear, for at times philosophical training will lead one to try to ascertain whether what was said is true, while theological skills may focus one on the manner in which different assertions have been formulated over the centuries, seeking (as Newman did so deftly) to find a pattern or drift in the permutation. Yet in other respects, philosophically trained in inquirers may prefer to focus on the sense of the formulations while theologians may be more concerned to ascertain their truth. However those predilections may display themselves in different cases, it is imperative that dialogic inquiries like the present one learn how to distinguish probing initiatives seeking understanding from those who propose a definitive creedal formulation. For dialogue especially serves understanding, where finding similarities and differences in formulations and in practices can lead to mutual illumination of one tradition by another. And that enhanced understanding will lead one more surely to judgments regarding one's own and other traditions, since judgment is inherently comparative, as one seeks always for a better way of expressing a revealed truth. (Aristotle's remarks on the relative accuracy of dialectical assertions—"human beings are animals"—and specific ones—"human beings are rational animals"— offers a simple case in point. Both are true, yet the second leads one more properly into the subject matter at hand.) So the pattern proposed here of a triadic structure for Abrahamic faiths will be realized quite differently in each, yet it is proposed to facilitate the "mutual illumination" which comparative inquiries can achieve at the level of understanding, which is at least indirectly relevant to the subsequent activity of judgment.

The next step in this comparative inquiry focuses on the community's reception of the revelatory word, and specifically on each community's way of distorting that revelation. I will call this trait a tradition's "shadow-side," adapting Jung's reading of individual psychology to the dynamics of a group. For Jung, one's shadow represents the individual dimension of the unconscious, stemming from conditions marking one's personal history. The shadow is normally exhibited in apparently inexplicable eruptions—"you just pushed his buttons!"—which are often more evident to those with whom we live closely than they are to ourselves. "Family-of-origin" therapy is designed to make us more aware of the sources of these distortions, as a way of alerting us to their presence and giving us skills to neutralize them. This dimension of the unconscious is not itself archetypal, but tied more particularly to our individual histories, and so more easily brought to consciousness. Yet we can remain quite oblivious to it, especially when we occupy a dominant position which demands less accommodation to others' needs or presence. Yet that hardly serves our own welfare, since left unchecked, such "shadows" can conspire to undermine our noblest aspirations. And what is most germane to our inquiry, it is these features which often shape our initial impressions of a person, whatever other virtues they may possess.

Adapting Jung's "shadow" to understand how religious traditions present themselves offers a way of detaching a tradition from its founding revelation. We can trace a faith community's "shadow side" by locating the distortion in the appropriating actions of individuals and groups, rather than in the revelation itself. Among the Abrahamic faiths, it can be said that Christianity casts the longest shadow, perhaps attributable to its prolonged hegemony in the west. (Recall how a dominant status can isolate the one dominating, rendering them unaware of how much they need the "other" to make sense of themselves—a key premise of this investigation.) The signs of distortion are especially evident in Christian attitudes toward Jews and toward Muslims. These sets of attitudes stem from quite different origins, with the Jews representing a continuing version of the "old" covenant which Christians believed to have been replaced by the "new," while Muslims came forward with a new revelation in the wake of the definitive revelation of the God of

Abraham, Isaac, and Jacob in Jesus. As a result, Christianity could find no theological space for either community, so oscillated between grudging toleration and outright persecution of Jews, while instigating the Crusades to rid the Holy Land of the so-called Muslim menace.

In each case, however, Jews and Muslims represented the "other" who could either call Christianity forth to a richer understanding of itself, or furnish the scapegoat which needed to be eliminated to lay claim to its privileged hegemony, secular as well as sacred. Jews, of course, did not pose the overt threat to that hegemony which the Muslim armies could, but by persisting as a worshiping community in the face of Christian recognition of Jesus as "the Messiah," they represented an even greater affront to Christian self-understanding. We can appreciate this in retrospect as we note how patristic metaphorical oppositions of "shadow/reality" or "flesh/spirit" prevailed over Paul's insistence that "God never takes back his gifts or revokes his choice" (Romans 11:29). It is the last phrase which Vatican Council II adopted in its effort to alter the inertial course of centuries of common Christian teaching that the "Old Testament" had effectively been superceded by the "New." While never enshrined in conciliar pronouncement as church doctrine, these recurring metaphors assured that most Christians adopted that attitude toward Jews. What assured the vilification of Jews, however, was the leitmotif of the Gospels that as Jesus' own people, they had nonetheless rejected him as "the one whom God had sent": "he came into his own and his own received him not." (John 1:11) Yet all of Jesus' immediate disciples were Jews, of course, so John's constant reference to "the Jews" as those with whom Jesus was locked in mortal combat is a thoroughly ambiguous reference, usually considered to denominate the power structure, although in times of Christian hegemony its reference became all too clear: all Jews. Moreover, were not the Gospels clear? Did Jews not bear collective responsibility for Jesus' death? In Matthew, they even took it on explicitly: "Let his blood be on us and our children" (Matthew 27:26).

The Gospels were never intended primarily as historical document, however, but rather as *kerygma* in the spirit of Hebrew *haggadah*: a story told so as to elicit a heartfelt response to God's saving action. In that spirit, rejection of "the one whom God has sent" by God's chosen people, and notably by their leaders, is directly reminiscent of the excoriations of Israel's canonical prophets, who never ceased to call their people accountable for ingratitude to the One who had singled them out, and for failing to "recognize the time of God's visitation." Yet again, it is one thing to excoriate one's own people, and another to vilify an alien people, which Jews quickly became, especially after Constantine. It must be said, however, of any tradition that the best interpretation of haggadic texts comes from the primary context in which they are heard: the liturgy. When John's gospel is read publicly on Good Friday, the assembled congregation is given a role which they take up with gusto: "Crucify him!" Repeated practice of this sort should insinuate in its participants the kerygmatic point of that (and every) Gospel: no one else but I/we is involved in this drama. Otherwise it could not be what it purports to be: the drama of our salvation. As an Anglican friend in Jerusalem loved to remark, when questions of assigning blame for Jesus' death emerged: "I should have thought that any Christian who blamed the death of Jesus on someone else had missed the point of the Gospels!" That is, anyone who had been formed in the practice of hearing the Gospels for the message they were designed to carry could not escape their personal implication, though all would try.

So Christians who would leave Good Friday services and torch the ghetto had indeed missed the point of the Gospel they had just heard, and perhaps were even encouraged to do so by the preacher. Yet this propensity to escape the implications of God's word intended for them puts Christians squarely within the condemnations issued by Israel's prophets to their own people. Indeed, however "new" the revelation of God in Jesus might be thought to be, the dynamics of its reception mirrors Israel's reception of the Torah. Indeed, this strategy dominated Christian writers throughout history, who mined the Hebrew scriptures for paradigms of their own journey of faith, as the Christian community adopted David's Psalms as the heart of its liturgical prayer. This pervasive practice gives the lie to any triumphal reading of the "new" testament as replacing the "old." For even if Christians must regard Jesus' coming as "fulfilling the scriptures," that fulfillment remains a promise in the lives of those incorporated into the new life bestowed in Jesus. Faith remains a journey, only to be fulfilled "on the last day." So existentially, if you will, Jews and Christians journey on similar paths of faith, united in reciting the Psalms as their nourishment for that journey. Their adherence to the goal will differ qualitatively as the mode of revelation differs, yet their way to that goal exhibits striking parallels. Once this fact is recognized as pervading Christian use of the Hebrew Scriptures, we can see how necessary are the people Israel to Christians becoming what they are called to become.

The relationship between Christianity and Islam differs from the one sketched out with Judaism on a number of counts. First, Christians do not share a book with Muslims as they do, in part, with Jews. Second, unlike Moses, whose Torah formed the heart of "the scriptures" on which Jesus based his mission, Muhammad emerged later as a prophet bringing a new revelation to those who had styled themselves as the "new Israel." Finally, Islam presented itself as the authentic and definitive revelation for all peoples, whereas Judaism was expressly confined to God's people Israel, despite proselytizing tendencies in Roman times. So Christianity and Islam were set in principle on a collision course, which turned into actual warfare as each religious community also staked territorial claims. A poignant example is the fate of the thriving Christian communities of North Africa, associated with Cyprian and with Augustine, in the wake of the lightning expansion of Islam within one hundred years of the Prophet's death. No one seems to know what happened to them, though the macabre pictures of Muslim warriors "spreading Islam by the sword" which stirred western imaginations to "holy wars" against them were certainly far from the truth. As diverse groups of crusaders were to experience themselves, Muslim troops normally engaged in warfare according to rules of engagement quite chivalrous in character. And as Bernard Lewis has remarked in collating Islamic views of the west, Muslims were wont to signal the superiority of Islam by noting how it did not need to be "spread by the sword"—a telling reversal of a stereotype, which should alert western Christians to the extent to which they have laundered the fact and impact of the Crusades out of their history.

But what about the Crusades? I have suggested them as a prime example of the "shadow-side" of Christianity as it encountered Islam. Can they not be more simply explained as economic historians are wont to do, and as a nearly inevitable outcome of the theological collision course just noted, coupled with rival territorial claims? After all, the "holy land" was the prize, where these contrary theological claims had to come in conflict. Historical explanation can never be monochromatic, however, so none of these alternatives is able to cancel out the others. What a

Christian reader finds so perplexing in the literature of the crusades is the way in which reflective spiritual leaders, like Bernard of Clairvaux, became caught up in the frenzy—people who could hardly have countenanced the excesses to which the "crusading spirit" incited collective marauding bands. Something more than economic gain or irredentism seems to have animated this prolonged movement, and prevailed over then classical Christian teaching regarding "just wars" and their conduct.

When we consider the paucity of medieval voices seeking to understand Islam as a way of faith—though a few do stand out, such as Peter the Venerable and later John of Segovia—and the readiness with which each side portrayed the other as "infidels," we cannot help but see Islam cast as "the other." And once that reaction-formation is in place, as we have noted with Judaism, nothing can be learned about one's own faith from that of the other. It is true that disputations were regularly carried on by Muslim and Christian intellectuals in Muslim lands, where the Qur'an itself enjoined an official tolerance toward Jews and Christians, yet disputations were seldom carried out in a dialogic spirit. Nor did the spirit of the time foster "dialogue," yet the ferocity of the Crusades, with their animosity toward Jews and Orthodox Christians en route to the Holy Land, hardly testifies to the spirit of the Gospels. Indeed, it seems that Islam afforded that "other" which activated in an especially acerbic way the "shadow-side" of Christianity, and there are abundant signs that it continues to do so today.

Yet some voices are beginning to explore the ways in which an appreciation of the dynamics of the Qur'anic revelation can illuminate fresh facets of Christian revelation, in the spirit of "mutual illumination." The early work of Anawati and Gardet effectively established the comparative study of Christian and Islamic theology, while the recent comparative study of Roger Arnaldez (Three Messengers for One God [Notre Dame IN: University of Notre Dame Press, 1996) brings that art to a fine point. On a more general level, Burrell and Malits' Original Peace (New York: Paulist, 1997) explores classical Christian affirmations from the focus on creation proper to Islamic theology, yet often eclipsed by the "salvation" narrative in Christian tradition. What may prove yet more telling than these intellectual explorations, however, are the signs of collaboration among Christians and Muslims as people of faith in a western ethos often self-characterized as "post-Christian" or "secular" in character. As Muslim communities begin to root themselves in pluralistic societies in the west, they cannot but feel an affinity with other religious groups in that society, but will also find themselves adapting to that western ethos in ways which in time will certainly affect Islam in its traditional milieu.

It is notably in those arenas in which the "secularization thesis" appears to be verified most starkly that its gains are increasingly being weighed against concomitant losses, as another generation begins to seek out the resources of their ancestral faith. Much as the human toll and ecological disasters in the wake of state Marxism dramatically displayed the underside of that enlightenment ideology, so a rapacious market economy is showing its underside across the globe. What is becoming clear is that nothing short of a transcendent faith can properly direct human development, or even (as John Paul II has argued in *Fides et Ratio* ["Faith and Reason"]) restore our faith in human reason. Yet the very communities which stand as vehicles of that faith have discredited themselves in their readiness to espouse an ethnic nationalism, demonize "the other," and even animate inhuman projects of "ethnic cleansing." Is not the challenge to religious communities in the millennium that we face one in which those same communities must so catechize their faithful that nationalist politicians will no longer be able to play the religion card?

Indeed, it is that very challenge which pushes theological inquiry into interfaith issues in our time. Some twenty years ago, in the wake of Vatican Council II, the renowned Austrian theologian, Karl Rahner, offered a radical re-periodization of Christian history in which symbolic dates emerged to bracket what he called nineteen centuries of western Christian history: namely, 70 and 1970 (*Theological Studies*, 1979). The first recalled the destruction of the Temple in Jerusalem and the eclipse of Jewish believers in Jesus by a flood of Greek converts, shifting the vortex of the movement to Rome. Coming as 1970 did in the wake of decolonization and the perspectives launched by Vatican II toward a more inclusive enculturation, Rahner regarded the slim document *Nostra Aetate*, treating of the Church's relations to Jews and to non-Christian believers, as the most prescient result of that Council. Other extensive deliberations of the Council had represented the fruit of decades of theological preparation, while *Nostra Aetate* responded to facts of history (including Auschwitz) for which Christian theology had been singularly unprepared, as it had also been for the extensive mission to "the Gentiles" signaled by 70 CE. It is hardly surprising that Christian theologians, trained within the parameters of the "western Christianity" exposed by Rahner, have been dilatory in appreciating his proposal, much less responding to it. For after all, his fresh periodization leaves the 16th century as a blip on the screen, while most western Christian theology has been fueled by that upheaval. Yet a salutary effect of secularization has been to make those intra-Christian divisions less relevant, as Christianity becomes polarized between an increasingly ecumenical *ecclesia,* where young people are less tolerant of Church boundaries, and groups grasping tightly an identity which sees both ecumenism and interfaith initiatives as threats to an "integral Christianity (or Catholicism)." This is an understandable response to a world in which we are invited to learn from others rather than demonize them, since "the other" will inevitably elicit both fascination and fear. Again, the capacity of the Christian revelation to be a resource for hope rather than fear offers the crucial test of this millennium.

The hopeful side of our proposal begins with each Abrahamic faith recognizing and acknowledging its shadow-side and begins to mine its tradition for the resources to neutralize those shadows. Here the inner creativity of each tradition can emerge, and in doing so present itself as a beacon in a world torn by conflict—conflict which these same religious groups had often animated. What is most telling about our times, however, is the fact that these resources are best discovered in conjunction with others; that interaction among people of faith will serve to uncover the resources for peace and reconciliation in each. We have already seen how groups firmly rooted in one tradition and able to reach out to others have renewed the face of both, as their collaboration led to a mutual illumination of each by the other. (See especially Scott Appleby's recent work which mentions among others the lay Catholic community in Rome, Sant' Egidio, and its work for reconciliation in diverse parts of the world.) The dynamic of these groups effectively belies the fears of those for whom such collaboration cannot but spell relativism or syncretism. "For authentic interfaith dialogue and effort, like friendships among persons of different faiths, cannot but strengthen the faith of each, as each comes to realize that the God whom they worship differently lies beyond our comprehension. Indeed, classical theologians of each of the

Abrahamic faiths, from al-Ghazali to Maimonides to Aquinas, all acknowledge that we can at best "imperfectly signify" the God who is creator of all-that-is, and that our faith formulations admit of unending development. In our time, that growth will take place within our traditions us as we interact with each other, learning how to share in different faiths—the challenge of our millennium.

J A M A L   J.   E L I A S

What Do We Want the Other to Teach About Islam?

Previous speakers and people in general discussion have brought up the point that it is important to be conscious of the audience when one is talking about one's own religion or another's. With that in mind, I want to begin by saying that my primary experience of teaching Islam is limited to 18- to 22-year-olds at a prestigious, private, secular, 4-year college in the United States. My students are predominantly white, upper middle or upper class, and very few of them come from religious backgrounds. Without having conducted a formal survey, I would guess that a quarter of my students are Jewish; and about ten percent are so-called minorities (which would be east-Asians, immigrant and foreign Muslims mostly from South Asia, and very few African-Americans). The remainder of the students come from a variety of Christian backgrounds. There are, in all, less than fifteen Muslim students out of a total student body of 1,600 at Amherst College. Most of these are nonpracticing foreign-born students. Only one is African-American. At my institution I am one of three faculty members who teaches anything to do with Islam or the Middle East.

Despite the fact that most of my students are ostensibly Christians and Jews, when I make any Biblical reference in order to clarify a point, I am often greeted with vacant stares from the vast majority of my class. I might also add that I do a fair amount of outreach work, what we call 'interfaith dialogue' here. In my experience, most Americans consider Islam and Muslims to be culturally foreign to them and approach Islam with a combination of ignorance and hostility. These experiences have convinced me that one cannot treat Islam in a similar way to the way one treats Christianity or Judaism in Western academic settings. I do not mean to imply that the case of Islam shares nothing with Christianity's view of Judaism or vice-versa, or to trivialize the very real antipathies that have colored the interaction between adherents of these two religions. I am simply saying that, in the view of most Americans, Christianity is certainly seen as an authentically European or Western religion. Judaism, too, has come to be viewed as a Western phenomenon. In contrast, Islam and Muslims are often viewed as belonging to a different civilization—a distinctly non-European one, and one which is hostile to the West. This is a complicated issue, not made easier by the fact that many Muslims view themselves also as separate from Western civilization. I will address some of these ideas before turning to what I consider to be the central points of Islam and its theology.

The encounter with the West is probably the most important event in the Islamic world in the last two centuries. The Crusades are important, but *the* meaningful encounter is really a recent one. The outline of what one needs to know about Islam presented here closely follows my textbook, *Islam*, which is available in five languages. For some reason it is selling very well in Ireland and China, which I cannot figure out!

I would like to emphasize that it is obvious in polemical literature and visible in other literature and art that there is an evolutionary continuity in the West's views of Islam from the period of the Crusades, through the Colonial period, into the present. During the Colonial period, European powers may have had a sense of superiority vis-à-vis their colonial subjects, but their attitude toward Muslims was different from that toward the Chinese or the sub-Saharan Africans. They never perceived the Chinese or the Africans as a genuine military and civilizational threat. There was no special place in hell reserved for a Chinese religious figure as there was for Muhammad in Dante's *Inferno*. This attitude has persisted over the last two centuries through notions such as the 'White Man's Burden' or European exceptionalism.

Of course, the category of "otherness" was applied to non-Muslims as well, but what set Muslims apart was that they were not a race or ethnicity. They were viewed as a civilization, the civilization that bordered Europe on all sides, except where Europe was bordered by the sea. In the opinion of many Muslims, the events of the latter half of the twentieth century bear out this view of the world, and it is not uncommon to hear Muslims observe that Colonialism is not over or even to say that the Crusades are not over. They see a European antipathy toward Muslims in German immigration policies, in the unquestioned support given to Israel, in the failure of the West to do anything about bringing war criminals to justice after the horrific war in Bosnia, in the absolute routine with which the most racist and offensive things are said about Muslims in the U.S. media, in the politics surrounding Turkey's attempts to join the European union, in the millions suffering due to the war in Iraq, and in many, many other things.

In observing Western attitudes, I have identified five points that seem the most problematic in attempting to understand Islam and Muslims. Some are characteristic of popular views of Islam; others are confined to the teaching thereof. And these five points are: 1) Islam is seen as essentially Middle Eastern and especially Arab; 2) Emphasis is placed almost exclusively on the classical tradition; 3) Islam is presented as an unusually ritualistic religion; 4) Islam is seen as oppressive toward women; and 5) Muslims are seen as violent. I do not have time to address all five points in detail, but the first three deserve some attention because they are common issues in the teaching of Islam and its theology.

I believe that a problem that is particularly acute in the U.S. is seeing Islam as exclusively Middle Eastern, and of seeing all Middle Eastern non-Israelis as Arabs. In part this is understandable since this region is where the religion started and where Islam's central holy sites are located. Furthermore, as a language of scripture, Arabic occupies a very special place in Islamic civilization and in religious usage. However, events of the 20th century, especially the identification of the Arab-Israeli conflict with Muslims in general, and the shutting off of substantial sections of the Islamic world during the Soviet era, have exacerbated this problem. I would like to point out that the overwhelming majority of Muslims live east of the Indus river, that most Muslims do not speak Arabic, and that the Muslim population of Indonesia is roughly equal to the entire population of Muslim Arabs. If one presented a statistical display of the median Muslim in the world, she would probably be a 16-year-old girl from Bangladesh.

The second point is more complicated because Muslims themselves participate in perpetuating this perception. This is the notion of an Islamic Golden Age, and the problem of people continuing to present the religion as one of the real or imagined era that extended from the 7th until the 11th century. However, many things have occurred in the Islamic world since then and to view these developments as somehow degenerate, illegitimate, or as a corruption of a pure, original Islam is misleading. This misrepresentation is related to my first point, since the big change that occurred at the end of the classical period was the increasing influence of non-Arabs as full-fledged contributing members of the Islamic community. The emphasis on the classical tradition trivializes the real religious lives of many people who do not participate in that version of the religion, but are, nonetheless, Muslims.

Many introductory textbooks about Islam make absolutist statements such as: 'Muslims pray five times a day,' or 'Muslims fast in the month of Ramadan.' I have never had the opportunity to gather empirical data on the subject, but the majority of Muslims certainly do not pray five times a day. If I were to hazard a guess, the majority of Muslims pray less than once a day. To say that they *must* pray five times a day is not only incorrect, but it also grossly misrepresents the nature of these people's religiosity and the relative importance they accord to ritual versus faith. The notion that one must pray five times a day as a ritual obligation, as if it were all or nothing, misses the point. The law is stated as an ideal and each Muslim chooses his or her relationship with God, the relationship between faith and works, and the importance of ritual in their lives.

The last two points are more an issue of cultural antipathy than they are pedagogical problems. I am particularly surprised by the visceral reaction that issues related to women seem to elicit among otherwise liberal and open-minded people in the U.S.—especially among educated women. Rather than try to find points of commonality with Muslim women's experience, I find many of my students (and other people I talk with) are intent on proving that Muslim women are universally and in every way worse off than women in the West, and that this situation is not the result of society or politics or economics, but of a religion: Islam. The curious fact is that Islam is particularly criticized for things that were, in fact, (and sometimes still are), aspects of Western civilization that citizens of the modern West would like to transcend. This is an important issue and I think it deserves some elaboration. It is the crux of at least half the problem in representing Islam and the West; namely, that Europeans try to situate Islam and Muslims in Europe's own past as blame-worthy primitives who need to be modernized and become *like* the West.

So the misguided logic would suggest that since Islamic law does not afford women absolute parity with men, it follows that women must be worse off in every legal way than they are in the West and that the Islamic religious status of women must be akin to and, in fact, worse than what it is in Christian canon law or in Talmudic law. So the myths abound: polygamy is presumed to be unregulated and absolutely licen-tious; women must not have any recognized religious status or even souls; female circumcision must be religiously mandated and universally practiced; menstruating women must be untouchable; every veiled woman must be the victim of oppression and if she feels otherwise, it must be the result of cultural brainwashing. The truth is, none of these things that I have just mentioned are true of Islamic law or society.

One of the problems with this situation is that the Western attempt to situate Muslims in the West's own past contributes directly to many Muslim attempts at self-definition. Muslims see themselves as heirs to one of the greatest civilizations witnessed in human history, and they feel that their religion has contributed in no small way to the develop-ment of that civilization. They believe that their religion is integrally bound to a way of living, to a civilization that they expect to be taken as an equal of Western civilization. At the same time, they frequently find it impossible to reconcile the sense of their own rich history and destiny with the fact that, at present, they are in no position to compete favor-ably with Western civilization in economic or military terms. Faced with undeniable Western dominance and the view that Muslims are in no way part of the Western world, they frequently strike apologetic and defensive poses regarding their religion. As such, Islam is seen as a reli-gion besieged by the West and that the only way to defend the religion is to circle one's proverbial wagons and retreat into some notion of a "pure Islam." There is a tendency among such Muslims to reject all Western influences, which they see as contaminants. In so doing, they frequently reject aspects of their own religion or culture which are shared with the West.

For individual Muslims who see themselves as beleaguered by the West, the only appropriate reaction is one of social and intellectual resistance. They see other Muslims who are appreciative of Western values or ideas as having surrendered and adopted a posture of defeat. Thus, contrary to how it is frequently presented in the West, Islam is not at all a monolithic religion, but rather one that is buzzing with internal dissent. What makes matters even more acute is that in Sunnism, the religion of the overwhelming majority of Muslims, there is no notion of a formal clergy or a binding canon of law. This has little impact on the basic doctrines of the religion and there are probably some advantages to not having a hierarchical clergy, such as diversity. But it also means that there is no easy way to resolve differences of opinion about how religion should be understood and implemented, nor are there any easy means by which people with strongly divergent views can separate out into denominations the way they do in Protestant Christianity. What this means in practical terms is that there is no denominational difference between the President of Bosnia, a rural woman selling chickens in a market in Indonesia, an Afghan fighter who is part of an insurgency in Kashmir, a suicide bomber who claims to be motivated by religion, or a stripper in a Turkish nightclub. And yet, their views on religion are hardly the same, and it is very misleading to present Islam as monolithic simply because they are all Sunni Muslims.

I realize that what I have said so far may not seem to address what one needs to know about Islam's theological tradition, but I believe it is necessary to address these issues because they underlie the presentation of Islam to Western audiences. Although Islam unquestionably comes from the same religious fountainhead as Judaism and Christianity, its present relationship with its siblings is dominated by the political circumstances of our time. Having said that, now I will turn to more theological issues.

The central shared characteristic of all Muslims is their belief in a God who sent a verbal communication called the Qur'an to a human prophet named Muhammad, who was born in the Arabian city of Mecca and died in the nearby city of Medina in 632. God, His ongoing involvement in His creation, and the human being's unique status as the only created thing whose opinion of God seems to matter to Him, lies at the center of Islamic belief.

The Muslim concept of God: God is commonly referred to by his Arabic name, Allah, but is also called 'the Lord.' Muslims in other parts of the world frequently use their own languages' equivalent word for God. They do not fixate on the term "Allah," although some have started to do so. Western scholarship in Islam has frequently presented the Muslim God as being stern and wrathful, and the relationship of human beings to Him as one of servitude largely motivated by fear of punishment and secondarily by a desire for reward in heaven. For many Muslims, however, the overarching characteristics of God are His nurturing mercy and compassion, and the ideal attitude of the human being toward Him should not be one of fearful obedience, but of gratitude. God's mercy and compassion are proven to many Muslims in everything from the wondrous complexity of the universe to the very fact of human existence. One of the most eloquent chapters of the Qur'an, Chapter 55, using both rhyme and meter, catalogs some of the wonders God has created and expresses a rhetorical amazement at the capacity of human beings to deny God's generosity. I will read a small translation of a section from it:

> The Merciful: He taught the Qur'an; He created man. He taught him an intelligent speech. The sun and the moon follow courses computed and the stars, plants and trees bow down in adoration. The sky has He raised high, and He has set up the balance of justice in order that you may not transgress. It is He who has spread out the earth for His creatures. There are fruit and date palms, producing bunches of dates; also corn, with its husks and stalks and sweet smelling plants. Then which of your Lord's favors would you deny?

There are numerous other places where the Qur'an speaks of God's mercy. "And He gives you all that you ask for and if you were to add up the favors of Allah, you would never be able to count them. Indeed, human beings are given to injustice and ingratitude." In the face of God's overwhelming kindness, disobedience to God becomes synonymous with denying his generosity, and evil is therefore the same as ingratitude.

Like the Qur'an, many Islamic theological writings see the entire universe as in a state of obedience to God's law, and the word 'Islam' literally refers to this state of surrender. Human beings are the only creations that have the capacity to disobey, and they do this by arrogantly thinking that they are self-sufficient—not needing God's support or guidance. There is a very interesting point here: when one looks at the description of God and God's relationship with creation, in the Qur'an God is a nurturer; God is a judge; God is a disciplinarian; God is a protector; God is a guide and ultimately He exercises a very parental type of role. God looks like a parent, but significantly, not once anywhere in the Qur'an is God referred to as a parent or a Father. This is a major difference in the scriptures of Islam versus Judaism and Christianity.

A commonly repeated Islamic tradition states that God is closer to a person than his or her jugular vein, implying that God permeates the cosmos. Islamic systems of ritual observance assume that there is a wakeful, attentive God who listens to and cares about each and every one of His creatures. As I have noted, many Muslims see Islam as submission to Divine law, and anyone who surrenders her or himself to this law is called 'Muslim,' the feminine being 'Muslima.' Religious and pious human beings often prefer to use the words 'Muhsin' and 'Muhsina' or 'Mu'min' or 'Mu'mina,' the former term applying to someone who does good deeds, and the latter to someone who believes or has faith. The word for faith is closely related to the words for safety, security and trust. For many Muslims, having faith automatically implies being in God's protection, secure within the principles of guidance that He has provided.

Muslims believe that God is One, which not only implies divine unity, but also a person's act of affirming that unity. This is a very important theological understanding because human beings participate at some level in the ongoing status of God as unique. It gives human beings a profound and active role in God's entire plan; participation in the religion is through an act—the act of affirming God as One.

Muslims also see their relationship with God as an intimate one in which God's creation of human beings is a blessing and His laws and strictures are not inflictions but an act of grace providing guidance in this life. Many Muslims hold the belief that our life in this world is actually a test for an afterlife. God has provided us with clear guidance through scriptures and prophets, so if we still choose to disobey, we deserve whatever unpleasantness awaits us in the hereafter.

The Qur'an speaks of a time before the physical creation of human beings, when they made a covenant by testifying to God's nature. "When your Lord drew forth from the children of Adam, from their loins, their descendants, and made them testify concerning themselves saying, Am I not your Lord? They said, 'Yes, we bear witness.' This, lest you should say on the day of judgment, Of this we were never mindful." This bearing of witness, or *shahada,* is the central concept in understanding the importance of human beings in God's plan because it puts them in the position of actively choosing to recognize God's nature and His relationship with them. The Islamic profession of faith is also called the *Shahada* and consists of uttering the statement: "I bear witness that there is no God but God, and I bear witness that Muhammad is the messenger of God." Frequently people have heard the statement that Muslims believe there is no God but God, but what often gets dropped is that one is also supposed to say, "I bear witness that there is no God but God." This is not a passive statement but an active one, not an abstract observation but an affirmation.

For many Muslims, the Qur'an is the single greatest sign of God in the physical universe. In fact, individual verses in the Qur'an are literally called 'signs.' The text refers to itself as guidance for the world—a clear sign for those who can understand. It provides instructions on how to live one's life and acts as a source of ethical guidance in the things for which it does not provide clear instructions. It is a common Muslim belief that, as God's final revelation, the Qur'an contains the sum total of what God plans to reveal to humanity. Therefore, behind the finite literal message of the Qur'an is an infinite reservoir of divine wisdom. The word Qur'an is derived from the Arabic 'to recite' or 'to read,' so the Qur'an is something like a recitation or a collection of things to be recited.

In the prophet Muhammad's understanding, and that of pious believers, the Qur'anic revelations came from heaven where they were preserved on a well-guarded tablet, a concealed supernatural book that existed in the presence of God. Muhammad did not become acquainted with the whole text of the Qur'an at once, but only with isolated sections of it. The Qur'an contains only a few obscure hints as to how it was communicated to Muhammad. In fact, it is from later Islamic text that we know how Muhammad would occasionally go into trances or at other times he would not, and how he would recite it to people around him.

Muslims believe the Qur'an is literally and exactly God's word. There has been considerable resistance to translating the Qur'an from Arabic into other languages until the last two centuries since the Divine Word cannot be perfectly contained in ink and paper. It is still common for bookstores not to write prices on copies of the Qur'an: the appropriate etiquette is actually to go up to the book seller and ask what the 'gift' for the book would be.

Muhammad believed that not only his prophetic mission but also the revelations of the earlier Hebrew prophets and the holy scriptures of the Jews and Christians were based on this original heavenly book. Thus, for Muslims the Qur'an confirms what was revealed earlier: the laws, which were given to Moses, the Gospel of Jesus, and other prophetic texts. All of this raises, in terms of relationships, a challenging and interesting situation because Muslims ultimately see themselves as the updated, revised edition, and in a sense superseding everything that comes before, while at the same time accepting these other scriptural texts as authentic. On that basis, Muslims have an affinity for Jews and Christians, but they do not quite comprehend why Christians would view this supercessionism or fulfillment theology as heretical.

Although the stories contained in the Qur'an and the concept of revelation through a series of prophets are shared with the Hebrew Bible and with the New Testament, the style of the Qur'an is different on two bases. First, the Qur'an is not written in prose or poetry—it is essentially rhyming prose, which makes it easier to memorize than regular prose and gives the verses a rhythmic aesthetic. Second, the Qur'an is not a book in the sense of having a narrative beginning, middle and end or a plot. It is a collection of discrete pieces of revelation and the long chapters occasionally combine pieces of revelation. There are no long, sustained narratives in the Qur'an. Many of the Biblical parallels are actually anecdotal in their reference. Genesis does not exist in the Qur'an so there is no fall of humanity and yet, Muslims have appropriated this and other ideas. The story of Joseph, which is not exactly the same as it is in the Bible, is the most sustained narrative in the Qur'an, and it is a beautiful story.

People read the Qur'an regularly. Those who cannot read Arabic learn the script and mouth the words; those who cannot read at all will pass their fingers along the lines and feel that somehow by doing so they are deriving benefit. As such, the Qur'an simultaneously becomes a source of prayer and a prayer in its own right; a guide for action as well as a ritual object. Muslims treat the Qur'an with great devotion and Qur'an stands, on which they are quite often ritualistically read, are some of the masterpieces of Islamic art.

In conclusion, Islam can be understood as the ongoing unfolding of God's plan for the universe, which he created and in which he placed human beings as the only creature with the sentience to recognize God's true nature. Two short sections of scripture are particularly valuable in providing a general understanding of how God is viewed by the majority of Muslims. These short sections are included here because they summarize well what Muslim notions are regarding the nature of God. The first is in itself a short chapter, 112, and the second one is a long verse from a long chapter, 2:255. The first: "Say: He is God, the one, the only. God the eternal, absolute. He begets not, nor is He begotten, and there is none like unto Him." The second: "God, there is no God but Him, the living, the eternal. No slumber can seize Him nor sleep. His are all things in the heavens and on earth. Who shall intercede with Him except as He permits? He knows that which is before them and what is behind them. Nor shall they compass any of his knowledge except as He wills. His throne extends over the heavens and the earth and He feels no fatigue in guarding and preserving them, for He is the Most High, The Supreme."

The first verse speaks to the overarching message of the uniqueness of God. The second one reminds us that although God is the sustainer of everything and quite self-sufficient, He has a throne. And having a throne implies that God has certain similarities with being human and is concerned with the actions of individual humans and is involved with all of human history.

PART II ~ WHAT DO WE WANT THE OTHER TO TEACH ABOUT
OUR THEOLOGICAL TRADITIONS?

For Further Discussion and Study

How are theological cornerstones such as the revelation of God, the oneness and unknowable mystery of God, covenant, Sabbath, ethical responsibility, Torah, codes of behavior, justice and compassion, prayer and fasting, worship, sacred time and space, holiness and holy people, wisdom, election of the community, and messianic vision understood by Judaism, Christianity, and Islam? Where is common ground, and where is divergence?

How can one teach about Judaism, Christianity, and Islam as valid and evolving in response to God's presence in the world, while also remaining true to one's specific faith commitments which may be contrary or contradictory to the other's? Why would one teach about the other and what could be the personal, social, or theological benefits?

Do the three Abrahamic traditions share a substantial common Scripture? How different are the parallel and common passages if one changes the order, context, or primary focus of the texts included in one's scriptures?

Some have suggested that concepts of grace and prophecy are common to Judaism, Christianity, and Islam. How are they similar, different?

What are some common misperceptions or stereotypes of Judaism, Christianity, or Islam?

Do Jews, Christians, and Muslims teach that discrimination of any kind, including religion, is forbidden and God desires diversity of religions in the world? Where are such teachings found?

What is the appropriate balance of describing one's religious identity with the other, rather than over and against the other? How does one deal appropriately and fairly with concepts such as election, fulfillment, or supercessionism when describing another's community or one's own?

For Action in the Community

What preparations and sensitivities can discussion group leaders have to present the other in a way that is adequate, fair and respectful, so that the other recognizes himself or herself in dialogue?

Are there opportunities to find points of concurrence by focusing on the responses (social, political, educational, religious practices, etc.) of each faith community to theological and ethical and issues more than on the theology of the Word, per se.

What are the advantages and disadvantages when living in a unique, set apart, committed religious community? What challenges and opportunities are associated with such a life when relating with the world?

In what ways can Jews, Christians, and Muslims be prophetic participants within society, while also retaining their unique religious identities and preserving their integrity in the midst of pluralism and some unacceptable Western values?

What Do We Want the Other to Teach About Our Historical Traditions?

D A V I D   L .   C O P P O L A

What Do We Want the Other to Teach About Our Historical Traditions?

A lthough this volume began by presenting ideas to foster interreligious dialogue and cultivate theological exploration and collaboration, perhaps the most important first task at hand is for Jews, Christians, and Muslims to confront together their heartbreaking histories. To remember accurately is necessary in order to deal with the past and hope for the future. Unless people are willing to remember and understand the other's pain and seek to repair the world, there can be no dialogue for reconciliation or peace. In this sense, the 1998 Vatican document, *We Remember,* is accurate in saying, "there is no future without memory" (p. 6). However, remembrance is never neutral and recalls the choices, actions, and events from the past that are meaningful and essential for a community's present identity and intended future destiny.

There is an astonishing amnesia on the part of some historians about the collective crimes of the last century, as if these crimes were normal and to be expected in the ordinary course of wars. Such unprecedented violence and cruelty leaves humanity with choices for peace or war, hope or despair, forgiveness or revenge, faith or doubt, and love or hate. A religious and moral memory is essential if Jews, Christians, and Muslims are to realistically shape a safe future. The human community cannot forget the mistakes of religions, nor can such historical memory be removed by improved political governments or rational arguments alone. Rather, intelligent, ethical, honest, and respectful efforts on the part of religious people will help to ensure that peace happens in the future through a

gradual building of trust and understanding through friendships and relationships that will allow healing and a new history to be established.

For these and other reasons, two conferences were sponsored on the
topic, "What Do We Want the Other to Teach About Our Historical
Traditions?" one in Edmonton, Canada, and the other in Bamberg,
Germany. Selected papers from both of these conferences are included in
this volume.

The Conferences in Edmonton, Canada and Bamberg, Germany

On March 19–21, 2000, the Center for Christian-Jewish Understanding
(CCJU) of Sacred Heart University, Fairfield, Connecticut, in cooperation with the Edmonton Interfaith Centre for Education and Action,
(EICEA) Alberta, Canada, sponsored a conference where Jews,
Christians, and Muslims participated in a dialogue at Beth Shalom
Synagogue. Over 20 scholars from Canada and the United States attended the proceedings with the additional attendance of graduate students
from Alberta University and several hundred observers who joined each
of the sessions spread over the three days. The conference included presentations by noted scholars with prepared responses, followed by discussion, critiques, and suggestions by all of the participants. Presentation
included an examination of the place and tradition of history from the
Jewish, Christian, and Muslim faith traditions on "What Do We Want
the Other to Teach About Our Historical Traditions?"

Before the conference formally began, a Harmony Brunch was held to
mark the International Day for the Elimination of Racial Discrimination,
which the United Nations had designated for March 21, the day in 1966
when South Africa's Sharpeville Massacre occurred. Canadian Senator
Douglas Roche, OC, and the president of the Canadian Multicultural
Educational Foundation, Robinson Koilpillai, CM, were the guest speakers. They both challenged the audience to rise above prejudice and indif-
ference and work to overcome systemic inequality in the world by seeking
justice and working for peace, especially through local synagogues,
churches and mosques. Later that evening, over 500 people gathered at
Edmonton City Hall to participate at an interfaith prayer service to com-
memorate the International Day for the Elimination of Racial

Discrimination. Representatives from 15 religious traditions offered prayers in the forms of readings, song, dance, ringing of bells, lighting candles, and chants. At the conclusion of each prayer, the congregation said together, "We affirm this prayer, celebrate our diversity and may peace prevail on earth." The mayor of Edmonton, William Smith, praised the citizens for working together for social justice and being a model for celebrating religious diversity. He said, "The walls that divide us must come down. The understanding you are building through the arts, religion, culture, knowledge, and commerce will have a global impact."

LIST OF PRESENTERS, EDMONTON, CANADA

Rabbi Lindsey Bat Joseph, Temple Beth Ora, Edmonton

Dr. Jamal Badawi, Saint Mary's University, Halifax, Nova Scotia

Dr. David Coppola, Center for Christian-Jewish Understanding of Sacred Heart University, Connecticut

Rabbi Joseph H. Ehrenkranz, Center for Christian-Jewish Understanding of Sacred Heart University

Dr. Andrew Gos, University of Alberta, Edmonton

Dr. Adrian Leske, Concordia University College, Edmonton

Neil Loomer, Ritual Director, Beth Shalom Synagogue, Edmonton

Right Reverend Victoria Matthews, Anglican Bishop of Edmonton

Rev. Clint Mooney, St. Matthew's United Church, Calgary, Alberta

Mr. Hasan Nazarali, Al-Waez, Ismali Muslim Community, Edmonton

Dr. Derek J. Penslar, Samuel Zacks Chair in Jewish History, University of Toronto

Dr. Saleem Qureshi, University of Alberta, Edmonton

Mr. Larry Shaben, president, Muslim Research Foundation, Edmonton

Dr. Leonard Swidler, Temple University, Philadelphia

The Center for Christian-Jewish Understanding also sponsored a second conference in cooperation with the University of Bamberg, Germany, on March 18–20, 2002, where Jews, Catholics and Lutherans participated in a dialogue at the University of Bamberg on the same topic. More than 30 scholars from Austria, Germany, Great Britain, and the United States attended the proceedings with the additional attendance of students from Bamberg University and dozens of observers who joined two of the sessions spread over the three days. The conference included presentations by distinguished scholars with prepared responses, followed by discussion, critiques and suggestions by all of the participants. Presentations included an examination of the place and tradition of history from the Jewish, Catholic, and Lutheran faith traditions on "What Do We Want the Other to Teach About Us?"

Bamberg, Germany, was chosen as the site of this conference because of the warmth and hospitality offered to the CCJU by the University of Bamberg community as well as Bamberg's varied and rich history. The city was founded in the Second Century CE, and in 1007, Bamberg became a bishopric, when the Emperor Heinrich II (973–1024) created an imperial residence. Of special interest to the organizers of the conference was the fact that many crusaders left from Bamberg to fight against Muslims in lands to the south and east, including Hungary and Austria, as well as the more infamous crusades to the Holy Land. Also, on the highest hill of the city is a large cathedral (built 1215–37) called the Dom. It contains both Romanesque and Gothic elements and is rich in sculptures and history. In particular, near the southeast end of the nave of the cathedral is a statue of two women depicting the "Church Triumphant" and the "Synagogue Defeated." A young, richly clad and beautiful woman represents the Christian Church, while a blindfolded, poorly dressed woman holding a broken rod symbolizes Judaism. Also, directly opposite is a statue of a beautiful young woman representing Mary, the mother of Jesus, and her cousin Elizabeth, the latter who is portrayed as a tired old woman. For medieval Christians, these two pair of women symbolized the triumph of the New Testament and Christianity over Judaism and the Old Testament and contributed to the notion that Christianity had superceded Judaism. Additionally, outside the Dom on its north portal, near the majestic sculpture of the 12 Apostles, who are standing on the shoulders of the 12 Prophets, is a figure in a pointed cap (which in medieval art signified a Jew), with a devil pulling his ears. This derogatory depiction of what was then a contemporary Jew vividly illustrates the contradictory attitude of many Christians toward Judaism. On the one hand, Jews were seen as a devilish people who rejected the Church. On the other hand, Christians realized that the Church was founded on the Jewish religion, without which Christianity would be meaningless.

Until the Second World War, when practically every Jew was imprisoned or killed, the Jewish community in Bamberg had been one of the most flourishing and influential centers in Europe. Recently, a small and slowly growing Jewish community has begun to be formed as Jewish immigrants from Russia settle in the area. After learning of this city's mixed history and observing the concrete reminders of supercessionism, the conference topic, as well as the conference site was judged to be a significant sign of hope for the future of interreligious dialogue.

On one evening of the conference, an interfaith concert by the "Inspiration Choir" was performed for the conference participants and interested members of the town at the 13th century building, Renaissance Hall, which had been newly restored. The concert theme was "Meeting Jewish Music." Nearly all of the members of the group were Christian and had committed themselves to understanding Judaism better by learning and performing Jewish music. The group was chosen by the CCJU as an excellent match for the conference theme because it had dedicated itself to "teaching" about the other by learning and performing the other's music. The evening was filled with warmth and celebration and some of the conference participants also contributed their musical talents by singing and dancing.

LIST OF INVITED PARTICIPANTS, BAMBERG, GERMANY

Dr. Ulrich Bauer, University of Bamberg

Rabbi Gilles Bernheim, Chief Rabbi of Paris, France

Professor Dr. Klaus Bieberstein, University of Bamberg

Dr. David Coppola, Center for Christian-Jewish Understanding of Sacred Heart University, Connecticut

Dr. Jon Gower Davies, University of Newcastle upon Tyne, Great Britain

Rabbi Michael Dushinsky, Ostrava, Czech Republic

Rabbi Joseph H. Ehrenkranz, Center for Christian-Jewish Understanding, Connecticut

Mrs. Chriss Fiebig, Bamberg

Dr. Christoph Heil, University of Bamberg

Professor Dr. Alfred E. Hierold, Dean, School of Theology, University of Bamberg

Professor Dr. Paul Hoffmann, University of Bamberg

Professor Dr. Wolfgang Klausnitzer, University of Bamberg

Professor Dr. Wolfgang Kraus, University of Koblenz-Landau, Germany

Ludwig Krempl, Focolare Movement, Nürnberg, Germany

Professor Dr. Verena Lenzen, University of Luzern, Switzerland

Dr. Herbert Loebl, University of Newcastle upon Tyne, Great Britain

Reverend Dr. Friedhelm Pieper, Martin Buber House, Heppenheim, Germany

Professor Dr. Martin Rothgangel, University of Weingarten, Germany

Professor Dr. Dr. Godehard Ruppert, President, University of Bamberg

Professor Dr. Hans-Joachim Sander, University of Salzburg, Austria

Rabbi David Sandmel, Beth Tfiloh Community High School, Baltimore, Maryland

Mrs. Barbara Schmitz, University of Bamberg

Professor Dr. Walter Sparn, University of Erlangen, Germany

Rabbi Bonita Nathan Sussman, Staten Island Rabbinical Association, New York

Rabbi Gerald Sussman, New York Theological Seminary, New York

Professor Dr. Lothar Wehr, University of Bamberg

Professor Dr. Erich Zenger, University of Münster, Germany

What Do We Want the Other to Teach About Our Historical Traditions?

For centuries, Jews, Christians and Muslims have mostly disputed. It is no small matter that they can even use the term conversation. They have a history, and it is God's presence that challenges them to show profound respect to one another. Jews, Christians, and Muslims all believe in a God who acts in history and communicates in history through events and people. The story of God's love gives breath, voice, and flesh to the bones of historical events and data. Similarly, God calls believers to discern the present signs of divine providence at work, as well as the ways in which the image of the Creator in humanity has been attacked and disfigured. By sharing what we want the other to teach about our history, we are making a covenant to trust and dialogue with each other.

As was discussed at the CCJU conference sponsored in Jerusalem on the topic of theology, the assumptions of modernity and postmodernity as well as the realities of diversity, pluralism, and relativism are important to understanding an accurate interpretation of history from the contexts of an insider's religious identity, theology, spirituality, aesthetics, and liturgy. The language of history describes important relationships and values for the community in a particular context and representation. The acceptance of many of the views of modernity and its growth in democratic societies has opened the doors for interreligious dialogue that can be based on human rights and mutual respect. Jews, Christians, and Muslims are uniquely positioned for dialogue because of recent reexaminations of each religion's identity in history, such as the Crusades, Inquisition, teachings of contempt toward the other, and the *Shoah*. On the other hand, by employing a historical critical method in interpreting faith and religion, one could run the risk of reducing memory and the important ethical insights and wisdom essential to a religious identity to mere historical coincidences.

It is difficult to know whether teachers of the other should emphasize more the teaching of the history of each religion or the history of particular Jews, Christians, or Muslims. Perhaps for children, religious history is best understood through the lives of holy people and how those people added to the presence and understanding of that community's identity and faith. For adults, historians and teachers of the other can act as witnesses to the truth of life as well as for those who have lived a good life following God. Time and space are the paths where God walks and is revealed to all. It is essential for the health and integrity of a faith community to remember and teach about the past in an adequate and respectful way. To remember the past means that adults challenge young people to recognize their part in history, especially their participation in prejudice or discrimination against others. It is also the time to recognize the tendency to fear and mistrust that which they do not understand. Racism, sexism, ageism are still present because of what people say and do, and because of what they do not say and do. An honest examination of conscience is appropriate because the God of History is involved in the events of every human life. This connection of all life to God in history reminds humanity to "resee," that is, respect, that all peoples are related and have dignity. Remembrance is never neutral and recalls the choices, actions and events from the past that are meaningful and essential for one's present identity and future destiny.

An important aspect to remember when teaching about the other's history is that religious history has not always been historical, at least from a scientific definition based on verifiable evidence and facts. It seems true that one's relationship with a particular religious history is just as important as the history itself since religious history has to do more with the ethical interaction of people and how they respond in justice and compassion to God's call. Thomas Cahill in the 1998 book, *The Gifts of the Jews*, has wrestled with the idea of expanding the notion of history beyond the simple repeating of facts. Cahill writes, "We normally think of history as one catastrophe after another, war followed by war, outrage by outrage—almost as if history were nothing more than all the narratives of human pain, assembled in sequences. And surely this is, often enough, an adequate description. But history is also the narratives of grace, the recounting of those blessed and inexplicable moments when someone did something for someone else, saved a life, bestowed a gift, gave something beyond what was required by circumstance" (p. iii).

Religious history of the other is best taught by a model where the other is present and one that is grounded on its own internal affirmations and memory of experiences with God, others, and the world. Such assertions and the contexts and interpretations related to them need to be explained by an insider and compared to interpretations of those from outside the community. In such a process, the histories of all three religions will be broadened and understood through the eyes of the other and will take on deeper significance in the task of repairing the world for each. By honestly teaching about one's own history and the history of the other, it is clear that that religion can be a positive force that can foster unity, a reality that has been achieved too infrequently. Nonetheless, the past can be overcome by the good deeds of the present.

Berlin
5 February 2002
The Federal President
Johannes Rau

Message of Greeting to the International Symposium
"What Do We Want the Other to Teach About Our Historical Traditions?"
of the Center for Christian-Jewish Understanding of Sacred Heart University
and the University of Bamberg
Bamberg, 18–20 March 2002

What do we want others to teach about our historical traditions? That is a difficult but also an extremely important question. We can only find the right answers if we ourselves have a clear image of our history and an idea of how others see us and how we see others.

In history few things have a greater influence than traditions which have grown over centuries. However, it is also true that in history there are aberrations and betrayals which cannot be predicted and which are very difficult to understand in retrospect, if they can be understood at all.

One can, indeed must, say here in Germany that the Holocaust was such a brutal betrayal. It was a complete breakdown in civilization. We must keep the memory of the *Shoah* alive. But it would be a mistake to regard the Holocaust as the sum total of German-Jewish history or the sum total of Jewish-Christian relations. We also want others to pass on the Holocaust as part of our history. However, we would also like our history before the Holocaust to be told. Only if Christians and Jews discuss their history in its entirety and not just parts of it will they have a common future. For this reason, too, meetings such as yours in which we examine our own Jewish and our own Lutheran and Catholic traditions are so important.

I wish you fruitful talks and encounters in Bamberg which will cause you to look back with gratitude and to look forward with hope.

Professor Dr. Dr. Godehard Ruppert
President, University of Bamberg

I would like to extend a warm welcome to you, both personally and on behalf of the Otto-Friedrich University of Bamberg. We are very pleased that the invitation to this international conference has met with such a good response and that it has brought such illustrious guests to our *alma mater;* such a fact alone gives rise to encouragement.

After the events of September 11, 2001, little in the realm of international and interreligious relationships is simply the way it was. As representatives of the German universities, we can only react with horror that some of perpetrators involved in this terrible act were graduates from German universities. On the other hand, we must make clear that the university needs to maintain an international character. Academia is, per se, international, and wherever it confines itself to national borders it endangers its ability to produce authentic scholarship. In my opinion, universities have to act as role models for society in the coexistence of people of different origins and different faiths. We have to demonstrate in our daily contact and in our working together with others that this coexistence actually works. In these times, it is more important than ever that German and foreign members of our university should not allow themselves to be divided. I must admit that I am proud of our record in maintaining this international character. The University of Bamberg ranks at the top of the German universities in terms of the percentage of its students who complete part of their studies abroad—a third of our students do so at present.

It also is part of my duty here today to impart some information about Bamberg and the area of Franconia. This campus and area offers an excellent framework for the topic of this conference due to the fact that numerous examples of coexistence from its history are apparent. For example, this is the town that benefited from the most important Jewish community in the whole of southern Germany. It was also famous in the 17th and 18th centuries for its Hebrew printers and its Talmud school and thus served as an example for the peaceful cohabitation of Catholics, Protestants and Jews. The National Socialist regime forced the closure of the university in 1939. The teaching of theology and philosophy began again in October 1945, but teaching was also carried out in the fields of law, political science and the natural sciences, not least because other university towns and cities in Bavaria had more serious effects of the war to deal with than Bamberg did. In our present day, the Jewish Museum in Schnaittach, founded in 1990, has the most important collection of artifacts from Jewish culture in the rural areas of southern Germany.

The University and its surroundings offer historical advantages and contemporary opportunities. In this era of globalization, we experience the strengthening of regions as a side effect of the ongoing globalization shaped by the economy and politics. This development points out the necessity of knowing the roots and traditions of the respective other party. Similarly, the Otto-Friedrich University of Bamberg represents both aspects in its present range of courses in teaching and research: research on ethnic and cultural studies of the regions and participation in the intercultural and interreligious dialogue, as well as in the international dialogue in the economic and social sciences.

I have often told students at the start of their studies that I hope they realize that *studium* in its range of meanings does not only mean "eagerness." In my opinion, one's studies should be a dialectical relationship of effort as well as leisure with friends. Bamberg offers the best conditions for both. I hope that you will experience something of this and that and wish you a successful and pleasant conference in Bamberg and at our university.

D E R E K   J.   P E N S L A R

Teaching Jewish History as Universal History

I. Introduction

W hat do I want others to know and teach about the history of my faith?" The answer is quite simple in principle, though complex in practice. I would like others to know and teach precisely what Jews should understand about their own history and culture. Historical knowledge is not valid unless it is universally accessible and demonstrable. Although a member of a faith-community is bound to bring a different perspective to the history of that entity than an outsider, all students should be able to agree on a fundamental historical narrative and can identify a common matrix of methodological and interpretive questions regarding causation, significance, and outcome of events.

I have spent my teaching career at secular universities (Berkeley, Indiana, and Toronto), teaching classes composed of Jews, Christians, Muslims, and nonbelievers. My students have come from a vast variety of ethnic and social backgrounds, and they have entered my courses with widely varying degrees of prior exposure to Judaism and Jewish history. Each student carries his or her own cultural baggage. Some are Jews from assimilated backgrounds; they see in history a means of strengthening their sense of collective identity. Other Jewish students are from Orthodox backgrounds; for them, university-level history provides an opportunity to move beyond the pietist worldview inculcated by the *heder* and *yeshivah* and understand Judaism within a global context. Some are Muslims, drawn to Jewish history by a desire to understand Israel, which they view with a mix of admiration, anger, and fear. And there are many types of Christian students, including, in addition to those motivated by mere curiosity, evangelical Protestants imbued with messianic philo-semitism, Roman Catholics who feel a certain kinship with Judaism's attachment to ritual and the Jews' strong ethnic consciousness, and, final-ly, and quite frequently, young Christians of all denominations who have fallen in love with a Jewish boy or girl and who want to better understand the culture into which they might be marrying.

The Christian students whom I have taught are overwhelmingly sympathetic to the Jews and Judaism; they might not know very much about the Holocaust, but they are deeply troubled by the relationship between their religious heritage and the greatest act of genocide in his-tory. On rare occasions, a Christian student will parrot anti-Semitic doc-trines picked up at home, e.g., the case of the pleasant young Indiana University basketball player who asked me, in all innocence, if his father was right that Jews controlled all the banks in the United States. Similarly, African-American students have asked about the truth of accusations made by the Nation of Islam that Jews dominated the African slave trade. I have answered these students' queries without recourse to apologetics, romanticization, or distorting self-criticism.

There is, then, one history for all students, Jew and Gentile alike. Moreover, there is only one history for students regardless of age. Obviously, children need to be given simplified views of history, but I believe that simplification should not justify distortion. Children have wide-ranging curiosity and powerful spiritual sensibilities. They ask penetrating questions and deserve thoughtful answers. If, for example, a Christian child asks me who is responsible for the death of Jesus, it serves no one's interests to repeat the old cliché that it was entirely the Romans' initiative and responsibility. Rather, the child can be told that although the Romans tried and executed Jesus, Jews and Romans alike feared Jesus because he seemed to challenge their authority. (This is an issue to which older children can easily relate.) If, to provide another example of a controversial issue, a Jewish child asks why there is so much fighting between Jews and Arabs in the Middle East, one can answer the question without denying either the Jewish or Arab claim to the land. That is, one can explain that Arabs lived in Palestine for many hundreds of years, that the city of Jerusalem is holy to them, and that when Israel was created many of them were forced to leave their homes. "But it says in the Bible that God promised Israel to us!" protested my daughter when I told her this. (My daughter was in third grade at a Jewish day school at the time.) So I explained to her that God has spoken to many people, not just the Jews, and that we have to learn about each other's holy books to find what we have in common, and not just what separates us. She seemed satisfied with that answer—at least for a while.

The same is true for adults, especially seniors, who often have the time and motivation to engage in serious study of the things that matter most to them. I have taught Jewish history in many churches and synagogues and have encountered varying levels of receptivity to the kind of universal approach I am advocating here. Some find it stimulating, others find it troubling, because for them history has been a vehicle for the affirmation of faith or identity, not an open-ended process of constant discovery, whose outcome may overturn as well as confirm long-cherished beliefs. Clearly, it is my obligation as a teacher to display sensitivity to their background and experience; for example, one does not talk about Jewish history to a group of Jewish Holocaust survivors of East European origin in exactly the same language that would be used for an assembly of Methodist retirees from the American Midwest. But although the style may vary, the substance remains the same. In one form or another, Jewish history, I believe, boils down to five essential points, with which all students of the subject, regardless of creed or age, should be acquainted:

1. The history of the Jews is the history of a great civilization. (I define "civilization," following the late scholar of Islam, Marshall Hodgson, as a "grouping of cultures [that] share consciously. . . literary and philosophical as well as political and legal values carried in lettered tradition.")[1] The centerpiece of the Jews' lettered tradition, their canon of sacred texts, led directly to the establishment of the world's most popular religion, Christianity, and inspired the founding of the world's second largest, Islam. Although Judaism is frequently referred to as the mother religion of Christianity, the two would best be described as siblings, sharing a common ancestor in the spiritual ferment that engulfed Palestine around the beginning of the Common Era. Although the

founders of Christianity were Jewish and imbued with Jewish beliefs, by the late first century, CE, Christianity and Judaism had parted ways. Judaism struck out on its own direction and developed the uniquely dynamic and worldly belief system known as Rabbinic Judaism. It accorded to human beings creative freedom in the interpretation of sacred texts while imposing upon the Jews a matrix of ritual activity that sanctified the everyday world. The centrality of the concept of salvific knowledge—gleaned from texts that were, in principle, obtainable by all—encouraged widespread male literacy, a flourishing of cultural production, and a fluidity of social relationships.

2. The dynamic quality of rabbinic Judaism was enhanced by the Jews' social conditions as a stateless, scattered, and primarily urban people. Deprived in the middle ages of land ownership (because of discriminatory taxation in the realm of Islam and the pervasive Christian ethos of the feudal system in Europe), the Jews lacked a hereditary aristocracy or a caste of serfs. The Jews were a people of burghers, concentrated in trade, and highly mobile, both geographically and socially. The elites of mercantile wealth and rabbinic learning overlapped and reinforced each other. The Jews' economic and intellectual ferment, never limited solely to the confines of Jewish society, came in modern times to embrace the societies in which they lived. The Jews—scarcely one percent of humanity at the beginning of the twentieth century and only one quarter of one percent at its end—have been overwhelmingly overrepresented in fields of creative endeavor, be they entrepreneurial, cultural, or academic.

3. The Jews' cultural and economic creativity is all the more remarkable given the persecution and discrimination that they have long endured. Jewish distinctiveness—at first religious, but over time, also economic and cultural—was a source of irritation among the Jews' host societies even in pagan antiquity. Islam tolerated Jews, as it did Christians, as a "people of the book," recipients of divine revelation, who would be accorded a safe, if inferior, position in Muslim society. Christianity, too, tolerated Jews, not out of a disinterested respect so much as vital, existential, need. Jews were to give testimony to the truth of Christianity by

the humbled circumstances in which they lived and their ongoing allegiance to the ancient Jewish Law, which Christianity revered while claiming to have superceded it. Moreover, the eventual conversion of the Jews to Christianity was seen as a necessary precondition for the Second Coming of Christ. The tensions inherent in depending upon a people scorned for having killed and rejected the Saviour were exacerbated by the Jews' economic concentration (caused in part by Christian pressure) in low-status occupations, the most famous of which was money lending. The image of the Jew as parasite and pathogen survived into modern times and, although mutated by the secularization of European society in the 19th and 20th centuries, provided the basis for the genocidal anti-Semitism of the Nazi regime and its acolytes.

4. Powerlessness is not a virtue in and of itself, nor does it bestow virtue. Ancient Israelite society was exceedingly violent, immersed in tribal war and murderous hatreds nursed by religious zeal. Postbiblical Jewish society was no more pacific or tolerant than Christendom or *dar al-Islam*. In the Middle East in the 8th century CE, rabbinic Jewish authorities clashed with Karaism, an anti-rabbinic Jewish sect. Medieval and early modern Jewish communities employed coercive force against backsliders (such as the philosopher, Baruch Spinoza). Rabbinic culture had strong misogynistic elements and frequently viewed Islam, and especially Christianity, with disdain. Modern Jewish society has featured numerous cases of internecine struggle, such as between the pietist *Hasidim* and their opponents in late 18th-century Poland, or between Orthodox and Reform Jews in 19th-century Germany. Finally, the Zionist movement and state of Israel have featured the brutality employed by any successful state-building movement, past or present. These facts are to be neither denied nor exaggerated, merely acknowledged as an inevitable part of the human experience.

5. The greatest challenge confronting contemporary Judaism is the dichotomy between a religious system forged in an atmosphere of relative powerlessness vis-à-vis Gentiles and the current world order, in which the state of Israel exerts considerable military and

political power. In this and many other ways, the Zionist project was revolutionary, an overthrow of the *ancien régime* of Diaspora-Jewish political and religious culture. Yet it is also true that many of the Zionist movement's goals, and the ways in which they have been achieved, reflect deeply preservationist impulses. Much of Israel's political, economic, and social structures, as well as many of its cultural norms, are remarkably consonant with those of the Diaspora communities of the nineteenth and twentieth centuries. Indeed, one could argue that Zionism was in many ways a counter-revolutionary movement, a defensive measure against assimilatory forces that were transforming modern Jewish society beyond recognition. Thus Israel, like all modern nationalist movements, is, like the Roman god Janus, a two-faced creature, with one side pointed toward the unknown future and the other gazing into the immemorial past.

I would like now to develop my arguments by dividing Jewish history into its ancient, medieval, and modern components, identifying in each case one or two particular conceptual problems that I have confronted in the teaching of Jewish history and believe to be central to understanding it properly.

II. Ancient Israel

Whenever I have taught surveys of Jewish history from antiquity to modernity, the first unit of the course—covering the period from the Israelites' origins to the origins of Christianity—has been the most difficult to teach. This is so because of the deep personal meaning of ancient Jewish history for the vast majority of students. The fundamental religious identities of Jews and Christians draw on a particular type of historical understanding drawn from the Hebrew Bible and Christian Scriptures, known to Christians as the Old and New Testaments respectively. This kind of understanding conceives of the scriptural narrative as a sacred history, that is, a demonstration of God's presence in history and a use of history to corroborate deeply cherished religious beliefs. Sacred history employs narrative as allegory; worldly events are shadows or reflections of meta-historical truths.

Sacred history is directly opposed to how I, as a professional historian teaching at a secular university, conceive of my discipline, which I will call critical history. The origins of critical history lie in the comparative and source-based historical methods pioneered in mid 19th-century Germany, and in large measure still employed to this day. Although scientific in its commitment to the systematic gathering and comparison of sources, as well as an ostensible claim to objectivity, critical history is also a deeply humanist discipline, empathetic with its subjects in a way that a chemist or physicist can not be. Critical history is the collective biography of humanity, a biography nourished by spiritual yearnings but also by countless other factors, material and psychological. Critical history does not deny the presence of the divine in this world but contends that the historical method of modern scholarship cannot detect its presence, any more than chemists dating the production of the Shroud of Turin can determine if the image it depicts was of divine origin.

If sacred history is allegory, then critical history is metonymy. No contemporary historian would be pretentious enough to claim that the events and interrelationships described by the historian are consonant with reality in its entirety. They are fragments of reality, representative of broader, as yet unknown and perhaps unknowable, dimensions of experience, and forged, thanks to the historian's artful sifting of evidence and narrative prose, into a unified, comprehensible form.

Thus, the teaching of ancient Israelite history introduces all students to the clash between sacred and critical history. To be sure, the line between the two is often blurry, for many of the great Christian archaeologists and Orientalists of the twentieth century made an a priori assumption that the biblical narrative was historically valid, and they interpreted their findings within this preexisting paradigm. Similarly, Israeli scholars of antiquity have often read the ancient data in order to conform to the Zionist master narrative about the Jews' ancient claims to the land and the historic necessity to struggle for its possession. In the mid 20th century, for example, both North American and Israeli scholars agreed that evidence of destruction in Canaanite villages (e.g., Jericho) from the turn of the second millennium, BCE, testified to the truth of the narrative in the book of Joshua about the Israelite conquest of Canaan. Moreover, the extent to which the narratives from Genesis appeared to reflect ancient Middle Eastern social and cultural practices was seen as confirmation of the fundamental truth of the Genesis narrative, even down to the historicity of the patriarchs Abraham, Isaac, and Jacob.

Since the late 1800s, scholars have assumed that the text of the Pentateuch consisted of strands, composed over many centuries and cobbled together only in the early Second Temple period. Over the past thirty years, the number and dating of these strands have become a source of constant controversy. Moreover, in recent decades scholars have increasingly questioned the value of the Hebrew Bible as a historical source given the paucity—at times the total lack—of corroborating documentation save for ambiguous archaeological remains. If there is no evidence to confirm any part of the Pentateuchal narrative, some scholars claim, that narrative must be seen as a purely literary source, a series of myths and tales crafted by a people to account for its origins and to justify its place in the world. When taken to its extremes, this approach takes on the name "Biblical Minimalism" and denies the historicity of not only the Pentateuchal narrative but even of the historical and prophetic biblical books as well. This new stream of biblical criticism, however, is not necessarily any less free of bias than its predecessor. Claims that the ancient Israelites emerged from within the indigenous Canaanite population, or that the United Kingdom of Saul, David, and Solomon never existed, can be motivated by an anti-Israeli animus that seeks to deny the Jews their historic and cultural claims to the land of Israel.

The claims of Biblical minimalists have been justly attacked. There is ample extra-Biblical evidence of the existence of the dual kingdoms of Judah and Israel after the breakup of the United Monarchy. The 1993 archaeological finding at Tel Dan of an inscription that may be read as "Beit David" might confirm the existence of the Davidic monarchy, although this piece of evidence seems to convince only those who are predisposed to believing in a real King David. Although the Bible must be read largely as a literary source, as a national epic, it has, like all national epics, undeniable historical value.

The difference between sacred and critical history of ancient Israel is *not* that the former is inaccurate and the latter presents objective truth. Scholars can be and often are believers of one kind or another, and their beliefs affect how they interpret the world. And even the most cool-headed scholar can make mistakes. The fundamental contrast between the sacred and critical historical paradigms, however, is that the latter is by definition open to self-correction, whereas the former is closed to it. Ancient Israel remains, if not a *tabula rasa*, then a *tabula obscura*. Every generation of scholars approaches it in a new way, and the findings of each generation are challenged by its successors. A responsible scholar of ancient Israel must admit that we simply do not know how much of the biblical narrative is historically valid. What is undeniable is the centrality of the Hebrew Bible as the underpinning of Jewish civilization. The historicity of Jacob, Moses, or David is less important than the religious system constructed in their name.

The clash between sacred and critical history is not limited, however, to the obscure, anterior regions of antiquity. The conflict continues to the end of the Second Temple period, an age well documented by late Biblical and extra-Biblical sources. I will illustrate his point through a discussion of the war of the 160s BCE between the Seleucid Greeks and the Jews of Palestine, led by the Hasmonean family, better known as the Maccabees.

When Jews celebrate the Hanukkah festival, they sing folk songs and tell stories to invoke the heroism and piety of the Hasmoneans, who in 167 BCE led a revolt against the Seleucid Greeks, whose emperor had desecrated the Jerusalem Temple and outlawed the practice of Judaism. But what do we make of the fact that after the conquest and rededication of the Temple three years later, and the defeat of the Seleucid army in Jerusalem in 162, the Maccabees continued to fight? Apparently they fought for total independence from their rulers in Damascus, although centuries of Jewish religious thought had legitimized Gentile domination over the Jews. They proclaimed a Hasmonean kingdom, although they were not descended from David, whose "branch," according to the biblical book of Zechariah, was divinely destined to provide the future messiah. They installed members of their family as high priest, although they were not descended from the line of Tsadok, the traditional source of the high priesthood. Thus although the Maccabees certainly fought for the Torah, they also fought for power.

These facts, known to the critical historian, have been extruded from Jewish sacred history. The biblical books of 1st and 2nd Maccabees, which tell the complete story, were excluded from the Jewish biblical canon, although they were preserved in the Catholic, and later Protestant, Bibles. But most Christians today know little about the Maccabees. I believe it is important for anyone learning about ancient Jewish history to know about the fate of the Maccabees after their great victory: the court intrigues, the civil wars, their adoption of the Greek language and many Hellenistic customs. And perhaps most important, we all need to acknowledge that the Maccabean revolt was as much an internal struggle between traditional and Hellenizing Jews, who favored a radical assimilation of Greek culture, as it was between Jews and persecuting Gentiles.

Understanding the truth behind the Hanukkah story demystifies Jewish history. We learn that in many historical situations, Jews have been dynamic actors as well as passive victims. We appreciate that power politics and court intrigue could characterize the Jews as they did the Jews' Gentile neighbors. While celebrating the strength of the Jewish spirit, we can recognize the Jews' ever-present potential for civil strife. Dissecting the many layers of the Hanukkah story also helps us appreciate the essence of the Rabbinic Judaism that was formed in the centuries immediately following the Hasmonean kingdom.

Between the first and seventh centuries CE, Jewish jurists in Palestine and Babylon formulated a vast body of ritual and jurisprudence known as the Oral Law. These jurists, known as rabbis ("masters" of Judaic knowledge), believed that the Oral Law had been transmitted to Moses on Mount Sinai but that they, and they alone, were authorized to authenticate and interpret it. One reason why the rabbis were reluctant to accord to the Maccabees a central role in historical memory was because the Maccabees had assumed the authority to make changes in Jewish Law, e.g., they authorized fighting on the Sabbath and proclaimed the festival of Hanukkah.

Another central aspect of Rabbinic Judaism, messianism, also plays into the Hanukkah story. The rabbis' vision of the future was of a Davidic dynasty ruling over an independent, harmonious Hebraic kingdom, itself a part of a world at peace and in recognition of the one true God. This vision of the end of days was utopian, unrealizable by human action alone, thus rendering it impossible for any mere approximation, or, in fact, for any worldly, historical phenomenon such as the Maccabean kingdom, to be given a place in Jewish collective consciousness. Thus for the rabbis, commemoration of Hanukkah needed to be restricted to the Maccabees' one undisputedly meritorious act: the restoration of the Temple, the cynosure of Jewish life, whose joyous rededication appeared all the more poignant to rabbis writing in the aftermath of its destruction by the Romans. But it was essential for the greatest victory of all to be the work of divine, not human power. Thus the miracle of the cruse of oil that lasted for eight days—a miracle related in rabbinic literature but not in the Books of the Maccabees.

Critical history should be respectful of its sacred counterpart even while rejecting its method and conclusions. The clash between critical and scientific history has continued throughout the ages because of the innate human need to find moral meaning and purpose in historical events. As the great Jewish historian Yosef Haim Yerushalmi has written, "There are myths that are life-sustaining and deserve to be reinterpreted for our age. There are some that lead astray and must be redefined. Others are dangerous and must be exposed."[2] The biblical narratives are, by and large, of the first sort: a mighty source of inspiration, comfort, and courage. But the Jewish historian must constantly be on the lookout for other, more baleful, types of myth. This brings us to a discussion of the Middle Ages, when Jews in Europe became the objects of demonic mythologization.

III. The Middle Ages

Historians of the Jews, and all the more so Islam and the Eastern religions, often feel uncomfortable applying to their own faiths forms of historical periodization originally developed by and for the Christian world. The very concept of a "Middle Age" is a Christian one, for it connoted a period between the first and second comings of Christ, that is, between ancient history, on the one hand, and the end of history, on the other. During the Renaissance, the tripartite division of time was altered to reflect the belief that Christendom had passed from an unenlightened Middle Age into a resplendent modern one, which embodied the humanist ethos of Greco-Roman antiquity. How, then, do the terms "ancient," "medieval," and "modern" apply to Jewish civilization?

If we associate ancient Judaism with the Israelite temple cult and medieval Judaism with the faith-system of the rabbis, then ancient Jewish history ended and medieval times began in the first century CE. Perhaps, instead, we should date the onset of medieval Jewish history to the decline of pagan antiquity and the triumph of Judaism's sibling religions, Christianity and Islam, for Jewish culture was indelibly stamped by its encounter with these two dominant faiths. If so, then medieval Jewish history began in the 4th century CE in the West and the 7th century CE in the East. This is not a mere chronological quibble, for taxonomy constructs the conceptual paradigms within which historical thinking operates. If medieval Jewish history is defined in terms of the development of rabbinic Judaism, then its motive forces are primarily internal. (After all, although the destruction of the Temple by the Romans hastened the growth of rabbinic Judaism, its roots lie deep within the Second Temple period itself.) If, on the other hand, we look to Christianity and Islam to define the onset of Jewish medieval times, Jewish history becomes a contingent phenomenon, dependent upon external forces.

Does Jewish history develop primarily according to its own inner drives or its encounter with the other? There is no easy answer to this question. It points to a clash between two different views of Jewish history, views that I can call "essentialist" and "contextualist" respectively. Students of Jewish history must understand both perspectives. On the one hand, they must reject Christian and Islamic supercessionism in any form and perceive medieval Jewish life as an indigenous cultural force. Moreover, if the patterns of medieval Jewish life frequently resembled those of their Gentile counterparts, the reason is not that the former were mimicking the latter, but rather that the two confronted similar situations and shared a common pool of intellectual resources. Moreover, although the issues facing Jews and Gentiles in medieval times often overlapped, at times they diverged as well. Thus the approach to medieval Jewish history that I advocate is best described as comparative rather than merely contextual.

A second fundamental issue in the teaching of medieval Jewish history has to do with assessing the nature of Jewish-Gentile relations. For the Jews, the Middle Ages were both fraught with danger and replete with opportunity. We must appreciate both of these aspects equally.

All too often, the history of medieval Jewry is understood according to what the great Jewish historian Salo Baron critically described as the "lachrymose view" of Jewish history. According to the lachrymose view, Jewish history prior to the modern age was one of unending misery. This view has been propagated by not only Jewish scholars but also well-meaning Christians, who look with justified horror upon the Church's anti-Jewish teachings, the burning of sacred Jewish books, forced conversions, libelous accusations of ritual murder and host dese-cration, expulsions and even massacres of Jewish communities. Violence was, unfortunately, endemic in medieval Christendom; acts of brutality against Jews must be placed against a background of what R. I. Moore has called a "persecuting society," obsessed, at least from the 13th century onwards, by fears of impurity and deviance, fears that led to systematic persecution of heretics, women, homosexuals, and lepers as well as Jews. Let us not forget that Muslims as well as Jews were expelled from Spain after the triumphant conquest of Grenada in 1492. And although Jewish converts to Christianity were specifically targeted for the cruelest of tortures by the Spanish and Portuguese Inquisitions, the so-called "new Christians" were never expelled, unlike the *moriscos*, Muslim converts to the faith of Rome.

I try to avoid the oft-repeated phrase that Jews were "second-class cit-izens" in medieval Europe. How can one say this of a time when the con-cept of citizenship—of membership in a political entity that conferred inalienable rights—barely existed? If the position of the Jews was inferior to that of the nobility or urban bourgeoisie, it was far superior to that of the peasantry, the vast bulk of the population. True, Jews lived in towns according to privileges granted by a ruling authority, but such was the legal basis of feudal society as a whole—conditional privileges as opposed to fundamental rights.

Furthermore, the legal, social, and economic privileges of the Jews in medieval Christendom varied considerably across time. In the early Middle Ages, the reigning Catholic doctrine was that Jews must of necessity live among Christians, albeit in a humbled state. In the 13th and 14th centuries, however, the Church changed its tune, arguing that Jews lived among Christians by sufferance (the official language was "Christian love") alone. When a renegade Crusader army massacred Rhineland Jews in 1096, the local authorities tried to protect them. Three centuries later, the patricians of Germany's cities joined the chorus of voices accusing Jews of poisoning wells and murdering Christian children for their blood. In Charlemagne's empire, Jews played major roles as international merchants, and in 12th-century England, Jewish bankers held mortgages on the estates of some of the realm's most powerful barons. By the 14th centuries, however, Jews had been reduced to petty money-lending, the more profitable banking positions long taken by Christians.

It is unfortunate that the history of Christian-Jewish relations in the Middle Ages is usually taught from the perspective of western Europe. The fact is that by the later Middle Ages, most of Christendom's Jews lived in the Polish-Lithuanian commonwealth, a multiethnic entity that offered Jews a relatively hospitable living environment. Although Jewish merchants faced considerable hostility from the burghers in western Poland's cities, Polish magnates encouraged Jews to colonize their vast estates in eastern Lithuania and Ukraine, thus creating the basis for a dense network of small towns (known in Yiddish as *shtetlakh*, sing. *shtetl*) with substantial Jewish populations. This became the core of Ashkenazic Jewish culture, expressed through the Yiddish vernacular and Hebrew sacred tongue, and which flourished for some three centuries before its obliteration by the Nazis.

Although the medieval Polish Church made some efforts to introduce the discriminatory legislation promulgated against Jews by the 13th-century popes, in practice Jews were rarely forced to wear the Jewish badge, nor were they economically marginalized as was the case in the West. Indeed, Jews were the pillar of the Polish manorial economy, buying and selling produce, managing noblemen's estates, and operating mills and taverns. During the 15th century, Jews expelled from the German lands were welcomed into Poland. During the Counter-Reformation, there was no parallel in Poland to the Jewish ghettos that were constructed in Germany and Italy. To be sure, Jewish life was never secure, even in the Polish-Lithuanian kingdom. In 1648, thousands of Jews in Ukraine were killed by supporters of Bogdan Chmielnitski, who saw in the Jews both the enemies of Christendom and the stooges of the hated Polish overlords.

Thus, the lachrymose view cannot be completely swept aside. It needs instead to be placed in an appropriate comparative framework. A similar, though in some ways opposite, observation must be made regarding Jewish life in the lands of Islam. In general, the legal status and personal security of Jews in the medieval Islamic world were higher than in Christendom. The most stunning example of Jewish success in *dar al-Islam* was 11th-century Grenada, where the Jew Shmuel ha-Nagid served as Vizier and commanded the kingdom's armies. But at times there has been a tendency to over-romanticize the "Golden Age" of Middle Eastern Jewry during the period of the Abbasid caliphate (8th–13th centuries), its Egyptian and Spanish counterparts, and the Ottoman Empire of the 15th through early 20th centuries. To be sure, Jews were vital to the economic life of the medieval Middle East, and, during the 1500s the Ottoman Empire welcomed tens of thousands of Jews expelled from the Iberian Peninsula. The Ottoman Empire became home to a flourishing Jewish cultural centre, speaking Ladino, the Judeo-Spanish dialect taken from the Iberian peninsula, just as the Jews of Poland spoke the Yiddish that had originated in high medieval Germany. At the same time, the Islamic world had its share of forced conversions (in North Africa, Yemen, and Iran). The Islamic tradition contained a good deal of anti-Jewish animus, some of it rooted in the Koran's depiction of Jews as a people of traitors and "slayers of prophets."

Medieval Christendom and *dar al-Islam* were ethnically and confessionally diverse, but they were not "multicultural," that is, accepting of different cultures and faiths as equally valid within a broad framework of natural- and positive-legal norms. Judaism was no different from its counterparts. Medieval Jewish thinkers considered it self-evident that their faith was the only authentic one and that the superiority of Judaism could be rationally demonstrated. Christianity was thought by many rabbis to be a form of idolatry. By the High Middle Ages that view had softened, most likely because of the need for medieval Jews, whose livelihoods depended on trade with Christians, to overcome talmudic prohibitions against doing business with idolaters. Although some medieval Jewish philosophers located common theological ground between the major faiths, Jewish mystics in Germany saw in the Christian world an ever-present source of moral pollution.

Jewish hostility to triumphant Christianity and Islam could be an important source of spiritual vitality. In the wake of the Crusader massacres of 1096, Ashkenazic Jews developed a commitment to martyrdom (*kiddush ha-shem*), a sort of inverted Christian chivalry, in which piety and bravery were expressed not via holy war against one's enemy, but rather by a willingness to commit suicide when faced with the choice between conversion to Christianity or murder at the hands of Gentiles. Sephardic Jews, bewildered by expulsions, forced baptisms, and torture at the hands of the Inquisition were attracted to the mystical mythology of the 16th-century rabbi Isaac Luria. Luria developed a Gnostic doctrine of a cosmological catastrophe that had caused God himself to be imprisoned by his own creation. The Chmielnitski massacres of the following century attracted Ashkenazic Jews to Lurianic mysticism, which became, admittedly with many modifications, the basis for the most successful pietist movement in modern Jewish history, East European Hassidism.

Medieval Jewish spiritual creativity was thus in part reactive, a product of interactions, frequently traumatic, with the Gentile world. But in keeping with my remarks at the beginning of this section, much of medieval Jewish life was internally driven. After all, Judaism had a rich mystical tradition going back to antiquity. The growth of Jewish legal commentary and codification certainly had parallels in other cultures but was not necessarily directly indebted to them. Medieval Jewish life was neither entirely indigenous nor contingent. Neither the essentialist nor the contextualist frameworks that I have mentioned above do justice to its richness and complexity. All the more so for the modern period, when Jews became intimately involved in virtually all aspects of their host societies yet maintained distinct religious, ethnic, and cultural features.

IV. Modernity

I am a modern historian, and most of my undergraduate teaching has focused on the 18th through 20th centuries. I have found that regardless of faith or ethnic origin, students tend to bring into the study of Jewish modernity an overwhelming fascination with one historical event: The Holocaust. My students have always been more absorbed by lectures on the Holocaust than any other subject. This fascination stems in part from noble sentiments: a desire to comprehend the causes of such an inhumane act and to prevent its reoccurrence; or feelings of vicarious identification with the victims and vicarious guilt about the actions of the perpetrators. Unfortunately, it can also reflect a desire for titillation in an era that has become desensitized to less spectacular forms of violence, a morbid obsession with Nazism, even a neo-pagan apocalypticism undergirded by deep anti-Semitic feeling. Anyone who has taught the Holocaust in a university setting has had unpleasant encounters with skinheads, white supremacists, and Holocaust deniers of various stripes.

The centrality of the Holocaust in popular perception of the modern Jewish experience has produced a serious distortion of history that I, as a teacher, labor to correct. Jewish history is, all too often, conceived in a deterministic, teleological manner; it is understood in reference to the Holocaust and interpreted as leading inexorably to that great catastrophe. In my teaching, I stress the contingent qualities of historical development, which, although explicable in terms of broad socioeconomic or collective-psychological forces, is not beholden to them. History has many futures. It is precisely this way of thinking that illustrates the magnitude of the horror of the Holocaust: modern Jewish history did not have to lead to Auschwitz because Auschwitz did not have to be built.

Furthermore, to what extent must the Holocaust, and by extension the history of modern anti-Semitism, be taught within the framework modern Jewish history? Aren't these subjects essential components of modern history writ large? To be sure, the history of Jewish life in the concentration camps and ghettos, acts of resistance and collaboration, and the impact of the Holocaust on Jewish communities worldwide must be an integral part of any course in modern Jewish history. But the Nazis' murderous anti-Semitism had nothing to do with real Jews; rather, it was a mixture of irrational phobias and fantasies. The Nazis drew upon both traditional Christian Jew-hatred and modern political anti-Semitism. The latter, which emerged in the 1880s, presented Jew-hatred as a systematic ideology, an "ism," a secular worldview on par with the great competing ideologies of the era, liberalism and socialism. Political anti-Semitism identified the Jews as responsible for all the anxiety-provoking social forces that characterized modernity: ruthless capitalism, revolutionary communism; avant-garde artistic modernism. Modern anti-Semitism was thus far more than yet another form of bigotry or xenophobia. It was, as the historian Shulamit Volkov has put it, a "cultural code," a signifier of social protest by individuals unwilling or unable to confront the real sources of their anxiety and despair.[3]

It disturbs me that it is often left to the Jewish historian, within the contours of a course in modern Jewish history, to teach courses on anti-Semitism and the Holocaust. Moreover, I want my students to come away from a course in Jewish history with a sense that the modern Jewish experience was in many ways a positive one. If one defines the history of modern Jewry solely in terms of the Holocaust, then it was a sorry spectacle indeed, a series of humiliations and atrocities leading inexorably to a vast valley of dry bones. But if defined in terms of spiritual and cultural creativity, political ferment, and ethnic solidarity, then Jewish history takes on flesh and blood and, for all its unique qualities, becomes not just the tragic tale of a pariah people, but the story of a people in the world, a world as beautiful as it is horrific.

How then should modern Jewish history be presented? It is the story of the Jews' engagement—at times enthusiastically receptive, at times hostile—with the new demands placed upon them and opportunities presented to them by the modern state. In West and Central Europe, Jews were forced to give up their long-cherished legal autonomy and to become fully subject to the laws of the state. In the late 18th and 19th centuries they were emancipated, freed of legal disabilities and, in time, allowed to take part in government and administration of the polities in which they lived. Jewish emancipation was part of the great modern project of human liberation that brought about the end of serfdom and slavery, the introduction of freedom of movement and contract, and the rise of representative government. Russia's Jews were not emancipated for the simple reason that Tsarist society was incapable of emancipating its people as a whole from the prison of feudal privilege and leading them into the light of inalienable freedom. Conversely, the brave new world of North America offered Jews considerable social and political freedoms from the start. As white property owners, they had a place in the new civil society of the United States and British North America.

The autonomous communities that had been the natural habitat for Rabbinic Judaism evolved into voluntary associations that Jews could enter or abandon at will. Jewish ritual and education had been predicated upon, and in turn promoted, social segregation between Jew and Gentile, but Jews increasingly attended public schools, abandoned Jewish vernaculars for the language of the land, and questioned the value of the dietary laws and Sabbath observance, which hindered social and economic relations with Gentiles. Some Jews assimilated entirely into Gentile society. Others, particularly in East Europe and Russia, developed a zealous Orthodoxy that rejected modernity in any form. Most fascinating, however, was the sizeable bloc of rabbis and lay leaders who forged a new faith, linked with Rabbinic Judaism yet qualitatively different from it.

The Jewish Enlightenment, or *Haskalah,* saw in modernity a challenge to Jews to construct a coherent and meaningful culture, rooted in classic texts yet open to innovation in science and other forms of secular knowledge. The result was a Hebraic revolution: in East Europe, the birth of modern Hebrew journalism and literature; and in the West, the application to classic Hebrew texts of the methods of modern academic scholarship. In Germany, the *Haskalah* inspired the development of Reform and Conservative Judaism, which abandoned certain aspects of traditional Jewish practice while cherishing others. The most influential exponent of German Reform Judaism, the mid 19th-century rabbi Abraham Geiger, rejected Orthodox accusations that Reform watered down traditional Judaism and mimicked Protestant practices. Rather, he saw Reform as a spiritually progressive force, the legitimate heir of Rabbinic Judaism, which captured its essence while casting aside its anachronistic features.

Although Conservative Judaism was more cautious in its approach, it too accepted the basic notion that Judaism was subject to historical change. Thus history, a subject of no particular value in traditional rabbinic culture, became central to 19th-century Judaism. Jewish scholars inspired by the Reform and Conservative movements produced monumental works of Jewish history. The greatest of them, Heinrich Graetz's eleven-volume *History of the Jews* (1859–73), remains absorbing and vibrant to this day.

Modern Jewish society, like its Christian counterpart, secularized without abandoning religious sensibility or social links with one's religious community. Moreover, although Jews in the West integrated into their host societies and thought of themselves as fully English, French, German, and so on, they maintained strong senses of Jewish ethnic identity. Jews continued to care for their own poor, ill, and aged; they built up dense networks of philanthropic organizations, involvement in which provided a secular form of collective identity. Acculturated Jews also had a sense of global Jewish identity. French Jews spoke of Jews worldwide as a "community of fate;" German Jews used the same term or the even more telling noun "Stamm," or ancestral community.

Jews also developed a rich political life. In the West, Jewish politics primarily took the form of associations representing Jewish interests to governments and to public opinion, e.g., the French *Alliance Israélite Universelle* (f. 1860); the American Jewish Committee (f. 1906). In

Russia, Jewish political activity was perforce more radical, given the oppressive nature of the Tsarist regime. The Jewish workers' organization known as the *Bund* was, in the first years of the 20th century, a pillar of the socialist movement in Russia. Orthodox Jews adopted the organizational techniques of modern mass politics to promote their interests. The ultra-Orthodox *Agudat Yisra'el*, founded in Germany in 1912, was particularly powerful in interwar Poland, where it won a plurality of votes in many Jewish communal elections.

Jewish political life took form within a dense, three-dimensional space defined by the axes of religious, national, and economic identification. The extremes of these axes were, respectively, Ultra-Orthodoxy and secularism, nationalism and assimilationism, and revolutionary socialism and bourgeois liberalism. There were Jewish political organizations representing virtually every conceivable permutation of loci along the three axes. The Zionist movement was, then, but one element in the vast matrix of early 20th-century Jewish politics. Similarly, its ambitious project of creating an autonomous Jewish society in Palestine shared many points in common with other attempts in the early 20th century to engineer Jewish homelands throughout the globe, e.g., Argentina (by the Paris-based Jewish Colonization Association) or Ukraine and Crimea (by the American Jewish Joint Distribution Committee).

Ultimately, though, only the Zionists succeeded in establishing a viable Jewish homeland. Jewish politics and social engineering, divorced from the politics of independent state-building, always failed. At the same time, it would be inappropriate to dismiss all other forms of Jewish politics or social engineering as merely stepping stones toward the realization of the Zionist ideal. The relationship between Zionism and other forms of Jewish politics should be conceived not in mathematical terms of unidirectional vectors but rather in biological terms of lateral evolution from a common ancestor. Zionism and other forms of Jewish politics were cousins, sharing a common ancestor in the economic misery and political insecurity of East European Jewry in the early 1900s.

Just as Jewish politics existed apart from Zionism, neither is there an inextricable and all-embracing link between the Holocaust and the creation of the state of Israel. A few years ago, a journalist was interviewing me about Israel, and she was astonished to learn that there had been Jews in Palestine before 1945. She had assumed that Palestine was handed over to the Jews as a gift by the United Nations as a form of reparations for the Holocaust. Although her ignorance was perhaps unusual, it does bespeak a general failure to appreciate the extent to which the state of Israel owes its existence to factors other than the Holocaust. By 1948, there were 600,000 Jews in Palestine; they had constructed a functioning political apparatus, national economy, and militia. When the United Nations' Special Commission on Palestine deliberated the future of that land, the Holocaust per se did not enter into their discussions. Rather, they viewed the land, rightly enough, as contested between two peoples, and the majority view (authored by, inter alia, Canada) was that the land must be divided between Jews and Arabs in order to prevent a descent into chaos. To be sure, the Holocaust certainly exercised postwar international public opinion, and the British were forced to bring the Palestine issue to the U.N. in part because of global outrage at the sight of Holocaust survivors interned in detention camps when caught en route to Palestine. But the partition of Palestine between Jews and Arabs was, first and foremost, a recognition of the successes of the Zionist movement to date, and without a half century of gruelling Zionist effort, no amount of international sympathy would have brought about the creation of a Jewish state.

The State of Israel, like all states, owes its existence to assertions, and at times excesses, of power. It engages in statecraft and wages war. Israel's actions toward Arabs have been, on the one hand, romanticized and obscured by Israel's champions, and, on the other hand, trumpeted and overblown by its enemies. But just as I have tried throughout this paper to present Jewish history as part of universal history, I ask that we consider the relations between Israel and the Arab world within the framework of nationality conflict, not abstract theology, and that we teach its history accordingly.

Israel is more than a state inhabited mostly by Jews; it is a Jewish state, bound to the modern Jewish experience as a whole. Modernity did not of necessity engender Israel, but Israel was born bearing all the scars of Jewish modernity. Israel is a contested land, not merely in terms of the conflict between Jews and Arabs, but also in terms of the unresolved clash between all the elements in the matrix of modern Jewish politics that I have described above. Socialism versus market capitalism, secularism versus Orthodoxy, integration into a global culture or isolation within what the Talmud calls "four cubits of the *halakhah*": all of these historic tensions are concentrated in one small, crowded space. As the poet Yehuda Amichai has written, Israel is "a package tied with string, bound together very tightly, and, sometimes, it hurts."

V. Conclusion

How one ends a historical narrative influences, via back-shadowing, one's perception of the narrative as a whole. It is not a mere pedagogic convenience, but a decision fraught with consequences, to end a class in Jewish history in 1945, in the aftermath of the Holocaust, or in 1948, with the creation of the state of Israel. Such endings retroactively project onto the course of modernity a lachrymose view of Jewish victimization or a blinkered view of Israel as the Aristotelian final cause of Jewish existence. Jewish history, like that of humanity as a whole, is openended; it is remade with every passing moment, as the present slides inexorably into the past.

Since the end of World War II, Israel has matured into a prosperous Mediterranean state, technologically sophisticated and, in large measure, heavily Westernized. It has produced a rich Hebraic culture, both secular and sacred, and its leading religious thinkers, e.g., the late Yeshiyahu Leibowitz, have struggled with the integration of the Jewish rabbinic tradition into the newly-spun fabric of Jewish empowerment. Israel's sunny Mediterranean climate is clouded, however, by its ongoing struggle with its Arab neighbors and with its own fissured identities.

The recent history of the Jewish Diaspora has been no less troubled. The Middle Eastern Jewish subcivilization all but disappeared with the mass immigrations to Israel in the 1950s. Most of the former Soviet Union's Jews have moved to Israel in the last fifteen years. The situation appears more stable in North America and West Europe, where the number of Jews has in recent decades remained constant, and Jews have experienced tremendous economic mobility. Yet low birth rates and significant levels of assimilation and intermarriage have caused the percentage of Jews within the total populations of the United States and other western lands to drop precipitously. In the wake of the Second Palestinian Uprising since September 2000, anti-Semitic attacks on Jewish property and persons have increased alarmingly. That said, there are many signs of cultural vitality among the Jews of the Diaspora, particularly in the United States, Canada, and France, and Orthodoxy appears to be flourishing.

The futures of Israel and the Jewish Diaspora are unpredictable; thus let their history be unfinished and the interpretation of that history be indeterminate. The historian must, of necessity, recognize the limit of her craft. History provides an empathetic understanding of the human experience, but it does not pretend to bear ultimate truths. History does not and cannot provide satisfying "foundational myths"—not if it wishes to retain any shred of pretension to critical detachment. The historian is an assayer, who tests the claims of ideologues in the scales of reason. Let us hope that in a world where the veracity of the Holocaust—perhaps the most thoroughly documented act in human history—is increasingly challenged, where historical consciousness has been all but eclipsed by the hegemony of a cybernetic eternal future, where the Orwellian nightmare of history written anew with every day has been realized by paper shredders and media "spin"—the assayer's task will not become a labor of Sisyphus.

Notes

1. Marshall G. S. Hodgson, *The Venture of Islam: Conscience and History in a World Civilization*, Chicago, 1974, I, 33.

2. Yosef Haim Yerushalmi, Zakhor: *Jewish History and Jewish Memory*, New York, 1989, 99–100.

3. Shulamit Volkov, "Antisemitism as a Cultural Code," *Leo Baeck Institute Year Book* XXIII (1978), 25–45.

MICHAEL DUSHINSKY

What Do We Want the Other to Teach About Jewish History?

I t gives me a great pleasure and an even greater honor to stand here today in this highly esteemed gathering. Our Sages command us "to open one's speech with a tribute to host's hospitality to scholars." Therefore, I would like to greet, to honor, and to give thanks from the depth of my heart to the revered Rabbi Joseph Ehrenkranz for encouraging me in my Jewish and interreligious work over the past few years and to Dr. David Coppola, who has been so helpful to me in preparing this paper. Both of them are from the Center for Christian-Jewish Understanding, Sacred Heart University, Fairfield, Connecticut, which hosts this conference. Of course, I greet and thank all of the participants here at the University of Bamberg and all who will read this paper.

What do we want the other to teach about us? There are difficult and complex sets of questions within the title itself. Who are the "we?" Is it the whole Jewish People today? Is it only scholars, academics, Rabbis? Is it Reform, Conservative, Orthodox Jews? And, if so, then which groups within them? Hassidim, Sephardim, seculars, or others? Is it the Israeli Jew, the Diaspora Jew, or do I have to speak, to answer, to act, to refer to and demonstrate the theme only according to me personally? Should I concentrate on this last point and ignore any other influences of others?

"Want." Why should I or we want anything? Is it my own wanting? Do Jews really want the "other" to learn or teach our history? I feel that I would want this to happen. But it is essential to bring to those who would listen, an authentic understanding and feeling of an "insider," rooted deeply in Jewish life, faith, practices, traditions, music, and teachings.

"The other"—or perhaps better, "others." Who are they? Why do they want to know, and more importantly, teach my history? I think the "others" are all people inspired with good will who would seek to understand and then teach authentic Judaism. The "others" who might read these papers to be gathered into a book will be clergy and religious leaders, seminarians and rabbinical students, religious educators and students taking interreligious courses on the undergraduate university level. The "others" will be teachers who may or may not be Jewish, who would like to see Judaism in a way that is true to the tradition but also expresses how that tradition is vital and lived today.

"To teach." To what extent must the teacher or the historian identify with the history that he or she conveys? Personally, I would ask my audience to be as empathetic as I am, and that includes not only detailed knowledge, but deep feeling too. How could I hope or expect the other to teach in such a way? It is very promising to see Jews, Christians—Roman Catholics, Lutherans and others—as well as Muslims as partners in dialogue who have agreed to respect each other enough to teach others' religious beliefs to the best of their ability. Also, it takes more effort and commitment from the person who humbly agrees to teach about another, rather than an academic enterprise that focuses primarily on learning for one's own knowledge or growth. My duty is to try to make a contribution, however modest it may be, to you my peers. My concern is that I authentically represent my forefathers, and therefore, my responsibility is somewhat overwhelming. My hope is to do them justice in my presentation.

"About our history." What do we see as history? Does our history remain in the past or is it an integral part of our present and future? The present is interpreted in light of how we understand the past. I do know that there is a strong connection in the three Abrahamic faiths to Revelation and G-d working in our history. This heavily impacts the way we understand the present that has been influenced by the past. And it is a lesson for the future.

It is a most difficult task to try to convey my thoughts and feelings about my history as a Jew, and it is particularly difficult to attempt to present the Jewish People as a whole in its interpretation of its history. The question that I have been asked to address is posed, therefore, in a very personal way and the matter of presenting Jewish history is indeed, a very personal matter. For me, history begins with the heritage of my Central-European Rabbinical family. It is the story of my late grandfather Rabbi Michael Dushinsky as Chief Chaplain in the Kaiser Franz-Yosef's army during the First World War. It is the fate of his Congregation in Rakospalota, Budapest, and its currently deserted synagogue, Miqve, school and cemetery. It is the life of his firstborn son, my late uncle Dr. Yechezkel-Edward Dushinsky. Having been born to an orthodox Hungarian patriot rabbi in 1899, he became an artillery officer in the Austrian-Hungarian army in World War I. This merit gave him the right, despite the "Numerus Clausus," to study medicine and dentistry. During the Nazi occupation of Hungary, for a lot of money and with his contacts as a physician, he managed to hide my cousins, his two baby daughters in a village outside town. It did not help. In that village they were caught and from there sent to Auschwitz to be gassed. He and my aunt Betty survived. They never had other children. He died at the age of 97 in Tel-Aviv under the photograph of his dear daughters. We mentioned their names on his tombstone.

Also for me, Jewish history is the fate of Rabbi Michael's youngest son, my uncle and mentor, Rabbi Professor Yerakhmi'el Ya'aqov, Eugene Jacob Dushinsky, who led that Rakospalota community through the Second World War. The Hungarian allies of Germany enslaved him in the mines of Bor, Yugoslavia. He was saved by Tito's partisans and joined them. He received the rank of colonel as Chief Chaplain in the Hungary's liberated, postwar army. Then he fled from the Communist regime to become Chief Rabbi of South Africa and a great Zionist leader.

For me, history is also my late Zionist father, Eliyahu Menachem Dushinsky, who settled in Tel Aviv in 1933, acquired Palestinian passports and hence caused me to be a proud born and bred Israeli citizen and soldier. And my late mother, Breindil Brachah ne'e Stein, born in Szighet, Transylvania to a Hassidic family, was a Zionist and came to Palestine in 1933 and married my father in Tel Aviv. Her brother, my late uncle Rabbi Shmu'el Be'eri-Stein, after losing his first family in the *Shoah*, he remarried. He was the first emissary of the Jewish Agency to the Jews of Ethiopia. His only daughter, my cousin, was born in Asmara. She is a white Ethiopian Jew. Later, he was Chief Rabbi in Finland and in the Netherlands, retired in Israel and passed away at the age of 90. Old and

154 ≈ Michael Dushinsky

young Ethiopian religious leaders were among those who mourned for him.

Jewish history is the survival of my People through four millennia. Both the private and the general histories are a vital part of my very being. Thus, I will now stay with those "events" of the past that bring meaning to me as a contemporary Jew. Part of the living Jewish history for me is the Creation, 5762 years ago by the L-rd, with "let there be light!" (Genesis 1:3), with the Tree of Knowledge and G-d's commandments that Adam and Eve disobeyed. An understanding of G-d's revelation to humanity begins in Noah and the seven Noachide Precepts, among them the sacredness of the life of human beings, compassion to animals and establishing courts. History is also the sins committed by the men and women of the Babylonian Tower, the Deluge generation, Sodom and Gomorrah, and the punishments the world suffered due to them.

From an academic perspective, Jewish history began with our ancestor Abraham, who discovered the oneness of G-d and proclaimed it to the world. The L-rd bequeathed him and his future generations the Land of Israel, my Land. History is the binding of his son Isaac and the angel who prevented that human sacrifice. This teaches me the origin of obeying the L-rd's will even if all seems to be lost. History is the story of Simon and Levi in Shechem—adherence to tradition even then—when they demanded *millah*, circumcision, that remained since Abraham, and the *mitzvah* was observed by all Jews voluntarily. History is the story of Judah and Tamar who kept the law of *yibbum*, levirate marriage. And within this story we find the origin of the House of David, the spark of the Messiah. History is the brotherhood and compassion between the twelve tribes in the story of Joseph. History is righteousness in the judgments of Potiphar and the Pharaoh in Joseph's time.

History is the Exodus from Egypt and the revelation in Mount Sinai. They mark the beginning of a journey of covenantal obedience to G-d that led to the 613 *mitzvot* of the Torah, given to us by G-d through Moses for all generations to come: "Everything that the L-rd hath said, we will do and we will listen to" (Exodus 24:7). History is the Books that remember and acclaim stories of great people and deeds: Joshua capturing the Promised Land, the Judges, the Prophets, the Kings, the Destruction of the First Temple in the 6th century BCE, the Babylonian exile, the Cyrus Declaration and the rebuilding of the Second Temple after 70 years.

Jewish history also remembers and includes Alexander the Great in Judea (332 BCE), the Diadochs Ptolmei and Seleucos, the revolt of the Maccabees (167 BCE), the Hasmonean household, and Jewish life during the Second Temple period. Jewish history is Pompius of Rome in Israel, the Pharisees, Sadducees, Essenes and Zealots, the Great Revolt, Josephus Flavius, Vespasian, Titus and the second Destruction in 70 CE, Rabbi Akiva and the Bar-Kokhba Revolt, the books of the Apocrypha, the Dead Sea sects and scrolls and the Mishnah.

History is the story through the centuries of the Jewry living and contributing to communities all over the world. History is also the the fate of communities in Germany, Poland, France, Spain, Russia, and a multitude of others in the Holy Land and all the exiles. Blood libels and expulsions, decrees and bloodshed, yellow stars, forced conversions, ghettos, pogroms, exiles, dispersions, hardships, the losses suffered by the State of Israel in its attempt to survive, thousands of destroyed and deserted cemeteries all over Europe, anti-Semitism, anti-Israelism, racism and the "noncemetery memorial" of the *Shoah* in Auschwitz and elsewhere are all part of the Jewish historical memory. Jewish history also gratefully remembers the Righteous among the Nations: the monarchs, popes, statesmen, monks, philosophers and all the Gentile lovers and defenders of Jews and Judaism throughout the centuries.

Jewish history is also the stories, the cultures, the religions and even the music of the great and small nations and empires of past and present and their relationship with Judaism and Jews: the Sumerians and Akkadians, Egyptians and Babylonians, Persians and Parthians, Greeks and Romans, Byzantinians and Arabs, Mongols, Japanese and Chinese, all the different Europeans, the French and the British, the Nazis and the Communists, and the Americans. History is how my people managed to live their own Sabbath, Festivals and Yom Kippur with their cultural traditions that uplift the soul, their own calendar, family purity and dietary laws, Torah education and charity, and all that keeps them unique.

And history for me is names like the biblical: Abraham, Isaac and Jacob, Judah and Joseph, Moses and Aaron, Deborah and Elijah, Isaiah, Jeremiah and Jonah, Ezra and Daniel; the Mishnah's, Shma'yah and

Avtalyon, Hillel and Shammai, Rabban Gamliel, Rabban Yochanan b. Zakkai, and Rabbi Judah HaNassi; the Talmud's, Rabbi Yochanan and Rabbi Shimon b. Laqish, Rav and Shmuel, Abbayye and Rava, Ravina and Rav Ashi; the commentators, codifiers, poets, philosophers, kabbalists, and scholars; the Ge'onim Amram, Haii and Saadia, Rabbi Judah Halevi and Rabbi Shlomo Gabirol (Avicebron), RaSH'Y and Rabbenu Tam, Rabbi Yitzkhak Al-Fassi and R'Y Migash, Rabbi Yehudah HeKhassid and Rabbi Me'ir of Rothenburg, RaMBa'M and RaMBa'N (Maimonides & Nachmanides), HaMe'iri and the RaSHB'A, Rabbi Moshe Isserlish and Rabbi Yossef Qaro, the Ga'on of Vilna and the Baal-Shem-Tov, the MaHaRa'L and the Chata'm Sofer, Khafetz-Khayyim and Ben-Ish-Khai, Rabbi Avraham Yitzkhaq HaKohen Kuk and Rabbi Moshe Feinstein. I humbly, but proudly call these people "my short sacred list." Its aim is to emphasize my view that this astounding phenomenon of the handing down of *halachah* and customs through the generations is living history to every Jew. We would not and we shall not exist as a unique people, a unique belief and a unique entity without a list such as this.

What then is the most important educational message of traditional Judaism that I want conveyed to others and by others? The answer is precisely that Judaism is a living and dynamic organism, that is inextricably linked back in an unbroken chain, since time in memoriam. To emphasize this point, allow me to focus on the insights of the most outstanding Jewish personality of the Middle Ages, Rabbi Moses Maimonides, known as RaMBa'M. He lived a life of faithfulness to G-d and his scholarship continues to influence Judaism to the day. It has been said about RaMBa'M: "From Moses to Moses never arose one like Moses" meaning from Moses, the receiver of Torah, until Maimonides there has never been another. Later generations have bestowed Maimonides with the title, the Great Eagle.

In the long introduction to his commentary of the Mishnah, which he wrote at an early age, and also in his short introduction to his Code of Laws which he finished in 1177, at 42 years of age, Maimonides detailed the order of the generations in delivering the Torah, the Oral Law, since the time of Moses. He also made it some of his "Thirteen Principles of Faith," which Jews sing and say twice daily before and after our morning prayers. By making these connections to former generations, he made a statement that Judaism is a religion and belief that is rooted and lived in history. He wrote the Book of the Precepts, Sefer HamMitzvot, in which he lists all precepts. There are 248 positive precepts and 365 negative ones. For each precept, *mitzvah*, the source in the Torah is presented followed by a description of its contents. RaMBa'M also makes distinct applications whether the mitzvah applies for Kohanim, Levyyim or Yisre'elim or for all; is it for men or women or for both; and whether it applies to a particular time and place or to all periods.

There were disputes during the 13th and 14th centuries, resulting in the burning of some of Maimonides' philosophic works. The Code of Laws, however, was left untouched. This monumental work was written in the most beautiful and accurate Mishnaic Hebrew, so that all Jews would be able to study it and relate it to their part in history. In every traditional Jewish home-library one will probably find his Code of Laws. Maimonides wrote his Code for all times and ironically his teachings remains the source and the rock for Jewish life until today. He and his teachings are a living history for every contemporary Jew.

Daily, Jews say and sing the twelfth Principle of Faith, one of the thirteen written by Maimonides. Jews went into the gas chambers with this verse on their lips. This is part of our recent Jewish memory, so it should be sung:

> I believe with perfect faith in the coming of the Messiah;
> and although he may tarry, I await daily for his coming.
> *'ani ma'amin be'emunah sheleimah bevi'at hammashiakh;*
> *ve'af 'al pi sheyyitmah`meah, 'im kol zeh 'akhakkeh lo bechol yom sheyyavo.*

This is the way I want the other to teach my history.

D A V I D   F O X   S A N D M E L

Understanding and Teaching Jewish History

Before I begin my formal response to Rabbi Dushinsky, let me first offer a few words of introduction to give you a sense of how I might approach our topic. I am a rabbi and I received my rabbinic ordination from the Hebrew Union College-Jewish Institute of Religion in Cincinnati, Ohio, and I am, therefore, a Reform or liberal rabbi. I am also an academic having just completed a PhD at the University of Pennsylvania where I studied the history and literature of Judaism and Christianity in the Greco-Roman world from a Religious Studies perspective. Finally, I claim some experience and expertise in Jewish-Christian relations. Both parents were active in Jewish-Christian dialogue. Among my earliest memories are Shabbat dinners and Passover Seders with priests and nuns as guests sitting at our table. More recently, I served as the Jewish Scholar at the Institute for Christian and Jewish Studies in Baltimore, Maryland, where I directed the project that produced *Dabru Emet: A Jewish Statement on Christians and Christianity*, which was published in September 2000. What I bring to a discussion like this is the passion of one who has committed himself to serving the Jewish people and the intellectual rigor of critical scholarship. There is some tension between these two perspectives that I try to balance, but I also feel they give me some insight into the dynamics of interfaith dialogue.

Rabbi Dushinsky's wide-ranging paper highlights the challenge of the topic we have been asked to speak about. I would like to focus on and expand upon several of the issues that he raised or alluded to in his paper, especially his meditation on the question that also serves as the topic of this conference: What do we want the other to teach about us? While sitting at my computer typing this last sentence, I made what I think is a revealing slip. Instead of the word "teach," I typed the word "think." So the question read, "what do we want the other to *think* about us?" When I saw this on the computer screen, I immediately deleted the mistake and typed in the correct word, and although "think" was no longer on the screen, that question remained in my mind and continued to intrigue me. At first, I thought that as an academician, my hope should be that others would teach about my tradition as objectively as is humanly possible, according to the most up-to-date scholarship, and that the learner would draw his or her own conclusions from the material that was presented. But I am also a Jew, a diaspora Jew, and in light of our history, what others think about Jews and Judaism also concerns me a great deal.

What makes a gathering of Jews, Christians, and Muslims and this discussion so important is that several Jews are being offered the opportunity to shape both the teaching and the thinking of the other. This is a remarkable revolution in interreligious relations that demonstrates that the perception both of the religious other and of the other's religion has undergone a radical transformation. In the past we—and here I mean all of us—defined the other from the perspective of our own particular tradition's frame of reference, using our own categories and terminology. The goal was not the accurate portrayal of the other, but rather to create an image of the other that made it easy to draw simple (often false) distinctions between "us" and "them" and to demonstrate that "we" were definitely superior to "them." The task before us that lies behind the topic question is quite different—it is to allow the others to define themselves, to make their self-understanding the standard for what we teach about them, to choose our words in such a way that if the other were standing in front of us, he or she would recognize themselves in what was being taught and not be horrified by stereotypes, caricatures, polemics, or even well-intentioned ignorance.

When we teach about the other, we must always imagine that other is standing in front us. As a Jew, if I am teaching Jews about Christianity, then I must imagine that one of my Christian friends is in the room. I should not say anything to this group of Jews that I would not say direct-ly to my Christian friend, or better, that my Christian friend would not say if he or she was doing the teaching. A Jewish scholar, Amy-Jill Levine, teaches New Testament at Vanderbilt University in Nashville, Tennessee. She relates that each year she brings one of her young children to her classes and she instructs her students, most of whom are Christian divinity students, to be sure that nothing they teach their students or their congregation would ever cause harm to this child. My colleagues and I used the same principle when we edited the book, *Christianity in Jewish Terms.*˙ Though, as the title shows, the book is written by and primarily for Jews, we asked Christian scholars to respond to each chapter as a "reality check." The specific assignment for the Christian respondents was to reflect on whether their understanding of Christianity was accurately reflected in the writing of the Jewish scholars. Indeed, I am tempted go so far as to say that in an ideal situation, "we" would not teach about the other at all. Rather, when we want to learn about other, we should invite the other into our classroom or into our pulpit to teach. The presence of the living, breathing other is itself a lesson that we can never duplicate. I recognize that there are many situations where this is either impossible or impractical, but I say it nonetheless, to underscore the delicacy, the challenge of teaching about the others as they would want us to teach about them.

Rabbi Dushinsky ruminated on the word "we"—he wondered which "we" was intended by the question, and he listed a number of possibilities for the identity of that "we." He said: "Is it the whole Jewish People today? Is it only scholars, academics, Rabbis? Is it Reform, Conservative, Orthodox Jews? And, if so, then which groups within them? Hassidim, Sephardim, seculars, or others? Is it the Israeli Jew or the Diaspora Jew?" I would respond to Rabbi Dushinsky's rhetorical questions because I believe it needs to be spelled out.

When teaching about Judaism, I believe it is essential to stress the variety, pluralism and the diversity that has characterized the Jewish community, not only today but in every period of Jewish history. Here I think the term "Judaisms" first used by Jacob Neusner is a useful concept. Neusner used the term to describe the vibrancy and variety of expressions of Judaism in the Second Temple Period, in part as a counterbalance to the once common tendency to describe Judaism in this period, the period that includes the life of Jesus, as a monolithic and petrified religion. Nothing could be further from the truth for that period or, for that matter, for any period of Jewish history. Dynamism and dissention have always been part of the Jewish reality. Even in Biblical times, we see religious conflict and diversity around issues such as centralized worship versus local shrines in the Josianic reformation in the 6th century BCE. A unique feature of the Mishna, as compared to any Jewish literature that preceded it, is that it preserved and even honored differences of opinion. I would suggest that this was a conscious choice on the part of the early *tannaim* in response to the catastrophe of the failure of the Great Revolt and the destruction of the Second Temple. In attempting to unite the fractious parties that had, in the eyes of the rabbis, contributed to the loss of Jerusalem, they tried to include as many opinions as they could. So unlike the literature of the Second Temple Period, which tends to see things in black and white, for example, the sons of light and the sons of darkness of the Dead Sea Scrolls, the rabbis tried to legitimize differences of opinion, at least within certain parameters.

In this regard, I would point out that Rabbi Dushinsky chose to concentrate his presentation of Maimonides on his *halachic* works, and mentioned only in passing his philosophical works, which, as the Rabbi stated, were burned in the 13th and 14th century. For those who may not be familiar with Maimonides, the controversy over his philosophical writing, over his *Moreh Nevuchim*, his *Guide for the Perplexed*, is another example of the diversity within Judaism. When I think of Maimonides, I think of him first as a philosopher, who in the tradition of the Arabic philosophy of his day, attempted to synthesize Judaism and neo-Aristotelianism, much as Philo had tried to synthesize Judaism and neo-Platonism in 1st century Alexandria. That Rabbi Dushinsky focused on Maimonides the halachist, and that I think of him first as a philosopher is instructive. In good rabbinic fashion, I can say that I am right and Rabbi Dushinsky is right. Or, to quote the Talmud, *elu v'elu divrei elohim chayim*, both this opinion and that opinion are the words of the living God.

Therefore, when one teaches about Judaism, one should be careful about any statement that begins with the phrase "Jews believe" or "Judaism teaches" for it cannot avoid being a gross oversimplification or generalization that does apply to all Jews in every time or place. Indeed, whether Jews or Christians, all of us must be careful about imposing a false unity of Jewish history and tradition. It may be useful to think of the Jews as a community of fate rather than a community of faith. That is, we Jews share a history, literature, ethical, and religious convictions, and perhaps, a culture, although we disagree vociferously about their meaning, authority, and significance. We feel a kinship with one another as Jews, even while we disagree on such fundamental issues as the nature of God or the content and meaning of revelation. In this regard, then, what makes a person a Jew is not only a matter of faith or belief as it is the recognition of belonging to an ancient people, to the extended family that, according to Genesis, is descended from Abraham and Sarah. It is being a member of the People of Israel or *b'nei Yisrael,* the children of Israel.

As a rabbi, I have worked with potential proselytes and I have made the point that "conversion" is not really an accurate translation of the Jewish concept of *giyur.* Conversion, at least from a Religious Studies perspective, implies a numinous experience that radically changes one's understanding of and relationship to God. In contrast, when a Gentile chooses to become Jewish, the process is more like becoming a naturalized citizen of country; it is being adopted into the family of Abraham and Sarah, and, over a period of time, learning that family's history and traditions. It is a family in which loyalty and commitment to one another is a primary value. As in many families, loving and defending the other members of the family is often quite different from liking them or agreeing with them, even on essential issues. Thus, another point in teaching about Jewish history and Judaism is stressing, not only the diversity within the Jewish community, but also that religion and faith are components, but not the totality of what Judaism is or what it means to be a Jew.

I also want to say a word, not about what one teaches, but rather *how* one teaches about Judaism. I would hope that others would be sensitive to the reality that teaching occurs not only in classrooms, but in other settings, as well. Focusing specifically on the Christian tradition, there is much teaching about Jews and Judaism that takes place through liturgy, hymnody, the lectionary, and even in church art, as can be seen, for example, in the message being communicated in the statues of Ecclesia and Synagoga that are found in the cathedral in Bamberg and elsewhere in European churches. Indeed, the challenge of changing liturgy and lectionary is much greater than changing what one teaches in an academic setting. But I think we must be cognizant that many more people will learn about Jews in church than in school. So Christians must ask themselves how the Old Testament is being read and preached as part of their worship. Is there any acknowledgment on their part that the Christian Old Testament is also the Jewish *Tanach,* that which Jews read and interpret differently than Christians? Insights from traditional Jewish midrash or from contemporary Jewish commentators might both enrich the understanding of the text and affirm that these scriptures can be read in rich and different ways.

Hymnody and liturgy are more difficult questions, for liturgy, music and song operate on a deep emotional level. It is most disturbing to Jews to go to a synagogue other than one's own, and not know any of the melodies. Hymns are like old friends. But precisely because they work affectively as well as cognitively, it is essential to be careful of the messages that they communicate. In English speaking countries, the words to a favorite Christian hymn in preparation for Christmas is, "O come, O come Immanuel and ransom captive Israel." Try to remove this hymn from holiday worship and one might have a congregation in revolt. But who and what is "captive Israel," what do these words teach and how do they influence how people think? Or what is the message when in some churches during the Easter vigil, the Old Testament readings are done in candlelight or darkness and then the lights are turned on for the reading of the Gospels. These examples are specific to certain churches, but they underscore the importance of examining carefully the kinds of teaching other than classroom instruction.

The lectionary is probably the most challenging aspect of worship. As most people know, there are many "difficult texts" regarding Jews and Judaism in the New Testament that have affected the historical relationship of Jews and Christians with disastrous results. In part, the onus is on the preacher who must not rely on the facile tropes of traditional homiletics, such as incorrectly contrasting the wisdom and compassion of Jesus with that of the legalistic and heartless Pharisees. Although the preacher can mitigate some of the challenges posed by difficult texts, I think it is also fair to ask whether certain passages should be read at all, or if they should be read without addressing directly the anti-Jewish sentiments that they contain. I know that there is much being done in this regard by many different churches. I merely want to emphasize that the messages that are communicated in worship, the teaching that takes place in that setting, must be congruent with what is taught in the classroom or contained in official pronouncements. I also recognize that no one is going to edit the New Testament, just as Jews are not going to edit the difficult passages of the *Tanach*. Liturgy, lectionary, and hymnody pose difficult challenges as well as opportunities to strengthen the positive advances in interreligious dialogue of late.

I would like to conclude by affirming that teaching about the other does not require us to compromise our traditions' commitment to what each believes to be ultimate truth. There are differences between Judaism, Christianity, and Islam (and between Judaism and other traditions) that should not be glossed over because we seek to understand each other better and avoid the hatred and violence that are part of our tragic history. Our traditions and beliefs are not interchangeable; as we said in *Dabru Emet*, they are "humanly irreconcilable." Our challenge is to teach those differences with humility and respect so that we can understand and appreciate the uniqueness of our own tradition and that of the other. In doing so, we can live with each other in peace and become a blessing to each other and the world.

Note

* *Christianity in Jewish Terms*, edited by Tikva Frymer-Kensky, David Novak, Peter Ochs, David Fox Sandmel, and Michael Signer. (Boulder, CO: Westview Press, 2000).

LEONARD SWIDLER

What Do Christians Want Jews and Muslims to Teach About Christianity?

Introduction

The first thing to be aware of about Christianity is that there have been, and are, many understandings and lived versions of Christianity. To begin with, there are three major branches of Christianity: Catholicism, Orthodoxy, and Protestantism. Further, some versions of Christianity have been more optimistic, some pessimistic, some absolutist, some tolerant, some other-world-directed, and some this-world-directed. However, in the latter half of the twentieth century most of Christianity took a dramatic turn in the direction of what might be called modernity. What I aim to do now is to present a general picture of that modern Christianity, and then point out some of the common ground that all three of the Abrahamic traditions, Judaism, Christianity, and Islam stand on together. But before I can turn to that fivefold Copernican Turn of contemporary Christianity, I need to trace the founding and subsequent trajectory of Christianity leading up to it, albeit in a most compact manner.

At the heart of all of the versions of Christianity stands the Jew, Jesus of Nazareth (or Yeshua ha Notzri, as he was called in his native Semitic tongue). Hence, to understand something of Christianity we must first understand something of Yeshua, and that in turn entails understanding something of the Hebrew and Jewish traditions.

Hebrew Religion

The ancient Hebrews thought and spoke in a theistic mode. Moreover, they eventually came to a monotheistic understanding, which became characteristic not only of their religion but also of the three major religions that sprang from their root: Judaism, Christianity, and Islam. The story of the development of the Hebrew religion is set down in "The Book" (*biblos* in Greek). In its beginning, it tells of one God who is the source and creator of all reality. The crowning point of creation was humankind, who was made in God's image, that is, someone who could know, could freely decide, and could love. In this tradition, everything that exists is good simply because it has being and this being springs from God, who is all good.

Then whence came evil? To the Hebrews, as to everyone else, it was obvious that there was evil in the world, indeed, in every human being. Their answer was that human beings themselves are the source of evil, for by their free will they can refuse to choose the good, and those choices are called evil. This understanding is embedded in the story of the "Fall" at the beginning of the book of Genesis: because humans did not follow the right order of their nature, their true "self," as created by God, in God's image, their nature became "disordered" in relationship to its own self and its creator, and hence in turn, to the rest of creation. Here was the first "domino theory." The way to live an authentic human life is to live according to one's authentic self, one's Image of God (*Imago Dei*, in Latin). Perceiving that true self, that *Imago Dei*, became difficult. However, after the Fall, according to the Hebrews, God arranged for special help to be made available, at least to the Hebrews, a "Chosen People," who in turn were to be "a light unto the nations." This special help was God's Instructions, God's Torah, on how to live a true human life, one in accordance with one's true self, the *Imago Dei*.

Thus, the Hebrew religion was basically optimistic, for the source of all reality was the one God, who was goodness itself, and God's creation was, as it says in Genesis, "good," *tov*, and at the end of the creation story, "very good," *mod tov*. But it also took account of the presence of evil in humans and prescribed its elimination by humans returning to their original authentic self, the *Imago Dei*, the clear path to which was indicated by God's Torah. And the heart of the Torah is justice and love, or even simply love, for, as Pope Paul VI much later said, "justice is love's minimum."

The summary of the Torah was the twofold commandment of love of God and love of neighbor, and the former could be carried out through the fulfillment of the latter, the love of neighbor. Then, who is the neighbor; who is to be loved? The Hebrew prophets appeared throughout the history of the Hebrew people to make it abundantly clear that what God desired was not "burnt offerings" but rather a just life. The prophets called for treating everyone fairly, but preeminently loving the oppressed, the powerless of society, specifically the poor, widow and orphan, the most vulnerable of society.

Judaism

In the first millennium before the Common Era, the Hebrew people became a united kingdom, and then suffered division into two parts; one of which, Israel, was largely destroyed in the seventh century BCE and the second of which, Judah, was carried off into Babylonian exile in the sixth century, only to return to rebuild Jerusalem. By this time, the Hebrews had rather firmly committed themselves to monotheism and more and more focused on carrying out God's Torah as the essence of an authentic human life. It is from this postexilic period onward that one speaks of Judaism. Later, around 167 BCE, the Pharisees, who have had unwarrantedly bad press in the Christian tradition, appeared on the scene. Among other things, they were responsible for prayers referring to God as a loving "Father" and such teachings as the resurrection of the body. But most of all, they showed the "way" (*halachah* in Hebrew) to lead a just life, a distinctly Jewish life, by laboring to make concrete the more general obligations found in the written Torah, the Bible. Eventually their specifying commentary came to be understood as the "oral Torah." It should be noted that for the Pharisees, as for Jews in general, the main question was not, "What must I think?" as it was for the Greeks and later for most Christians, but rather, "What must I do?"

The Pharisees, of course, were not the only Jews at the beginning of the Common Era who laid claim to have the right teaching on how to live an authentic human, Jewish life. There were others such as the

Sadducces, Essenes, Zealots, Hellenists, among others. One of those "others" was the Galilean Jew, Yeshua ha Notzri, who in many ways was close to the Pharisees, but also critical of them, as would be appropriate in his tradition.

Yeshua of Nazareth

As noted, Yeshua was a Jew, religiously as well as ethnically. He was born of a Jewish mother, studied the Jewish Scriptures (the Hebrew Bible, of course, not the New Testament), was addressed as "rabbi," carefully kept the Torah, or Law. Like the Pharisees, Yeshua also specified the general great twofold commandment of love of God and neighbor; all his teaching and all his stories were aimed at making God's instructions—God's Torah—concrete. And similar to other Jewish prophets, his followers called him a prophet because he epitomized the love of neighbor in reaching out to the powerless: When asked, who is leading an authentic human life, who will "enter into the kingdom of heaven?" he answered, "Those who give drink to the thirsty, food to the hungry, clothing to the naked. . . ." (Matthew 25:31–46). For Yeshua, because he was a good Jew, the main question was not, "What must I think?" but "What must I do?" In brief, the "Good News," the "God-spel," that Yeshua taught was that the Reign of God was near, indeed, "within you" and that letting God reign in their lives would lead them to joy now, and "in the world to come." Thus, the first followers of Yeshua, who were Jews, found in him a special "way" (*halachah*) to "salvation" (the term comes from the Latin *salus,* meaning primarily a full, healthful, whole, and therefore (w)holy life) by what he thought, taught, and wrought. They sensed in him an inner wisdom and authenticity (what he "thought"), which issued in his extraordinarily insightful and inspiring teachings (what he "taught"), which in turn were reflected in his self-emptying life, and death, for others (what he "wrought").

Yeshua made it clear that although he understood himself called to address in his lifetime the "children of the House of Israel," his notion of neighbor was broad: It included not only one's geographical neighbors, one's relatives, one's ethnic fellows; but it even included one's enemies, as the story of the Good Samaritan graphically illustrates. Yeshua attempted to even break through that most ancient pattern of oppression—sexism—by welcoming women as followers, even to the point that some ancient writers claimed this was one of the reasons for his condemnation! The first followers of Yeshua obviously grasped the heart of what he "thought, taught, and wrought," though unfortunately, his feminist example faded from Christian view until this century.

Despite the view that the end times were near, the followers of Jesus did not understand the "way" of Yeshua (*hodos* in New Testament Greek, similar to *halachah* in Rabbinic Hebrew) to be one of preaching "in the sky by and by." Rather, the fulfillment of the commandment to love God could be accomplished only through the fulfillment of the commandment to love one's neighbor: "If any one says, 'I love God,' and hates his brother, he is a liar; for he who does not love his brother whom he has seen, cannot love God whom he has not seen" (1 John 4:20).

Christology

Yeshua clearly was an extraordinary charismatic teacher, healer and prophet. But some of his first followers saw something else very special, very Jewish, in him; they saw him as the Messiah (*christos* in Greek), the Anointed One, who, as promised in the Scriptures, would free Judea from the despised Roman military occupation. But he did not. Instead, the Romans crucified him. At first, Yeshua's followers were crushed. Two of them were reported to have said, "But we had hoped that he would be the one to set Israel free" (Luke 24:21). But the power of Yeshua was too great for it to end on the rock of Golgotha. For his followers, Yeshua rose bodily from the dead and further empowered them to go forth to preach his "Good News."

But what about the messianic claims of Yeshua's followers for him? He did not become the new political king of Israel. They, or at least some of them, did not drop the messianic claims, they transformed, spiritualized the understanding of Messiah. Moreover, as the "Way" of Yeshua moved from a Jewish to a Greek world the Greek term "Christ" grew in usage and importance, and it became fused with another Jewish title given to Yeshua, namely, "son of God." The latter, which was a term used by Jews to refer to kings and holy men, was meant in a relational or metaphorical way. However, in the Greek world the metaphorical title, "son of God," moved in a few centuries to the ontological title, "God the Son," as reflected in the Trinitarian formula of the Council of Nicaea (325 AD).

One way some theologians have described this shift in understanding and expression is that the early followers of Yeshua saw in him a transparency of the divine. He appeared to them to be so radically open to all being, including the root of being, God, that he was completely filled with Being. Thus, he was a human meeting point of the human and the divine, an enfleshment, the incarnation of the divine. In this way Yeshua becomes for Christians a model of how to live an authentic human life. In him they meet ultimate reality, the divine, so that in a preeminent way he is for them the door to the divine, the one that informs all others.

At the same time, it is also clear from the New Testament, especially from the writings of Rabbi Saul (later called St. Paul) and John's Gospel, that there was a tendency early in the history of the followers of Yeshua to be more Christocentric than theocentric, that is, a tendency to focus the disciple's gaze more on the mediator, Christ, than pointing to God (Theos). This did not mean that Paul and John forgot about God and concentrated solely on Christ. It does mean, however, that in their writings there is a great emphasis on reaching God through Christ, whereas in the Synoptic Gospels (Mark, Matthew, and Luke), which mainly portray Yeshua's teaching and actions, the stress is more on God rather than on Christ. Moreover, it is important to note that Paul overwhelmingly talks about, not Yeshua, not Jesus, but about Christ, Jesus Christ, Christ Jesus. For Paul, most often Christ was not a concrete human person, but much more a spiritual force or life, so that he could write things such as, "I live now not I, but Christ lives in me." This notion of a "spiritual life" entering into one's own interior life fit quite well with the Semitic way of understanding and speaking of the world.

A Christian must choose Yeshua and his way if he or she wants to be a Christian, because for such a follower, the Jew, Yeshua of Nazareth, is the key to the meaning of life and how to live it. It is obvious that he must be spiritualized in a variety of ways so he can be interiorized in a person's life and consequent external behavior. A Christian can build his Christian life on the foundation of Yeshua—on what he thought, taught, and wrought—as a model, and having thus been inspired, strive to live accordingly and at the same time understand and refer to that interiorized life as Christ, as Paul did, for example.

The Christian Religion and Its Development

By the fourth century, and even before, the religion of Yeshua had largely become the religion about Christ. It was no longer simply Yeshua's "way;" it had become Christianity, the state religion of the mighty Roman Empire. In the ensuing centuries, the Christian Church spread throughout the Roman Empire and eventually beyond it. It took on many of the elements of the Greco-Roman culture, including a strong emphasis on "what to think," generating a plethora of lengthy creeds. These creeds were the source not only of unity but also of divisions. Each time a new creed was insisted on, a new division was enacted and many of the divided churches still exist today.

A large and unfortunate division occurred in 1054 with the split between Eastern and Western Christianity, usually known as Orthodox and Catholic Christianity. This was further followed by another major division of Western Christianity in the sixteenth century known as the Protestant Reformation. Each of these three major branches of Christianity took a rather absolutist view and insisted that they were the only ones who were correct and true, and the others who differed from them were consequently wrong. Of course, for almost all Christians, non-Christians were considered even more wrong!

The Christian West, Modernity and Global Civilization

Modernity is characterized by a focus on this world, on freedom, by a critical turn of mind, and eventually a historical sensibility. This began to happen in Western Christendom with the Renaissance and accelerated with a series of revolutions as Christendom evolved into Western Civilization, and is now emerging into Global Civilization: The sixteenth century World Discovery Revolution, the seventeenth century Scientific Revolution, the eighteenth century Industrial Revolution, the eighteenth/nineteenth century Political Revolutions, the twentieth century

Information Revolution, and the third millennium Dawn of the Age of Global Dialogue.

In effect, the twentieth century began in 1914 with the beginning of World War I, hit its nadir in 1939–45 with World War II, and ended in 1990 with the fall of the Berlin Wall and the end of the Cold War. About two-thirds of the way through, momentous changes began to surface, starting in a number of instances in America, but not limited to there. In fact, the 1960s was a momentous turning point in time for the entire world: 1) American Catholics broke out of their isolationist approach to religion in the election of President Kennedy; 2) the American civil rights movement began a transformation of the Western psyche; 3) the antiwar, environmentalist, antiestablishment and related movements in the West brought global transformation to a fever pitch; 4) through the Second Vatican Council (1962–65) the Catholic Church took a dramatic turn and leapt into what might be called modernity, and edged even beyond. It is to that last event I want to now turn, for it must be recalled that the Catholic Church has over one billion of the world's population of six billion. If Catholics are significantly changed and each of them interacts with non-Catholics in important and ethical ways, two-thirds of the world would be significantly impacted.

A Fivefold Copernican Turn of the Catholic Church

Some refer to this dramatic turn in the Catholic Church as a Copernican turn, for, as in the 180-degree turn in astronomy led by Copernicus from geocentrism to heliocentrism, much of Christianity through Catholicism has made a dramatic turn in the last four decades. That fivefold turn included: 1) the turn toward a historical sense; 2) the turn toward freedom; 3) the turn toward this world; 4) the turn toward inner reform; and 5) the turn toward dialogue.

First, for centuries the thinking of official Catholicism was dominated by a static understanding of reality. It resisted not only the democratic and human rights movements of the 19th and 20th centuries, but also the growing historical, dynamic way of understanding the world, including religious thought and practice. That changed dramatically with the

Second Vatican Council (1962–65) where the historical, dynamic view of reality and doctrine was officially embraced.

Second, the image Catholicism projected at the end of the 1950s was of a giant monolith, a community of hundreds of millions who held obedience in both action and thought as the highest virtue. With Vatican II, however, this constraining image and reality was utterly transformed. Catholics became aware of their "coming of age," and with it their freedom to think and choose as adults, as well as the corresponding responsibility of such choices. This was clearly expressed in many places, but the clearest document was *Dignitatis Humanae*, the "Declaration on Religious Liberty."

Third, until recently, salvation was understood exclusively to mean a person's going to heaven after death. As such, Catholicism tended to be more concerned with the next life than this one, and was often removed from issues of social justice. But that focus shifted radically with Vatican II, especially as reflected in the document, *Gaudium et Spes*, "The Church in the Modern World," which launched a concern for shaping a just world in this life.

Fourth, since the Protestant Reformation of the 16th century, the internal Catholic Church leadership was strongly opposed to even the use of the word "reform," to say nothing of the reality. But Pope John XXIII called for the Second Vatican Council and spoke about "throwing open the windows of the Vatican" to let in fresh thought. He called this effort to bring the Church up to date an *"aggiornamento."* Indeed, the Vatican II documents even used that painful word, "reformation." In *Unitatis Redintegratio*, "The Decree on Ecumenism," the Council declared, "Christ summons the Church, as she goes her pilgrim way, to that continual reformation of which she always has need;" and "All [Catholics] are led to . . . , wherever necessary, undertake with vigor the task of renewal and reform;" and all Catholics' "primary duty is to make an honest and careful appraisal of whatever needs to be renewed and achieved in the Catholic household itself."

Fifth, especially since the 16th century, the Catholic Church has been caught in a kind of solipsism, talking only to itself, and shaking its finger at the rest of the world. Again, Pope John XXIII and Vatican II changed an inward-looking posture to an outward one. Ecumenism was formerly forbidden and now "pertains to the whole Church, faithful and clergy alike. It extends to everyone" ("The Decree on Ecumenism"). Pope Paul VI issued his first encyclical letter, *Ecclesiam suam*, in 1964 on dialogue:

> Dialogue with children is not the same as dialogue with adults, nor is dialogue with Christians the same as dialogue with non-believers. But this method of approach is demanded nowadays by the prevalent understanding of the relationship between the sacred and the profane. It is demanded by the dynamic course of action which is changing the face of modern society. It is demanded by the pluralism of society, and by the maturity man has reached in this day and age. Be he religious or not, his secular education has enabled him to think and speak, and conduct a dialogue with dignity (#78).

At Vatican II, Catholics were taught in the "Constitution on the Church," the "Declaration on Religious Liberty," the "Decree on Ecumenism" and the "Declaration on the Relationship with Non-Christian Religions" that to be authentically Christian, Christians must a) cease being limited by their tribal forms of Christianity—they must stop their fratricidal hate; b) they need to recall their Jewish roots and the fact that the Jewish people today are still God's chosen people—for God's promises are never revoked; c) they need to turn from their convert-making among Muslims, Hindus, and other religious peoples and turn toward bearing witness to Jesus Christ by their lives and words, and toward helping Muslims be better Muslims and Hindus better Hindus. This will make Christians love their own liberating traditions not less, but more, for these traditions will then be even more fully Christian.

Jewish-Christian-Muslim Dialogue

I would like to reflect here further on dialogue. As the term is used today, dialogue is characterized as encounters between persons and groups with different religions or ideologies. In the past, when different religions or ideologies met, it was mainly to overcome or to prove the other wrong and to teach the other because each was completely convinced that it alone held the secret of the meaning of human life. More and more in recent times, people of good will and of different religions and ideologies have slowly come to the conviction that they did not hold the secret of the meaning of human life entirely unto themselves and that in fact, they had something very important to learn from each other. As a consequence, they approached their encounters with other religions and ideologies not primarily in the teaching mode, holding the secret of life alone, but primarily in the learning mode, seeking to find more of the secret of the meaning of life. That is dialogue.

The question we are addressing in this series of dialogues is why it is important, beyond this general reason, for specifically Jews, Christians and Muslims to enter into dialogue. The impetus for dialogue in the contemporary world has come mainly from Christians and then from Jews. Thus, it is natural that when Islam enters into dialogue, it is most likely to first be with Christians and then Jews. To be sure, there is need for dialogue between Islam and Hinduism, and even Buddhism, as well is underlined almost daily in the newspaper reports of mutual hostility and killings in Kashmir, India, and elsewhere. But it is overwhelmingly the encounter with the other two Abrahamic religions, Judaism and Christianity, which has been the motor driving Islam toward dialogue. As a prolegomenon to understanding why this is true, it is important to list at least some of the major elements these three Abrahamic religions have in common.

Elements the Abrahamic Religions Have in Common

First, all three religions come from Semitic roots and claim Abraham as their originating ancestor. Second, the three traditions are religions of ethical monotheism, that is, they all claim there is one, loving, just, creator God who is the supreme source, sustainer and goal of all reality and expects all humans, as beings created in the image of God, to live in love and justice. In other words, belief in God has ethical consequences concerning oneself, others, and the world. This is a common heritage of the three Abrahamic religions, which is by no means shared by all elements of the other major world religions. Third, the three traditions are historical religions, that is, they believe that God acts through human history and that God communicates through historical events, through particular human persons—preeminently Moses for Jews, Jesus for Christians, and Muhammad for Muslims. Historical events—such as the exodus, crucifixion, and *hijrah*—as well as individual human agents do not play the same central role in many other world religions, as, for example, in Hinduism and Taoism.

Fourth, Judaism, Christianity, and Islam are all religions of revelation, that is, they are convinced that God has communicated—revealed—something of God's own self and will in special ways through particular persons, for the edification, the salvation, or for the humanization of all humanity. In all three religions this revelation has two special vehicles: prophets and scriptures. In Judaism, the men prophets Isaiah, Amos, Hosea, Jeremiah, and the women prophets Miriam and Huldah, etc., are outstanding "mouthpieces" of Yahweh, and the greatest of all the prophets in Judaism is Moses. For Christianity, Moses and the other prophets are God's spokespersons and also within the prophetic witnesses in early Christianity are Anna (Luke 2:36–38), and the two daughters of Philip (Eusebius, Eccl. Hist. III.31). Most of all, Jesus was originally understood to be a prophet, although most Christians later came to claim much more than prophethood for him. For Islam, the Jewish and Christian prophets are also authentic prophets, God's revealing voice in the world, and to that list they add Muhammad, the seal of the Prophets.

For these three faiths God's special revelation is also communicated in "The Book," the "Bible." For Jews, the Holy Scriptures are the Hebrew Bible or *Tanakh*; for Christians it is the Hebrew Bible and the New Testament; and for Muslims it is a selective inclusion of some of Jewish and Christian scriptures as well as the *Qur'an*, which is corrective and supercedes the first two. For Muslims, Jews and Christians have the special name: "People of the Book."

There are many more things that the Abrahamic faiths have in common, such as the importance of covenant, law, faith, and community. But just looking at this brief list of commonalties will provide us only with an initial set of fundamental reasons why it is imperative for Jews, Christians, and Muslims to engage in serious, ongoing dialogue.

If Jews, Christians, and Muslims believe that there is only one, loving, just God in whose image they are created and whose will they claim to try to follow, then they need to face the question of why there are three different ways of worshiping the same God. Obviously that question can be faced only in dialogue. Also, if Jews, Christians, and Muslims believe that God acts through human history, through historical events and particular human persons, then they need to face the question of whether all religiously significant historical events and persons are limited to their own histories. In other words, do Jews, Christians and Muslims believe that they have God in their own historical boxes or by their own principles, does God transcend all limitations, including even their sacred historical events and persons? Finally, if Judaism, Christianity, and Islam believe that God is revealed to humans not only through things, events, and human persons in general, but also in special ways through particular events and persons, then they are going to have to face the question of whether God's will as delivered through God's spokespersons, that is, the prophets and the Holy Scriptures, is limited to their own prophets and scriptures.

In concrete terms, Jews will have to reflect on whether Jesus and the writings of his first Jewish followers (the so-called New Testament) have something to say about God's will for humankind to non-Christians. Jews and Christians will have to reflect on whether the prophet Muhammad and the *Qur'an* have something to say about God's will for humankind to non-Muslims. Muslims already affirm the importance of the Jewish and Christian prophets and scriptures. These questions, and others of serious importance concerning the ultimate meaning of life, can be addressed only in dialogue among Jews, Christians, and Muslims. Once this is recognized, however, it also becomes clear that all the questions just listed which challenge the absoluteness and exclusivity of the three Abrahamic traditions' claims about truth, history, prophets, scriptures and revelation, could also apply to the non-Abrahamic religions and ideologies, such as Hinduism, Buddhism, and Marxism.

Different Dialogues, Different Goals

Pragmatically, one cannot engage in dialogue with all possible partners at the same time. Moreover, all the goals of one dialogue with a certain set of partners can never be fulfilled by another set of dialogue partners. For example, the goal of working toward denominational unity between the "Lutheran Church in America" and the "American Lutheran Church" would never have been accomplished if Catholics had been full partners in that dialogue with Lutherans. Or again, Jews and Christians have certain items on their mutual theological agenda, e.g., the Jewish claim that the Messiah has not yet come and the Christian counterclaim, which will not be adequately addressed if Muslims are added as full partners. And so it goes with each addition or new mix of dialogue partners.

There is a special urgency about the need for Christians to dialogue among themselves to work toward the goal of some kind of effective, visible Christian unity: the absurdity and scandal of there being hundreds of separate churches all claiming "one foundation, Jesus Christ the Lord," is patent. The need for intra-Jewish dialogue I will leave to my Jewish sisters and brothers to inform me about, but it nevertheless appears noticeable in general. However, for Christians, dialogue with Jews has an extraordinarily high priority that cannot be displaced, and where it has not been both initiated and continued, that exigency demands to be addressed with all possible speed and perseverance. If nothing else, the twentieth-century Holocaust of the Jews in the heart of Christendom makes this dialogue indispensable.

Nevertheless, there is something similar, though not precisely, to a relationship of parent and offspring which could incline Jews to enter into dialogue with Christians, and Christians with Muslims. Furthermore, there are today many reasons for Jewish-Christian dialogue with Islam that flow from the reality of the earth now being a global village and the unavoidable symbiotic relationship between the Judeo-Christian industrialized West and the partly oil-rich, relatively non-industrialized Islamic world.

Expectations from Trialogue

A special word of caution to Jews and Christians entering into dialogue with Muslims is in order. They will be starting such a venture with several disadvantages: 1) the heritage of colonialism, 2) ignorance about Islam, 3) distorted image of Muslims, and 4) a culture gap.

The vast majority of Muslims trained in Islam's beliefs and thought are non-Westerners, which means they likely come from a country that was until recently a colony of the West. Many Muslims are still traumatized by Western colonialism and frequently identify Christianity, and to a lesser extent Judaism, with the West. Jewish and Christian dialogue partners need to be aware of this and move to diffuse the problem. Jews and Christians will need to make a special effort to learn about Islam beyond what was required for them to engage in the Jewish-Christian dialogue, for in the latter they usually knew at least a little about the partner's religion. With Islam they will probably be starting with a negative quantity, compounded from sheer ignorance and massive misinformation.

Most often, the Western image of a Muslim is a gross distortion of Islam. Indeed, it is frequently that of some kind of inhuman monster. But the Ayatolla Khomeni distortion of Islam is no more representative of Islam than the Rev. Ian Paisley of Northern Ireland is of Christianity or the Jewish murderer of Israeli Prime Minister Yitzak Rabin is of Judaism. Most difficult of all is the fact that a huge cultural gap exists between the great majority of Muslims and precisely those Jews and Christians who are open to dialogue. In brief: Islam as a whole has not yet experienced the Western "Enlightenment," or "modernity," and come to terms with it, as has much of the Judeo-Christian tradition, although obviously not all of it. Only a minority of Muslim Islamic scholars will share a "deabsolutized" understanding of truth needed to be able to enter into dialogue with "the other," that is, to converse with the religiously "other" primarily to learn from her or him. This means that many attempts at dialogue with Muslims will, in fact, be foundational efforts and a preface to true interreligious dialogue. Frequently such attempts will be not unlike a so-called "dialogue" with many Orthodox Jews or evangelical Christians or with Roman Catholics before Vatican II. But these foundational efforts and discussions must be experienced in order to reach authentic dialogue. There is no short cut. Surely the words of the Second Vatican Council and Pope Paul VI included above apply in this case to all Christians and Jews and Muslims, who "must assuredly be concerned for their separated brethren . . . making the first approaches toward them . . . . Dialogue is demanded by the pluralism of society, and by the maturity man has reached in this day and age. Be he religious or not, his secular education has enabled him to think and speak, and conduct a dialogue with dignity." (*Ecclesiam suam* #78) It is toward that end all Christians, Jews, and Muslims are urged to strive, first among themselves, and then with each other in pairs, and then all together.

Hans-Joachim Sander

God's Own History:
The Pastoral Process of Revelation

History offers the Church the opportunity and pastoral challenge to present God to the world. I dare to propose this as a Catholic abstract about the meaning of history for Christian faith. From this perspective, Catholic doctrine solves a problem the Church had to struggle with for centuries; namely, in a pastoral approach, the Church stands on the side of the eternal God and at the same time is deeply within an ever-changing world. The Church need not be disrupted by a power struggle to immunize itself against the real historical situations of people and can lead them to God without seeking to fight against approaches of other religions. On the contrary, Christians can find a language for the power of God, which can heal all wounds and create new life within the powerlessness of human beings and peoples suffering in history. Confessing faith in the eternal God means to look for the signs of the times revealing the decisive events for a human future or the danger of inhuman developments. The pastoral nature of the Church is born of the creative tension between the Gospel and the signs of the times. A pastoral contact with history frees Catholic theology to be curious about other religious traditions and their insights into the inner relationship between God and history. Pastorally conceived, history is concerned with making the world into a better place for human beings, and therefore is a fitting context for dialogue between Christians and other religions and also among themselves.

For the Catholic Church and Catholic theology, to come to terms with this framework of history is a major step, since it was not an invention of Catholics to consider history as a basis for faith, religion, and God-talk. On the contrary, for most of their modern existence the Catholic Church and Catholic theology have tried to step aside as soon as it was confronted by religious arguments out of history. In the grammar of the Catholic world, one would look upon the Church and its faith as powers that transcended history. Both were viewed as elements in the world and in history, of course, but fundamentally they were thought of being nonhistorical so as not to be looked upon as products of social and mental developments but as realities with an eternal nature. To understand what Catholic theology and doctrine have to say about history, one has to begin by analyzing history as a 'not-subject.'

1) The Not-Subject History—a Constitutive Element for the Church in Modern Times

For the modern Catholic Church, i.e. the Church after Reformation, there were reasons to avoid history in relation to Christian faith. Arguments out of histories and historical developments are always critical and these arguments could give the impression that faith and God are relative, especially as they confront plurality. Relativity means powerlessness to some extent; plurality means accepting the other to some extent. And powerlessness and otherness were not ideas the Church was eager to embrace after the Reformation. The ecclesial strategy to present the Church was *societas perfecta*, i.e., a complex analogy that rejected the model of the up-and-coming national states and their ever-growing influence. A *societas perfecta* is not constituted by history but by an ahistorical idea. In the case of the Church, this idea has a transcendental, theological origin; it is an idea of God. Therefore, the Church claimed to be a religious community with a transhistorical character. This religious community ought to be treated and had to be shaped as a social complex out of its own authority and rights, under the leadership of its own chosen personnel, territorial integrity, and with unique truth-claims not to be the subject of open debate by outsiders, and especially not open to a completely enlightened discourse. A strict line had been drawn between the inside and the outside of this religious community. History belonged to the outside. The relativity of history could be the subject of ecclesial interest in relation to the world but it must not be brought into the inside as an ecclesial factor for this religious community. Such relativity was thought to certainly lead to the damage of the eternal purity of the truth which resided inside the Church.

It is easy to understand that, for most of the modern times, the Catholic tradition strictly tried to avoid this relativity and feared plurality. Catholic theology did not take part in the developments of the modern natural sciences or in the critical reviewing of the history of Holy Scripture. After the trial against Galileo Galilei, theology was not considered any longer as a serious partner in discourses about nature, which discussed the position of human beings in the universe in a relative and reduced way. Exegetical scholarship of the Old Testament and New Testament remained a more or less Protestant project until the encyclical *"Divino Afflante Spiritu"* in 1943, by Pope Pius XII.[1] It was not by chance that while historicism held the intellectual leadership in Europe, Darwin's evolution-theory uttered convincing arguments and data about the origin of life on this planet, and the theory of relativity became the most exciting perspective on the Universe; in theology, neoscholastics dominated the subjects to be treated and the debates to be followed. And neither these subjects nor those debates would raise serious points about the importance of history for dogma, the reality of evolution in faith-matters, or the meaning of relativity for God. The simple reason is that scholasticism is not able to take history seriously enough for presenting God's presence in historical developments. Scholasticism deals with history only indirectly, in terms of authority. We will come back to this concept, which may be productive for another subject.

Only a very few theologians like the Dominicans Marie-Dominique Chenu and Yves Congar and the Jesuits Henri de Lubac and Karl Rahner were realizing that the relativity of history and the plurality of historical experiences give an excellent opportunity to present the universality of the Christian faith and the meaning of its doctrine for the others.[2] This universality cannot be presented without serious debates with other people—ideas and realities outside of the Church. Such a debate urges one to deal critically with one's own truth-claims. At the same time, the acceptance of plurality in history opens up a closed religious society for the truth-values of ideas and realities outside of the

Church. Acceptance of this relativity creates deeper relations with other religions and a higher respect for the historical experiences of other Christian denominations.

In the Catholic Church and theology, this did not happen before the end of the modern era. It belongs to the recent history of the Church that the Catholic tradition respects history as a primary locus to search for truth about God and on behalf of God's own presence in the world. This respect is one of the major achievements of the Second Vatican Council. This Council took place in the name of derived history and it discovered the bearing of historical concerns on the truth of Catholic doctrine while including the perspectives of others. At the Council's very beginning, Pope John XXIII urged the bishops to respect history as a "teaching master of life" and warned them not to follow those who viewed the world as nothing but decadence and evil. The pope saw that the Church had to take a major step to understand more deeply its own Christian faith and to present it to people over the world in a more convincing way.[3]

The Council fathers followed the pope's vision and confronted the Catholic Church with a historical problem: the Church became the major subject of the Council. And under this confrontation with historical reality, the Council discovered the plurality of the Church and the value of otherness for its existence in God. The Church undertook a twofold self-examination: *ecclesia ad intra* and *ecclesia ad extra*, i.e. "Church, what do you present to yourself about yourself" and "Church, what do you present to others about yourself?" Originally a plan of the Belgian Cardinal Suenens, this two-sided plurality became the cornerstone of the Council's doctrine. It led to the Council's two constitutions on the Church, the dogmatic constitution, *Lumen Gentium* [Dogmatic Constitution on the Church] and the pastoral constitution, *Gaudium et Spes* [Pastoral Constitution on the Church in the Modern World]. Both deal with history and develop a doctrine out of a specific history of God relating with his people. *Lumen Gentium* presents God's solidarity with his own people wandering through its history; it looks into the Church's own path through the history of humankind to discover God's presence.[4] *Gaudium et Spes* presents God's solidarity with every human being wandering through his or her own existence; it looks outside the Church to discover God's presence.[5]

What *Lumen Gentium* teaches is that God's history is with his people, beginning with the people of Israel, a people he called to himself and guided through the ages to be fulfilled at the end of time. This history is the history of the Church. The Church is the "People of God" constituted by the mystery of God's presence in the community, but also constituted by all that hinders the Church to realize fully and completely what God's own history with his people means for humankind. This means that the Church continually needs to be sanctified.[6] In other words, in *Lumen Gentium*, the Church learned to look at itself and its ambiguous history— the Church finds sinners in its inner reality and is, at the same time, the holy Church deeply in need of purification. The Church has to follow the way of penitence and renovation again and again.[7] Jesus Christ is God's own history with humankind, but it is a history of the risen Christ from out of time and a history of the crucified Jesus from within time. In analogy to Jesus Christ's two natures, the Church lives its own history out of a human and out of a divine element. The Church's existence is realized in a historical and a transhistorical process, its reality presents a historically ordered society and a Christological mystery.[8] Being the Body of Christ, the Church is a social being with a historical being and a transhistorical becoming.

What *Gaudium et Spes* teaches about history is that God's history is with every human being. It is a special history: the vocation every woman, every man, every child has received as a free gift from God. There is a divine seed in every human being and the Church seeks to cooperate with all humankind to build a community of brothers and sisters with equal rights to life.[9] This divine vocation is not specifically prescribed but can be interpreted as a call to every human being to become a full human being. Everyone is called by God to behave humanly and not to behave ahumanly or even to act by inhuman deeds. This vocation is a history of God with every human being and the Church has to serve this history. So whatever deep human experience or dangers of inhumanity that people are confronted with, the Church must be open to and realize its history in solidarity with the histories of all people. In consequence, the Gospel cannot be presented by the Church without its relation to history. The Church must address those events that have a significant meaning for what is human and what is inhuman in the present time. These significant facts in history are the "signs of the times." In discerning and realizing these signs right now, the Church is led into a contrast between history and the Gospel, and this contrast opens up God's presence in history as well as the human meaning of the Gospel.[10] On the other hand, this process is constitutive for those actions that are significant for the history Christ has built for the Church. This twofold constellation was called "pastoral" by the Council. Pastoral processes are constitutive for the Church in the actual world.

This is the appropriate doctrinal framework for Catholics to approach history. This teaching, pastorally shaped by Vatican II, is the first and primary answer for the question: "What Do We Want the Other to Teach About the Catholic Historical Tradition?" This teaching has built a *locus theologicus* (a locus for theology) to wrestle with history in terms of God, Christ, and the Holy Spirit and to shape religion in a manner necessary for the faith of the Church. God's pastoral relation with humankind and his presence in relation to the signs of the times constitutes a history that transforms the Church from a purely religious community to primarily a pastoral one.[11]

The pastoral perspective also solves the challenges of relativity, plurality and relativism to the Christian faith. The community of faith lives in deep solidarity with all peoples, with every human being on earth. It cannot find its own inner and outer actuality by God and in front of God if this community avoids others. Who they are, how they live, what they are suffering from, what they are longing for—all of these things are the subjects for a pastoral transformation of history. In the pastoral framework, one's own history does not necessarily come first. Rather it is God's history with humankind in the first place. So, the Church is always a secondary historical consideration when compared with the first. It is this pastoral turnaround of doctrine that enables the Church to engage in a real and intense dialogue with other religions. At the same time, dialogue takes on a realistic character and will have a pastoral meaning, or it will not be able to change the world into a better place for people and their relationship with God. From this perspective, one can freely examine the major issues of the religious community of the Church that have been marked by history. Some examples are the issues of the Church's origin, the nonidentity between Scripture and Tradition, papal infallibility, human rights and religious pluralism. In all of these matters, the pastoral nature of doctrine makes

a significant difference. Of course, one has to start with what comes
first.

2) Jesus and the Kingdom of God—Religious Origin
and Difference of Christian Faith

In the Catholic tradition, the Gospels have always been given preference
before Paul's letters. The perspective of the Kingdom of God had a deeper impact on the Church than justification. "Kingdom" marks a concept
of power and justification, not one of powerlessness. In the Kingdom of
Heaven there is the presumption of ruling people, whereas in justification
the individual is given dignity and the choice to respond to God in faith.
However, Jesus' Gospel of God's Kingdom and Paul's teaching of the risen
Christ are not contradictory to each other. Both are linked by a healing
mixture of power and powerlessness, which is a specific Christian perspective and may be common ground for ecumenical discourse among
Christians. Nevertheless, both messages imply a contrast, which in special contexts, may grow to intellectual, cultural and political difficulties
and did so in the past. These harsh difficulties do not necessarily come
out of the perspective of powerlessness in front of an overwhelming history of sin, but rather out of a perspective of power in front of an overwhelming concurrence of power.

The constellation of Jesus with his Kingdom of God and Paul with his
teaching of justification brings forward another problem of plurality and
relativity caused by history. One of the reasons that the Catholic tradition is linked much deeper with the Kingdom of God than a longing to
be justified comes out of the communitarian aspect of Jesus' history. Jesus
was surrounded by a community of followers (disciples) and his words and
deeds prestructured this community. Both are an experience of power.
The Church started up from these historical experiences and looked upon
itself as faithfully and loyally fulfilling the will of Jesus for all peoples' history. This position gave to the Church a historical identity and a basis for
a will-to-power in human history after Jesus' death. In the first centuries
of Christian era, this will-to-power saved the Church while suffering from
bloody oppression. It was understood that whatever happened was God's
will. The early Christians realized that their life in God could not be

stopped by an opposite will of any emperor on earth. The history of God's people would not lie in the hands of temporary powers and forces. As Saint Augustine put it, Christians are the *civitas Dei* (city of God), not to be identified with *civitas terrena* (city of the earth); but at the same time Christians could not be separated from earthly problems in a dualistic Manichean-like manner. The solution was that the historical destiny of the Church must therefore lie in the hands of an atemporal power. We will return to what this power is all about.

After Constantine, the ecclesial will-to-power would grow into a greater historical horizon. It was the timely impetus of a religious community looking for intellectual and political leadership on earth. This resulted in the millennial struggle between Christians and non-Christians, between pope and emperor, between representatives of the Church and the different peoples on earth, between the Reformation and Counter-reformation, between the Holy See and the national states, between revolution and restoration, between science and faith, between the Enlightenment and Scholasticism, between integralism and democracy, between the working poor and clerical moralists, between fundamentalism and modernism, and between mission and religious pluralism. One of the major aims of Christians, especially Catholics, was not to be overpowered by any other religious, social, cultural, or political power. In this historical struggle, the Church conquered one powerful position after another until the beginning of the modern times at the end of 15th century. But this time in history, under different circumstances and in a more pluralistic context, the Church had to give up position after position in terms of power. These experiences deeply and negatively shaped the Church's attitude toward secular history in modern times. They were understood as a depravation of God's own history with humankind. For example, it was quite difficult for a theologian like Karl Rahner to defend a position relating the secular history and the history of salvation to each other. Rahner did not say that they were more or less the same. But he saw an inner relation between both and encouraged the Church to realize God's anonymous presence in the midst of secular history.[12] Until Vatican II this position was vigorously attacked by the theological and ecclesial mainstream. The pastoral turnaround of Vatican II changed the picture completely.

A historical event like Vatican II cannot be explained by a historical logic; this would be an idealistic, Hegelian-like misunderstanding of the open field of history. Nevertheless, one can name systematic reasons why this process materialized. Jesus had primarily taught about and stood for the Kingdom of God, not the institutional Church that had developed over time. Both are intertwined with each other but they are not identical. As a consequence, one has to relate the Kingdom of God to the Church, but this relation contains a historical problem since the Kingdom of God has an eschatological quality. The Kingdom of God cannot be fully realized now, although its presence right now is what is most important for us to consider. There is a relation, and at the same time, a difference between being and becoming. This difference has to be accounted for when looking to the meaning of history for Christians. This has a large impact on the historical problem of Christian faith itself. Whatever power Christians are able to accumulate in the history of humankind is not necessarily the actual status or sign of the Kingdom of God, a kingdom for which Jesus gave his life and out of which God has revealed his Christological character. The power the Church is obliged to seek historically is the power of the Kingdom of God and not the earthly power of *civitas terrena*. But the Kingdom of God is a reality of historical power since "Kingdom" represents power. But the grammar of this power is based on powerlessness. Jesus' Sermon on the Mount in Matthew 5 functions that way. So, the major difference between the Church and political powers is not set by a different will-to-power but by the grammar this will has to pay attention to in Jesus' example.

The power of the Kingdom of God does not fear powerlessness but evolves out of it. This grammar is very important to solve a historical problem that is even more difficult than the relation between Church and the Kingdom of God. This historical problem is Jesus himself and the relation of the Church to him. Jesus represents the historical origin of the Church. Without his existence there would be no Christian faith, no Christian community and no ecclesial history. But this historical origin implies a special religious problem. The founder of Christianity is not a member of the ecclesial community starting with his history. Jesus was a Jew, not a Christian. And it appears that he had no intention whatsoever to be someone else in religious terms. As far as we know, he wanted to and did remain a Jew his entire life. The very founding figure of the Christian community does not stand in the midst of this community but—historically speaking—witnessed outside of it. This is very disturbing for Christians to encounter, and it has been a source for violence.

For a long time, Christians tried to close and destroy the gap between Jesus the Jew, and themselves, the non-Jews. This resulted in Christians fighting and overpowering Jews and Judaism in the history of Christian Europe. This was a strategy of power. And it failed completely in human history.[13] The religious gap between Jesus the Jew and Christians following Jesus cannot be closed, especially not by means of historical power. But it can be lived with by means of powerlessness. Powerlessness is a historical concept for the restored and proper relation between Jews and Christians; i.e., Christians cannot do anything else other than accept this gap between Jesus and their own religious community as God's will. Historically and systematically Jews represent the otherness of the Christian faith. This otherness is the historical basis for Christians themselves. The otherness does not mean that Jews have to be forced to be incorporated into the Christian Churches but that these Churches have to look to be accepted by Jews. Jews can live religiously without relation to Christians; they can live out of their own religious relationship to God in historical terms. But Christians cannot exist in the tradition of their historical origin without a welcoming relation with Jews. This is the Christian powerlessness in history. But this powerlessness brings them close to the very founding figure of their historical existence. For Christians, the Jews are the necessary historical bridge to Jesus.

This does not mean that Christians have to become Jews or have to become Jews first before becoming Christians. And this does not deny Paul's concept that all people have an independent access to the resurrected Jesus. On the contrary, Paul's concept of a mission to all people (1 Corinthians 9) remains the religious strategy Christians must employ throughout history. But neither does this mean that the Jewish origin of Christians is past history. There exists a major power standing between Jews and Christians. This power is not Jesus. Jesus is standing on the Jewish side; his historical position is not in-between. The power attacking all relations between Jews and Christians is violence, a short history of violence by Jews against Christians and a very long history of violence by Christians against Jews. Without resisting this power, violence will rule over every positive, healthy relation between both religions. When one deals honestly with the question of historical guilt and confronts one's religious community with the violence that has stood and continues to stand between Jews and Christians, one is resisting the power of violence. This subversive action is a religious task. At the same time, this resistance is building the bridge for Christians to come to Jesus the Jew. In this sense, there is no future for Christians without clearing up the history they have in common with Judaism. Christians can use this bridge as soon as they realize and present their sins to Jews. Without naming their historical sins toward Jews, Christians will lose their historical origin. This is a harsh truth for Christians but it is redeeming from the terrible habit of resentment. Resentment feeds all kinds of triumphal attitudes over the failure of others and opens the door to violence. Religions that run into situations of concurrence with each other risk being lured to resentment against each other. One has to take this danger into account if one aims at a successful and creative religious dialogue.

There is no religion without weak points and without real religious strength. For a dialogue between religions that is led by a pastoral aim, there is only one possible strategy: to search for the religious strength of the other. The strength of the other is of great interest, especially for Catholics after Vatican II. The pastoral redefinition of doctrine by Vatican II cannot work with resentment against others but encourages solidarity with all human beings and welcomes the contrast in the signs of the times and the Gospel. The pastoral effort depends on the ability to realize the genuine human situation and to find ways to improve the living conditions for all people. For Catholics, the religious strength of the Christian faith does not depend on the weakness in the faiths of other religions, especially not in the case of the Jewish faith. In fact, the pastoral strength of Christians is to realize and to accept the strength of the other. This is not an act of philanthropy, owing to a civilized behavior in modern pluralistic societies, but an act of religious necessity, even an act in the religious self-interest of Christians. In realizing and accepting this strength of the other, Christians can realize their own weaknesses and can learn how to overcome them.

For Christian-Jewish dialogue this is a very important point. Christians can never avoid religious relations with Jews, simply because Jesus was a Jew. In the past, there was too much resentment from Christians against Jews. In societies with Christian majorities, there was a forceful interest to seeing that Jews were powerless. As soon as Jews found ways to gain social and political power, the Christian majority found ways to counter strike this power. Anti-Judaism and anti-Semitism are strategies with such an aim; it is not by chance that they are full of resentment. They cannot be political forces without nurturing resentment against Jews. Of course, it is possible that there is weakness even in the Jewish religion. But for Christians with a pastoral perspective toward the other, it is not this weakness that is the proper focus of Christian-Jewish dialogue. For Christians, the strength of Judaism and Jews is important and any weakness is a reality to be dealt with by Jews. But their strength is a true value for Christians. In a dialogue between Jews and Christians it belongs to the strength of Jews to have a living memory of the violence that Christians have unleashed on Jews for centuries. By realizing this strength, Christians have the opportunity to be confronted with their own guilt. This guilt can become a religious weakness of Christians and give birth to new resentment unless there is repentance. The strength of Jews forces Christians to find ways to confess this guilt and to overcome the destructive force of resentment.[14]

This structure of being close to the strength of the other by setting a distance to a false history in one's own tradition is significant for the Christian faith. It even marks the concept of revelation that Christians are obliged to present in the history of humankind.

3) Scripture and Tradition—Discursive Continuity and Discontinuity of Christian Revelation

Revelation is a key concept for history in the theological tradition. It is in itself a historical event, because it is done and communicated by language. It is not essential for revelation to be an actual spoken word but it has to be something that can be presented. There is no language without context or without representation. Both are historical facts. If there exists a revelatory language that has meaning to realize who and what God is, then God has a history of his own. It is not a history like that of humans with a clear beginning and a definite end in time. It is a history of language with a real context and an actual meaning for human beings. It is not a history meaningful only for Christians or something like a specific

Catholic history, but rather, God's history touches the entire human race. This history is a gift for all people to live a more human life.

In the case of revelation confessed by Christians, this language is a twofold affair: Scripture and Tradition, the Bible and the dogmatic tradition of the Church. For a long time many thought that these were identical with the revelation itself. But if so, then one has to face a difficult problem: Which of the two languages is more revelatory? Which is more powerful in terms of revealing God? Which has more force for closing the gap between God and the world? This has been a major subject between Protestants and Catholics since the Reformation. It is the question of *"sola Scriptura,"* the word of the Bible alone, and on the other hand, the question of Scripture and Tradition with a higher value placed on Tradition. For centuries this problem separated the major Christian denominations. Each thought to stand for the only truth and therefore, each denomination sought to claim more authenticity and authority to present God. At the same time, these claims for a higher authority in the language of revelation meant more power-claims over the other. The religious wars in Baroque Europe are a result of these claims.

In Vatican II, the dogmatic constitution, *Dei Verbum,* Catholics found a solution for this thorny problem: they gave up the strategy that there is more power in one of these languages and decided that both languages must be interwoven with powerlessness. They have to be treated as language forms to bring revelation to the hearers of the Word. But the revelatory event is not the Bible itself and not Tradition itself. Neither of the two has the power to be the complete manifestation of God. Scripture can be treated simply as a book and this cannot be stopped by the force of Scripture itself. On the contrary, the method, historical criticism, was developed by people working with the Bible. And Tradition can also be treated simply as a history of religious ideas and there are no means in Tradition to overcome such a treatment.

Nevertheless, in both there is revelation and in both one can experience the power of revelation. But no Scripture and no Tradition have the power of revelation alone. Revelation itself is God presenting himself and designating his will of salvation for every human being. There is revelation in Scripture and in Tradition, but in the sense that they are forms to communicate this revelation to people all over the world and through all times still to come. They belong to the transmission of Divine Revelation.[15] Therefore, Scripture can always be a critical counterbalance toward Tradition. In this sense, the critical enterprise of biblical scholarship is a gift for the systematic enterprise of dogmatic theology. Otherwise the communication of revelation and revelation itself can be dangerously mixed with each other. So, neither by Scripture nor by Tradition can one get an unbroken hold of God's revelatory power. It is a pastoral strategy to be confronted with revelation itself in terms of powerlessness. It is God presenting himself to humans as a friend.[16] No one is the owner of revelation but everyone can be inspired by it through Scripture and Tradition. In this pastoral framework of revelation another controversial problem can be solved, namely the special truth claims in the papal grammar of Catholic tradition.

4) Authority and Infallibility—Ecclesial Topology of Catholic Doctrine

At the beginning, I said that Catholics did not employ history as a basis to present God because they feared the relativity inherent in such an enterprise. But of course, Catholics were confronted with the problem of history like any other religious community in modern times. In the modern period, no religious standpoint could avoid dealing with history. During the 16th century, a relevant question became the discussion of how arguments are able to produce authority, especially after the Reformation because the unity of history had come to an end; the one truth for all had fallen apart into different truth claims. By searching for *loci theologici*; i.e., searching in theology for a language with authority in terms of God's presence on behalf of faith, theology began a new intellectual enterprise. It is that what is now called "dogmatic." Doing Godtalk in dogmatic terms is a modern product and it results from a new historical era.

Papal infallibility belongs to this program of the *loci theologici*. Doctrine and Dogma in the Catholic faith is understood in the tension of history and eternity. Infallibility stands for a locus to be active in history by terms of faith. Whatever proposition of faith is marked with the authority of papal infallibility, must have authority within history. Its truth is not "produced" by the pope but the pope can and has to trust in the truth of this proposition. If the pope produced the truth then history would not matter. But this is not the doctrine of papal infallibility, although it is often misunderstood in this way. Such a misunderstanding must read authority ahistorically and mixes it with power. In practical terms, a proposition of faith is not true because the pope says so, but rather, the pope can define and has to define a proposition if it is true. Vatican II adds a pastoral character to doctrine and raises the need of people to find a public voice in situations of social, political and religious danger for their humanity and the necessity of the pope to confront the world with the truth about this human situation. So, human rights become a major field for papal pronouncements. In this perspective, religious dialogue is no longer an intellectual enterprise between scholars of religions but has to be viewed as a social and religious contribution to the welfare of humankind.

The doctrinal authority of the pope is a strong help for promoting the importance of religious dialogue. In the case of dialogue between Jews and Christians this is already a historical fact. Papal authority was necessary for the religious paradigm shift of Catholicism toward Jews.[17] If the pope wants to improve this dialogue, no one in the Catholic Church can stop it. But the pope has to do it and did it because of pastoral considerations. Without this dialogue, the truth of Christian faith cannot be presented in the world of our times. Slowly and convincingly this dialogue has become a *locus theologicus* of our times.[18] As a consequence, the dialogue between Jews and Christians presents an older dogmatic perspective: history is the place to act with infallibility. Therefore, the pope is a historical figure and is able to represent the doctrine of the whole Church in the present situation of history. But at the same time, history is the problem for papal infallibility. Whatever is presented with such an authority has to be presented within a historical situation. So, it has to remain an authority within history and has to deal with the authority of history itself. Papal infallibility is necessarily related to pluralism. It cannot work without pluralism.[19] It is not an ahistorical power in the sense of absolutism. It means a historical power in the sense of pastoral relativism and this does not deny its ability to stand up for real truths.

5) Human Rights and Plurality of Religions—Historical Confrontation and Opportunity for a Catholic Identity in Postmodern Times

In the modern times humankind had to learn a harsh lesson. If one does not respect the elementary rights of every human being in society, the horror of violence will rule and in the end everyone will be victimized by this violence.[20] These rights are the human rights. They are not a product of historical powers; i.e., states, religions, churches, or economies. On the contrary, they come out of a powerless resistance against such powers. And this struggle is far from over. The invention of human rights by the powerlessness of basic human resistance against public violence was a harsh lesson for the churches to learn too. There is no religious community in the modern Christian tradition that has not violated elementary human rights in its religious history. So, for the Church, it is a major step to respect and champion human rights, because such a stance helps to overcome a sinful history and pattern. In Vatican II, the Catholic Church had the courage to take this step and even accepted a schism for the recognition of religious freedom as a divine commandment. Inevitably, human rights do mean relativity for the claims of any religious community, especially for the claim to be the sole religious power for people.

Religious truth claims have to be presented from a different perspective if human rights are to be respected by a religious community such as the Church. In the Catholic tradition we are standing in the midst of this historical process that is far from over. Two recent examples point to positive advances in authentically presenting Catholic truth claims. First, the Catholic Church does respect the plurality of religions and of religious truth claims. The doctrine of Vatican II—the declaration about religious freedom, *Dignitatis Humanae,* and the declaration about the relationship of the Church with non-Christian religions *Nostra Aetate*— empowered this kind of recognition. This means that Catholics are called to treat with respect all human truths that other religions have found in their history. This respect is owed to the pastoral enterprise. Second, the Church recognizes its historical guilt in relation to other religious people and violations of their human rights. Without a confession of guilt, the truths of the Catholic historical tradition cannot be presented convincingly or with integrity. Pope John Paul II's reconciliatory act at the Day of Pardon on March 12, 2000, significantly empowered this enterprise.[21]

This act is owed to the pastoral framework of the Christian faith. The Church has taken an important historical step toward the future locus of the Christian faith in the midst of humanity. These two examples are significant for the future of the Catholic tradition in terms of its authentic historical memory and future identity. Based on these initial advances, there is hope that the Catholic historical tradition will have meaning for humanity in general because it gives a small hint for God's own history within human history.

Notes

1. Cf. Henrici Denzinger, *Enchiridion symbolorum definitionum et declarationum de rebus fidei et morum, quod emendavit, auxit et adiuvante Helmuto Hoping,* edidit Petrus Huenermann, editio xxxvii, Freiburg: Herder, 1991, 3825–3831 (Denzinger-Huenermann).

2. Only as one example: Marie-Dominique Chenu, *La Parole de Dieu.* Vol. I: La Foi dans l'intelligence. Vol. II: *L'Évangile dans le temps,* Paris: Cerf, 1964.

3. ibid., Nr. 15, 135–137.

4. *Lumen Gentium,* n. 2, Denzinger-Huenermann, 4102.

5. *Gaudium et Spes,* n. 2, Denzinger-Huenermann, 4302.

6. *Lumen Gentium,* n. 9, Denzinger-Huenermann, 4122.

7. *Lumen Gentium,* n. 8, Denzinger-Huenermann, 4120.

8. *Lumen Gentium,* n. 8, Denzinger-Huenermann, 4118.

9. *Gaudium et Spes,* n. 3, Denzinger-Huenermann, 4303

10. *Gaudium et spes,* n. 4, Denzinger-Huenermann, 4304

11. For further discussion of this distinction cf. my publication: nicht ausweichen. Die prekäre Lage der Kirche, Würzburg: Echter, 2002.

12. Cf. Rahner's third thesis: „Die Heilsgeschichte deutet die Profangeschichte." (Weltgeschichte und Heilsgeschichte, in: Karl Rahner, Schriften zur Theologie, vol. 5, Einsiedeln: Benziger, 1962, 115–135, 129)

13. Cf. Rainer Kampling (ed.), "Nun steht aber diese Sache im Evangelium…" Zur Frage nach den Anfängen des christlichen Antijudaismus, Paderborn: Schöningh, 1999. Cf. also the older enterprises of Franz Mußner for a "Theologische Wiedergutmachung," especially: Franz Mußner, Traktat über die Juden, second ed., München: Kösel, 1988.

14. The declaration of Vatican II about the Relationship of the Church with Non-Christian Religions *Nostra Aetate*, is the decisive step toward a dialogue that overcomes resentment toward the Jews. The focus of this declaration lies in the strength of the Jewish religion and of the lasting relationship between God and the Jews. The Christians are described as *"Abrahamae filios secundum fidem"* (n. 4, Denzinger-Huenermann 4198); they depend on the strength of the Jewish faith. In consequence the Church had to stand up against resentment toward the Jews: *"Judaei tamen neque ut a Deo reprobate neque ut maledicti exhibeantur"* (ibid.). The tribute to this resentment by Christians during the history of the Church is not yet thoroughly discussed in *Nostra Aetate*. Pope John Paul II's lasting contribution to the Christian-Jewish dialogue is the naming of this guilt at the Day of Pardon in March, 2000.

15. Cf. Caput II „De divinae revelationis transmissione" of the Dogmatic Constitution about the divine revelation *Dei Verbum*, Denzinger-Huenermann, 4207–4214.

16. Cf. Dei verbum n. 2, Denzinger-Huenermann, 4202.

17. The doctrinal basis for Vatican II's declaration *Nostra aetate* was the importance Pope John XXIII issued to this subject; his famous welcoming address to a Jewish delegation in 1960 is much more than an anecdote. His words, "Son io, Giuseppe, il fratello vestro! (It's me, Joseph, your brother)" was a sign for the path the dialogue between Jews and Catholics may realize and still has to realize. With Pope John Paul II's many dialogues with Jewish religious leaders this doctrinal strategy has become irreversible in the Church.

18. Cf. Rolf Rendtorff/Hans-Hermann Henrix (ed.), Die Kirchen und das Judentum. Vol.I: Dokumente von 1945 bis 1985, third ed., Paderborn/Gütersloh: Schöningh/Gütersloher Verlagshaus, 2001. Especially in the last decades the increasing quantity of official texts by the major Christian Churches is impressive, cf. Hans Hermann Henrix/Wolfgang Kraus (ed.), Die Kirchen und das Judentum. Vol. II: Dokumente von 1986–2000, Paderborn/Gütersloh: Schöningh/Gütersloher Verlagshaus, 2001.

19. Papal infallibility and papacy in general are subjects to a new theological discourse. This is a result of the invitation by the Pope toward all Christian denominations to discuss the role papacy may play for all Christians. Cf. John R. Quinn, The reform of papacy. The costly call to Christian unity, New York: Crossroad, 1999. See also Hermann J. Pottmeyer's proposal for a ‚primacy in communion', in Hermann J. Pottmeyer, Toward a papacy in communion. Perspectives from Vatican I & II, New York: Crossroad, 1998. From my point of view, the meaning of pastoral relativity is underestimated in this discussion.

20. Cf. Alain Finkielkraut, Verlust der Menschlichkeit. Versuch über das 20. Jahrhundert, München: dtv, 2000.

21. Cf. http://www.vatican.va/news_services/liturgy/documents/ns_lit_doc_20000312_prayer-day-pardon_ge.html.

CHRISTOPH HEIL

God's Own History: A Response to Hans-Joachim Sander

I would like to offer some remarks about the Catholic historical tradition from the viewpoint of biblical interpretation. First, it is important to recognize that the Catholic Church did not take into account the historical dimension of faith until late in the 20th century. Of course, this ignorance was not without foundation in the New Testament. On the dome of St. Peter's in Rome, the words from Matthew 16:18 are inscribed, "You are Peter, and on this rock I will build my church, and the gates of Hades will not prevail against it." The words and their placement in St. Peter's gives a combined message of the church as a super-historical, timeless entity, already in the New Testament![1] This is true, however, only in an unhistorical perspective, which was the dominant position of the Catholic Church. This perspective took Matthew as the first Gospel, written by the apostle Matthew. The more natural and universally accepted model that Mark was the first Gospel and that Matthew 16:18 was a later, post-Easter addition, was first considered by the Catholic Church in the encyclical, *Divino Afflante Spiritu* (1943) and in the Second Vatican Council's Constitution on Divine Revelation, *Dei Verbum* (1965).

In 1994, the Pontifical Biblical Papal Bible Commission issued a document on "The Interpretation of the Bible in the Church."[2] The document explicitly rejects a fundamentalist reading of the Bible and recommends historical and literary-critical approaches. However, if one observes how unhistorically official Vatican documents treat the Bible, one wonders how serious the Roman Catholic magisterium takes its own Biblical Commission. So, the instance of Matthew 16:18 is a good example how historical investigation—or the neglect of it—can improve or harm theological statements and pastoral approaches. Professor Sander's paper provides an important and necessary correction by allowing the historical dimension to play a decisive part in theology, which makes theology more human and more attentive to the needs of individual, concrete people.

The Catholic Church has long identified itself as the institution founded by Jesus to embody the Kingdom of God on earth. And it has identified its own tradition with the intention of Holy Scripture. Both identifications have led to a triumphalistic, self-assured theology and pastoral method. It is to be regarded as great progress that the Catholic Church has revisited and sought to correct the historical distance between itself and Jesus the Jew, his proclamation of the Kingdom of God and the Holy Scriptures. This includes a new, honest view by the Catholic Church in its relation to Judaism. Much progress has been made recently, but much more needs to be accomplished.

Another important point that Professor Sander presents is that a historical approach allows for development and progress in defining the Catholic faith. The New Testament does not deal with concepts such as human rights or religious pluralism as they are understood in the modern world. Only after the Catholic Church allowed for new insights given by God in the course of history, was the acceptance of human rights and religious pluralism possible. This acceptance is still fragile and disputed, but the Second Vatican Council laid the foundation on which the Catholic Church must proceed.

Judaism is credited with being open to and articulating God's self-revelation in history with his people. The Jewish tradition is the prime example for how the historical dimension of faith contributes to a better understanding of God and others. Christian theology is well-advised never to marginalize this historical inheritance from Judaism. Thus, the main point of convergence Professor Sander's paper presents to Judaism's and Protestant Christianity's understanding of history is that finally Catholic Christianity is prepared to take the historical dimension of faith as seriously as they do. The Second Vatican Council marks the official paradigm change for the Catholic Church in accepting this historical dimension. Of course, individual Catholic theologians had long before stressed the importance of a historical understanding of faith and church, a historical understanding of the development of creedal formulas, but not before the Second Vatican Council did the Catholic Church officially accept this approach.

The challenge that Professor Sander presents to interreligious dialogue is the admonition to hold fast to the historical dimension of faith in a time when history is abused, relativized, deconstructed, decolonialized, etc. To be sure, many new hermeneutical approaches have their merits and they help to correct problematic attitudes in older paradigms. It was always an open secret that historical texts convey history as much as their author's intentions. After World War II, the redaction critical approach in biblical studies aimed at finding the biblical authors' theologies and social contexts. So this is not new. A new temptation lies, however, in the attitude that there is nothing else in the biblical texts than their author's theologies and contexts. Without a historical approach, every biblical author's own view is valid unto itself. As such, the quest for a hierarchy of truths is made impossible. Research about Jesus, for example, becomes impossible since one would only have the evangelists' stories to draw from. Unfortunately, the institutional Magisterium and its theologians could be tempted to welcome such an approach, since if there is no historical criterion to decide between what is central and marginal in biblical traditions, then the religious institution will decide for everyone. Thus postmodernism and apologetic, uncritical theology could form an unholy and unhealthy alliance.

I am not advocating the naïve historicism of the 19th century. We have certainly made progress in our historiographical methods and approaches. But Jewish and Christian (and Muslim) theologies can only gain by using a critical, sober historical approach to understand their own traditions. The historical dimension challenges us to accept the development and human character of our faith, which corresponds to a God who reveals himself in history to average people like you and me. The Hebrew Bible, Septuagint, New Testament and Talmud did not fall from heaven. And the religious institutions that are based on those texts have no exclusive copyright of them. To keep the distance between foundational texts and religious institutions in mind allows for healthy self-correction by the institution itself. Only then are the texts are allowed to inspire and criticize the religious institution. An unhistorical concept of identity of text and institution means that the institution will eventually fail its own mission, its reason for its own existence.

Professor Sander also emphasized the idea of "powerlessness," which is inherent in using the historical approach in theology. By taking their histories seriously, Jewish and Christian theologians are indeed challenged to accept their own powerlessness vis-à-vis the revealing God. As in Jesus' parables or in the apostle Paul's doctrine of justification, God is acting as the subject of history and invites us to be humble and faithful disciples.

The historical approach is best suited to enhance understanding and cooperation between Jews and Christians, and also between Lutheran and Catholic Christians. We should acknowledge the clear distinction between historical reconstructions and developments and how each of us interprets those reconstructions and developments. In the case of scholarly investigation, the biblical or historical scholar should not try to be a better systematic theologian, although the systematic theologian should take exegetical and historical insights seriously as the foundation and inspiration for her or his work. Both the historical and the systematic approaches have their own right, and both can learn from each other. But a perfect harmony between them is not the ideal; the ideal is critical exchange and dialogue.

The exegetical and historical disciplines are indeed, a good example of how Jews and Christians can work well together. Think about Jewish and Christian authors in the Anchor Bible Commentary series and in the new Herder Theologischer Kommentar zum Alten Testament series. In New Testament studies, the cooperation of authors from different denominations is common in the Evangelisch-Katholisher Kommentar series and in the Okumenischer Taschenbuchkommentar series. At exegetical or historical conferences such as the Society of Biblical Literature's annual meetings, there is excellent cooperation between Jewish and Christian scholars. The differences, however, must become visible when the exegetical and historical data is interpreted in a systematic fashion. Key historical concepts, such as the primary events of Revelation, Scripture, Tradition, faith, covenant, and community are viewed differently in Jewish, Lutheran, or Catholic statements of faith. The agreement in exegetical/historical reconstruction, but disagreement in the interpretation of it, must be made transparent and must be endured. This dichotomy can be seen, for example, in the reception of the Joint Declaration on the Doctrine of Justification, which was jointly issued by the Lutheran World Council and the Roman Catholic Church in 1999.

A broad consensus on the exegetical and historical developments corresponds to a disagreement about what the exegetical and historical data mean for today. Beginning with the dissertation of Hans Kung on Karl Barth's concept of justification (published 1957) and followed by many contributions by Catholic exegetes and historians, there has been a growing rapprochement of Catholic and Lutheran understanding of justification. If one reads the recent commentaries on Paul's letter to the Romans, for example, the differing interpretations are no longer caused by Catholic-Lutheran controversies. This is real progress. However, the limits of a purely exegetical consensus become visible when this agreement is pressed against the Procrustean beds of denominational creedal formulas. Perhaps it is too optimistic, but for me a solution is only possible by rearticulating those creedal formulas in a new, contemporary language informed by history and inspired by the Bible. If not, we risk losing the developmental and human character of our faith and the opportunity to respond with intelligence, integrity, and courage to the mission entrusted to us by God who continues to reveal himself in our world.

Notes

1. Compare Vögtle, Anton: Zeit und Zeituberlegenheit in biblischer Sicht. Zur Grundlegung des Selbstverstandnisses der Kirche in dieser Weltzeit (1965), in: Ders: Das Evangelium und die Evangelien. Bitrage zur Evangelienforschung (Kbant), Dusseldorf: Patmos, 1971, 273–295.

2. Compare The Interpretation of the Bible in the Church, ed. J. L. Houlden, London: SCM, 1995; Die Interpretation der Bibel in der Kirche. Das Dokument der Papstlichen Bibelkommission vom 23.4.1993 mit einer kommentierenden Einfuhrung von Lothar Ruppert und einer Wurdigung von Hans-Josef Klauck (SBS 161), Stuttgart: Kath. Bibelwerk, 1995.

W O L F G A N G   K R A U S

What Do We Want the Other to Teach About the Recent History of Protestant-Jewish Dialogue?

From November 5 to November 10, 2000, the synod of the Evangelical Church in Germany (*Evangelische Kirche in Deutschland*, EKD) met in Braunschweig.[1] The synod was followed by a publication called "A Statement on Christians and Jews, 50 Years after the Declaration of Weißensee." The publication referred to a text which marks a tremendous turning point in the development of Protestant-Jewish relations in Germany: the declaration of the synod of the EKD in Berlin-Weißensee, which was passed in April 1950.

Today, more than 50 years later, we are looking back and we are trying to recall what has been achieved in the Protestant-Jewish dialogue of the last 50 years. Examining the reasons for the often fatal attitude of the Church toward Judaism, the Declaration of Berlin-Weißensee admits that the church was "involved in the systematic destruction of European Judaism by the fateful tradition of alienation from and hostility toward Judaism. This theological tradition made attempts to form a new relationship with the Jewish people very hard and led to a delay."[2]

This is a rather cautious statement. Klaus Haacker, New Testament scholar in Wuppertal, had expressed the same facts with more detail in his essay, "The Holocaust as a Date in the History of Theology:" "The contribution of the Christians to the Holocaust was presumably mainly the spreading of a naive anti-Judaism, which was almost universal, and which paved the way for the militant, racist anti-Semitism. This naive anti-Judaism cannot be overcome with a programmatic philo-Judaism, but only with a patient and complete inspection of the whole theological tradition of the church."[3] I hold the view that Haacker speaks rightly of a "date" in the history of theology. I am picking up the semantics of the word referring to its Latin root when saying: it is something that has been given, it is a task that has been set. Thus, examining the shortcomings and failures of the church in regard of the Holocaust was the most important step toward a new beginning of a Christian-Jewish dialogue.

The main reason why the Protestant churches came up with a reassessment of Christian-Jewish relations after 1945 was the realization that church authorities and Christian theology had been involved in the millionfold murder of Jewish people. Haacker claims that the naive anti-Judaism, which had spread among Christians, made the paralysis of church and theology regarding the genocide understandable. He also says that it was naive anti-Judaism that paved the way to militant anti-Semitism. Haacker does not speak of a direct link between the ecclesiastical anti-Judaism and the racist anti-Semitism. However, we do have to be aware of the relation between the two. It is not an easy task at all to overcome old traditions, even if they have always been wrong. Only a "patient and complete inspection of the whole theological tradition of the church" can make a new beginning possible.[4]

Being aware of this terrible time in history, which overshadows Christian-Jewish relations up to this very day, I have often been amazed about the fact that there is a dialogue between Christians and Jews at all. I am grateful for this dialogue. In order to maintain and strengthen the dialogue, it is essentially necessary to be constantly aware of the mistakes of Christian Theology regarding Judaism. One major mistake was a Christian ecclesiology that denied Israel's continuing election by God. I will deal with this crucial point in detail toward the end of this paper.

This paper is divided into three parts: I) the most important stages of the Protestant-Jewish dialogue since 1945; II) the development during the last two decades; and III) some important perspectives for Christian-Jewish dialogue in the future.

I. Where Do We Come From? Stages Since 1945

In order to regain contact with the international ecumenical movement after 1945, German Protestant church leaders were forced by their ecumenical partners to express somehow that the churches in Germany had a share of the blame. In October 1945, such an admission was attempted in the so called Stuttgart Confession (*Stuttgarter Schuldbekenntnis*):[5] "Endless suffering was brought upon peoples and countries by us. . . . We accuse ourselves of not having stood up more courageously, of not having prayed more faithfully, of not having believed more happily and of not having loved more dearly."[6] In my opinion, this is not a confession, but a list of shortcomings. And the crime against the Jewish people did not play a role in this text of 1945.

Another confession from the time after the Second World War, the so-called 'Word of Darmstadt' (1947) was more precise in naming the guilt. But the murder of the Jews was not mentioned either. In 1948, the so-called Council of brothers of the Evangelical church in Germany (*Bruderrat der Evangelischen Kirche in Deutschland*) passed a declaration which was called "Word concerning the Jewish question."[7] The council clearly speaks about the guilt of the Christians concerning the Jews. Disappointingly, it goes on to name all false traditional theological aspects of Israel's rejection: Israel[8] had crucified its Messiah and thus lost its election and its position as the chosen people. Therefore, it was the church that had been turned into the chosen people. Israel was under the curse of God and therefore a constant warning for the Christian community not to mock God. To treat the *Shoah* as a mere warning was an unbearable offense not only to Jews and thwarted the document's intended purpose. Moreover, the declaration was lacking a fundamental questioning of previous Christian positions. Church authorities tried to carry on where they left off in 1933. After 1945, only few churches issued words of repentance, which went beyond the general statements of the Stuttgart Confession.[9]

A reorientation on the level of the Evangelical Church in Germany began with the declaration of the synod of the Evangelical Church in Germany (EKD) in Berlin-Weißensee in 1950. The declaration constitutes a major turning point. Seven issues were mentioned, which have had a tremendous impact on all further developments. These seven subjects dominate the conversation even today.

1) Jesus the Jew
2) the Church—consisting of (former) Jews and gentiles
3) God's enduring promise to His chosen people Israel after the crucifixion of Jesus
4) the Christians' responsibility for the persecution and death of
   (the) Jews
5) Christians are asked to accept God's judgment
6) the rejection of anti-Semitism and
7) the plea for eschatological completion together with the saved
   Israel

"God's promise to His chosen people, Israel, remained unchanged
after the crucifixion of Jesus."[10] This point of view, which occurs in the
Berlin-Weißensee declaration for the first time in an EKD document,
has become dominant in almost all ecclesiastical declarations. God's
promise to *Israel* to be His chosen people remains valid.[11] The covenant
has not been terminated. However, these ecclesiastical declarations did
not yet reflect the predominant opinion of theological teachers and
church members. This is the reason why those declarations could only
function as a prospect, but not as a description of the status quo.

We could sum up the conflicts in Christian-Jewish relations of the
1960s with the heading: dialogue versus proselytizing. This time was
mainly dominated by the conflict between supporters of the dialogue
and supporters of the mission among the Jews.[12] There were people, especially on the Lutheran side, who rejected the core statement of the declaration of Berlin-Weißensee.[13] Looking back, we have to admit that
sometimes they argued in strange ways.

Following an international consultation of the Lutheran World
Federation (LWF) in Logumkloster, Denmark (1964), the 'Study-
Committee for Church and Judaism' of the Evangelical Church in
Germany (EKD) was established in 1967, and the 'Study Group Church
and Judaism' of the United Evangelical-Lutheran Church in Germany
(VELKD) in 1968. In 1975, the first EKD study of the EKD-study-com-
mittee "Christians and Jews" was published.[14] It was a central aim of this
study to make a consensus among Protestants possible. This study was
another major step after Berlin-Weißensee. Even its structure was different from what had been issued before. It contains three parts: 1) The
reflection on common roots of Jews and Christians, and an important

decision on fundamental principles: Jews are considered to be partners of Christians and not to be recipients of Christian goodwill; 2) The partings of the ways, which deals with the different interpretations of the Old Testament/Hebrew Bible and with Jewish as well as the Christians' self-understanding as God's chosen people; and 3) Christians and Jews today have strong possibilities for developing their relationship.

The EKD study commission is significant, because Jewish members have been included in the discussions from the very beginning. So it has not just been Christians reflecting on their relationship toward Judaism, but the study has been a common task for Christians and Jews. The EKD study of 1975 helped to cope with the burdens of the past and made it possible for Jews and Christians involved in dialogue to meet as partners.

During the 1980s, several declarations were passed by various Protestant regional churches in Germany, starting with the Evangelical Church of the Rhineland in January 1980. The resolution of the synod of the Evangelical Church of the Rhineland was a very important step in the development of Christian-Jewish dialogue.[15] It was a resolution of a church synod that had legal power, and not simply a commission's study such as that of the EKD in 1975. The resolution of the synod of the Evangelical Church of the Rhineland was the first attempt to go beyond the description of the status quo. It had the same motto as the EKD study of 1975: "Thou bearest not the root, but the root thee" (Rom 11:18).[16] Various statements in the synod's resolution have given rise to vehement debates. Examples include:

1. The historical necessity of a renewal of the relationship, mainly because of the *Shoah*.

2. The perception of Jesus as "Jew, as the Messiah of Israel, and the saviour of the world, who joins the gentiles with God's people."[17]

3. The statement that the church was being included in God's covenant with Israel through Jesus Christ.

4. The statement concerning the church's mission among the Jews. The resolution says that there has to be a difference made between the church's testimony toward Jewish people and the mission to the gentiles.

5. Finally, the understanding of Israel's continuing existence and its homecoming to the promised land, as well as Israel's regained existence as a state being a sign of God's faithfulness.

Several regional Protestant Churches have followed the Evangelical Church of the Rhineland by issuing statements right after the synod's resolution of 1980. Up to now, all churches of the Evangelical Church in Germany (EKD) and of the Council of the Reformed Churches have begun processes over the last two decades, which have led to declarations of synods and church leaders. These processes have mainly been initiated by work groups and committees. The first study of the EKD "Christians and Jews" of 1975 and the "Resolution of the Synod of the Evangelical Church of the Rhineland" of 1980 were significant for the development during the 1980s. Most additional reflection in other German churches was based on either the approval or the rejection of the statements issued in these texts. During the 1980s, several other regional churches, besides the Church of the Rhineland, issued declarations about the Christian-Jewish relationship.[18] After 1990, more churches issued declarations on this topic.[19] With one exception these texts were newly published in a collection from 2001.[20]

II. Where Are We? Developments Since 1990

The declaration of the Lutheran European Commission Church and Judaism (*Lutherische Europäische Kommission Kirche und Judentum*, LEKKJ) of 1990[21] and the second EKD study "Christians and Jews: The Theological Reorientation of the Relation Toward Judaism" of 1991[22] led to a new stage. With the declaration of the Lutheran European Commission Church and Judaism (LEKKJ), the Lutheran Churches in Europe followed suit after consistently having been more reserved than the Reformed Churches and the Churches of the Union (United Churches). The second EKD study of 1991 was another milestone in the Christian-Jewish dialogue. It mainly deals with the conceptions of the church and the Jewish people as God's chosen people. In this study, we find a nascent New Testament ecclesiology. Since the publication of these texts, a basic consensus has begun to emerge within the churches of the EKD and the Reformed Council. This consensus can be described by the phrase: 'the election of Israel as God's people remains valid.'[23] Even if one states that this topic is still controversial in scholarly theology, there was not a single ecclesiastical statement during the 1990s in which this basic consensus would have been questioned. However, the consequences drawn from this consensus vary.

Two theological questions played a special role in the declarations of the 1990s: Firstly, how can we think of the participation of the church in God's covenant? Secondly, how do we address the question of proselytizing? In its 1980 resolution, the Evangelical Church of the Rhineland tried to answer the first question when saying that through Jesus Christ the church was integrated in God's covenant with Israel.[24] This can hardly be appropriate and scarcely any other church followed this example.[25] As far as the question of mission among Jews is concerned, there is a consensus among the churches that belong to the EKD or to the Reformed Council: proselytizing is rejected by all churches but one: a minority vote of the church council in Württemberg.[26] Study groups of regional churches and councils have documented this change of perspective by changing their names.[27] The discussion, however, is far from being over. On the contrary: there was a fierce discussion in the run-up to the 'German Protestant Church Congress' (*Deutscher Evangelischer Kirchentag*) of 1999.[28] There are still a few groups in favor of proselytizing,[29] but their impact on the Christian-Jewish dialogue is rather small, if not insignificant.

The fact that the Christian-Jewish dialogue has led to changes in the church order, and especially in the constituting articles, deserves particular attention. The Evangelical Church of the Rhineland again was the first to change its church order in 1987,[30] by mentioning the dialogue between Christians and Jews as an obligation for the Church as a whole and as a necessity for all congregations. The Evangelical-Reformed Church was the first to change its constitution in 1988.[31] After that, other churches also changed fundamental articles of their church constitutions.[32] It is striking that there are only a few Lutheran Churches among them.

I would like to give an example, of the significance of these changes by citing the central passage, which the churches of Berlin-Brandenburg and Pommern inserted in their constitutions: "She (the Church) recognizes and recalls that God's promise for his people Israel remains valid. . . . and recognizes her obligation to take an interest in the course of the Jewish people. She (the Church) is connected with it (the Jewish people) in listening to God's commandments and in the hope of the completion of the kingdom of God."[33]

Another stage in the renewal of the relation of the churches toward Judaism will hopefully follow the third EKD study "Christians and Jews. Steps Toward a Renewal of the Relation Toward Judaism"[34] which was published in the year 2000, and the declaration of the Leuenberg church community[35] of 2001. On the one hand, the EKD study includes topics on covenant and proselytizing, which are still in need of discussion. On the other hand, the study names specific areas in which Jews and Christians can work together in a secular world. The study was only published in 2000. The time that has passed since the publication of the study is not yet long enough. We will have to wait and see which impact this study and the Leuenberg statement will have.

The peace process in the Middle East is of great significance for Christian-Jewish relations. The Protestant churches accompanied the process with statements and declarations. The 1991 Gulf War was a political event that caused various reactions by churches. In this context, it became obvious that the solidarity of the church with the Jewish people cannot be expressed without a clear approval of the state of Israel.[36]

Finally, it is significant to state that several church councils reacted immediately to right-wing anti-Semitic riots. It is also important to mention that churches issued statements concerning the integration of Jews in Germany coming from former Soviet states. These statements show a new awareness of concerns for the Jewish Community in Germany.[37]

If we look at the topics of the declarations of the last two decades, we can state that the following issues were of particular interest:
- the lasting connection of the church with the Jewish people,
- the continuing election of the Jewish people,
- the refutation of anti-Semitism /anti-Judaism,
- the question of participation in the covenant,
- the position not to withhold the diverging opinions between Christians and Jews,
- the question of the church's witness to the Jews,
- the question of how to assess the state of Israel theologically,
- the consequences of the dialogue for our everyday lives.

III. Where Are We Going? Perspectives and Topics for Future Conversations

What I have depicted so far is the situation based on official declarations of the regional Protestant churches and the Evangelical Church in

Germany (EKD). I think that there is reason to say that significant progress has been made within the last decades. It is now important to pass on the insights that have been gained in cause of the process to the local congregations. Here, the new thinking needs to be established so that we can come to a new form of Christian-Jewish relations. We are still at the beginning, or to speak with the title of a book: 'On the Way to a New Beginning.'[38]

I would like to list five issues, which I think to be of particular importance on the way to a new beginning.

1. The problem of anti-Judaism

Without any doubt, there are passages in the New Testament that—on a first glance—contain anti-Jewish polemics. There are different historic reasons for this fact. It is our task to work with these texts in a hermeneutic way that tells us how to deal with the crucial passages. This enables us to understand:

- anti-Jewish polemics as a phenomenon of detachment (detachment of the subsidiary religion from the parent religion, cf. Mark 12:28–34; Matthew 22:34–40),
- anti-Jewish polemics as indices of disagreements between Christian and Jewish communities in the time of the New Testament, which can be shown by sociohistorical exegesis (cf. Matthew 22:1–14; Luke 14:16–24),
- anti-Jewish polemics as a reaction to the events of the year 70 AD: the destruction of the Temple (cf. Matthew 22:7),
- anti-Jewish polemics as a temporary faux pas (cf. 1 Thessalonians 2:14–16),
- anti-Jewish polemics as a way to cope with the traumatic experience of division (cf. John 8:31–47; 9:22; 12:42; 16:2).

Theology will need to teach how to differentiate between texts written by a suppressed minority (in times of the New Testament) and deeds of a political majority (since the time of Constantine). Concerning the interpretation of the polemical texts, there are several tasks for theology: Firstly, theologians will need to demonstrate that these anti-Jewish polemics within the New Testament have to be understood within the context of the historical time and not as propositions of eternal truth. Secondly, these passages have to be seen as an expression of rejected love, filled with emotions, and not as statements about the nature of Jews and Judaism. Thirdly, the authors of these polemical texts come from a Jewish background. There has to be differentiation between those polemics and statements coming from people in the following centuries not rooted in a Jewish background. Fourthly, we must not forget the interest of the church to define itself as the true heir of the Old Testament. Finally, we must learn to distinguish which statements within the New Testament are of greater or lesser importance and which ones are essentially problematic.

Is anti-Judaism essential to Christianity? Is anti-Judaism the left hand of Christology? In a debate with the Jewish scholar David Flusser, conducted in the periodical *Evangelische Theologie* in the 1970s, the Protestant New Testament scholar Ulrich Wilckens spoke in favor of considering anti-Judaism inherent to the system of Christianity. Wilckens spoke of it as if anti-Judaism was theologically necessary.[39] The New Testament scholar Günter Klein followed the same line.[40] Similarly, but with a quite different aim, Rosemary Ruether wrote, "We have recognized that the anti-Jewish myth was neither a superficial nor a secondary element of Christian thinking. The foundations for anti-Judaism were laid in the New Testament."[41]

Looking at the position of the apostle Paul, I consider this evaluation inappropriate. I would even say it is theologically incorrect. Naturally, one must admit that in Matthew or John, for example, the view of Judaism should be seen as depending on a particular Christological approach. But Paul himself shows in Romans that Christological argumentation must not necessarily sound anti-Jewish— although I admit this has certainly been seen differently in the traditional interpretations of Romans. Rosemary Ruether asks, "Is it possible to say Jesus is the Messiah without simultaneously saying implicitly and the Jews must be damned?"[42] And my answer is, yes, it is perfectly possible, as Paul demonstrates in the letter to the Romans. The problem of anti-Judaism becomes even more complicated if we turn to questions of religious pedagogy and homiletics. But this would be a topic of its own.

2. Israel's/the Jewish people's continuing election as a fundamental concept in the hermeneutics of Scripture

As I already said: almost all ecclesiastical documents of the last twenty years mention the "continuing election of the Jews as God's people."[43] However, this does not mean that a consensus has been reached on this topic within Protestant theology. Let me demonstrate this with just one quotation, although there would be many more examples. A well-known exegete concludes from the fact that the church is being called "God's chosen people" in the New Testament (Romans 9:25f; 1 Peter 2:9; Revelations 1:6) that "Israel was substituted by the church."[44]

The problem derives from the New Testament itself. In the New Testament, various conceptions of the Jewish people as God's chosen people exist side by side in an unbalanced way.[45] It is not easily possible to bring them down to a common denominator. On the contrary, they reflect an *unfinished problematical issue*, which was not resolved uniformly even in the New Testament period and had to be left open.[46] The question of who were God's chosen people played a decisive role after the crucifixion and resurrection of Jesus. The answers given, however, varied.[47]

The reason for these variations is that most New Testament texts were written in a time when the relationship between Christian congregations and Jewish synagogues was extremely tense. After the Jewish War against Rome (66–70 CE), Judaism had to redefine its identity without its former center, the Temple. At the same time, Christianity had to define itself within the Roman Empire and vis à vis Judaism. During this time there were fights about the heritage of the Old Testament. Some extreme expressions within the New Testament can only be explained within this context (cf. Matthew 23; John 8:39–47; 9:22).

We find a totally different statement in Romans 9–11. It is the only text within the whole New Testament in which the relations between Church and Israel are treated as a topic of its own.

Romans 9–11 is a popular text within Christian-Jewish dialogue and it is often quoted. But why should we relate to Romans 9–11? Why should we not start our theological reflection with John 8 or Matthew 23? This is a question that demands critical examination and a theological decision. According to Paul, the Gentiles called by Christ have an equal right to belong to the eschatological people of God because of baptism: they are children of God, descendants of Abraham and thus heirs of the promise (Galatians 3:26–29; Romans 8:14–17). But for Paul this does not exclude the Jewish people from remaining the people chosen by God (Romans 9:1–5; 11:1ff, 28ff). Thus, Paul is the only writer in the New Testament who has explicitly done justice to the problem of God's chosen people in its double form, to the question of the "Church" and of "Israel/the Jewish people." However, in order to reach the solution expressed in the letter to the Romans, Paul too, followed highways and byways, which are reflected in different arguments in his letters. Even he could only solve the problem after several attempts (cf. 1 Thessalonians 2,14–16; Gal 4,21–31).

This is the decisive problem that Paul tried to solve—and, in my opinion, did solve—in the letter to the Romans: How can the conception of a lasting promise of God to the Jewish people continue to exist alongside the message of the redemption of all people through Christ alone, especially when one considers Israel's persistent rejection of Jesus as the Messiah? Does this mean that the doctrine of the election of Israel stands against Christology? We should not underestimate the sensitivity of this problem. Other New Testament authors also recognized the problem. When they dealt with this particular issue, they generally argued that Israel as God's chosen people had been substituted by the Church. That was not at all Paul's view in the letter to the Romans, a letter that is rightly estimated by exegetes as the summit of Paul's theological thinking or as his *"summa evangelii."*

The special feature of Paul's approach is that Paul describes God's righteousness as revealed by the coming of Christ (Romans 3:21). This event triggered the question of whether God's promises to Israel were still valid (Romans 9:1ff; 11:1). God's righteousness, in the sense of his faithfulness to the covenant, does not let go of Israel even though Jesus is not recognized as the Messiah by the majority of Israel. In his faithfulness to the covenant, God will lead Israel to final salvation by means of the "Deliverer of Zion" (Romans 11:26f). In this way, the doctrine of justification itself, which is often interpreted as being irreconcilable with the continuing election of Israel, becomes the possibility for maintaining the *solus Christus* at the same time as the validity of the divine promises to Israel. The answer to which Paul comes in the letter to the

Romans differs from those in the first letter to the Thessalonians (esp. 1Thessalonians 2:14–16) or in the letter to the Galatians (esp. Galatians 3:15–22; 4,21–31). There is a controversial debate about whether one can speak of a development in Pauline theology. But the point at issue is not the term "development;" it is much more important to recognize that, in the letter to the Romans compared with the statements in I Thessalonians and Galatians, there is a conscious correction or withdrawal of arguments.

The important theological, critical, and hermeneutic problem concerning the doctrine of justification, as it is presented in the letter to the Romans, is to demonstrate whether the Pauline approach found there is an appropriate expression of the Gospel of Jesus Christ. This is the question that must point the way for our reflection. What is at stake is nothing less than objective theological criticism in the Bible itself. By demonstrating in Romans 11:25–27 that Paul is speaking of the salvation of "all Israel," only half of the problem has been solved since we are left with the problem of Jesus being rejected by the majority of Israel (G. Strecker, H. Räisänen et al).[48] There are several questions to be answered: Does the conclusion of Romans 11 fit into the overall context of Romans 9–11 and of Romans 1–8? Does Romans 9–11 only constitute the discussion of a question which arises in Paul's biography or is it an expression of what must be said according to the apostle's doctrine of justification? In the latter case, these statements would have brought us to the heart of his theology. But then how do Paul's other statements about Israel fit in? And how should we define the relation to other New Testament views where there is no reference to all Israel being saved? And finally: the Christian Bible comprises the writings of the Old and New Testaments. How should the Pauline statements and the (sometimes contradictory) statements of other New Testament authors be seen in the context of the Bible as a whole? To put it in a nutshell: If the objective theological necessity of the statements in Romans 11:25–27 (and also 11:28ff; 15:7–13) cannot be demonstrated within the context of the Pauline theology of justification, then there are no conclusive reasons against marginalizing them in a psychological or some other way.

Then it is also not difficult to unhinge the popularity of this text and the insistence on its statements—which is often found among those involved in Christian-Jewish dialogue. Is Romans 11:25–27 exceptional or can it be seen in the context of Paul's theology and general biblical statements? Is it an appropriate expression of the Gospel of Jesus Christ—and therefore an appropriate expression of the charity and the righteousness of the God of Israel, with all the consequences this has for the church and for Christian theology? We are now at the heart of the debate. And here, a theological decision is required which, in my view, can only be: In the letter to the Romans Paul indicates the criterion for our relation to Judaism; God has not rejected the people that he had previously chosen (Romans 11:2). The source of this statement is at the heart of the Pauline doctrine of justification and it is a genuine expression of the Gospel of Jesus Christ.[49]

3. Israel as an integral part of Christian ecclesiology

According to Romans 15:7–13, Jesus did not *fulfill* God's promises made to the fathers, but he *confirmed* these promises. Christ came into the world in order to become a servant of 'the circumcision' (i.e. of the Jews) with the aim of confirming the promises made to the fathers. This means that Israel remains God's people because of God's promise. Also in times of destruction and suppression, when there is no visible sign for the election, it remains nevertheless real.

According to the New Testament, the church was chosen to belong to God's people through Jesus Christ. Therefore, Judaism cannot only be seen as the historical root of Christianity, but has to be seen as the continuing partner vis-à-vis God. Judaism, as a living religion, is a permanent challenge to the church's understanding of itself. This could be one reason for the defensiveness against a fundamental renewal of the Christian-Jewish relationship, which unfortunately still exists in certain circles. The EKD study of 1991 demanded that the church must express its self-understanding in such a way that Israel's self-understanding is not demoted.[50] This is an important task, but only one part of the challenge that is still ahead of us. It is one thing to recognize that Christianity has Jewish roots. To some, even this recognition has not come easily. It is another thing to express one's own self-understanding in a way that does not demote the Jewish people, i.e. the chosen people. It does fundamentally question the Christian identity if it is recognized and admitted that the Jewish people must constitute an integral component when formulating the church's understanding of itself.[51]

When the church recognizes that God has established a lasting relationship between Israel and himself, the church must realize that it does not stand alone as "God's chosen people," and for precisely this reason Israel must necessarily be included in the description of the Christian identity. A real partnership with Israel as the chosen people must necessarily create a Christian self-definition which has to include Israel. A Christian self-definition which excludes Israel appears inadequate. Here, we still have much to learn from Paul (cf. Romans 15:7–13). In other words, an adequate Christian ecclesiology can only exist if it also includes the first chosen people of God.[52]

4. The Jewish aspect of Christology

A famous statement by the German scholar Julius Wellhausen says: "Jesus was not a Christian, he was a Jew." This statement still sounds strange to some Christians. Christian art has always portrayed Jesus as if he was one of the artist's contemporaries. To give an example: In the Church of the Annunciation in Nazareth, there are different representations of Mary and Jesus as a child. Mary and Jesus look like the inhabitants of the countries where the pieces of art were made: They look like Europeans, Africans, South Americans, Asians, etc. Such representations of Jesus are justified by the claim to portray Jesus as a 'true human being' who offers the possibility of identification for all people in the world. But still, we must not forget the Jewish identity of Jesus.

Hans Joachim Iwand, a famous German Lutheran theologian, wrote in a letter to the Czech theologian, Josef Hromádka in 1959, in which he looks back to the struggle between the church and the state in Nazi times:

> We did not see clear enough . . . that the attack on Jews met Him, Jesus Christ himself. We stuck to Jesus as a human being, but we considered irrelevant that Jesus was a Jew. We considered it irrelevant in a dogmatic sense and in the sense of a general ethical humanism. We saw

the inner connection between the old and the new covenant less clearly and less sharply than our opponent did, who discovered the weakest
spot in our modern Christianity. In this case the veil lay upon the eyes
of the church rather than upon those of the synagogue. We did not see
that we should lose our ecumenical state as church and that we would
have lost it by being cut off from our Jewish roots. . . . The souls of
those who did not betray their Jewish friends were sheltered by this
confession.[53]

So the search of the Jewish Jesus is not just an eccentricity of very
few theologians, but it is a theological necessity. The question about
Jesus within Judaism has been pushed forward on the level of exegesis
during the last decades, without having reached a consensus yet.[54] In
consequence, the question has to be asked, whether New Testament
exegesis has tried (in a fatal attempt) to separate Jesus from Judaism by
overrating the criterion of differentiation, promulgated by some New
Testament scholars.[55] Jesus was always interpreted in a way that
allowed us to distinguish him categorically from Judaism. It is very difficult to break with the rigid belief that Jesus had overcome the Law or
Judaism itself. I, however hold the view that we can only learn about
who Jesus was by seeing him for what he was: a Jew. In order to do so,
we will need to work on New Testament studies as well as on Judaic
studies constantly and patiently in the future. If we want to do Jesus of
Nazareth justice, we need to place him where he belonged: in his
Jewish environment.

The Jewish dimension of Christology makes us aware of another
aspect: Originally, the doctrine of the Trinity was worked out in order to
enable us to hold on to the unity of the God of Israel and—at the same
time—to the revelation in Christ and the work of the Holy Spirit. This
was the aim of the dogma formulated in Constantinople in 380/1 CE.
The Christian practice of praying sometimes makes me doubt whether
this connection is seen correctly. Christian prayers address the triune
God. They must not arouse suspicion of tritheism. The church fathers
said: we pray to God, in the name of Jesus, through the Holy Spirit.
People addressing Jesus with their prayers have to keep in mind the basic
aims of the doctrine of the Trinity—and, eventually, look for adequate
way of prayer.

5. Transformation of the Christian claim of absoluteness into eschatological terminology

Christian theology needs to recognize that it is not sufficient to declaim that salvation has come in Christ. Theology needs to spell out what that means and in doing so, it must not glibly ignore experiences of suffering and of the absence of salvation. Christian theology must translate its statements about the salvation that has come in Christ, into eschatological terms in a way that continues to make these statements clear so that they cannot be confused with ontological affirmations.[56] We have been saved—but in hope! (Romans 8:24) Or, as it is expressed in 1 John 3:2: What we will be has not yet been revealed. Outwardly, salvation is not yet visible.

In 1 Corinthians 15:25, Paul states that Christ has been set in his ruling position but he has not yet made his rule prevail. So Paul's statements about the presence of salvation have the character of prolepsis and anticipation. This concept makes it possible to maintain the dignity of both beliefs: salvation through the coming of Christ as well as the integrity of Israel. This does not mean that the salvation that has come in Christ is reduced, but it is expressed more precisely. What is the reality of salvation? Here I would speak like Martin Luther about a "reality in the word," the reality of the promise. The biblical message states, that at the end of time, there will be a visible establishment of God's kingdom, the prevalence and recognition of the divine name. And here, the Jewish and Christian traditions are very similar: Zechariah 14:9 (On that day the LORD will be one and His name one), the final verse of synagogue worship, and 1 Corinthians 15:28 (God will be all in all) have the same aim in mind. In this eschatological hope Christians and Jews are not far from one another.

The last paragraph of the Jewish declaration *Dabru Emet* says that Jews and Christians have to work together for peace and justice in today's world.[57] In Koblenz, where I taught, we had a conference in 1997, which was entitled: "Bioethics and the Understanding of Humanity in Judaism and Christianity." Jews and Christians, theologians and scientists, came together for three days and discussed the questions posed by modern biotech engineering and the tremendous opportunities which are given to us by the biotechnological developments. At the end of the conference, we formulated a joint statement on these questions. We observed that, in spite of our different opinions in several theological issues, we are united in our understanding of humankind and in our understanding of creation. And we are united in our obligation to work against the temptations of the world of today and modern technologies. We saw it as our obligation to say together what it means, that humanity was created in the image of God. This is just one example that shows how Jews and Christians can work together for peace and justice in our world by maintaining the dignity and integrity of the religious beliefs of Judaism and Christianity. May there be many more in the future.

Notes

1. It might be helpful to mention that in German Protestantism we find regional churches in the different states of the Federal Republic of Germany. Some of them are Lutheran, some are Reformed, and some are United Churches (Lutheran and Reformed together). All of these churches belong to the Evangelical Church in Germany, an umbrella organization, the EKD (*Evangelische Kirche in Deutschland*). The Lutherans organized themselves in the United Evangelical-Lutheran Church in Germany (*Vereinigte Evangelisch-Lutherische Kirche in Deutschland*, VELKD). The Reformed churches form the Reformed Council (*Reformierter Bund*). The United churches form the Evangelical Church of the Union (*Evangelische Kirche der Union*, EKU). These Churches are members of worldwide organizations such as the Lutheran World Federation (LWF) or the Ecumenical Council of Churches (ECC). Until 1991, the churches in the German Democratic Republic formed the Council of Evangelical Churches of the GDR [*Bund der Evangelischen Kirchen in der DDR*, BEKD-DR]. In this article, I will focus mainly on the situation in Germany, discussing both Lutheran and other Protestant churches, while I will only touch on other Protestant Churches from all around the world. One additional note: the use of the word "evangelical" in the names of German churches differs from the use of "evangelical" in the US context.

2. *Cf. H.H. Henrix/W. Kraus*, ed., Die Kirchen und das Judentum. Dokumente von 1986–2000, Paderborn: Bonifatius / Gütersloh: Gütersloher 2001, 940, E.III.75'.

3. *Klaus Haacker*, Der Holocaust als Datum der Theologiegeschichte, in: *E. Brocke / J. Seim*, ed., Gottes Augap-fel, Neukirchen-Vluyn: Neukirchener 1986, 137–145: 145. For all translations of German texts given in this

article the author is responsible. I thank Karin Lange and Steffen Link from Saarbrücken for their substantial help—not only to improve my English.

4. cf. fn. 3.

5. The official title is: „Erklärung gegenüber den Vertretern des Ökumenischen Rates der Kirchen". Cf. R. Rendtorff/H. H. Henrix, ed., Die Kirchen und das Judentum. Dokumente von 1945–1985, Paderborn: Bonifatius / München: Kaiser 1988, 528f.

6. Cf. U. Schwemer, ed., Christen und Juden. Dokumente der Annäherung, Gütersloh: Gütersloher 1991 (GTB 790), 85.

7. "Darmstädter Wort zur Judenfrage", cf. R. Rendtorff/H.H. Henrix, ed., Die Kirchen und das Judentum. Dokumente von 1945–1985, Pader-born: Bonifatius / München: Kaiser 1988, 540–544.

8. When 'Israel' is mentioned here and in the following texts, the term is always meant as a theological concept, not as the state of Israel.

9. E.g. the Evangelical-Lutheran Church of Oldenburg (6. Nov. 1945, cf. Henrix/Kraus, E.III.32' Anhang, 683–685) and the Protestant-Lutheran Church of Sachsen (17./18. April 1948, cf. Schwemer, 91f). Also some organizations besides the official churches' synods, e.g. the ‚Kirchlich-theologische Sozietät in Württemberg' (cf. Rendtorff/Henrix, E.III.3), and the ‚Bruderrat der Bekennenden Kirche von Berlin' (cf. Rendtorff/Henrix, E.III.4), published words of repentance in 1946.

10. Text in Rendtorff/Henrix, 548f.

11. In my opinion, the restricted interpretation of R. Rendtorff, Hat denn Gott sein Volk verstoßen?, ACJD 18, München: Kaiser 1989, 22f, whereas not Israel's election but only God's eschatological promise is held up, is not justified.

12. Cf. Rendtorff/Henrix, E.III.18, 555–557; E.III.19; 576–578.

13. Cf. e.g. Rendtorff, Hat denn Gott, 22 Fn. 21.

14. Cf. Rendtorff/Henrix, E.III.19, 558–578.

15. Cf. Rendtorff/Henrix, E.III.29, 593–596.

16. This motto already came up in a text on the relations of Christians and Jews by Karl-Heinz Becker, a minister of the Evangelical-Lutheran Church in Bavaria, written in 1934! I thank Axel Töllner, Nuremberg, for his notice. He is dealing with this text in his dissertation on the so-called 'non-arian' pastors in the Evangelical-Lutheran Church in Bavaria between 1933 and 1945 which is on the way to publication in the Kohlhammer publishing house in Stuttgart.

17. Cf. Rendtorff/Henrix, E.III.29, 594.

18. The Evangelical Church of Baden (1984), the Reformed Church of Bavaria and North-West Germany (1984), the Evangelical Church of Berlin-Brandenburg (1984), the Evangelical Church of Pommern (1985), the Evangelical Church of Württemberg (1988), the Evangelical Church of Westfalen (1988), the Evangelical-Lutheran Church of Sachsen (1988), the Evangelical Church of the Palatinate (1990), the Evangelical-Lutheran Church of Mecklenburg (1990), and the Reformed Council (1990).

19. The Evangelical Church in Hessen and Nassau (1991), the Evangelical-Lutheran Church in Oldenburg (1993), the Evangelical Church of Westfalen (1994 and 1999), the Evangelical-Lutheran Church of Hannover (1995); the Evangelical-Lutheran Church of Kurhessen-Waldeck (1997), the Evangelical-Lutheran Church of Bavaria (1998), the Regional Church of Lippe (1998), the Evangelical-Lutheran Church of Mecklenburg (1998), the Evangelical Church of Württemberg (2000), and the Evangelical-Lutheran Church of Nordelbien (2001).

20. H.H. Henrix/W. Kraus, Hg., Die Kirchen und das Judentum. Dokumente von 1986–2000, Paderborn: Bonifatius / Gütersloh: Gütersloher 2001. The text from the Evangelical Church of Westfalen, 1988, is published in the book of U. Schwemer, Christen und Juden (see fn. 6), 145–151.

21. Cf. *Henrix/Kraus*, E.I.2'.

22. Cf. *Henrix/Kraus*, E.III.24'.

23. Cf. *Henrix/Kraus*, E.III.24', 635f.

24. Cf. *Rendtorff/Henrix*, E.III.29, 594.

25. An exception is the statement of the Reformed Council, cf. *Henrix/Kraus*, E.III.19', 608f.

26. Cf. *Henrix/Kraus*, E.III.73', 937f.

27. Cf. *Henrix/Kraus*, E.III.27'; E.III.30'; E.III.74'.

28. Cf. *Henrix/Kraus*, E.III.69'; E.III.73'.

29. Cf. *Henrix/Kraus*, E.III.36'; E.III.46'.

30. Cf. *Henrix/Kraus*, E.III.4', 556.

31. Cf. *Henrix/Kraus*, E.III.9', 567f.

32. The Synod of the Reformed Church in Bavaria and North-West Germany, 1988, the Evangelical Church of Hessen and Nassau, 1991 (*Henrix/Kraus*, E.III.25'), the Evangelical Church of the Palatinate, 1995 (E.III.40'), the Evangelical Church of the Rhineland, 1996 (E.III.47'), the Evangelical Church of Berlin-Brandenburg, 1996 (E.III.54'), the Evangelical Church of Pommern, 1997 (E.III.57'), the Regional Church of Lippe, 1998 (E.III.68'), the Evangelical-Lutheran Church of

Oldenburg, 2001, the Evangelical Church of Baden, 2001, the Evangelical-Lutheran Church of Nordelbien, 2002. The Evangelical Church of Westfalen and the Evangelical-Lutheran Church of Braunschweig are in the process of discussion about whether and how they should change their constitutional articles.

33. Cf. *Henrix/Kraus*, E.III.54', 766; E.III.57', 779.

34. Cf. *Henrix/Kraus*, E.III.72', 862–932.

35. Cf. http//www.jcrelations/stellung/kirche-und-israel-01.htm.

36. Cf. *Henrix/Kraus*, E.III.34'.

37. Cf. *Henrix/Kraus*, E.III.31, E.III.67, E.III.76.

38. Cf. *W. Kraus*, Hg., Auf dem Weg zu einem Neuanfang, München: Claudius 1999. I have also to admit, that the consensus we are beginning to see in various church statements has not been reached on the level of university theology either.

39. *David Flusser*, Ulrich Wilckens und die Juden, Evangelische Theologie 34, 1974, 236–243; *Ulrich Wilckens*, Das Neue Testament und die Juden. Antwort an David Flusser, Evangelische Theologie 34, 1974, 602–611.

40. *G. Klein*, Christlicher Antijudaismus, Zeitschrift für Theologie und Kirche 79, 1982, 411–450.

41. *R. Ruether*, Nächstenliebe und Brudermord. Die theologischen Wurzeln des Antijudaismus, ACJD 7, München: Kaiser 1978, 210 (first published in English under the title: Faith and Fratricide).

42. *Ruether*, Nächstenliebe, 229.

43. cf. fn. 23.

44. *Hans Hübner*, Biblische Theologie des Neuen Testaments II, Göttingen: Vandenhoeck & Ruprecht 1990, 309.

45. Cf. *Henrix/Kraus*, E.III.24', 651–662.

46. Cf. *Henrix/Kraus*, E.III.24', 661.

47. Cf. *W. Kraus*, Paulinische Perspektiven zum Thema 'bleibende Erwählung Israels', in: *ders*. Hg., Christen und Juden. Perspektiven einer Annäherung, Gütersloh: Gütersloher 1997, 143–170: 144ff.

48. Cf. the articles mentioned in: *Kraus*, Paulinische Perspektiven 158 fn. 41 and 159 fn. 45.

49. Cf. *W. Kraus*, Das Volk Gottes. Zur Grundlegung der Ekklesiologie bei Paulus, WUNT 85, Tübingen: Mohr 1996, esp. 290–333.

50. Cf. *Henrix/Kraus*, E.III.24', 661f.

51. Even the Jewish roots of Christianity can degenerate into a merely historical memory.

52. I suggested that they include this aspect in the text of the first draft of the EKD declaration concerning the 50th anniversary of Berlin-Weißensee in year 2000 (cf. above fn. 2). It would have been another major step, comparable to the step that was taken in Berlin-Weißensee in 1950. The EKD was not able to make a decision in favor of this suggestion.

53. *Hans Joachim Iwand,* Brief an Josef L. Hromádka, 8.6.1959, in: *ders.,* Briefe, Vorträge, Predigtmeditationen. Eine Auswahl, hg. von Peter-Paul Sänger, Berlin (Ost): Evangelische Verlagsanstalt 1979, 122–133, 126. The text goes on: "We came across an astonishing secret. But the price. Was it not too high? Who is going to take away the blame from us and our fathers—where it began? What must happen so that we can put this behind us? How can a people that has rebelled against Israel and against its God become clean again?"

54. Cf. on this topic *Karlheinz Müller,* Forschungsgeschichtliche Anmerkungen zum Thema 'Jesus und das Gesetz', in: Martin Karrer / Wolfgang Kraus / Otto Merk, ed., Kirche und Volk Gottes, FS Jürgen Roloff, Neukirchen-Vluyn: Neukirchener 2000, 58–77, and the literature mentioned there.

55. Cf. on this question: G. *Theißen/D. Winter,* Die Kriterienfrage in der Jesusforschung. Vom Differenzkriterium zum Plausibilitätskriterium, NTOA 34, Göttingen: Vandenhoeck & Ruprecht / Fribourg: Universitätsverlag 1997.

56. Cf. G. *Baum,* Foreword to Ruether, Nächstenliebe, 24.

57. Cf. *Henrix/Kraus,* J.8', 974–976: 976.

JAMAL BADAWI

What I Want the Other to Teach About Islamic History and Faith

All praise is due to Allah who is the sole creator, sustainer, and cherisher of the universe; and may his peace and blessings be upon his last messenger and prophet, Muhammad, and upon all prophets and messengers who preceded him in history. My dear brothers and sisters, I greet you with the greeting of all the prophets in its most complete and beautiful form, may the peace, blessings and mercy of Allah, God, be with you all.

I wish to start off by thanking the organizers and the inspirers and all the attendees of this conference in Edmonton, Canada, who participated in this very worthwhile dialogue. I would like to indicate that this morning I am speaking on behalf of some Muslims, but not all. I will try to deal with issues that I believe have common acceptance among the majority of Muslims. Most particularly, I will be making references to the *Qur'an* which is regarded as the first and primary source accepted by all Muslims of all schools and applying certain rules of exegesis that are recognized by almost all Muslims.

I have five basic topics to present: 1) Islam and Muslim are not necessarily identical terms; 2) Islam as a universal faith of all of the prophets; 3) Connections between the Abrahamic faiths from an Islamic perspective; 4) Islam and pluralism; and 5) Common misconceptions about *jihad* and Islam.

Introduction

We are living in a generation of humanity that is able to leap on the moon, yet is unable to walk on earth living with one another in peace, justice, and human love—even though God is loving for all his creation. There is a plethora of problems that humanity is facing today—economic, social, and political—and those problems appear on all levels from the family to the world at large. At the heart of the problems though is a spiritual vacuum in the lives of many people.

We also are living in what is appropriately called a "global village" with a great deal of interdependence, and that is where interfaith dialogue and relations play a pivotal role in bringing people together. In fact, I would like to clarify at this juncture, again referring to the *Qur'an*, how interfaith dialogue is viewed. The *Qur'an* is dialogical by nature. Let me offer a few examples. In Chapter 3:64 there is an open invitation to the People of the Book—particularly Jews and Christians—to come to the common term or common denominator between themselves and Muslims, namely to worship none but Allah. The word "Allah" in Arabic simply means the one and only true universal God of all. It implies that we will not associate others with God in his exclusive, divine attributes.

The mode of that dialogue is also explained in Chapter 29:45–46, which basically instructs Muslims not to argue with the People of the Book except in ways that are best, most effective, and most courteous. Also, that same part of the *sura* (chapter) provides a guide for Muslims in dialogue to try to capitalize on common ground, since one cannot force people to believe the same way as another. Muslims are encouraged at least to look at the common ground and say, "We believe in what has been revealed to us and what has been revealed to you in its original form. Your God and ours is one in the same, and unto whom we all submit."

Chapter 34:24 speaks about the attitude to approach another in dialogue. The *Qur'an*, says that even when people discuss their differences, they do not begin by saying, "I've got the truth, I am right, and you are wrong, and let me tell you how you're wrong." Rather, there is a firmness balanced with openness where the Muslim is to say "You and we could be either guided or in manifest error," implying: so let's discuss this, look at the evidence, and reason together. I must say before I leave this point that the same attitude that the *Qur'an* recommends for interfaith dialogue should also govern the actions of intra-faith dialogue. If that spirit of tolerance and understanding is required between different faiths, all the more should it be promoted also within various groups of people who claim to belong to the same faith.

Islam and Muslims

Islam and Muslims are not identical any more than Christianity and Christ or Christianity and Christians are identical. Similarly, Judaism and the action of Jews or some Jews are not identical. Muslims can be "Islamic" to the extent they abide by the behaviors and ethics that are taught by Islam in its pristine original sources. Any lapses on the part of Muslims historically is their fault, not Islam's. Individual Muslims lapse but Islam does not.

There are two primary sources for Islam and both are believed to be authentic revelation. The first is the *Qur'an*. The Prophet Muhammad—peace be upon him—reported that *Qur'an* is the verbatim word of God dictated through the agency of the archangel Gabriel. Since the *Qur'an* is the exact word of God implies that no human being, even the greatest of prophets, has any right to supersede or to cancel it, or else one would be claiming to have greater knowledge and wisdom than the Creator. A second primary source of revelation for Islam and Islamic jurisprudence, is known as *sunnah* (sometimes called *hadith*): the teachings, the words, actions and approvals of Prophet Muhammad, which is believed also to be revelation, but the words are not the words of God. They are Muhammad's own words and unlike the *Qur'an* which is completely authentic, there are degrees of authenticity in the *sunnah*. A *hadith* is a narration about the life of the Prophet or what he approved, as distinct from his life itself, which is the *sunnah*.

The secondary sources, however, are not infallible and they apply reason in the light of the text and spirit of the Islamic law in order to come up with solutions or answers to different problems with the variations of time, place, and circumstances. This process materializes into a legal opinion. It is not uncommon for one to find more than one legitimate jurisprudential opinion presented or advocated by two equally qualified scholars or even the same scholar, depending upon the situations or settings.

I believe this process is relevant to some of the issues concerning how faith can be relevant in the daily lives of people today. Much like the solar system—constantly in motion while at the same time exhibiting a dynamic of stability in orbit—there are certain things that are constant in Islam while Muslims respond and interact with the forces of modernity. In fact, if one looks at how the *Qur'an* itself was revealed, its nature was one of dynamism. It was an interactive book—interactive revelation—not an abstract concept. Often revelation comes to the prophet in response to a question directed to him about an event in society while he was guiding the communities in Mecca and Medina. The revelation of the *Qur'an* spans about 22 years amidst the events of history—war, peace, marriage, divorce, all kinds of situations on the social, political, and economic levels, and the *Qur'an* is intended to guide humanity step by step on its road. Again, the *Qur'an* is not an abstract book, it is interactive and relevant by its very nature.

Can the Muslim come in humility to engage in dialogue with others with the purpose of not instructing them, but learning from them? Since dialogue is a human effort and will be prone to fallibility and imperfection, there is also the possibility that good can arise from it. So there is no problem in participating in a dialogue. In fact, the prophet Muhammad taught his followers to look for wisdom with others. He said that wisdom is the lost property of the believer and wherever a person finds it, he or she is most deserving of it. So, there is no restriction to dialogue and learning from others, so long as one is not diverted from the basics of his faith or compromised in those essentials.

Islam Is a Universal Faith of All of the Prophets

Islam and Muslims as people are not tied to a particular geography or ethnic background. Islam is, in its nature, a generic, universal faith. Unfortunately, I have seen instances where even some universities have classified Islam under eastern religions with Hinduism and Buddhism. It is understandable that many people would consider Islam an Arabic religion or Middle Eastern. And yet, historically speaking, both Judaism and Christianity began as Middle Eastern religions. Many people are surprised to learn that Arabs are a minority among Muslims—no more than 20 percent—of a population of approximately 1.3 billion or one fifth of humanity. The largest Muslim country in the world, Indonesia, has about 200 million people. Approximately 120 million Muslims live as a minority in India—a number that is twice as much as the total population of the largest Arab country, Egypt.

The term "Islam" comes from the Arabic root, S-L-M. These three letters are also found in Muslim, and mean peace, submission to Allah, or surrender. If a person is true to his or her faith and has peace with God, and thus, peace from within, then he must have peace with all of the creation of God—humans, with their variety of beliefs and cultures, animals, plants, and the environment. But, that kind of attitude can only be achieved if the person willingly and consciously chooses to obey God and submit to his will. Such an attitude is at the core of the message of all the prophets.

For that reason, some people may become puzzled when they read in the *Qur'an* that prophet Abraham was a Muslim. I remember someone asking, "Abraham was a Muslim even though he lived and died centuries before Muhammad was even born? That's like saying Thomas Jefferson loved Kentucky Fried Chicken." He failed to understand that the term "Islam" has two meanings. Of course, Islam refers to what Muslims believe and follow as revealed by the Prophet Muhammad. But the second meaning is one referring to that which all of the prophets followed to achieve peace through submission to God. So, in this second sense, all the prophets were Muslims because they submitted themselves to the will of God. In fact, one could say that the whole universe is Muslim. The sun, the moon, and all things submit to God, except that as humans we have the freedom of choosing to submit or not.

Abrahamic Connections of Islam to Judaism and Christianity

Some people have raised the question about the relationship between the *Qur'an* and the Bible, or more broadly, between the teachings and beliefs of Islam and those of its two sisters—Judaism and Christianity. Some people might be tempted to conclude simply that Jews believe in the Torah, Christians believe both in the Hebrew Scriptures and the New

Testament, and that Muslims believe in both plus the *Qur'an*, as if the *Qur'an* was no more than a supplement or rehashing what has been said in the Torah or the Old Testament and New Testament.

First, the *Qur'an* does not use or refer to the terms equivalent to Bible, Hebrew Scriptures, or Old or New Testament. The *Qur'an* does refer to the leafs or manuscripts of Abraham, presumably now gone. The *Qur'an* also speaks about the Torah in Arabic, but it is unlikely that the term is meant in the same way our Jewish brothers and sisters understand the term. When the *Qur'an* refers to Torah, there is a restricted definition that Torah means exclusively what Moses received on Sinai, nothing more.

The *Qur'an* also speaks about what most translators call "the psalms of David." I defer to the biblical scholars, but I do know that there is a dispute as to whether all the psalms of David were written by David. Whatever the case, when the *Qur'an* refers to the psalms, it refers only to what David received. Similarly, according to the *Qur'an*, only the words that Jesus himself spoke are authentic teaching—not the biographies about Jesus written by his followers, nor the religious experiences of those who encountered that beautiful personality and reported the feeling, but exclusively what Jesus himself said, provided it is authentic. So, it is important to be precise when we make comparisons. To say that the *Qur'an* is a continuation is, in one limited sense, true, but it came to confirm what remained intact of the Bible and be like a guardian over the previous scriptures—a guardian that is taking the liberty to clarify and indicate where misinterpretation of God's message might have taken place—to sift through what the prophets actually received by way of divine revelation and what their followers articulated or elaborated, making a clear line of distinction between both (Chapter 5:47–52).

I have read that some people say that Muslims believe the Bible is corrupted and not to be accepted, that nothing is true about it. If this indeed were the case, what did the *Qur'an* come to confirm? If the entire Bible had no value, no importance, no authenticity whatsoever, why does the *Qur'an* say that it came to confirm what remained intact of that Bible? The presumption here is obviously clear that there are things that a careful Muslim looking into the Bible will find consistent with the teaching of Islam and the *Qur'an*. The most obvious example is the *Shema Israel*, found in Deuteronomy 6:4, "Hear O Israel, The Eternal is our God, the Eternal is One." Muslims agree completely that Allah is the one and only God eternal. On the other hand, of anything that is found in the Bible that is totally opposed to what is in the *Qur'an*, the Muslim would very politely say, "This is what I believe to be the word of God and the word of God supersedes human ideas and theology." And regarding texts in the Bible that neither contradict nor have been confirmed by the *Qur'an*, the prophet taught we cannot accept them or reject them. It may have divine origin or it might be someone's opinion, so we must leave it in abeyance.

So, with these understandings, we see similarities and parallels, but not in the usual way that Islam is often portrayed—with Judaism and Christianity as the original branches of a tree from which Islam draws its identity. Obviously there is a very strong connection between Christianity and Judaism since Jesus was a Jew and taught Torah. However, from a Muslim's perspective, another conception could be to have God at the center and have that same God reveal to Noah, Abraham, Moses, Jesus and Muhammad, and all other prophets in world history, especially since the *Qur'an* has been revealed directly from God.

There are many uniting things between the three Abrahamic religions—belief in the one true God, prophets, belief in revelation and scriptures and taking responsibility for our deeds in this life, a code of ethics, and a belief in the hereafter. One does not have to be in the physical lineage of Abraham to claim to belong to Abraham. One of the most beautiful expressions in the *Qur'an* says that those who have the greatest claim on Abraham are those who follow him and his teachings (See chapter 3:67–70).

Islam and Pluralism

Does the history of normative Islam accept plurality; namely, living with others and showing respect for the rights of others, not treating them as inferiors or persecuting them? In Chapter 4, the *Qur'an* instructs all humankind to be dutiful to the Lord who created us from a single soul and of like nature, and of both of them he multiplied multitudes of men and women. Notice that the passage does not say all Muslims or all believers, but all mankind. The same instruction—to all mankind—

appears in Chapter 49:13, where we were created from a single pair of a male and female. This means that we are all one family. True, there are different branches and sometimes we disagree and fight with each other, but this happens in families and ultimately, we are one family. Chapter 49 continues by saying that God made us into nations and tribes so that we may come to know and recognize one another, although the most honored in the sight of God is not based on gender, wealth, color, or nationality. The most honored in the sight of God is one who is most righteous.

Earlier in the *Qur'an*, Chapter 30:22, it explains the variations of human languages and colors as a sign of the power of God creating diversity, not for superiority or inferiority, but as signs of his power, mercy and compassion. The creation of heavens and earth and the variations in the languages and complexions of people is, as I like to put it, a bouquet of flowers where the white flower is beautiful in its own right, so is the red, the yellow, and the pink; but more beautiful are all of them together. That is what one can derive from the *Qur'an* and its stances on human brotherhood.

But, within the scope of human brotherhood, we have also the People of the Book. This is a complimentary title given in the *Qur'an* to distinguish them from other religions that do not have as much in common with Islam as they do. People of the Book are those whose religion is based on revealed books or revealed scriptures. One of the most amazing things in the *Qur'an* is found in Chapter 5:5, which indicates the proper Muslim attitude toward the People of the Book who are living in peace with him. It allows for the women of the People of the Book to marry a Muslim, which is a form of interfaith marriage. And it also says that animals killed by the People of the Book for food are acceptable for Muslims to eat, whereas he is not supposed to eat meat that is slaughtered by a person who is an atheist or polytheist. So the relationship between Muslims and People of the Book goes well beyond a polite or courteous relationship to one where both can share food and also be a part of the same family.

And then, in the same chapter, some quote another verse in the *Qur'an* out of context and sometimes the translation is incorrect. There are some translations that say to the believers, do not take Jews and Christians for your friends. That is erroneous. The original context and

Arabic meaning implies that Muslims should not take alliance with Jews and Christians for the sake of their own defense. In other words, Muslims must defend themselves.

But, perhaps one of the most important issues is the question of plurality. According to the text of the *Qur'an*, there is an assumption of living with people of other faiths and other religions—and that is God's design. In Chapter 118 it says that if God or Muhammad had willed it, he would have made all people one nation or one community of believers. It is true that Christians will believe that they should share the good news and Muslims will feel that we have to share the good news. However, the difference is that is it one thing to share the good news and quite another to try to force someone to believe. We do not understand why people differ but we are convinced that plurality is part of God's design. Therefore we have no right to condemn one another or to mistreat each other.

From this acceptance of plurality as God's will, two important concepts follow: universal justice and dignity. The *Qur'an* speaks about the importance of speaking truth and acting justly even if it goes against one's self interest or one's family. In fact, justice must be extended even to one's enemy. Chapter 5 says that not even hatred should dissuade one from doing justice. This is because Muslims must be witnesses of God who witnesses all things.

In the arena of law, there is a concept of *vhimme*, which means "covenant," implying the covenanted people who possess the covenant of God and his messenger, that by virtue of being a minority, certain rights shall be granted. This is different from a democracy. In Islamic law by making this distinction, giving a special status to the *vhimmes*, the covenanted people, it means that God has given them these rights and as such, no majority rule can revoke those rights because this is the covenant that the God has given. They can go to their own religious courts for proper justice.

Since Islam is a complete way of living—religious, economic and political—it presumes also a righteous community or a righteous society that establishes justice and looks after the needs of everyone. In addition to the tremendous contributions to the areas of science over the past 650 years, Islamic civilization has also developed a compassionate view of humans in society. According to Islamic law, all citizens—Muslims and

240 ap   Jamal Badawi

non-Muslims alike—are entitled to what we call today social security. An Islamic state finances this kind of program by paying a *zakat*, which is a tax and also a religious duty, one of the pillars of Islam. So not to offend other members of the community, non-Muslims were asked to pay a *jizya*, a tax to assure that they would be beneficiaries of protection and support in their sickness, poverty or old age. The *jizya* was not a punishment for not being Muslim. When there has been unfairness in Muslim societies, it is not because of the Islamic system. It is because of unfair rulers who at the time were unfair to Muslims and non-Muslims alike.

Jihad and Islam

I would like to look carefully at some common stereotypes and challenge them. The first is the notion of *jihad*—mistakenly called holy war—which brings to mind images of terrorism and senseless violence. There is no single occurrence of the term "holy war" in the entire *Qur'an*. *Jihad* means to exert effort. According to the *Qur'an* and the teaching of the prophet, there are different levels of *jihad*. First, on the individual level, one struggles within oneself for self purification and obedience to God.

Second, *jihad* also appears on the social level, and the *Qur'an* describes itself actually as a means of *jihad*. A Muslim is to make *jihad* with the truth that is contained in the *Qur'an*. It is quite common also for a person to make *jihad* with his tongue or *jihad* with his pen, that is, one must exercise restraint when tempted to be uncharitable. Actually, the *Qur'an* also describes charity as *jihad* and says to make *jihad* with one's property or wealth.

Third, there is also *jihad* in the battlefield, and according to the *Qur'an* it is for self defense and a last resort to fight against oppression. Although going to the battlefield may become necessary, it is not desirable, and Muslims share with everyone the hope and the desire that there would be no war. But the reality of human life past, present and possible future is quite different. For Muslims to rightfully engage in war, peaceful means of resolution must have been attempted and this is the last resort; there must be a purification of motives—which does not permit duty, pride, nationalism or superiority to be the guiding motive; and the war must be declared publicly by a legitimate authority. There is also clear instruction by the prophet and his successors that noncombatants must be spared—women, children, old people, religious people, farmers minding their fields, and even the mutilation of animals.

To conclude, I would want others to teach that Muslims respect the right of others to differ with them, and that Islam can never be forced on another. I believe that the principles of Islam rooted in the *Qur'an* and the Prophet have guided Islamic history, and will continue to guide the way that righteous Muslims live in the world. The future offers us a wonderful opportunity to focus on issues of common concern such as peace and justice. And, in my humble view, peace and justice are like the two wings of a bird. Without both wings, freedom and dignity will fail. It is my great honor and pleasure to be a participant in this very noble effort to move in that direction. There is no better time than now. Peace be with you.

PART III ~ WHAT DO WE WANT THE OTHER TO TEACH
ABOUT OUR HISTORICAL TRADITIONS?

For Further Discussion and Study

What is the process or method by which one accurately expresses through limited language what is most important to the greatest number of people of a religion? Who decides what is important historical revelation? Are contemporary events less important than past ones? What are the values and the shortfalls of the historical-critical approach in adequately describing all of religious experience?

Are religions prone to teaching more about transhistorical, eternal beliefs rather than temporal events? Why, why not? What are the advantages or limitations of a methodology that takes history seriously as a primary category in hermeneutics and revelation?

How do Judaism, Christianity, and Islam understand their historical roots? What are the primary stories or events that are central to the other's identity? How were these stories or events chosen? What are the diverse historical expressions within each of the religions of Judaism, Christianity, and Islam?

Are Jewish, Christian, and Islamic histories in concert with other histories? Where and why do the subjects and goals of religious history differ? What are the possible ways to teach about the other's history and historical tradition without situating them in a Western timeline and analysis?

For a history of interreligious dialogue itself, examine some of the prominent documents, namely, the 1947 Seelisburg Statement, *Nostra Aetate* (1965), the Lambeth Conference (1988), the World Council of Churches (1988), "We Remember: A Reflection on the *Shoah*" (1998), and "*Dabru Emet:* A Jewish Statement on Christians and Christianity" (2000). All of these sources and many others can be found on www.ccju.org.

Judaism, Christianity, and Islam share a chronological historical relationship and encountered each other negatively or violently at different times throughout history. How can we teach about the other as an ongoing valid religion today without pointing to times in the past that would situate and demean the other as a relic or cultural prisoner of the past?

Describe the principal holidays, festivals, and life-cycle events that recall the historical events that connect the present religious community to the ongoing story and history of each religion.

How do Jews, Christians, and Muslims balance the religious, cultural, political, eschatological, and national dimensions of their faiths?

How is Jewish, Christian, and Islamic history tied theologically to land, for example, in the case of the State of Israel, Holy Land, Palestine?

How is it possible to overcome the asymmetrical cultural and political relationship between Jews, Christians, and Muslims? Are the Jewish partners too disadvantaged in numbers to meaningfully and authentically participate? Are Christians believed to be imperialist crusaders by the others? Are Muslims unfairly portrayed as a violent, foreign culture resistant to dialogue or exchange of ideas?

How have Jews, Christians, and Muslims dealt with Enlightenment and modernity in their theology, identity, mission, ethics, anthropology, ecclesiology, and spirituality?

For Action in the Community

Are historical studies the proper starting point for Jewish, Christian, and Muslim relations, or is social justice, ethics, scriptural study, spirituality or theology more appropriate? What is best for this specific dialogue group and why?

What are some of the stereotypes of the other? What are the ways educators can present other religions fairly without comparing the best of one's religion and the worst of the other's? How does one overcome the negative stereotypes based on the other's or one's own religious extremists who may be prone to violence and oppression?

How can Jews, Christians, and Muslims interpret and productively respond to the signs of the times, such as: secularization, industrialization, economic disparity among people, immigration, urbanization, and the rapid expansion of information?

Describe how the other engages its sources and applies them to the ethical demands of daily life. How is that similar or different than your own religious tradition?

Is it possible to describe oneself as is, rather than over and against others? Is it possible for Christians to understand Jews and Muslims outside the categories and contexts of European history?

What would be your short sacred list that exemplifies the depth and breadth of your religious history as an individual and as a religious community? For example, name your most important or favorite ideas, stories, values, laws, prophets, holy people and leaders who have contributed to your living religious history.

How can dialogue partners effectively and respectfully deal with historical revisionists?

Jews and Christians have been developing and refining a dialogue for the past forty years. As such, there are many Jewish-Christian documents that have begun to deal deeply with Jewish and Christian concerns. There are also very recent statements and efforts (such as these conferences) to meaningfully include participation by Muslims. How can Judaism and Christianity invite and engage the believers of Islam in a more concerted way?

Is it possible to institutionalize in a curriculum each religion's memory together with the other, so that creation, the seven Noahide laws, the commandments, etc., can lead people closer to peace and salvation? Why, why not?

What are the various informal or unconscious ways that religions teach about the other that require more careful attention? For example, history, laws, worship, art, songs, others?

PART IV

What Do We Want the Other to Teach About Our Prayer and Liturgy?

D A V I D   L .   C O P P O L A

What Do We Want the Other to Teach About Our Prayer and Liturgy?

Conference in Rome, Italy

On March 13–15, 2002, the Center for Christian-Jewish Understanding (CCJU) of Sacred Heart University, Fairfield, Connecticut, sponsored a conference at the Dionesian Center at Villa Piccolomini, Rome, entitled, "What Do We Want the Other to Teach About Our Prayer and Liturgy?" The conference began with remarks by Dr. Anthony J. Cernera, president of Sacred Heart University, and Rabbi Joseph H. Ehrenkranz, executive director of the CCJU. Rabbi Reuven Kimelman, professor of Near Eastern and Judaic Studies at Brandeis University, Waltham, Massachusetts; Cardinal Carlo Maria Martini, Archbishop of Milan; and Sheikh Professor Abdul Hadi Palazzi of the Cultural Institute of the Italian Islamic Community, Rome, presented papers to an audience of more than 200 people. Papers included philosophical, theological, and liturgical considerations from the Jewish, Christian and Muslim faith traditions on "What Do We Want the Other to Teach About Our Prayer and Liturgy?" At the end of the lectures, each presenter was given the opportunity to respond to questions.

The format for the following day of the conference included responses to the papers by noted scholars followed by discussion, critiques and suggestions by a group of 30 scholars and participants from Europe and the United States. Graduate students from several universities in Rome, as well as representatives from the Sisters of Sion and the Focolare Movement joined for each of the sessions.

On one evening of the conference, the film, *Desperate Hours*, directed by Victoria Barrett, was shown. About 40 people joined the conference participants at the Villa Piccolomini, and several representatives from the Italian press attended. The film documented how the government and the people of Turkey helped to save the lives of European Jews by giving them citizenship papers as well as places to resettle during World War II. At a public reception that followed, Dr. Coppola facilitated a discussion that lasted two hours.

LIST OF INVITED PARTICIPANTS

Rabbi Tsvi Blanchard, Director of Organizational Development, CLAL, New York

Professor Giovanni Bonsanti, Esq., Office for Islam, Order of the Knights of the Holy Sepulchre

Dr. Anthony J. Cernera, Sacred Heart University, Connecticut

Dr. David L. Coppola, Center for Christian-Jewish Understanding of Sacred Heart University, Connecticut

Khadija Rosaria De Maria, Council of Muslim Women, Italian Muslim Association, Rome

Mrs. Istina Di Corte, Focolare Movement, Rome

Rabbi Dr. Riccardo DiSegni, Chief Rabbi of Rome

Rabbi Joseph H. Ehrenkranz, Center for Christian-Jewish Understanding of Sacred Heart University, Connecticut

Rev. Dr. Joseph Farias, Drew University, New Jersey

Avv. Guglielmo Guerra, Italian Muslim Association, Rome

Sheikh Dr. Ali M. Hussen, Italian Muslim Association, Rome

Kalim Karim Hussen, Federation of Muslim Students, Italian Muslim Association, Rome

Cardinal Walter Kasper, Commission for Religious Relations with the Jews, Vatican City

Farid Naimi Khan, Italy-Afghanistan Fellowship, Counselor for Asia, Italian Muslim Association, Rome

Rabbi Dr. Reuven Kimelman, Brandeis University, Massachusetts

Rabbi Joseph Laras, Chief Rabbi of Milan

Cardinal Carlo Maria Martini, Archbishop of Milan

Marzuk Marzio Mostarda, Italian Muslim Association, Office for Islam Order of the Knights of the Holy Sepulchre

Sheikh Professor Abdul Hadi Palazzi, Cultural Institute of the Italian Islamic Community, Rome

Dr. Margaret Palliser, OP, Sacred Heart University, Fairfield, Connecticut

Lisa Palmieri-Billig, Anti-Defamation League, Italy, Rome

Rev. Dr. Charles Parr, Catholic University, Washington, DC

Rabbi Abraham Piattelli, Rabbi of the Great Synagogue, Rome

Dr. Ombretta Pisano, Sidic Center, Rome

Rabbi David Rosen, International Council of Christians and Jews, Jerusalem

Lucy Thorson, NDS, Sister of Sion, Rome

Mechthild Vahle, NDS, Superior General, Sisters of Sion, Rome

What Do We Want the Other to Teach About Our Prayer and Liturgy?

To understand the prayer life of a vibrant religious tradition, one would have to read about, experience, and understand the two narratives of public prayer and individual spirituality. Of all the topics in this volume, prayer and liturgy is the most difficult to understand and to teach about the other. This difficulty is not due to an unwillingness on the part of believers to share prayer or to pray for each other, nor is it that Judaism, Christianity, or Islam practices incomprehensible, esoteric rituals. Rather, the experience and reality of prayer and liturgy is only completely known by the "insiders," those who know and believe what they are praying from an intellectual, emotional, cultural, and moral perspective. These complex and beautiful layers of encounter with God individually and in community impel people to choose with whom they share their lives and what direction their lives take. The papers that follow in this section are helpful for setting the stage for further exploration into the mystery of prayer, but much more joint study needs to be pursued in the areas of prayer and liturgy, aesthetics and the Scriptures of each religion. Several additional themes emerged from the conference.

First, in one sense, prayer and liturgy are a conversation, a relationship and relating of God's people to God, the world and others. This conversation asks about and reflects an individual's and a community's destiny and meaning in response to God's revelation. Participants during the conference on prayer and liturgy critically examined how ideologies have separated us from seeing the other as someone who conscientiously prays with God. In the past, by acting as if God did not listen to the prayers of the other, or was only focused on one particular group, this has diminished a fuller experience of the presence of God's apprehension in every worshipping community. Instead of worshipping God as the One who is above all, the effect of claiming God exclusively for one community's prayer has had the unfortunate result of seeking to domesticate and control God and God's capacity for revelation.

Second, in addition to inspiring faith, liturgical symbols can also prevent us from praying more deeply, especially if those symbols evoke feelings and actions that are immoral, such as anger, prejudice, haughtiness and violence. The cross, for example, is a paradox and a stumbling block to some, as well as the central symbol to inspire prayer in others. One participant said, "Symbols, images, art, music, beauty, are beyond the rational. They are visceral and are lodged in our marrow." The worship setting and the liturgical context of symbols are powerful remedies to counter the secular abuses of religious symbols throughout history and at present. Also, it was noted that the placement of a building within a community as well as its specific architecture are symbols that speak to the hearts of believers. The participants agreed that prayer is fostered through a building's attention to sanctuary, holiness, reflection, community, hospitality, liturgical movement, pilgrimage, beauty, transcendence, light, and educational elements (statues, stained glass, inscriptions etc.). However, it was also pointed out that historical circumstances have led to many places of worship being built as fortresses and overbearing monuments to particular leaders. Such symbols remain, but contemporary religious symbolic communication to the community has the opportunity for a renaissance. For example, when a religious community builds a house of prayer in conversation with the other religions of a city, rather than proceeding with the intention of "outdoing" or overwhelming the other houses of prayer, then all will benefit from such cooperation.

Third, the *Shema Israel:* "Hear O Israel: the Lord our God is one, and you shall love the Lord your God with all your heart, and with all your soul and with all your might" (Deuteronomy 6:4–5), can be a starting point for prayer. This prayer helps the person in prayer to focus on the proper relationship of humans to God in a God-human partnership to repair and perfect this world. The Abrahamic faiths all believe in the oneness of God and God's desire for unity and peace among all people.

Such belief has potential for praying for each other as well as coming together to pray.

Fourth, Catholics need to pay attention to the visceral impact of liturgy on Christian formation, especially since the Mass is the context in which most Catholics are able to engage their faith tradition most regularly. Christians have often asserted the dictum *lex orandi, lex credendi*. However, it is also important to remember that the Church's *lex credendi* (rule of belief) may require changes in the *lex orandi* (rule of prayer), especially as Christians have come to understand their relationship with others and God more deeply. This is particularly important in the growth of the Church's relationship with the Jewish people, which was articulated in the corrective and reformative efforts of the 1965 Vatican II document, *Nostra Aetate*. The document calls Christians to celebrate their "intrinsic bond" with the people and faith of Judaism and their respect for Muslims. "Sounding the depths of the mystery" that is rooted in these "spiritual ties," *Nostra Aetate* (# 4) suggested that Catholics revisit their liturgy in this new light. Some of the Catholic participants noted that it was probably a fair criticism that Catholic liturgical documents are slow in coming to reflect this deeper understanding of the Catholic-Jewish relationship. Without adequate catechesis in the Catholic community, for example, the traditional "Reproaches" employed in some Good Friday services, the "O Antiphons," some liturgical hymns, as well as the liturgical usage of polemical New Testament texts, such as Matthew 27:25 or the Apostolic speeches in the beginning of the Acts of the Apostles, may be construed as a denigration or supersession of the Jewish people. While acknowledging the differences in the leadership structure of Catholics from Jews and Muslims, the participants of the conference agreed that it would be of great value to furthering the dialogue process if additional efforts, suggestions and encouragement also came from Jewish and Muslim faith communities.

Fifth, several people raised the importance of each person's being nourished in his or her own community of faith. When or if guests join a congregation to pray together, it is not appropriate to tinker with that faith community's integrity and traditional worship by watering it down. Certainly one's sensitivity is heightened and an authentic sense of hospitality is rightfully extended but the presence of the other serves as an invitation to be authentic in one's worship of God. When we are secure in our commitments, we can be open to those of other faiths. For example, at the start of the World Day of Prayer for Peace at Assisi in October 1986, Pope John Paul II said that he was "a believer in Jesus Christ and in the Catholic Church, the first witness of faith in Him, but. . . it is in fact, my faith conviction which has made me turn to you."

Sixth, one participant said that there is a rich Christian liturgical heritage that needs to be cautious about misappropriating Jewish celebrations or creating syncretistic rituals. This is especially difficult for Christians who grew out of a Jewish milieu and Jewish prayer tradition. The challenge remains for Christians and Jews to neither cloud their differences nor overreact by objectifying each other by placing the other on pedestals. At the same time, numerous points of connection between Jews, Christians, and Muslims were raised, particularly with regard to prayer, piety, fasting, wisdom, the unknowable mystery of God, and prophecy as a gift. Also, liturgical expressions that are common to all cultures and religions—processions, preaching, times of silence, chanting, music, art, gestures and body movements, liturgical vestments, liturgical environment, incense, light, dance, bells—have different meanings depending on the context of the prayer, but they are all "dialects" in the human vocabulary used to worship God that may be shared.

Seventh, the three Abrahamic traditions share a substantial common Scripture. In Judaism and in Islam, the Word of God is primarily revealed in the Torah and the *Qur'an,* while in Christianity that same Word is understood in the person of Jesus Christ. There is the natural predilection towards the metaphysical when explaining the Word, whether as eternal, preexistent *ruah, dabar,* Wisdom, prophecy, or the Word made flesh, or the Word made Book. These understandings surface the need for a more textured theory of revelation in relationship to the ways we teach about each other's prayer and liturgy. In particular, interreligious dialogue might uncover more points of concurrence by focusing on the response of the faith community in prayer and social justice, more than on the Word, per se. This proper response to God of the community could, in turn, lead to deeper prayer and enlivened liturgy.

Eighth, a further opportunity for study and prayer is the cooperative exploration of a more extensive interreligious theology of one's life as a journey or pilgrimage of prayer. The conference participants noted that prayer and pilgrimage are enduring themes for all three faith traditions and a common theological backdrop and religious experience leading to God. At Jerusalem, Rome, Mecca, and many other destinations, one leaves his or her place of security, journeys to a sacred place, despite danger and risk, and experiences a feeling of equality with other pilgrims. The pilgrim comes before God's presence in a new way and performs a sacred duty or celebration that transforms him or her. It was noted by the participants at the conference that Psalms 120–134 are hymns of pilgrims walking up to Jerusalem where they were greeted by the residents, "Blessed are you who come in the name of the Lord!" It was also suggested that Torah is a pilgrimage, belief is a pilgrimage. For the Christian participants, pilgrimage is also a model for life and the Christian journey focused on Jesus. Prayer and contemplation is a pilgrimage towards God, whether God's Holy Mountain, or internal Seven-Storey Mountains, or the journey of prayer that one may take on one's prayer carpet. Finally, it was pointed out by one of the participants that for many people, pilgrimage becomes real in their witness of social justice and serves as a remedy for exaggerated, overspiritualized faith.

Ninth, one participant reminded the group that it was God's presence that challenges all religions to show profound respect to one another. As such, God's presence challenges us to seek further understanding on many important questions that still remain. Examples include: Does the wideness of God's mercy call into question our own narrowness? Because the Abrahamic faiths take history seriously, there are often strong connections between culture, faith, and civilization. Can we begin to eliminate the elements of supersessionism in our prayers and liturgies while remaining faithful to our beliefs? Can prayer unite us? How many ways are there to the One and only God? Does God distinguish between our prayers? Is there still a place in our faith traditions for prophetic prayer? Is there a unity that transcends our particularity that can be expressed in prayer and liturgy? Do we gather together and pray, or gather to pray together? Whatever we decide in our local and universal faith communities, have we forgotten in our newness of this relating, the time and place for silence and contemplation together? Can we allow time to reflect, to be quiet, to listen to inspired readings, to sing?

Finally, it is clear that individual prayer is a necessary preparation for authentic dialogue and study to take place, especially if one's prayers are fundamental individual and communal processes that remember and celebrate who an individual is and who we are called to be as people of faith. As such, prayer is about responsible relationships. Through prayer and meditation, we open ourselves to God and each other. Prayer and meditation help to bring to the surface transcendental values, which can inspire ethical action for justice and peace that counters materialism and disrespect for life. Prayer leads us to recognize the other as an equal, perhaps even a sibling. In short, there is a divine dimension to the dialogue process and if entered with reverence and respect, dialogue can be a sacred encounter pleasing to God.

R E U V E N   K I M E L M A N

What Do We Want Others to Teach About Jewish Prayer and Liturgy?

Jewish prayer is marked by its multitude of blessings, its understanding of the body and soul, its advocacy of the love of God, and its vision of redemption. With regard to the body, it underscores the religious significance of the workings of the body and its relationship with the soul. With regard to the love of God, it works out the relationship between the love of Torah and the love of God. With regard to redemption, it presents a three stage development starting with the individual moving to the community or people of Israel and ultimately incorporating all of humanity. All three themes appear in the daily liturgy in this order respectively.

The Body and the Soul

The following blessings are recited upon awakening and after all body eliminations. Its regular recitation spurs awareness to what degree we are at least our bodies. It states:

> Blessed/praised are you, Lord our God, Sovereign of the universe, who with wisdom has fashioned the human, creating within him openings and closures. It is well-known to you that were one opening to close down or one closure to open up one could not exist in your presence a single moment. Blessed/praised are you, Lord, healer of all flesh who sustains our bodies in wondrous ways.

This blessing is juxtaposed to one expressing gratitude for being granted a pure soul. It goes as follows:

> My God, the soul you gave in me is pure. You created, you formed it, you breathed it into me; you keep body and soul intact. And you will in the future take it from me and restore it to me in the hereafter. So long as the soul is within me I thank you, Lord my God, God of my ancestors, Master of all creation, Lord of all souls. Blessed/praised are you who restores souls to lifeless exhausted bodies.

The first blessing helps us experience our body as a delicate assembly of divine marvels. Its intricate assembly of portable plumbing manifests an ingenious design attributable only to the great Designer. Its recitation after urination and defecation makes us aware that the delicate balance between well-being and illness is a function of a well-operating body. Precisely at the moment of greatest vulnerability we become aware of its great viability. The blessing reinforces the idea that the body partakes of the wisdom of God. Indeed, through it one realizes that the divine image exceeds one's soul. On the contrary, it is the interplay of matter and spirit that places us on the borderline of the divine.

The second blessing underscores that the soul implanted in us is in mint condition—any marks on it are our own. This awareness often inspires a lifelong sense of gratitude within us and maybe even longer since the mini-reunion of body and soul upon awakening in the morning anticipates the great awakening that awaits us in the future.

Why, one may ask, does the liturgy begin with a prayer for the body followed by one for the soul? Why two separate blessings as opposed to integrating the two into one? Apparently, each has its way of helping us to become aware of ourselves. Together they present us with a sense of self that includes both coordinates. We are the juncture between body and soul, not the battlefield. In saying both prayers, we feel no hostility between matter and spirit, only polarity. Never quite sure whether we are more an ensouled body or an embodied soul, we are happy to be trustees of two gifts, caretakers of both. Reciting both blessing reminds us that our personhood evolves out of the interaction of body and soul, just as water is the combination of hydrogen and oxygen, for a body without a soul is a corpse and a soul without a body is a ghost.

As all official blessings, the first blessing begins "Blessed are you, O Lord our God, King of the universe." This beginning reinforces the idea that in prayer, one's sense of self has three coordinates: God, community, and humanity which can be charted as follows:

"Blessed are you" = self – God

"O Lord our God" = community – God

"King of the universe" = humanity – God

Judaism seems to have a blessing for everything. Many people find that blessings evoke in them the awareness of living in God's world. The blessings serve to awaken their consciousness to see the world as God's temple. According to the Bible, it is sacrilegious to appropriate objects from the Temple for personal use. If the whole world is the Lord's Temple, one might fear that all is off limits. Judaism teaches otherwise. When we utter a blessing, we become a resident of God's Temple and within the precincts of the Temple, we may partake of all its objects. If my mind and my lips are in the right place, nothing is off limits.

Blessings help Jews to see ourselves as guardians rather than landlords of the universe. With this in mind, we realize that reaping benefits from the world without proper acknowledgement is similar to an act of stealing. Acknowledging God's Lordship grants us entrée to his entire domain. No aspect of the world is devoid of spiritual resonance. As Elizabeth Browning invited us to see: "Earth's crammed with heaven, And every common bush afire with God; But only he who sees takes off his shoes; the rest sit round it and pluck blackberries." By taking off our shoes we are able to see.

Further, "See and thou shall praise" is the leitmotif of the blessings. As Isaiah urged us, "Lift high your eyes and see who created these." (40:26) Is not the divine handiwork visible if one were but to lift up one's eyes? Does not all creation rhapsodize its Maker. Through blessings, creation is both noticed and exalted. Indeed, it is sanctified, for what is sanctification if not the perception of the connection with the divine? Thus, we are to recite 100 blessings a day to satisfy minimum daily spiritual requirements. Some say that the number corresponds to the hundred sockets that held together the structure of the ancient tabernacle. By reciting daily a hundred blessing, the spiritual structure of creation becomes transparent.

These blessings take note of good smell and taste, rising up and lying down, the intake of food and the elimination of waste. Blessings also celebrate the spectacle of lighting, falling stars, majestic mountains and stretches of wilderness. The roar of thunder has its praise, the sight of sea and rainbow its response. Beautiful animals, indeed beautiful people, elicit blessings as do trees in blossom, the new moon, new clothing, new houses (some even say the first taste of legitimate sexual delight) and on and on. Indeed, we will be held accountable, says the Talmud, for forgoing those pleasures that God would have us relish.

"For the sake of making life as superlatively polished as the most sublime work of art," advised Henry James, "we ought to notice the ordinary." Through diurnal blessings, the common, the mundane become permeated by the extraordinary and the sacred, and the routine becomes special.

The Love of God

The second blessing is the morning recitation of the *Shema* ("Hear O Israel, the Lord our God, the Lord is one") which makes the case for the election of Israel as an expression of God's love. The argument is contained in the first half and last part. The conclusion is encapsulated in the peroration:

1. With everlasting love have you loved us, O Lord our God
2. With great and exceeding compassion have you cared for us.
3. Our Father our King, for the sake of our ancestors who trusted in you
4. As you taught them the statutes of life
5. So grace us by teaching us.
6. Our Father, merciful Father, have mercy upon us
7. by making our hearts understand, discern, listen, learn, teach, appreciate, do, and fulfill all the words of your Torah in love.
8. Enlighten our eyes in Your Torah and make our hearts cleave to your commandments.
9. Unite our heart to love and to revere your name.
....
10. You have chosen us from among all peoples and tongues
11. You have granted us access to your great name.
12. [To praise/acknowledge you and declare your unity] out of love. Blessed are you, God, who chooses his People Israel out of love.

The version that opens with the declaration of the beloved, "With everlasting love have you loved us, O Lord our God" inverts God's profession of love in Jeremiah 31:3—"With everlasting love have I loved you"—in order to serve as Israel's acknowledgement of divine love. The liturgy, following Jeremiah (31:3) grasps revelation as God falling in love forever with Israel. Such love is attested to by the gift of the Torah pointedly called "the statutes of life," in which God is entreated to grace Israel by teaching them as he taught their forefathers. By presenting the Torah and its teaching as gifts of love, the blessing promotes its conclusion that God "chooses his people Israel in love."

The addition of the love motif to that of the Torah distinguishes this blessing from the standard blessing on the Torah. The latter opens with blessing God for having "chosen us from among all the nations and given us His Torah," and closes with blessing God for "giving the Torah," without any mention of love. Moreover, in contrast to presenting the Torah and its commandments as obligatory accompaniments of the covenant, they appear here as expressions of God's beneficence.

The parallel blessing of the evening service also stresses the link between love and teaching. Adhering to the syntax of the Hebrew, it translates as follows:

1. With everlasting love the house of Israel, your people, have you loved,
2. Torah and commandments, statutes and laws, us have you taught.
3. Therefore, Lord our God, when we lie down and when we rise up,
4. we shall speak of your statutes and rejoice in the words of your Torah and in your commandments forever,
5. for they are our life and the length of our days,
6. and we will recite them day and night.
7. May your love never depart from us.
8. Blessed are you, O Lord, who loves his people Israel.

The parallel syntax and Hebrew rhyme scheme of lines 1 and 2 converge illustrating that God's election-love is expressed through teaching Torah and commandments. Lines 3 and 4 reinforce the idea that God's everlasting love (*olam*), as expressed through such teaching, is reciprocated by a commitment on Israel's part to rejoice and study the teaching and commandments forever (*le'olam*). As with the morning version, so the evening version presents the loving God as a teaching God. The appearance of a pedagogical relationship as a metaphor for love is quite remarkable. One would have thought that the appropriation of Jeremiah's use of "everlasting love" would have triggered off analogies of connubial or parental love to express the relationship of God to Israel as does Jeremiah himself. The absence of other expressions suggestive of the connubial relationship found in Isaiah, Jeremiah, Hosea, or the Song of Songs is clear evidence that their love metaphors are not those of the blessing. Even those of Deuteronomy and Jeremiah, which do provide much of the language of the blessing, lack the pedagogical image. Whether or not the metaphor of God as a loving teacher is of liturgical coinage, it achieved its most prominent expression through the liturgy.

Why did an educational metaphor gain pride of place over a nuptial one? The deployment of a pedagogical image instead of a marital one for the language of love is all the more perplexing in view of the significance of the marriage metaphor for the biblical covenant. For our purposes, the relationship between God and Israel undergoes three major developments. In Deuteronomy, the relationship is primarily described in terms of ancient suzerainty pacts or treaties. In the prophets, the marriage metaphor predominates. In the liturgy, the theme of reciprocal love is presented through a teaching metaphor. Since God becomes Israel's loving husband long before becoming a loving teacher, it is surprising that the teacher metaphor won out notwithstanding the availability of both marital and pedagogic metaphors for the revelation on Mt. Sinai.

The absence of the marriage metaphor may be attributed to its difficulty in serving effectively as an analogy for both love and sovereignty. Teachers more easily command fealty, exercise mastery, and elicit love. Moreover, the image of the beloved as student may be responding by anticipation to the command that the love of God be reflected in the instructing of children/students as found in the first two biblical sections. If love is reciprocated by teaching, then it might well have been initiated by teaching. To quote Wordsworth's Prelude: "What we have loved, others will love, and we will teach them how."

Finally, the idea of portraying revelation as an act of teaching Torah confirms the rabbinic idea of teaching Torah as an extension of revelation. The biblical books helpful in tracing the image of God as a loving teacher are Deuteronomy, Isaiah and Psalms. In Deuteronomy, Moses is the teacher and God is the commander. In Isaiah and Psalms, God is also a teacher. A midrashic treatment of the verse from the Psalms (119:68)—"You are good and beneficent, teach me your laws," exemplifies the type of teaching that led to the liturgical image.

David said to the Holy One, blessed be he, that God was good and beneficent to them [Israel] in every matter and he taught them his Torah and commandments and laws as it says, "I am the Lord your God, teaching you for your own good, guiding you in the way you should go. If only you would heed my commands." (Isaiah 48:17–18) The statement of David from Psalm 119:68, "You are good and beneficent, teach me your Torah;" along with the citation of Isaiah (48:17), "teaching you for your own good," epitomize the ideology of our blessing. By rereading the revelation as portrayed in Deuteronomy through the prisms of the Psalms and Isaiah—with their idea of a beneficent, teaching God—the blessing opens the way to perceiving the teaching of Torah as an expression of divine love. After all, if God's beneficence entails teaching Torah, his love can do no less.

Having established that God's love entails teaching Torah, let us look at the terms for the Torah in the next line. Line 2 consists of four curricular subjects: Torah, commandments, statutes, and laws. These four appear as a unit four times in Scripture. Their order here matches that of 2 Chronicles 19:10. Their context of revelation, however, matches that of the other three, namely, 2 Kings 17:34, 37, and Nehemiah 9:13b, all of which refer to the revelation of divine law. Indeed, Nehemiah 9:13b is preceded by the telling phrase, "You came down on Mt. Sinai and spoke to them from heaven" (9:13a), which is exactly the backdrop of the blessing. Similarly, a Genizah version of the festival liturgy, which could easily double for the second blessing of the *Shema*, cites the same verse from Nehemiah after stating, "You chose Israel . . . and brought them close in love around Mt. Sinai." The order of the four also points to the practice of linking Torah with commandments, and statutes with laws, a practice that turns out to be an inversion of the way they are paired in 2 Kings 17. The inclusion of all four terms reinforces the Sinaitic setting of the blessing wherein the giving of Torah was first grasped as an expression of love as well as the position of Deuteronomy (4:14) that other statutes and laws were promulgated along with the Decalogue.

The other innovation of the blessing consists in orientation line 5— "for they are our life and the length of our days"—to the study of Torah as well as to the commandments. In Deuteronomy 6 and 30, this phrase refers to observance of the commandments alone without any mention of the study of Torah. Moreover, Deuteronomy 30:20 predicates residence on the land upon the keeping of the commandments, saying: "By loving the Lord your God, heeding his commands, and holding fast to him, you shall have life and length of days upon the land. . . ." In contrast, the blessing omits any reference to the land while underscoring the significance of Torah study by affirming that "we will recite them day and night." The idea of reciting the Torah day and night alludes to Joshua's admonition to keep the Torah constantly in mind—"Let not this book of Torah cease from your lips, recite it day and night" (1:8), and the description of Psalm 1:2 of the man who delights in the Torah by reciting it day and night.

In rabbinic parlance, the term "recite" became the technical term for the articulation of the *Shema*. By associating "they are our life and the length of our days" with the twice daily recitation of the *Shema*, line 5 confirms the rabbinic position of fulfilling the biblical mandate of constant involvement in Torah study through reciting the *Shema* day and night. By excluding any reference to the land and by introducing the study of Torah, and the love of God as expressed through the teaching of Torah, the unit of verses was formulated to sound fully biblical while accommodating the Torah-centered agenda of the Rabbis.

Both morning and evening versions of blessing advocate the study of Torah and the heeding of its commandments as the means of disclosing divine love. The juxtaposition of the request for enlightenment in the Torah and for help in cleaving to the commandments with the request for the unification of the heart in the love of God is not without significance. By so linking the two, the morning version presents both study and observance of the Torah as paths leading to the love of God. The Torah and the commandments serve the dual function of expressing divine love and of providing the means for its reciprocation. It is through sensing divine love that its human counterpart is sparked. God gave us Torah and commandments out of love. By complying with them, we can come to requite that love. The repetition of "love" in the morning blessing, fairly evenly distributed among the beginning, middle, and end, weaves its way through the whole passage. Indeed, the first and last word is "love." These ubiquitous glimmerings of love are also refracted in what appears in some versions as a nuance of Psalm 86:6— "Unite our heart to revere your name"—to "unite our heart to love and to revere your name" (line 9). The inclusion of love here underscores the love of God in contrast to the oft-mentioned love by God elsewhere in the blessing.

Blessing holds that experiencing the grace of guidance provided by the commandments leads to the conclusion that they were given in love. In contrast to the position that compliance with the commandments expresses love for God, blessing maintains that compliance with the commandments engenders such love. Nonetheless, blessing goes beyond noting the typical reciprocal love between God and Israel as found in the following midrash: "Israel says: 'You shall love the Lord your God,' and God says to them: 'With everlasting love have I loved you.'" The priority of God's unconditional love is thrown into relief when contrasted with an example of God's conditional love such as the following midrashic statement: "Whoever loves God and complies with His commandments and teachings, God also loves him." By positioning this blessing about God's love before the *Shema's* demand to love God, the point is made that we are to love the God who loved us first. As love is best aroused by the awareness of being loved, the commandment to love God becomes liturgically an act of reciprocity—"the love of the lover," to use Rosenzweig's expression. It is God's love of Israel that produces a God-loving Israel. Thus, the blessing goes on to entreat God to render one capable of returning the love. Clearly, the experience of being loved nourishes the capacity to love.

The second section of the *Shema* and the second blessing both seek to bring about compliance with the commandments. Their approaches, however, diverge. What the former achieves through threats of punishment, the latter achieves through assurances of love. The punishment motif is entirely absent from the blessing framework. Positive reinforcement alone serves as its motivation. Through such motif conversion, a pact of loyalty became a covenant of love, thereby transforming a biblical affirmation of fealty into a liturgical expression of ardor.

Redemption

The theme of redemption permeates Jewish liturgy. As above, the example below derives from the daily liturgy. It is taken from the *Amidah*, where a form of this prayer appears in every Jewish statutory service. The primary theme of the *Amidah* is redemption. The focus is on blessings 17 and 18 which complete the drama of redemption, the former through God's return to Zion and the latter through his universal acknowledgement. Blessing 17 concludes: "May our eyes behold your merciful return to Zion. Blessed are you, O Lord, who restores his presence to Zion." It is followed by blessing 18's theme of God's universal acceptance. Together they conform to a motif that recurs throughout the Prophets and the liturgy, especially on the High Holidays; namely, that the precursor of the universal recognition of divine sovereignty will be God's return to Zion.

The argument of blessing 18 on the subject of God's universal recognition deserves special attention. It begins: "We praise [*modim*] you," followed by a listing of examples of divine beneficence that elicit thrice daily praise. The central part of the blessing goes as follows:

1. We will thank you
2. and tell of Your praise
3. for our lives which are in your hand
4. and for our souls which are entrusted to you
5. and for your miracles which are daily with us
6. and for your wonders and kindnesses at all times.

Strophes 1 and 2 lay out our intention; strophes 3–6 state the reasons why. The whys are divided into two categories: strophes 3 and 4 express gratitude to God for our lives and souls; strophes 5 and 6 enunciate praise for God's miracles and wonders. Thus, 1 is to 3–4 as 2 is to 5–6, making for an a-b-a-b structure. According to this construction, the blessing says: We will thank you for our lives that are in your hand and for our souls that are entrusted to you. And tell of your praise for your miracles which are daily with us and for your wonders and kindnesses at all times. The blessing concludes, saying: "For all of these [i.e., strophes 3–6] may your name be blessed, exalted, and extolled, O our King, continually and forever," followed by the expectation that "all the living shall worship you." What began as "we praise/acknowledge you" culminates in "all the living shall praise/acknowledge you." God is exalted threefold: at all times, for all time, and by all. As a bridge between the particular and the universal, the blessing pointedly lacks any reference to distinctively Jewish grounds for thanks and praise of the divine. Its inclusive perspective invites all to share in recognizing the divine margin common to all human life.

Some even extend the "all" of "all the living" forward in time to include the resurrected and others extend it vertically in space to include heavenly beings. But it is precisely the extension of the "all" horizontally to all humanity that lets the *Amidah* share in the common liturgical climax of the universal acknowledgement of divine sovereignty. The shift from our acknowledgement of God to his universal recognition frames much of the eschatological core of the rest of the liturgy. The best-known example is the linking up of the *Aleynu–Al Kain* sections of the Rosh Hashanah kingship liturgy which, as the *Modim* of the *Amidah* begins with Israel alone bowing in worship (*modim*) and concludes with all humanity following suit upon their realizing the sovereignty of God. The shift from us to everyone is reflected also in the rabbinic midrash of the *Shema* verse: 'The Lord is our God,'—for us; 'the Lord is one,'—for all humanity. 'The Lord is our God'—in the present period; 'the Lord is one'—in the future period, as its says, 'And the Lord shall be king over all the earth, on that day the Lord shall be one and his name one.' Unlike non-eschatological liturgies that tend to move from the universal to the particular, eschatological liturgies, such as the *Amidah*, tend to move from the particular to the universal.

In sum, the *Amidah* as a whole advances from personal through national to universal redemption, each stage involving the progressive realization of divine sovereignty from self to community/people to humanity. This process of progressing from self to humanity through the people/community is such a liturgical staple that it frames some of the most prominent elements of the liturgy such as Psalm 145, the *Shema* verse, and the blessing formula.

In conclusion, it might be said that it is precisely our awareness of ourselves as body and soul which enables us to love, and be loved by God and look forward to redemption.

TSVI BLANCHARD

Response to Rabbi Reuven Kimelman

The paper presented by Rabbi Reuven Kimelman is extraordinary. Of course, there is always more to add and inevitably, a basic Jewish approach to anything, especially prayer, must emphasize certain themes, the ones which lead to deeper questions. On the one hand, when people articulate their spirituality through their theology, there tends to be an emphasis on the distinctiveness of traditions. On the other hand, when people talk about the *human* situation or spiritual experience that provokes the desire to do something positive, they then talk about the human situation. Rabbi Kimelman's talk was on the public communal prayer, which is found in liturgical classical texts. My presentation will focus on the private spiritual life. I believe that in order to understand the prayer of any religious tradition, one would have to include both the public and the private aspects of prayer, and one understanding of the tradition would be inadequate without the other. In sum, Jewish liturgy and the Jewish spiritual life are two complementary expressions of Jewish prayer.

To begin, while public religion proclaims and talks about the sacred texts, the language and content of private religion is more about anecdotes. When Jewish people got together, they often told stories of sages and saints. I understand saints in all traditions to be those who make the traditions alive to their members. It is these stories of spiritually unique people that help keep the tradition living and vibrant. Traditions, by virtue of being traditions, are always receding into the past. It is the lives of sages and saints that help make our traditions real and present to us.

The renewal of interest in Jewish spirituality that began about 30 years ago was heavily focused on scriptural text study. It also had a misguided overemphasis on Jewish mystical texts as an alternative to rabbinic Judaism. By now, of course, much of this emphasis has passed away. The renewal that is most powerful now has to do with the rediscovery of the spirituality available in traditional Jewish sources and their use in non-orthodox settings, for example, traditional religious meditation, song, and dance. Today, there is a conscious Jewish search for spiritual experience.

Perhaps the center of all prayer and the center of all human life (because life can become prayer) is *Kavannah*—mystical *intention*. In later Jewish piety, the notion of spiritual intention is re-understood as purity of motive. For example, there is a story about a very holy man, the founder of Hasidism, an 18th-century religious movement. He traveled with his disciples, and they came to a synagogue when it was time for the afternoon prayer. They were about to enter when the master stopped and looked into the room. The disciples watched and wondered what to do. Why was he waiting? Why wouldn't he go into the room? After some time passed, he said to his disciples, "I cannot go in. It is too crowded in there." He somehow knew the words of prayer that had come out of the mouths of the congregants who had been in the room. They had been thinking about a business deal or how to saddle a horse or what they were going to say to their spouse. These prayers filled the room, but because of the wrong *Kavannah*, there would be no place for these prayers to go. Hence there was no room left for the master. This focus on intention lies at the heart of teaching about Jewish prayer. It has to do with purity, and in the end, the task is somehow to find a way in which one transcends the demands and concerns of the present situation and gives one's heart fully to God.

Here is another story about pure intention: Imagine that a king, that is God, gave two tasks, one to one servant and one to another. The first servant's job is to cut precious stone. The king said, "If you cut these stones, be very careful of how you do it. And, when you have finished cutting these stones, I will give you as your reward whatever extra is left over." To the second person, "Your job is to clear out the king's storage rooms. Get rid of all the rubble I do not need. At the end when you finish, you will get as a reward whatever is left over from your job."

Ordinarily one would think the stone cutter is the lucky one. He finished the job and received gems as payment. And, the other poor guy, he has to clean out the storage rooms and what does he receive as a reward? He gets the junk. And yet, this is a mistake. The person cleaning out the junk knows that he will receive nothing and has nothing to look forward to. The only reason he is doing his task is because the king asked him to do it. The person cutting the precious stones will probably spend all of *his* time thinking about the reward of leftover gems. The "junk cleaner" becomes a model for ideal spiritual prayer. Prayer is an activity that purifies because the person learns not to desire the reward of precious stones, but instead to "get rid of the junk." The "junk" inside the human being is to be transformed by what is left over when it is gone, namely, more room for God.

In Judaism, private prayer has the ability to improve the world through the transformation of the self to serve God alone. Jewish prayer emphasizes purity of motive and intent, a striving to avoid complicating the activity of prayer by having ulterior motives. We teach: beware false promises that your prayer will reward you with an enormously successful life. The heart must sincerely love God without ulterior motives. The object of prayer is God and God alone.

This is not easily done. Most people come to prayer for mixed motives. Of course, we prefer to come to prayer by enjoying the desire to serve God in a positive way. But prayer in pain and tears is also acceptable. If a person is afflicted by trouble, suffering, poverty, or pain, bear in mind that what has happened is a powerful reminder to pray to God who is present in the world and engages with the human condition despite all of its poverty and pain, despite its exile from the Garden of Eden. If one can come to prayer for love of God alone, that is best. But many people cannot do so. They need to begin with pain, then search to move from their pain to love of God. Purity of heart is not necessarily something with which one needs to begin. One can also begin with motives that are less noble and animated such as, "This hurts, and I want it to go away," or "I feel lost for a moment or separated, and I need to reconnect with others."

During prayer, people sometimes think about doing something that is wrong. The more they think about it, the more interesting the sin becomes. They get lost in the thought, and the next thing they know, they snap out of their thoughts at the end of prayer and discover that the experience has actually been sinful. People can respond to it by telling themselves to repress sinful thoughts. And yet, the Jewish tradition of prayer is not fundamentally about repressing one's thoughts. Ultimately, one cannot expect to deal with human nature without embracing the physical. Rather than driving one's evil impulses away during prayer, the tradition encourages one to allow all thoughts into prayer and then slowly and gently stop from giving them the power that comes from our curiosity and confusion. We need to stop investing in these sinful thoughts and transform them by "resting them" in God's presence.

Take as an example a man daydreaming about a woman. What is he going to do with this daydream in prayer? As he is thinking that the woman is beautiful, he may slowly allow it to become clear that if God created this woman and she is beautiful, then God must be even more beautiful because God is the source of all beauty. This classic Platonic reflection moves away from a particular instance to the general idea of beauty as a whole, from fragmentation or distraction to wholeness and focus. An alternative is to take the erotic and the idea of beauty and then refocus it upon one's wife. Certainly, the erotic and the mystical go together, in most traditions. A Jewish emphasis is to take the erotic and then to embody it in one's wife so that, for example, sexual relations between husband and wife on the Sabbath become an affirmation of the divine-human unity. We do not seek to overcome the body. Rather we embrace the physical in order to experience the spiritual. Some have suggested the example of a candle inasmuch as the wick cannot burn unless there is wax, and the wax is the body. The body is a necessary element to achieve spiritual enlightenment. (This is not easy to do, but if one has a loving spouse it may be possible; of course, without such love, it is disastrous.)

So we can see that even erotic attractions are a piece of the greater whole. One of the advantages of prayer, that attempts to connect directly to the presence of God through the search for wholeness, is that our heart gradually develops the kind of methods of contemplation that move towards purity. Instead of assuming that we start with purity, we assume that we are going to journey towards it, but not without contemplation. Contemplation takes our lived experience and forms it into a loving and beautiful reality. In prayer, one can know that he or she is having an experience of God's presence and one can experience the removal of boundaries that gives way to a wholeness—something that can no longer be recognized as temporal. I suggest that Christians and Muslims are also no strangers to this experience.

In prayer we are attempting also to participate in the kind of experience that transforms whatever stands in the way of God's Will. Prayer can move us beyond notions of being trapped in our ego and its sense of personal suffering, loneliness, or in a desire for personal gratification. Through prayer we can get past these traps to see suffering as something that we share as part of the human condition, as part of the world condition. We may even see this connection in prayer as something that completes, corrects and repairs the world. God becomes present in the world in something akin to a feminine presence (*Shechinah*). Of course, there is holiness and wholeness in all creation, but sometimes God appears to us to be at least as "self-divided" as we are. Prayer allows us to put those seemingly divided parts back together. God appears to us as both mercy and judgment, and in prayer both mercy and judgment are brought together.

We all come to life with the most primitive theology: God is a large parent who always loves us, always takes care of us, always smiles on us, and thinks we are terrific. For most human beings, that infantile theology of childhood stays in place until they experience their first profound loss. Then they become enraged that someone important has been taken away from them.

In Hasidism, in Jewish mysticism, a person works through this anger by beginning with it. One imagines at some profound level the *imago*, the image of the parent can never be eliminated. But the individual must return to this image constantly and transform it. We want to please our parents. We want them to smile and to love us. But, everyone has parents and everything one sees—even the birds and the trees—everything has a source, "parents" so to speak. And moving outward in contemplation, the world as a whole, also has a source, "parents." Gradually one moves from the desire to please one's biological parents, to the desire to unify that which is separate in the world and thereby, "please" the whole human family, even God. In this case, one's search is to unify that which is fragmented on both the levels of intellect and of meditation. In Hebrew, these are *yichudim*, contemplative unifying of apparent opposites.

But Hasidic prayer is not simply that a person thinks these thoughts. The person experiences and deeply feels in his or her entire being the exile of humanity and God. They experience unification, and the desire to provide satisfaction. This kind of spiritual movement is about the entire person being drawn together with others to God, leaving behind one's individual being and coming to recognize ecstatic joy. In Hasidism, for example, there is often singing and dancing and in the end, the participants are full of joy. Why is this important? I once attended a Pete Seger concert in New York. Everyone was singing and I was together with my friends singing along with this great American folk singer. We were all having a terrific time, and we really saw and felt a kind of peaceful unity. Similarly, in mystical prayer, we begin by being caught up in the experience of singing and dancing together, and for a moment we leave our individual selves, our egos behind. For a moment, the boundaries between things that make us seem separate are gone. For a moment, the need to be restricted to one's personal biography is gone, although one's personal biography still finds a place in the larger biography of the universe as a whole. For a moment, one does not think about community as an interesting idea, but as an actual experience of ecstasy with God. It is momentary, but it is real.

There is more than this community unity. I think Muslims and Christians have no trouble identifying with the need for being solitary and seeking solitude as part of their prayer experience. Similarly, in the Jewish tradition there is a belief that it is important for humans to talk to God every day in the vernacular by themselves, individually, telling God everything that is on their minds, seeking God and asking help from him. This is not a contemplative act. This is not an attempt to gain ecstasy by understanding the universe in a more profound way. In some Hasidic traditions, one goes off alone, outside the city, in an attempt to seek God in solitude. Once there, the person sits and pours out his or her heart to God using his or her native tongue. Speaking in the tongue that moves you, one will experience feelings that are beyond formal language. This is an intimate kind of personal prayer that is not ritualized prayer. In fact, it is deliberately deritualized and deliberately "deautomates" the self. In essence, it attempts to annihilate the self by stepping into a situation of dialogue with God where one discovers that dialoguing with God leaves the person profoundly changed, the way all good dialogue changes people.

Although good interpersonal dialogue starts with the condition that nothing about the other must be changed, nonetheless as we truly come to understand another, he or she will change us. And if one has not known this wonderful experience, then get married and watch it happen. When we begin to talk with others without fear, there is no way in any intimate relationship that the participants can remain the same, unless he or she is incredibly rigid—a person that rigid would not be interested in dialogue to begin with. Similarly, when we talk to God and pour out our hearts to God, we also change. Of course, the criticism of this kind of prayer is that it is nothing more than free psychoanalysis where one talks to God for an hour every day and there is no bill. Unlike your psychiatrist who supposedly knows the truth and will one day review with you the "true interpretation" of yourself, God says nothing. Nonetheless, I believe that there is a transformative process active in constantly reaching out to another who, in this instance, is seen as a personalized God. Only in solitude and solitary talk with God, our creator, can we abolish all our lost and evil traits to the point where we completely negate our material existence and become reabsorbed into our elevated spiritual roots. Of course, there is always prayer beyond talk. I do not know of any religious tradition that does not cultivate the capacity for silence as preparation for prayer as well as an active expression of prayer. Many prayers focus upon liturgy and many of us can suffer from too many words, but the ultimate praise to God is through silence.

To conclude, being devoted to God through a purity of intention is a starting point and also an ending point to the place where one is going, namely purity of heart. One achieves purity of heart through contemplation and the search of ecstasy by understanding fully what the universe is actually like—the condition of exile and separation that brings us to prayer. This begins with one's own life, body, feelings, worries, desires, and is transformed gradually into a larger picture. This can happen in two ways—either by directly contemplating a religious theory, which in prayer becomes more than a concept, that becomes one's life direction. Or this can also take place by direct and unmediated conversation with God in a solitary and secluded place, which also transforms an individual. In all of these things, do not trust me. Seek the face of God to test these things for yourself. Test these ideas by checking the traditional sources, but more important, by trying, using, and seeing the ways in which these reflections could be an integral part of your personal prayer life. The more profoundly it resonates with parts of your own tradition, the more profoundly we will discover that understanding the other, understanding those people we thought were different from us, is just as much a way of connecting to others—and it is truly possible to connect on the deepest levels—as it is a way to distinguish ourselves from others. This is not a totally imaginary world. It is only once removed from the real world, and finding the imaginary world may turn out to be the salvation of the real one.

CARDINAL CARLO MARIA MARTINI

What Do We Want the Other to Teach
About Catholic Liturgy and Prayer?

Thank you very much for your warm reception and openness to grow in understanding. I greet all of you with peace. I feel privileged and honored to be able to participate in this effort by a Catholic university to promote interreligious dialogue and understanding. But, I also have to confess that I feel somewhat inadequate to speak about this topic. Of course, I love prayer and liturgy and I have some practical experience of Catholic and Christian prayer and liturgy, but I am neither a theologian nor a liturgist. I am a simple bishop who has served God through and in the experience of daily prayer and liturgy.

I am enthusiastic about the topic and I understand the title, "What Do We Want The Other to Teach About Our Liturgy and Prayer?" in the most simple way. I feel this is a very important topic and an excellent approach. I will begin by recommending some sources on Catholic prayer and liturgy, followed by some misunderstandings that I would like the other not to commit. I will conclude with some simple and foundational ideas concerning prayer and liturgy.

I would like to indicate some readily available sources through which a member of another religious community could gain simple and clear ideas about Catholic prayer and liturgy. First of all, the Constitution on the Sacred Liturgy (*Sacrosanctum concillium*) is still the best summary available on the liturgy. It was promoted in 1963. A second document I would suggest is the Catechism of the Catholic Church in the sections dedicated to liturgy. Especially on the Eucharist, I recommend numbers

1135 through 1209 and from number 1345 through 1419. Also, I think the sections devoted to Christian prayer, numbers 2559 to 2865, which includes an explanation of what is called the Lord's Prayer are the best pages written in recent times about Christian prayer. And, finally, I would suggest one other document, a letter from the Congregation for the Doctrine of the Faith, issued in 1989 called, "A Letter on Some Aspects of Christian Meditation." In these documents, one can find a true and simple explanation of what I will now summarize by emphasizing a few ideas, which I consider from my experience to be important points to avoid misunderstandings and to promote accurate mutual knowledge. I shall emphasize five items—two on liturgy and three on prayer.

First, liturgy constitutes a vital part of Catholic experience and consists of rites and prayers which are in themselves noble and simple, and therefore, accessible to ordinary people, especially after Vatican II when local churches began to celebrate liturgy in the vernacular. Nonetheless, liturgy remains always a deep mystery. A profound understanding of what is going on in liturgical action is achieved only gradually and partially in the course of one's entire life. In other words, I am not sure that I understand exactly and completely what is going on in a Eucharistic service. I have still to learn a great deal with God's continual direction. A reason for this mystery is that liturgy in the Catholic understanding is not primarily a human action, but is a response to the risen Jesus Christ in his Church and through his Church. In other words, I would say that Jesus, during his life, experienced and offered prayers, including praise of God with deep joy and exultation. In a similar way, today his community is assembled around him and united with him in his glorious life praying, rejoicing, and thanking God. Although he remains invisible, he is present through signs such as bread and wine. Therefore, Christian liturgy is intentionally simple and visible, but remains mysterious and, in a sense, inaccessible.

A second point: The Eucharist, the Real Presence of Jesus present in the form of bread and wine among his people gathered in liturgical worship, is the source and summit of Christian life. The Eucharist is where we draw our strength and courage as well as our inspiration and hope as we journey towards the heavenly banquet. I will not go further explaining the Eucharist as such, which is the center of Christian liturgy, nor would I desire that it should be explained in a first attempt to show what is Christian liturgy. I understand Eucharist as something so mysterious that it can be grasped adequately only by living a fully Christian life. Therefore, to avoid misunderstandings, I will not go further but to say that the Eucharist leads Christians to the heart of God and it is a love that is immeasurable.

Third, similar to Christian liturgy and worship, prayer is a great mystery. I think I have prayed all my life, but I find it difficult to explain exactly what happens when I pray. When I pray, there is certainly an activity of body and mind, an activity of speaking and thinking. But, at its deepest levels, prayer is an action of God's Spirit in us. In prayer, we become one with the Risen Lord through his Spirit who moves the heart and tongue to prayer. Also, we do not readily or frequently experience the deepest levels of this action.

Fourth, prayer may be understood as an elevation of the mind to God or as a request of something from God. In this second sense, prayer is a request where a Christian believes that his or her prayer is effective, is working in a mysterious way, but that the effect may remain unknown. And this causes anxiety or suffering for many Christians who pray because it is impossible to understand the ways of God, even by earnestly-praying Christians. Nonetheless, Christians who pray trust that God accepts their prayers and responds to them, giving to them what is best for the body and soul, and for those for whom they pray. But Christians are often not sure what would be best for them or those they are praying for. So prayer becomes an exercise of faith and hope without any expectation of an immediate reward.

Fifth, Christian prayer should not to be understood or confused with a kind of psychologically deep experience. Christian prayer is offered through a human mind and body, but transcends them. Prayer requires giving oneself to God's mystery and requires surrendering to God's action without the pretension of controlling what is experienced. In this sense, prayer is an exercise of pure faith and hope, not of intellectual or psychological human achievement. The latter may be good and fruitful, but there is not the same sense of satisfaction or deep fulfillment as when one comes into contact with a direct and conscious experience of God's love and action.

I have mentioned these five points to help avoid misunderstandings about Christian liturgy and prayer. However, by mentioning these possible misunderstandings, I have already alluded to some positive aspects of Christian liturgy and prayer, but I will limit myself to a few remarks, first on prayer and then on liturgy.

Christian prayer is manifold and can assume many forms. I dare to say that there are more types of prayers in the world and in the history of Christian spirituality than types of leaves on all the trees of the world. But one form of prayer that is particularly important to Christians comes from the influence of the Hebrew Bible, notably the Psalms. To understand Christian prayer as it was and as it is, one must consider the examples of prayer contained in the Bible, especially the Psalms. Christians are very grateful to our Jewish brothers and sisters for the treasury of the Psalms, which we have gratefully received from them. Christians pray psalms at every Eucharistic liturgy and every time they pray the Liturgy of the Hours, for example, at Morning and Evening Prayer. The Psalms have also given great comfort to those at wake and funeral services. For prayer to be Christian prayer, the person praying must be in some union with Jesus Christ, which is why even the Psalms are read in light of the risen Jesus Christ who is the fullness of revelation for Christians.

The 1989 document on Christian meditation which I mentioned earlier, summarizes some further characteristics of true Christian prayer. First, Christian prayer is founded and dependent upon Christian revelation, and therefore, with the revelation of God's glory shining through Jesus Christ. All the teaching of the Church about God and Jesus Christ and human salvation should be mentioned in order to understand Christian prayer. But, this goes beyond the scope of this paper. In any case, I would emphasize that Christian prayer is always performed in union with the Church, the faith of the Catholic Church, and in the midst of the Communion of Saints and their understanding of Christian life. Further, a central line of Christian prayer is the request, "Thy will be done," which is part of the Lord's Prayer and is the prayer of Jesus before his Passion began. Every Christian prayer has to be measured with this rule: Is this bringing me to a real identity with God's will? We say from and through the heart, "Thy will be done."

Finally, I shall say a few words on the liturgy. Although liturgy is celebrated every day in the Christian community, a most special and sacred day for Christians is the day of Sunday, which recalls for Christians the resurrection of Jesus Christ from the dead. Sunday is the Sabbath, the main day of the week for the celebration of the Eucharistic liturgy. Christian liturgy invites active participation and celebration by the entire community, although there are different functions within the Christian community. There are ministers who have special functions as leaders to act in Christ's person for the service of all members of the Church. But liturgy is not private prayer or devotion, but is the participation of an entire community praying together. The liturgy is celebrated by people who have received the Sacrament of Baptism in union with Jesus Christ, and it is connected with the offering of one's life and one's intentions to God's glory. As such, there is a strong union between liturgy and the everyday life that people lead according to the law of love. Both liturgy and the challenges and blessings of everyday life go together. If there is a disconnect, then the liturgy has become too removed, as if an abstract, unrelated drama, or the Christian community has failed to respond appropriately to the conversion called for by the Word of God proclaimed in the liturgy.

The liturgy is filled with symbols, words and actions that refer primarily to Christ's saving actions when he lived among us. Christian liturgy uses various forms to express or mediate prayer, such as music, dance, and sacred icons as means and ways to represent the invisible and ever-present God. But, even with the use of these mediations, honor and glory and adoration are given only to the invisible God. The Eucharistic meal and the proclamation of the Word of God in the Scriptures are the center around which these other noble forms gather.

The liturgy is also celebrated according to different times of the year, which is called the liturgical year. There is a liturgical calendar, which may have differences according to different rites or traditions within the Church. For instance, in my dioceses of Milan, we do not follow the Roman rite, the Roman calendar. We follow another rite called the Ambrosian rite (from St. Ambrose), and so is done in many different churches, especially in eastern Christianity. In any case, this calendar reflects the Christian view of the history of salvation and especially reflects on the events of the Jewish people in the Hebrew Bible and the saving acts of Jesus Christ as they are recounted in the Gospels. Throughout an entire year, the main facts of the People of God and of Christ are recalled in the course of the Christian liturgy. The liturgical calendar also remembers especially Mary, the mother of Jesus, and many

Christians who are considered to be martyrs or saints. They were human beings, but in them we honor God who has sanctified them with the grace of his Spirit, and we see in them an example of life according to the teaching of Jesus.

I have presented a few points that I believe will help others teach about Christian liturgy and prayer. I think that dialogue among religions is more vital than ever, especially in order to show that religion is opposed to every kind of violence. An effective dialogue requires time, listening and understanding in order to be sure that we have grasped truly what the other thinks. Therefore, I consider this theme to be of the greatest importance and relevance. Ultimately, however, our efforts will only bear fruit if they are motivated by the love of God and authentic respect for the dignity of our neighbor. This means that we—all God's people—must pray tirelessly for each other to follow God's will in our lives.

DAVID L. COPPOLA
MARGARET PALLISER, OP

What Do We Want the Other to Teach About Christian Prayer and Liturgy?

Jesus Christ: The Center of Christian Prayer and Liturgy

At the heart of all Christian prayer and liturgy lies a mystery: the incarnate Word of God, Jesus Christ, Son of God and risen Lord of history. To begin to understand Christian prayer, one must see it as both an expression of and response to God's self-revelation in the person of Jesus of Nazareth and the fullness of Christ's Body, the Church. In their prayer and liturgy, Christians are joined *to* Christ and *in* Christ. Like Saint Paul, they proclaim that it is the "Christ who lives in me"[1] who offers praise, worship, and supplication to God.

God's Self-Revelation in Human History

For Christians, as for Jews and Muslims, God is the Creator of the universe and is actively involved in the lives of human beings. God has revealed wonderful things, acting in human history in significant and meaningful ways, and this same God continues to communicate to humans through events, or revelation, to this very day. This divine activity transforms human history and encourages people to live lives of integrity, courage, and love.

Christian prayer and the substance of living the Christian life is based on an openness to the ever-increasing revelation of God at all times and places. Christian prayer begins and ends in a relationship with the Trinity; one God, three persons, Father, Son, and Holy Spirit. Each person of the Trinity is fully God in a coequal, coeternal, infinite, and indivisible relationship with each other. This mysterious, loving relationship is described in Church teaching as *perichoresis*, a "dancing" in and around the table and returning to the starting place, wherein all three persons of the Trinity mutually share in the life of the others, and none is isolated or disconnected from the actions of the others.

Christians are drawn into the loving relationship of the Trinity in prayer and liturgy. A Christian's prayer arises in response to gifts that God has given, and the liturgy is the community's participation in the Divine Liturgy, the "dance" of the Trinity. As Father, God calls forth the creation of the universe. Jesus Christ, begotten of the Father before all time, is the Word become incarnate, who walked among humanity and shared the good news of salvation. Jesus prayed that his followers would be one: ". . . as you, Father, are in me and I in you, that they also may be in us, that the world may believe that you sent me."[2] The Holy Spirit, the Comforter and Counselor, illuminates the mind and enkindles a Christian's desire to pray. In his letter to the Romans, Saint Paul talks about the Spirit who ". . . helps us in our weakness; for we do not know how to pray as we ought, but that very Spirit intercedes with sighs too deep for words."[3] An example of the revelation of the Trinity is found in the gospel according to Matthew:

> And when Jesus had been baptized, just as he came up from the water, suddenly the heavens were opened to him and he saw the Spirit of God descending like a dove and alighting on him. And a voice from heaven said, "This is my Son, the Beloved, with whom I am well pleased."[4]

One of the most fundamental prayers of Christians, called "The Sign of the Cross," is both a reminder of the ignominious death that Jesus suffered for the redemption of the world as well as an attestation to the full revelation of the Christian God: One uses one's right hand, lightly touching the forehead, the heart, and the two shoulders, to trace a "cross" on oneself while saying, "In the name of the Father and of the Son and of the Holy Spirit." This simple, yet profound gesture, is used both publicly and privately to begin liturgical celebrations and times of individual and communal prayer.

The Christian's Response to Revelation: Prayer and Ethical Living

The revelation of God's Trinitarian life of love calls the believer to respond by living a life of holiness, a life of faith, hope, and love in ever-deepening relationship with God. Christians are invited to live in covenantal community, faith, law, love, justice, and witness. Individual believers create space and opportunity for prayer as they seek to repair the world by their words and good deeds. Liturgy and worship are the response of the community of believers to God's gift of life and God's overtures of love.

Similarly to Jews and Muslims, Christians look for signs of God's presence in their daily lives. Whether God's revelation is experienced through the Scriptures, Tradition, leaders, holy persons, liturgy, nature, or the critique of unjust situations or structures, prayer remains an essential activity that helps believers continue on their journey toward holiness.

Holiness is not solely the work of an individual's disciplined meditation and prayer, although setting time aside for prayer and meditation inevitably opens one to God's will. Christians are called by God to holiness through the community of faith, the Church. The pilgrim People of God have the responsibility to follow God's will in their time and, as appropriate, to support and challenge members of the community to live lives worthy of their calling by Jesus. Christians also have a special responsibility to work for social justice and to care for the poor and the outcast. As such, social justice and apostolic work can also be seen as a form of prayer, doing God's work of redeeming and improving the world. The Christian's mouth and hands become God's vessel to speak truth and work for the good. To discern the proper course of action to take in the world requires constant prayer—communication with God and openness to God's word.

Jesus, the Source and Center of All Christian Prayer

For Christians, the person of Jesus of Nazareth was God's perfect self-revelation in a particular time and place. Just as those who walked and talked with the Jesus in first century Palestine came to know God's love through their personal experience of the historical Jesus, the Christian comes to know that same God through the person of the risen Jesus Christ.

As a devout Jew, Jesus had a deep relationship with God whom he called *Abba*, "Father," a relationship marked by personal prayer in solitude as well as public prayer in the synagogue. Faithful to the teachings of his religion and conscientious in fulfilling his responsibilities within it, Jesus prayed in the synagogue often and was actively involved in the discussions and arguments about the religious issues of his day.

Little is known about the early life of Jesus, suggesting that his life was that of a normal, working-class Jew living in Palestine at a time when the Romans ruled. Later in his life, Jesus was led by God to become a public preacher, teacher, and healer, and was often called "Rabbi." He preached a simple message: "The time is fulfilled, and the kingdom of God has come near; repent, and believe in the good news."[5] One summary of his teaching is known as The Beatitudes:

Blessed are the poor in spirit, for theirs is the kingdom of heaven.
Blessed are those who mourn, for they will be comforted.
Blessed are the meek, for they will inherit the earth.
Blessed are those who hunger and thirst for righteousness, for they will be filled.
Blessed are the merciful, for they will receive mercy.
Blessed are the pure in heart, for they will see God.
Blessed are the peacemakers, for they will be called children of God.
Blessed are those who are persecuted for righteousness' sake,
    for theirs is the kingdom of heaven.[6]

Jesus gathered followers around him, and he taught them by word and deed. When they asked him, "Lord, teach us to pray,"[7] Jesus gave his disciples what is probably the most recognized Christian prayer. Followers of Jesus pray the "Our Father" or "Lord's Prayer" often in their private individual prayer, and they recite it together at almost every public worship service:

Our Father, who art in heaven, hallowed be thy name;
Thy kingdom come;

Thy will be done on earth as it is in heaven.

Give us this day our daily bread;

And forgive us our trespasses

As we forgive those who trespass against us.

And lead us not into temptation,

    but deliver us from evil. Amen

This most privileged of Christian prayers also illustrates the deep Jewish roots that Jesus drew upon in his relationship with God as well as his strong focus on forgiveness.

After Jesus was put to death by crucifixion by the Romans and was raised to new life, his early followers gathered in community to pray. Although they experienced adversity and even persecution, these early followers drew their strength and inspiration from Jesus who sent them his Holy Spirit to guide them on their journey. Fearlessly, the disciples of Jesus preached about he who had been raised from the dead as the one to whom all could look for redemption. Most, if not all, of these early disciples were Jewish, and they continued their Jewish practices with the additional distinction of believing in Jesus as the Messiah, the Christ ("anointed one"). They participated in the temple services, shared the stories of his life and teachings, and gathered together for meals during which they commemorated the "breaking of the bread"[8] (now known as "Eucharist"); they also shared their material goods with those who were less fortunate, especially widows and orphans.

The stories and teachings of Jesus were initially spread by word of mouth. Along with some Jewish liturgical and synagogue practices, these stories and teachings became the basis for public worship for Christians. Eventually gathered together in collections resulting in four classic texts—Matthew, Mark, Luke, and John—, the gospel[9] places Jesus at the center of a follower's life as the source and inspiration of that life. To this day, Christians look to Jesus as their model, doing as he had taught and acted, even to turning the other cheek to an aggressor and praying for one's enemies.

One traditional way to summarize the ways that a follower of Jesus should act is articulated in what are known as the corporal and spiritual works of mercy. The corporal works of mercy are to 1) feed the hungry; 2) give drink to the thirsty; 3) clothe the naked; 4) visit the imprisoned;

5) shelter the homeless; 6) visit the sick; and 7) bury the dead. The spiritual works of mercy are to 1) admonish the sinner; 2) instruct the ignorant; 3) counsel the doubtful; 4) comfort the sorrowful; 5) bear wrongs patiently; 6) forgive all injuries; and 7) pray for the living and the dead.

Christian Liturgy—The Prayer of the Church, the Body of Christ

In his thoughtful reflections included in this volume,[10] Cardinal Carlo Maria Martini, SJ, emphasizes that Christian prayer, especially within the liturgy, is profoundly mysterious. In order to begin to grasp the nature of Christian liturgy, one must approach another of the great mysteries of the Christian faith: the Church as the Body of Christ.

As Christianity matured with the guidance of the Holy Spirit, the community gradually discerned deeper meanings about the mystery of Jesus, the Word of God become flesh, who has "pitched his tent among us."[11] By the fourth century, Saint Augustine was preaching and teaching about Christ in three ways: as the eternal Word of God, Second Person of the Trinity, in and with the Father; as the Word Made Flesh, the incarnate Son of God; and as the *Totus Christus*, the Whole Christ in the fullness of the Church.[12] Christians respond to God's self-revelation in Jesus not only by prayer and good works, but also by participating in the mystery of Christ as members of his Mystical Body, the Church, which unites head and members, both on earth and in heaven. This mysterious union of Christ and his Body is source of the Christian mystical prayer and the Church's rich liturgical and sacramental life.

The early Christian prayer forms were deeply rooted in the Jewish prayer tradition and Scriptures. Over time, prayer, liturgy, and sacraments developed to reflect the central place of the Paschal Mystery (Christians' belief in the suffering, death, and resurrection of Jesus). The Christian Sabbath became Sunday in remembrance of the day of Jesus' resurrection from the dead. Christians gather on Sunday each week for the celebration of the Eucharist to recall the life, death, and resurrection of Jesus.

For Catholic Christians, the sacrament of the Eucharist both signifies and, at the same time, causes that which it signifies: the Body of Christ—the Christian community and its unity. Just as many grains of wheat make one loaf and individual grapes are pressed to make one cup of wine, so individual Christians become one living body—the Whole Christ, his Mystical Body. By their participation in the celebration of the Eucharist, Christians become all the more that which they already are, the Body of Christ. This understanding of Eucharistic participation reflects a theology that sees the Eucharist as both the sacrifice of Christ and the sacrifice of the Church. Christians offer themselves along with Christ.[13] A recent articulation of this theology can be found in the theme of the 2005 Synod of Bishops: The Eucharist—source and summit of the life and mission of the Church.

Often publicly celebrated in the Christian community, the sacraments are privileged rituals that both celebrate and affect the Christian's relationship with God and with the other members of the faith community. The sacraments of initiation into the Christian community are Baptism (welcoming the new member, often infants, into the community), Eucharist (coming to the table of the Lord), and Confirmation (assuming the responsibilities of a full, adult member in the community). Other sacraments in some Christian churches include Reconciliation (asking for God's pardon for sins), Matrimony (the covenantal commitment between a couple, the Church, and God), Holy Orders (public ordination to ministry and leadership), and the Anointing of the Sick (to strengthen members of the community struggling with their health).

The central role of the Jesus in the life of the believer, as well as in all of human history, may be best captured in the concluding phrase of many of the prayers of the liturgy and sacraments, where the prayer is made "through Christ our Lord. Amen." This centrality of Jesus' life, death, and resurrection was also reflected in the evolution of holydays and liturgical seasons, e.g., Advent, Christmas, Epiphany, Lent, Holy Thursday, Good Friday, Easter, Ascension, and Pentecost. A feature of Catholic liturgy and its calendar is the remembrance as well of Mary, the mother of Jesus, and the saints—human beings who lived exemplary lives of prayer and good works and who continue to inspire Christians to see God's presence shining through their humanity. A traditional prayer, part of which can be found in the Gospel of Luke,[14] recalls the angel Gabriel's announcement to Mary that she had been chosen to be the mother of the Savior:

> Hail Mary, full of grace! The Lord is with thee;
> blessed art thou among women,

and blessed is the fruit of thy womb, Jesus.
Holy Mary, Mother of God, pray for us sinners,
now and at the hour of our death. Amen.

The Christian Community's Life of Faith

It is safe to say that one cannot be an individual Christian—at least not
for long. At its core, Christianity has a conviction that God's revelation
is best experienced in the faith community. Communal faith statements
or creeds appeared as early as the second century. One of the first codified
statements of Christian belief is known as the Apostles' Creed:

> I believe in God the Father Almighty, Creator of heaven and earth;
> and in Jesus Christ, his only Son, our Lord; who was conceived by the
> Holy Spirit, born of the Virgin Mary, suffered under Pontius Pilate, was
> crucified, died, and was buried. He descended into hell; the third day he
> arose again from the dead; He ascended into heaven, is seated at the
> right hand of God, the Father Almighty; from thence He shall come to
> judge the living and the dead.
>
> I believe in the Holy Spirit, the Holy Catholic Church, the
> Communion of Saints, the forgiveness of sins, the resurrection of the
> body, and life everlasting, Amen.

In addition to official communal statements of belief such as creeds,
Christians understand their communal prayer or liturgy as an attestation
of their belief. The ancient Christian principle, "What the Church prays,
the Church believes" (*lex orandi, lex credendi*) highlights the importance of
communal prayer as a form of catechesis and transformation. Therefore,
much time and attention is paid to the preparation of the Christian liturgy. Those involved in the different ministries or roles during the service
(hospitality ministers, presiders, readers, eucharistic ministers, preachers,
musicians, etc.) often view their part as a sacred service or prayer to God
on behalf of the community. Care is also taken to prepare the worship
space in the proper seasonal environment, symbols, art, etc.

Despite the propensity of Christianity to codify its public prayers
into official books and translations, there is a remarkable diversity in the

celebration of public prayer. On the local level, communities celebrate their faith through their own unique expressions of common prayer and celebrations of faith: Days of Reflection and Renewal, blessings, Morning and Evening Prayer (Liturgy of the Hours), Scripture sharing groups, prayer meetings, parish songfests, festivals, processions, and retreats. Additionally, in the Catholic Church the many spiritual traditions practiced by communities of religious men and women (Augustinians, Benedictines, Dominicans, Franciscans, Jesuits, etc.) offer deep and refreshing wells of prayer and resources for the Church. It should also be noted that, as Catholics and the Churches of the Reformation continue to grow closer together in their understanding of theology as it relates to the Word, their forms of prayer and liturgical celebration continue to evolve based on this new relationship of mutual respect.

As a final note on communal prayer and worship, Christians believe that Jesus Christ came to redeem the whole world. As such, there is often an emphasis placed on the salvation of souls during communal prayer, with Jesus as the sole agent. The salvation of souls is seen as the way that God's reign of peace on earth will be accomplished.

The Individual Prayer Life of Christians

Having explored Christian liturgy as the prayer of the community, we will now focus briefly on the more individual and private prayer life of the Christian. Note that we are avoiding the use of the phrase "personal prayer" because one's person is deeply involved in both communal liturgy and private individual prayer. Whether one prays as an individual or as a member of the community, authentic prayer is always personal.

The depth of one's unique personal relationship with Jesus is known only to God, and the path to which he or she is led by God is most sacred. A person's conscience is his or her most sacred core and sanctuary, and it is in this sacred space that God speaks. There are innumerable paths to holiness, but what is clear is that they all have times of solitude, retreat, reflection, renewal, and prayer as part of the journey, treasured times which, in turn, lead one back into the world to help to repair it.

Christians are encouraged at a young age to pray informally to God, asking for guidance and protection. This intimate and direct form of communicating with God helps adults also as they seek to recenter their daily lives in the world in God. As a Christians mature in the faith, they also learn traditional prayers and devotions, exercises that have inspired countless generations of Christians before them. Examples of traditional devotional forms of prayer include: grace (or "blessing") before and after meals, quiet meditation, devotional reading of the Scriptures, family prayers, bedtime prayers, Stations of the Cross (recalling the journey of Jesus on the way to his death), rote prayers, spontaneous prayer, Eucharistic devotion, the rosary, novenas, meditation walks, retreats, sacred music/hymns, and pilgrimages. All of these devotions may be practiced in the company of others. It is also important to note that the concerns of one's personal faith journey and home life are always included in the community's public worship.

To conclude, we would like to leave the reader with a prayer. Recorded in Luke's gospel, "The Magnificat" is a beautiful prayer of praise whose Jewish roots are evident. Placed on the lips of Mary as she awaits the birth of her son, these words inspire the Christian to follow God's will in humility and courage, trusting that God's reign of mercy, justice, and peace will dawn.

> My soul magnifies the Lord,
> and my spirit rejoices in God my Savior,
> for he has looked with favor on the lowliness of his servant.
> Surely, from now on all generations will call me blessed;
> for the Mighty One has done great things for me, and holy is his name.
> His mercy is for those who fear him from generation to generation.
> He has shown strength with his arm;
> he has scattered the proud in the thoughts of their hearts.
> He has brought down the powerful from their thrones,
> and lifted up the lowly;
> he has filled the hungry with good things,
> and sent the rich away empty.
> He has helped his servant Israel,
> in remembrance of his mercy,
> according to the promise he made to our ancestors,
> to Abraham and to his descendants forever.[15]

Notes

1. "I have been crucified with Christ; and it is no longer I who live, but Christ who lives in me" [Galatians 2:19b–20a]. NOTE: All scriptural passages in this paper are taken from the *New Revised Standard Version Bible*, © copyright 1989, Division of Christian Education of the National Council of the Churches of Christ in the United States of America. Used by permission. All rights reserved.

2. John 17:21.

3. Romans 8:26.

4. Matthew 3:16.

5. Mark 1:15.

6. Matthew 5:3–10.

7. Luke 11:1–4. Cf. Matthew 6:9–13.

8. "They devoted themselves to the apostles' teaching and fellowship, to the breaking of bread and the prayers. . . . All who believed were together and had all things in common; they would sell their possessions and goods and distribute the proceeds to all, as any had need. Day by day, as they spent much time together in the temple, they broke bread at home and ate their food with glad and generous hearts, praising God and having the goodwill of all the people." Acts 2:42, 44–47a.

9. The literal meaning of *gospel* is "good news."

10. See immediately preceding chapter by Cardinal Martini: *What Do We Want the Other to Teach About Catholic Liturgy and Prayer?*

11. "And the Word became flesh *and lived among us*; and we have seen his glory, the glory as of a father's only son, full of grace and truth." [John 1:14] Literally, "and pitched his tent among us."

12. The earliest teachings on the "Body of Christ" can be found in the letters of Saint Paul (Corinthians 1 & 2, Ephesians, Romans, Galatians). The term "Mystical Body" did not appear until the Middle Ages and became especially popular in the last century as a result of Pius XII's encyclical on the Church, *Mystici Corporis* (1943).

13. "The Eucharist is also the sacrifice of the Church. The Church, which is the Body of Christ participates in the offering of her Head. With him, she herself is offered whole and entire." *Catechism of the Catholic Church*, No. 1368.

14. Luke 1:28, 42.

15. Luke 1:46–55.

ABDUL HADI PALAZZI

What Do We Want the Other to Teach About Islamic Prayer and Liturgy?

In the name of God, the Merciful, the Compassionate: Peace, God's mercy and his blessings be upon all of you. I want to thank the Center for Christian-Jewish Understanding of the Sacred Heart University of Fairfield, Connecticut, for arranging this distinguished interfaith conference, and the Centro Dionysia, Rome, for hosting all of us in this marvellous place.

What I find particularly significant in our meeting is the idea of focusing our attention on how the other sees and teaches about us, on how the members of other religious traditions understand and interpret the sense of our methodology of worship. The Prophet Muhammad, peace be upon him, used to say, "Prayer is the cornerstone of Islam," and I think this can also be extended to Judaism and Christianity, and to many other religious traditions. Inside the Catholic tradition, for instance, we find the idea of the deep connection between the way of praying and the contents of belief, between *lex orandi* and *lex credendi*, and in general, one can say that prayer is exactly the context in which our belief is changed into action, in which the believer puts himself in touch with the One who is the object of his faith and the inspirer of his actions.

The first obstacle one finds in trying to explain the role of prayer and liturgy in Islam is connected to language. Normally one translates "prayer" with two concepts in mind which, in Islam, are quite different from each other; i.e., the ritual prayers (*salah* in Arabic), which must be performed in Arabic, according to detailed rules of purity, at appointed times with fixed formulas and a specific orientation of the body; and spontaneous prayer (*du'a'*), which is not dependent on particular rules and by which the creature can ask his Lord whatever lawful things he is in need of and in whatever languages he likes. With a certain percentage of approximation, one could translate *salah* as "service" and *du'a'* as "supplication." This would permit us to say that by his supplications, a Muslim is offering to God a praise that is human and fallible, while by his daily service he is offering God the praise through which God praised himself in the glorious *Qur'an*. The recitation of *Qur'an*, and in particular of its opening chapter (*al-Fatihah*) is in fact an essential part of each service, while the conditions of purity and the positions which the worshipper takes during the service are also prescribed in it.

By mentioning this point, we are referring to what is common to the three Abrahamic faiths. The central rites of each of the three religions— *tefillah* in Judaism, the liturgy in Christianity, and *salah* in Islam— includes the idea of offering to God not only our actions, our hopes, and our submission, but mainly his own Word, to the point that the service is not exactly a gift to him, but rather a restitution to him of the Word through which he created the whole universe. In Judaism and in Islam, the Word of God is essentially manifested in the form of the Torah and of the *Qur'an*, and this is the reason why their recitation has such a central point in Jewish and Islamic services, while in Christianity that same Word is not understood as transcendentally manifested in a revealed Book, but rather in the person of Jesus Christ. So, the liturgy of the Word in a Catholic Mass, for example, has a role that is preliminary to the Eucharistic liturgy, which is conceived as the offering of the Word of God on the altar as a sacrifice. The common point between the three religions is in understanding the service as restitution to God of the Word of God, which implies a participation of the creature to the same divine nature, but the manifestation of the Word is not understood by Christianity in the same way as it is understood by Judaism and Islam. Consequently, a Jew and a Muslim find no difficulty to immediately understand the similarities between their respective daily services, but they could find some difficulties in understanding the similarity which nevertheless exists between those services and a Catholic Mass. In the same way, a Catholic could be inclined to see in Jewish and Muslim services the mere repetition of words and prayers, without a palpable nature of offering, and even less of offering to God his own divinity.

This also explains how the passage from one language to another does not alter the nature of the Mass, as demonstrated by the Liturgical reformation and the introduction of vernacular languages after the Second Vatican Council, while the attempt to use languages different from Hebrew or from Arabic would necessarily alter the nature of the services in Orthodox Judaism and in Islam. This brings us to another difference: in Orthodox Judaism and Islam, the language of revelation is itself part of the revelation, which involves both the letter and the meaning of the Holy Book. A *targum* of the Torah in Aramaic or in any other language is not the Torah itself, but rather a human interpretation of the revelation. In the same way, Muslims believe that the *Qur'an* cannot be translated into another language, and that a so-called "translation of the *Qur'an*" is not a real translation, but rather an explanation of the meanings in a language that is different from Arabic. Islam also teaches that the *Qur'an* has seven levels of understanding, each of which is disguised by the level that precedes it. A translation of the meaning necessarily concerns the literal level only, which is the most external of the meanings; i.e., the one that is understood by every person who reads the *Qur'an* while knowing the Arabic language.

There have been some cases where the Muslim communities of Europe found some difficulties with non-Muslim editors of the translations of the meanings of the *Qur'an* in French, German, English, etc. From one point of view, printing an edition of the meanings of the *Qur'an* with the Arabic text was too expensive, and not conceivable for a publication intended for the general public. But from another point of view, the Muslim communities refused to give the title "the *Qur'an*" to a book that did not contain the original Arabic text, and insisted on the title, "Translation of the Meanings of the *Qur'an*," which the editors did not find palatable for the public, and considered it as a sort of eccentric and pedantic fixation. The issue was not so simple. In most of cases, the editors were not able to understand that, according to Muslims, a text including the translation of the meaning of the *Qur'an* in another language was not "the *Qur'an*" at all, but only its fallible interpretation. In the same way, the attempt of Mustafa Kemal to compel the Muslims of Turkey to read "the *Qur'an* in Turkish" during their services was a total failure, since not only the theologians, but also the laypeople understood that by doing so, one would lose the offering to God his Word, of praising God by the praise through which he praised himself.

This helps us to understand how the same notion of revelation is not identical in Islam and in Christianity. Christianity understands revelation as the divine inspiration of human authors, who wrote in their language, from their culture and with their intellectual background. Translating the contents of Christian revelation into new languages has no tragic consequences, and neither does the introduction of the vernacular into the liturgy. Latin was neither the original language in which the New Testament was written, nor the language spoken by Jesus or by the early Christian community. Latin was not a sacred language but rather, a liturgical language introduced at a certain stage of the development of the Church and in a period in which it was the *lingua franca* of Europe. At a time when this language is not spoken widely anymore, and the number of those who understand it is limited, the introduction of native languages could sensitively increase the participation of the believers to the liturgy. On the contrary, in Islam (similar to Hebrew in Orthodox Judaism), Arabic is not only a liturgical language, but a sacred language. Revelation is conceived as a communication, not only of the meanings, but also of the grammatical form. It is through the revelation of the *Qur'an* that one of the many dialects spoken by Arabs became a language that is spoken and understood from Morocco to Iraq. The revelation changed Arabic into the language of a nation, and its nature as language of the revelation of the *Qur'an* also prevented Arabic from evolving into different national languages.

As for the opening chapter of the *Qur'an* (*al-Fatihah*), it contains a synthesis of the whole book, and as noted earlier, its recitation marks the beginning of every daily service. It has a role in Islam that is analogous to that of the *Shema'* in Judaism and of the "Lord's Prayer" in Christianity, and is divided into two parts. The former contains a mention of the divine names, while the latter is a request of guidance and of protection against deviance. Its words mean:

1. In the name of Allah, the Merciful, the Compassionate
2. Praise be to Allah, Lord of the Worlds,
3. The Merciful, the Compassionate,
4. Master of the Day of Judgment.

5. Thee we worship and Thee we ask for help.
6. Guide us to the straight path,
7. The path of those whom Thou hast favored, not the path of those who earn Thine anger, nor of those who go astray.

Abu Hurayrah, one of the Companions of the Prophet Muhammad, narrated that he heard him say: "God, mighty and sublime is he, had said:

> I have divided the service between Myself and My servant into two halves, and My servant shall have what he has asked for. When the servant says: "Praise be to Allah, Lord of the Worlds," God says, "My servant has praised Me," and when he says, "The Merciful, the Compassionate," God says, "My servant has extolled Me." When he says, "Master of the Day of Judgement," God says, "My servant has glorified Me." When he says: "Thee we worship and Thee we ask for help," God says: "This is between Me and My servant, and My servant shall have what he has asked for." And when he says: "Guide us to the straight path, the path of those whom Thou hast favored, not the path of those who earn Thine anger, nor of those who stray," God says, "This is for My servant, and My servant shall have what he has asked for."

This mention of divine answers to the recitation of the creature leads us to understand in which sense the service is considered an intimate colloquium between the creature and his Creator. After completing the reading of al-Fatihah, the worshipper adds other verses from the Qur'an, and then bows, to show that he has not added anything to the praise which Allah gives to himself, but as only manifested by means of his created tongue, the uncreated Word which—according to Islam—is one of the divine attributes. After bowing, the believer stands again, and while coming back to the erect position says what means, "God listens to the one who praises him." This is a further clarification of the intimacy with the Divine Essence that is reached by means of the service, since God is not actually listening to the words of his servant, but rather to his own Word, which descended upon the tongue of his servant. As a consequence of this divine epiphany, the same individuality of the creature is temporarily abolished, and the worshipper prostrates with his forehead to the ground, symbolically coming back to the earth he came from. No individuality can stand in front of God, and the prostration represents a condition of extinction (*fana'* in Arabic) of the created nature, which is like a temporary mirage, like a contingent shining which made God's light manifested. Even so, extinction in God is not conceived in Islam as a permanent condition, but as the first stage, which in the Islamic terminology is referred as "the journey from the creation toward the Truth." It is immediately followed by subsistence in God (*baqa'*); i.e., by the "journey from the Truth toward the creation." After being extinguished in God, the creature is sent back to himself, and this is represented by the seated position, which follows the prostration. That subsistence through God, the coming back to one's createdness while remembering the precedent, relative union with God, is itself transitory, and is followed by the stage in which the creature is again extinguished through the "extinction of the extinction" (*fan'u-l-fana'*), which is represented by a second prostration.

These changes of status are obviously symbolic only for the wide majority of the believers. They represent the spiritual journey from the creation to the Truth and from the Truth through the creation, but this does not mean that each Muslim actually performs a spiritual journey during each of his daily services. Even so, Islam admits that the spiritual journey during the service has an ontological reality for the *awliya'*; i.e., for that category of beings that basically corresponds to the *tzadikim* of Judaism and to "saints" of Christianity. The same idea of a magic carpet in the folklore of the Islamic world and in popular Islamic literature (for instance, in "One Thousand and One Nights") hints at this same truth. The carpet stands for the place were the worshipper stands for the daily service, and the notion that someone can fly on a carpet is a sort of materialized transposition of the notion of spiritual journey.

These hints lead Muslims to seek the "secrets of the service" which should limit the tendency of those orientalists who deal with Islam as a mere "legalistic religion," as a religion which knows no priesthood, no rites and no sacrifice. In reality, by referring to *salah* as mere "prayer," and not as a Dominical service, its specific ritual depth is greatly undervalued. Probably this undervaluation of the ritual nature of the Islamic service depends on how differently ritual is conceived in Catholicism and in Islam. A Catholic Mass is centered on the Eucharistic sacrifice, but has plenty of accessory elements that concur with its celebration, such as special garments for the priest and for the deacons, incense, hymns, physical postures during the service, etc. From a technical point of view, the Islamic service has complex conditions, prerequisites, rules, etc. Each of the classical treatises of Islamic law opens by a series of chapters dedicated to the water with is used for the ritual washing and for the ablution which precedes the service, to the different daily services, and to their compulsory or optional constituents. On the other hand, Islamic rituality is concentrated in the person of the worshipper himself. His body, his mind, and his heart are all that are necessary for the service, which can take place in a mosque, a room, or even in an open space. Even the carpet is not an essential element of the service, but is only conceived as a means to ensure the ritual cleanness of the place were the worshipper puts his forehead.

Strangely enough, those same orientalists who tend to reduce the role of the daily service to "prayer" and who, in general, completely ignore those symbolic aspects of the service to which we have referred, are nevertheless inclined to describe Islam as a "legalistic religion," and tend to limit Islam to its legal system, the *Shari'ah*. On the contrary, the *Shari'ah* is only one aspect of Islam. It is a religion that is formed by *Shari'ah* (law), *Tariqah* (path), and *Haqiqah* (truth). While the *Shari'ah* deals with those external deeds that a believer performs with his body, the *Tariqah* deals with the inner disposition in performing those same deeds, and the *Haqiqah* deals with that knowledge of God that is the goal of both *Shari'ah* and *Tariqah*. *Tariqah* is also known as *Tasawwuf*, i.e., Sufism, which is, in respect to the *Shari'ah*, the kernel of a nut in relation to its nutshell. *Shari'ah* without Sufism is incomplete and mutilated, in the same way that Sufism without *Shari'ah* is. None of them—if isolated—represents the totality of Islam. One can say that all the deviations which historically took place inside the Islamic world arose from attempts to isolate one of those elements from its necessary complement. One of the early jurists of Islam, Imam Malik Ibn Anas, used to explain this reality by saying, "Whoever abides by Sufism without Law becomes a libertine, and whoever abides by Law without Sufism becomes corrupted, while whoever studies Sufism and Law together finds the Truth."

Another of the early jurists, Imam Muhammad Ibn Idris as-Shafi'i, clarified this same principle in one of his quatrains:

"Don't be exclusively a jurist or exclusively a Sufi:
For God's sake, I am giving you sincere advice.
The Law-only man lacks sincerity, while the Sufism-only one is
ignorant.
How is it possible for someone who is ignorant to prosper?"

The *Shari'ah* without Sufism is like a corpse without a soul, and Sufism without the *Shari'ah* is like a disincarnated soul which suffers from its separation from the body. The one who knows the *Shari'ah* without knowing Sufism will only perform void rituals, whose significance is inaccessible to him, while the one who knows Sufism without knowing the *Shari'ah* will not even know how the daily service must be correctly performed. That is the reason why, from the beginning of Islam until today, Islamic scholars have repeatedly dealt with the complement between "the science of the exteriority" and "the science of the interiority." In many cases—the most famous of which was Imam al-Ghazali—those whose authority was in matters of Law were also among the most outstanding representatives of Sufism.

At the beginning of the eighteenth century, a region of Arabia called Najd saw the emergence of Wahhabism, a puritanical and literalist sect which considered Islam "degenerated," and proposed a "reform" to be imposed on Muslims by means of coercion, terrorism and indiscriminate massacres. One of the goals of the Wahhabi movement was to reduce Islam to a mere formalism, bereft on any spiritual depth. The alliance of the Wahhabis, originally a gang of semi-illiterate desert marauders, with the British Empire in its war against the Ottoman Sultanate, led to the creation of the Kingdom of Saudi Arabia and to the appointment of the descendants of those marauders, the royal House of Sa'ud. The belief of the Wahhabis' official religion of the Saudi Kingdom was so primitive and narrow-minded that it did not spread outside of Arabia. The situation started to change with the discovery of oil, which made the House of Sa'ud one of the richest families of the world and a financial power in the worldwide economy. Saudis massively invested in Wahhabi propaganda, first in the Arab world, then in the Indian subcontinent, and finally, in the West. Paradoxically, the existence of the Soviet Union prevented the spread of Wahhabism to Uzbekistan, Kazakhstan, Turkmenistan, and Tajikistan, to the point that in the Arab world of today, the influence of

Wahhabism and modernism has considerably spread while Islam in the Soviet Muslim Republic survives in its pristine form.

Wahhabism has many of the features of Islam as conceived by the orientalists: is literalist, legalistic, rejects every form of Sufism, and reduces the practice of religion to the passive assimilation and mechanical application of rules. Nevertheless, in the eyes of Muslims it has a main defect: it is not "Islam" but rather an anthropomorphic cult which started three hundred years ago, and was rejected by the most eminent Muslim theologians. The orientalistic prejudices associated with the Wahhabi propaganda are preventing many Westerners from understanding traditional Sunni Islam, and from realizing the role Sufism has played in Islam since its beginnings. The consequence is that, apart from a very restricted group of specialists, most Westerners completely confuse Islam with Wahhabism and attribute to Islam those attributes that are notions of the Wahhabi belief.

With the constitution of al-Qa'idah and of the Taliban regime of Hamas, Wahhabism has returned to its primitive methodology. Like terrorism and indiscriminate carnages permitted the Wahhabis of old to occupy the Holy Places of Islam in Mecca and Medina, so the neo-Wahhabis of today are conceiving the idea of conquering the whole world by the same means. And they invest in the international network of terror by applying their profits derived from oil trade. If the Wahhabism of old was a menace for the Muslim inhabitants of Arabia, contemporary Wahhabism has become a menace for humanity as a whole. In front of that menace, in front of pseudo-religious legitimization of violence, bloodshed and terror, an increase in interfaith dialogue—especially among the Abrahamic faiths—is the best answer which can be given to those who plan to abuse the truth of Islam and to legitimize murder and terrorism "in the name of God." An interfaith dialogue that does not include the need for a joint defense of a common front against the menace of the pseudo-religious legitimation of terrorism is destined to be reduced to a mere scholastic debate; and the serious risk is that representatives of pro-terror extremism may find a way to get involved, even in interfaith dialogue, thus getting legitimized as authentic "religious representatives."

While I have dedicated most of this paper to clarify the distinction which exists in Islam between service and supplication, between ritual prayer and spontaneous prayer, I want to conclude by hinting at another form of prayer, *dhikr*, the continuous mention of the Divine Names. *Dhikr* in Arabic has the sense of "remembrance," and remembering God, being aware of his presence in all the circumstances of our life is what Islam considers to be the goal toward which all the acts of worship and all the religious practices are finalized. In this sense, one can say that the *dhikr* of God is the quintessence of worship: the daily service is not prescribed because of the positions which the body assumes, because of its fixed times but because of the remembrance of God which it causes. The same applies to fasting or to the pilgrimage to Mecca and to every other Islamic prescription. When a Muslim walks, sits or lies down, and then starts remembering God by mentioning his names in a low or in a soft tone, he abides by the ritual which includes and substantiates all the other possible forms of worship. Every other form of worship is subjected to rules and limitations, but the *dhikr* is not. One can go on making *dhikr* while walking, working, while performing any other of his daily activities, and without any need to stop them. This excellence of *dhikr* in respect to other forms of worship—even in respect to the service—is clarified by the *Qur'anic* words which mean:

> Recite what is revealed to thee of the Book and raise the service. Verily the service restrains from shameful and unjust deeds, but nevertheless the remembrance of God is surely the greatest form of worship, and God knows what ye do. And dispute ye not with the People of the Book except for the best, unless it be with those of them who inflict wrong. Say to them: 'We believe in what was revealed to us and in what was revealed to you. Our God and your God is One; and to Him we submit. (29:45–46)

Significantly enough, this proclamation of the excellence of the remembrance of God upon all other forms of worship is immediately followed by instructions concerning the Abrahamic dialogue. Useless disputes and diatribes must be avoided, and emphasis must be put on what unites us, our common faith in the Divine revelation, on the awareness that the God of the Jews, of the Christians, and of the Muslims is One God. Thus remembering God immediately means remembering the deep link which unites us. Moreover, remembering God also means to remember that he is a God of peace, and that He is peace. *As-Salam*, peace, in Arabic is both the common greeting and one of the ninety-nine Beautiful Names of God. When we great each other by saying "peace be upon you," this does not simply mean wishing that the other lives safely and is safeguarded from war, but also wishes that God be upon him, inspire peace into his heart and make his milieu an abode of peace. In this spirit, I would like to end by reciting one of those supplications which the Prophet Muhammad, peace be upon him, used to repeat after each of his daily services, and which many Muslims go on repeating after their services until today:

> O God,
> Thou art Peace and Peace comes from Thee,
> And Peace cometh back to Thee.
> Let us enter,
> Our Lord,
> In the abode of Peace
> And grant us access to Heaven.
> Thy abode is an abode of Peace,
> May Thou be blessed and exalted,
> Thou art the Owner of Majesty and Generosity.
> Amen.

ALI HUSSEN AL-BADAWI AS-SIDDIQI

Sufism, the Inner Dimension
of Islamic Spirituality

ೞ In the name of God, the Merciful, the Compassionate ๛

Imam Qushayri, the author of the great Sufi compendium Rasa'il, understands Sufism in the sense of purity (*safa*); i.e., the purity of inner and outer life, and says that "purity is something praiseworthy in whatever language it may be expressed and its opposite, impurity (*kadar*), is to be eschewed." In support of purity he cites a tradition (*hadith*), which explains the meaning of Sufism and affords proof for it: Abu Hujaifa told us that once the Holy Prophet Muhammad visited us and his face showed us that he was deeply perturbed. He said: "The best part of this world is gone and only its *kadar* (impurity) remains." Consequently death is now a boon for every Muslim.

Imam Ghazzali, under the heading "On the Way of the Sufis" in his book, *Al-Munqidh min-al-Dalal* (*Rescuer from Error*) states: "When after acquiring proficiency in these sciences, I turned my attention to the methods of the Sufis. I came to know that their method attains perfection by means of theory and practice. The gist of their knowledge is to mortify the self and acquire freedom from baser passions and evil attributes so that the heart may get rid of the thought of anything save God and to embellish it with Divine remembrance."

During the days of his academic fame and glory, Imam Ghazzali gave up his literary pursuits, and the job of judge (*Qadi*). Adopting the ways of Sufis he wandered alone in the forests. During this period of his asceticism, someone met him and asked for a legal decree on some problem.

He said to him, "You have reminded me of the false times. Had you approached me when I was engaged in literary pursuits and was a *Qadi*, I would have issued a decree in the matter." The eminent imam now considered the lessons of the schools as worthless and he viewed that period as false and a time of destruction. Such truth is expressed by the words of the Persian Sufi-poet, Rumi:

> O heart, thy high-prized learning of the schools,
> Geometry and metaphysic rules,
> Yea, all but lore of God is devil's lore:
> Fear God and leave this lore to fools.

In explaining Sufism, Abu'l Hasan Nuri says, "Sufism is the renunciation of all selfish pleasures." A Sufi is usually free from greed and lust and knows that, as long as he is a victim of lust, he is imprisoned. He must make himself subservient to God's will, thus his greed and lusts will be annihilated. He is well aware that following the dictates of desires and lusts is misleading and is destructive. As a translation of the meaning of the *Qur'an* says, "And follow not the lusts, for they will mislead thee from the path of God." [*Qur'an*, 6:19] Similar good advice was offered by Bayazid Bustami in this couplet:

> Listen to a good word of the Sage of Bustam
> Spurn the lure of the grain if thou carest not to fall into the net.

Abu Muhammad al-Jurayri writes, "Sufism is the building up of good habits and the keeping of the heart from all evil desires and passions." To Muhammad bin al Qassab, "Sufism is good manners which are manifested by a better man in better times before a better nation." Muhammad b. Ali has expressed the view that Sufism is goodness of disposition; he that has the better disposition is the better Sufi."

It is clear, then, that according to these Sufis, Sufism is the purification of the senses and the will. It is the effacement of one's desires in the will of God. It is the building up of a solid wall between the pure self and the lure of passions and desires. It is, in a word, "self-discipline," beyond the avoidance of what is forbidden and the performance of what is ordained.

Al-Kalabadhi thus sums up their "doctrine of the duties imposed by God on adults." [The Sufis] are agreed that all the ordinances imposed by God on his servants in his Holy Book and all the duties laid down by the Prophet (in the *hadith*) are a necessary obligation and a binding imposition for mature adults, whether he be a veracious believer (*Siddiq*), or a saint or a gnostic, even if he may have attained the furthest rank, the highest degree, the noblest station, or the most exalted stage. They hold that there is no station in which a man may dispense with the prescriptions of religious law, by holding permissible what God has prohibited, or making illegal what God has declared legal, or legal what God has pronounced illegal, or omitting to perform any religious duty without due excuse or reason, which excuse or reason is defined by the agreed judgment of all Muslims and approved by the prescriptions of the religious law. The more inwardly pure a man is, the higher his rank and the nobler his station, so much the more arduously he labors with sincerer performance and a greater fear of God. In this sense, Sufism is at the highest aspect of Islamic discipline, which builds up the character and inner life of the believer by imposing certain ordinances and duties, obligations and impositions, which may not be abandoned in any way by any man.

The Prophet Muhammad was sent to "instruct" humankind "in Scripture and wisdom and to sanctify them." The Sufis keep these "instructions" before their eyes; strive their utmost to perform what has been prescribed for them to do and to discharge what they have been called upon to do, subsequent to that prescription. The *Qur'an* says; "And those who fight strenuously for us, we will surely guide them into our way." And again: "Oh ye who believe! Do your duty to God, seek the means of approach unto him and strive with might and main in his cause: that ye may prosper." Believing in these exhortations, the great Sufi Sidi Yahya said; "the spirit of gnosis will never reach thy heart, so long as there is a duty owing to God which thou hast not discharged!" Thus, Sufism, in the words of Abu' Ali al-Rudhbari, is "giving one's lust the taste of tyranny" and "journeying in the pathway of the Holy Prophet."

From another perspective, Sufism means building one's inner life. Junayd has defined a Sufi as "dead to his self and alive in God." He passes away from what belongs to himself and persists through what belongs to God. When he is dead in relation to his own self, he becomes alive in his relation to the self of God. Husayn b. Mansur al Hallaj thinks that a Sufi is, "singular in his being, he neither accepts anybody nor does anybody accept him." He feels the immediate presence of God alone within and senses the presence of God without and his mental faculty gets rid of the thought of anything save God and is totally captivated by God: The eye does not see anything except God! Predication of everything is of Him only. When 'Amr b. 'Uthman-Makki was asked the meaning of Sufism he replied: "A Sufi is alive to the value of time and is given every moment to what that moment demands." As another Sufi-poet, Ahmad Jami, says,

> O votary of earthly idols feign,
> Why let those veils of flesh enwrap thy brain?
> Tis folly to pursue a host of loves;
> A single heart can but one love contain!

Abu Muhammad Ruwaym described Sufism: "Sufism is nothing else save submitting one's own self to the will of God. A Sufi becomes dead to his self-will and God Almighty's will alone enters in him and as a consequence of it, he has no wish of his own, neither does he want, desire or yearn for anything. In the words of Shaykh al-Ghawth al-A'zham Abdul Qadir al-Jilanithe, a Sufi is "at rest in body, contented in mind, and broad-chested. His face beams with the light of God, with an enlightened heart and he is oblivious of all things due to his nearness with God." In calamity and in affluence, he considers God Almighty alone to be the real agent, the real doer, and does not accept any other being as cause or instrument. Shibli says: "A Sufi is severed from the world (*khalq*) and connected with God (*Haqq*) alone, as God Almighty had said to Moses, "I have chosen thee for Myself (for service) and have disconnected thee from others." Later addressing Moses He said: "By no means canst thou see Me." And so, the end and aim of a Sufi's life is God alone; he loves God alone; his thinking, meditation and prayer are for God alone. He is ever ignorant of everything except God and when he thinks of God alone his mind is purified. In this sense he finds himself attached to God and disconnected with everything except God. He is totally captivated by God alone! When people see him involved in acts of charity toward other human beings, animals or plants, he is simply contemplating God's creation for God's sake. Again Rumi says:

> Of my soul's union with this fleshly frame,
> Of life and death thou art the end and aim.
> I pass away: thou only dost endure
> When I say "me," it is "thee" I mean to name.

All the above definitions of Sufism lead us to conclude that its teachings are not limited to purification of the will and senses, but that it also confers on us nearness to God, as a consequence of which a Sufi being lost his sense of self subsistence loses himself in the self subsistence of God. He feels the immediate presence of God in all things that exist. His knowledge and actions are guided by God alone.

The first step of a Sufi is to teach a traveller on the path how to be released from the clutches of desires or lusts (hawa), how to emerge out of his own individual sphere of knowledge and enter into the knowledge of God. This part of Sufi teaching could be expressed in these words: God alone is our deity (ilaha); i.e., God alone is our master, Lord, and our Helper. We worship God alone and to him we ask for help in all our wants and desires. (Qur'an, 1:5)

From the viewpoint of worship, we are cut off from everything except God and we express our humility and surrender before him alone. This conviction in the supremacy and lordship of God almighty purifies man of all the baser attributes and embellishes him with all the other nobler qualities—his heart is freed from unbelief, idolatry, hypocrisy, heresy, and sin, and is filled with faith, monotheism, truth, and virtues. Sufism means a sanctification of heart and when the Islamic faith imparts to us the knowledge that God alone is our deity, that him alone should we worship and that he is the One we should ask for help, the question then necessarily arises in our minds, "Where should we seek this God whom we worship and before whom we express our humility and subjection?" Sufism offers a reply to this question in the light of the Qur'an and the Prophet's hadith, and it is also called "the knowledge of the nearness of God" (Ilm-i-qurb). The Sufi who is conversant with the knowledge of nearness knows the secret of the relation between the Truth and his creation, God and the phenomenal things, the secret of nearness and proximity, immanence and transcendence, firstness and lastness, outwardness and inwardness of God. Not only does he know this secret, but he feels the immediate presence of God within his own self. Now he is dead to his self and consequently we can call him the one whom God has drawn near to him (*muqarrab*).

In chapter 56 of the noble *Qur'an*, men are sorted out into three classes: 1) The Companions of the Right Hand (*Ashab-al-Maimana*); 2) The Companions of the Left Hand (*Ashab-al-Mash'ama*); and 3) Those nearest to God (*Muqarrabun*). The Companions of the Right Hand are "Those who believe in the Unseen," are "steadfast in prayer," and "have assurance of the hereafter" in their hearts. The Companions of the Left Hand are "those who reject faith and go after false gods." The *Qur'an* describes them as "Those who bartered guidance for error" and "have lost their true direction." This classification is, thus, according to the knowledge out of which spring their actions, knowledge of the right path and knowledge of the wrong path. But who are the *"Muqarrabun?"* They are not simply the Companions of the Right Hand only, otherwise they would have not been in God and he, by his Spirit, lives in him. Because God is, the *Muqarrab* is, without Him, he can do nothing and is nothing. Realizing his innate nature and being confirmed in the knowledge of his "poverty in spirit" (*faqr*), the Sufi regards all created beings as dead and thus "total disappointment from what is in the hands of people" is created in his mind. He regards God Almighty alone as the doer and submits himself to the will of God.

The goal of Sufism is thus the realization of the immediate presence of God. As you have seen, the sources of these teachings in the Islamic tradition are contained in the *Qur'an* and the *hadith* of the Prophet Muhammad (God's blessings and peace be upon him). Sufism is never merely a theory, but is always a presence. And even learning about it, by hearing a preliminary explanation such as this, is regarded as the first step along the path. This is said to happen even when the listener does not fully realize it, even when he only supposes to be listening to a lecture, a conference or a similar academic program.

In Sufism knowledge is identical to the object to be known, and this is the reason why the one who teaches the basic principles of Sufism and the one who listens are considered as already being in the company of all the Sufi Shaykhs of the past. Moreover, because of the argument, when this level is reached, the angels come down from heaven and God's pres-ence (*Sakinah*) surrounds all of those who are present encompassing them. This now causes me to be silent in your company and to listen for a message from Heaven, which is normally covered by the many sounds of ordinary life. May God bless us all.

PART IV ~ WHAT DO WE WANT THE OTHER TO TEACH ABOUT
OUR PRAYER AND LITURGY?

For Further Discussion and Study

What is prayer? How would you describe both its public and personal characteristics? Does each religion encourage the balance of public liturgical prayer and private prayer as part of the whole of religious life, or are people drawn in excess to private revelations and rituals or to unconscious public practices?

Acknowledging the intrareligious nuance of each religion, describe the central rites of each of the three religions. How should a person prepare his or her inner self for prayer? Is there any physical or spiritual purification to be performed before prayer? In what ways do these three religions understand prayer as a process of purification?

What are the primary sources for prayer and liturgy in each religious tradition, e.g., Scriptures, tradition, prayer books, religious life, law codes, etc.? Does public worship emphasize more the scriptural texts and traditional rubrics, while personal prayer tends to be more informal, anecdotal, and inspirational through human stories in each of the religions? How important are the Scriptures to prayer? Is study of Scriptures also prayer?

How important is the remembrance of holy people in the prayer of each religion; e.g., prophets, saints, sages, etc.? What are the principal feasts, celebrations, and commemorations in the liturgical calendars of each religion?

What are the daily prayers for each religious tradition and what is the general purpose of the prayers? Does the one who prays expect an immediate response or reward in any of the faith traditions?

What is the importance of blessing in each religion? What is the importance of redemption in each religion's liturgy? In addition to the experience of public worship, what are the educational components of prayer in building faith and identity?

What is the importance of a specific language in mediating God's presence and revelation in private or public prayer; e.g., Hebrew, Latin, Arabic, etc.? What is the proper place of translations of the Scriptures for personal reflection and prayer?

Does each religion describe the experience of prayer akin to a spiritual journey where individuals go from one spiritual place to another?

In what ways can prayer be understood as the heart's reaching out to God in love? What is mysticism? What is meant by surrender or self-emptying to God in each religion?

Are there renewals of prayer and spirituality occurring in each religion? How are they manifested: meditation, contemplation, ecstasy, song, dance, Scripture study, prayer meetings?

What is the relationship of the body to prayer? How does each tradition understand transcending, transforming and living in one's body at the same time of prayer? What are the appropriate contexts for asceticism, dancing, spontaneous song, prostrations, etc.?

Describe the various spiritual traditions practiced by communities of religious men and women in each religious tradition. Do men and women have a different way of praying privately and publicly?

How would each religion describe the divine dimension of prayer; i.e., how much of it is God speaking through the one who prays? Does God's Presence/Spirit within us speak through us, making us one with God? Does each religion teach that God listens and answers one's prayers even before the prayers are asked?

Holiness is more than a learned theory or prescription of actions to achieve. How would each religious tradition describe and encourage holiness through prayer? Does prayer necessarily lead to the renunciation of all selfish pleasures and the apprehension of the absolute presence of God?

For Action in the Community

What are appropriate ways for us to pray together? When are appropriate times and who can be respectfully invited?

How can we support and participate appropriately in the different kinds of prayer and approaches to prayer for stages in an individual's faith life, such as birth/initiation, maturity/responsibility, repentance/forgiveness, marriage, leadership, illness, death?

Visit a local place of worship other than your own. Afterwards, ask about the significance and importance of the rites and prayers with someone from that synagogue, church, or mosque.

What are your personal prayers or devotions of your home/family? Explain to the other why they are important to you. How do these prayers relate to your religion's public, communal worship?

Where and how can we teach that those who pray in God's name for violence that violence is not central to that religion's teaching? How can we support ourselves or others to stand up and speak against injustice committed in the name of religion?

Is it possible to promote in each religion a public prayer that is more compassion-oriented than justice-oriented for those who have committed crimes? Why or why not?

How can Jews, Christians, and Muslims work together to highlight the importance of Sabbath and marking sacred time and space? Is it possible to plan local calendars so that the principal liturgical seasons and central high holidays of each religion are respected? What would those seasons and holidays be?

PART V

What Do We Want the Other to Teach About Our Ethical Traditions?

D A V I D   L .   C O P P O L A

What Do We Want the Other to Teach About Our Ethical Traditions?

The Conference

The Center for Christian-Jewish Understanding (CCJU) of Sacred Heart University sponsored a symposium March 31–April 2, 2003, at Sacred Heart University, Fairfield, Connecticut. The conference, "What Do We Want the Other to Teach About Our Ethical Traditions?" is part of CCJU's ongoing work to promote dialogue and understanding. This was the final of five conferences with Jews, Christians and Muslims focusing on the topic, "What Do We Want the Other to Teach About Us?" Forty scholars and religious leaders agreed to participate in this symposium. Papers were presented, after which there were prepared responses and general discussion by all of the participants. Presenters included Rabbi Eugene Korn, Rabbi Barry R. Friedman, Dr. John Elias, Dr. Brian Stiltner, Dr. Asad Husain, Dr. Mohammad A. Siddiqi, and Imam Dr. Kareem Adeeb. In addition to the participants, several faculty, staff, and students from Sacred Heart University attended one or several of the sessions.

In addition to the sessions led by the scholars and religious leaders, there were two events that were also open to the public. First, Rabbi Tsvi Blanchard, Director of Organizational Development at the National Jewish Center for Learning and Leadership (CLAL), New York, spoke about the necessity and importance of interreligious dialogue. His lecture was followed by a reception in the lobby of the Pitt Center where a cultural exhibit, "World Religions, Universal Peace, Global Ethic," was being featured. The exhibition invited the viewer to explore the spectrum of world religions to have a better understanding of the importance of their ethical messages for present-day society. With the help of short text panels, quotations, photographs and other illustrations, the exhibition introduced principles for a global ethic through which world religions could better understand each other and bring them closer together.

On Tuesday, April 1, the Fairfield County Jewish Chorale of Fairfield, Connecticut, offered a moving performance of religious music that was followed by a rousing concert by the Newark Boys Chorus. The Newark Boys Chorus School, founded in 1969, is a private school located in Newark, New Jersey. Known as Newark's "Musical Ambassadors," the Chorus has been heard throughout the world and its interreligious message rang clear and true that evening.

LIST OF INVITED PARTICIPANTS

Imam Dr. Kareem Adeeb, American Institute for Islamic and Arabic Studies, Stamford, Connecticut

Dr. Judith Banki, Tanenbaum Center for Interreligious Understanding, New York

Dr. Adena Berkowitz, New York

Rabbi Tsvi Blanchard, National Jewish Center for Learning and Leadership (CLAL), New York

Dr. John Clabeaux, St. John's Seminary College, Massachusetts

Dr. David L. Coppola, Center for Christian-Jewish Understanding of Sacred Heart University, Connecticut

Rabbi Joseph H. Ehrenkranz, Center for Christian-Jewish Understanding of Sacred Heart University, Connecticut

Dr. John L. Elias, Fordham University, New York

Rabbi Barry R. Friedman, Temple B'nai Abraham, New Jersey

Dr. Tikva Frymer-Kensky, Divinity School, University of Chicago, Illinois

Mrs. Deborah Goldberg, Interfaith Council of Southwestern Connecticut, Stamford, Connecticut

Rabbi Emanuel S. Goldsmith, Congregation M'Vakshe Derekh, New York

Dr. Frances Grodzinsky, Sacred Heart University, Connecticut

Dr. Hugh Talat Halman, University of Arkansas, Arkansas

Imam Abdul-Majid Karim Hasan, Muhammad Islamic Center, Connecticut

Dr. Sohail Hashmi, Mount Holyoke College, Massachusetts

Dr. Frank Henderson, professor emeritus of Newman and St. Stephen's, Edmonton, Canada

Rabbi Mitchell M. Hurvitz, Temple Sholom, Connecticut

Sr. Phyllis Kapuscinski, NDS, Institute of Judeo-Christian Studies, Seton Hall University, New Jersey

Dr. Colleen Keyes, Tunxis Community College, Connecticut

Rabbi Eugene Korn, Anti-Defamation League, New York

Dr. Ahmad Moen, Howard University, Washington, DC

Imam Sulayman S. Nyang, Howard University, Washington, DC

Rev. George Papademetriou, Holy Cross Greek Orthodox School of Theology, Massachusetts

Imam Izak-El Mu'eed Pasha, Masjid Malcolm Shabazz, New York

Rev. Thomas P. Ryan, CSP, Paulist Office of Ecumenical and Interreligious Affairs, New York

Rabbi David Fox Sandmel, KAM Isaiah Israel Congregation, Illinois

John Schramm, St. Francis of Assisi Men's Roundtable, Connecticut

Dr. Claudia Setzer, Manhattan College, New York

Dr. Mohammad A. Siddiqi, Western Illinois University, Illinois

Dr. Brian Stiltner, Sacred Heart University, Connecticut

Dr. Michael Ventimiglia, Sacred Heart University, Connecticut

Dr. Fayette Veverka, Villanova University, Pennsylvania

What Do We Want the Other to Teach About Our Ethical Traditions?

Most people seem to be able to agree broadly about what the good society would be, what the good life in that society would be, and what it would mean to be a good person. Certainly, there are intra- and interreligious disagreements on some levels, but strong consensus is found among religious and nonreligious people that humans share "common sense" conceptions of morality based on some form of the golden rule. For Jews, Christians, and Muslims, shared ethical themes include the invitation to love God and neighbor, to act with justice toward others, to follow God's commandments, and to be responsible stewards of creation, among others. For those who have embraced the Noahide Laws and Mosaic covenant, the cry of the other cannot go unheeded, which makes the pursuit of justice in this world crucial. The ethical revolution by the Abrahamic faiths in defense of the weak, poor, widow, orphan, and stranger has changed the face of human history and the way history is contextualized, told, and judged.

Although Jewish, Christian, and Muslim ethics developed out of common foundational experiences of revelation from God who invited humans into covenantal living (ethical monotheism), each has its unique history of development of ethical traditions, as well as distinct methodologies and prioritizing of authoritative sources employed in ethical decision-making and action. Even the universal religious command to love one's neighbor or brother, for example, would have different nuances, understandings, and narrative expressions in each religious tradition that cannot be immediately and simplistically equated.

Jews, Christians, and Muslims communicate ethical traditions because God has chosen to be in relationship with them and such a relationship by its very nature requires an appropriate response. Over time, as this covenantal relationship developed, the responses of communities have taken on a classic and normative status that allows future generations to deepen and expand its relationship and identity. It would seem, for example, that ethical reflection, dialogue, and the common pursuit of social justice are all shared elements of a fundamental and necessary process that illustrates who each person is in relationship to his or her community of faith as well as the community itself. How one acts, communicates, thinks, and feels is the substance of personal identity. For the individual believer to respond to God's invitation and say, "Here I am," is to stand in line with Abraham, Moses, and the many prophets who helped to shape a common ethic from which Judaism, Christianity, and Islam drew inspiration and guidance. In a sense, this response is an act of conscience and is a process of consciousness of one's identity and unlimited value in the eyes of God. Similarly, ethics and morality are inextricably interwoven in a community's conceptualization of its identity and the recognition of the sanctity of human life as the starting point of ethics.

Religious identity that is based on notions of the good society and the moral person in relationship with God is often expressed in terms of law. Judaism, Christianity, and Islam acknowledge the need for law in common, but also see the need to remain faithful and consistent to their own revelations and convictions. At the core of law and the religious values contained in law is that community is a place where virtuous lives can be lived; and there are those who are chosen to speak for the community as leaders and authoritative voices of interpretation. Laws help to put into service a normative ethic that supplies the values or standards by which persons are to live their lives while balancing freedom, responsibility, right judgment, choice, growth, justice, and mercy.

At the ultimate conclusions of each religion, Judaism, Christianity, and Islam assert truth claims that are mutually exclusive. And yet, if each community refrains from triumphal expressions about its witness of the truth, then other cooperative efforts can be pursued together, especially on the level of ethics and social justice, working together for peace and justice. Jews, Christians, and Muslims can learn to respect each other in principle based on their common recognition of one supreme God who calls them to ethical living in covenantal community.

In our time, there are many moral issues that affect millions of people, such as hunger, disease, homelessness, injustice, lawlessness, discrimination, and oppression. However, probably the most important ethical issue, inasmuch as its negative effects are exponential, is the issue of war and its use to initiate or resolve conflicts. The complexities of historical and cultural circumstances, the struggles against military oppression, and the ambiguities of wars for national liberation or proposed manifest destiny have significantly increased the urgency of interreligious dialogue for the sake of peace. Although each tradition promotes peace as a primary ideal ethic, and the scope of influence for each tradition has been unequal, each has been involved in violence and wars and has sought to find a rationale for an ethical or just war, usually in the context of self-defense or of defending the weak. Many pacifists contend that, in a nuclear age, it is impossible to meet the conditions for a just war. For an in-depth treatment of strategies to achieve peace through interreligious dialogue see *Religion and Violence, Religion and Peace* (2000), and *Religion, Violence, and Peace: Continuing Conversations and Study Guide* (2004), both published by Sacred Heart University Press.

Finally, Jews, Christians, and Muslims are immersed in secular cultures that idolize the secular. Such cultures have the effect of nullifying values or preferences of truth claims in the public forum. In response to secularism, members of each faith tradition need to develop together appropriate theological, philosophical, humanistic, and political ethics that advance the common good in ways that do not exclude the other traditions and maintain the distinctiveness of its own.

E U G E N E   K O R N

Jewish Ethics:
Foundations, Development, and Future

Until modern times no one had attempted a systematic account of Jewish ethics. Rabbinic authorities were generally not philosophers who quested after systematic constructs. On a deeper level, the absence of systematic Jewish ethics is probably attributable to the fact that Jewish tradition never considered ethics an autonomous subject matter or mode of inquiry. In fact, there is no indigenous Hebrew word for 'ethics.' Jewish ethics is embedded in Jewish law and theology, and only a modern would see Jewish ethics as isolated. In describing Jewish ethics therefore, I will attempt to formulate what philosophers call a "rational reconstruction," i.e., a logical tapestry weaved from many different strands of Jewish literature, law, liturgy, and theology. Systematizing Jewish ethics is made more difficult by the fact that Jewish ethics is strongly pluralistic and consequently cannot be formulated as a universal apodictic system similar to Euclid's geometry or even Aristotle's ethics.

Although a modern product, a systematic presentation of Jewish ethics contains great value to Jews and gentiles alike. For Jews, it can shed light on the relation between formal *halakhah* and ethics. For Christians, it can assist in correcting their traditional polemical notions of Judaism and Jewish values. For Muslims, it may help counter anti-Jewish political rhetoric that has arisen around the tragic Israeli-Palestinian conflict. And for thinkers of all backgrounds, it can assist in resolving the age-old problem of defining Jewish tradition and culture.

The Essential Components of Jewish Ethics

Jewish ethics can be seen as having three fundamental components or dimensions.[1] The first is scriptural imperatives and formal law. These are usually detailed prohibitions or prescriptions of specific behavior in particular circumstances. Sometimes the Bible is a bit too general, so the talmudic rabbis had to flesh out the specific situations and behavior to which these imperatives apply. Honoring one's father and mother (Exodus 20:12) or not infringing on a neighbor's property or business (Deuteronomy 27:17) are cases in point. Just how does one display honor? How much competition is fair when it reduces another's profits? The Talmud proceeded to define in careful detail how one could fulfill these imperatives.

The second level is that of overarching values. Examples of these generic values are the Divine image implanted in all human beings (Genesis 1:26), peace (Isaiah 57:19), holiness (Leviticus 19:1), justice (Deuteronomy 16:20), love of neighbor (Leviticus 19:18), and a general concept of moral rightness and goodness (Deuteronomy 6:18). These values run throughout with specific behavioral imperatives and are the intermediate purposes of their implementation.

The last level, which may be termed the *summum bonum* of Jewish ethics, is the ultimate vision that animates the entire system. This is the beautiful messianic dream of a society suffused with peace, justice, and knowledge of God, and is the dream that Jews are obligated to help realize within human history by virtue of their covenant with God. It may be helpful, therefore, to describe Jewish ethics by using a metaphor traditional to both Judaism and Christianity. Jewish ethics is similar to a tree. Its branches are specific positivist laws, its trunk is formed by overarching values, and its roots are the ultimate messianic dream which nurtures the entire living body.

Positivistic Imperatives

Legal imperatives constitute the starting point and first level. Commandment (*"mitzvah"*) is the central category of Jewish life and culture, giving Jewish ethics a strong deontological character. These positivistic imperatives flow from the sacred biblical covenant contracted between God and the Jewish people, and hence there is little influence—if any at all—of natural law considerations in formal *mitzvot*. For example, in contrast to Catholic teaching on sexuality and reproduction, Jewish sexual ethics are driven by the value of fulfilling the *mitzvah* imperative, not how God structured nature. Since Jews have a legal duty to procreate, if a woman has blocked fallopian tubes, it is a religious duty to seek artificial reproductive methods (e.g. IVF). If nature poses a problem, it is a religious imperative to "get around" the natural blockage. If pregnancy would endanger the life of a woman, then birth control is warranted since preserving life is a penultimate value and Judaism seeks to avoid sexual abstinence, seeing it as injurious to mental and spiritual health. The fact that such methods deviate from the way that prescientific humans reproduced or engaged in sexual activity is irrelevant for Jewish ethics. I believe these examples are representative within the entire system of *mitzvot*.

Jewish ethics is consequently behavior- and act-oriented. "Give to the poor," "Do not murder," "Do not stand idly by while your neighbor is in danger," "Do not work others on the Sabbath," are hallmark forms of Jewish ethics. The system does not strive for contemplation (*ala* Plato or Aristotle), metaphysical unity (*ala* mystics) or intention/authenticity (*ala* existentialists), but for empirical behavior that has salutary effects on society and its individuals.

It is important to stress that while traditional Jews take scriptural imperatives most seriously, traditional Jewish ethics is not fundamentalist or literalist. Even Orthodox Jews insist that while Scripture is divine, its interpretation is given over to human judgment and reason. (The Talmud[2] even goes so far as to claim that the talmudic rabbis dramatically told God to "stay out" of a debate on a point of Jewish law, since after the revelation at Sinai, the Torah no longer resides in Heaven.) Jewish exegesis always employs rationality and considerations of the above guiding values to determine the normative meaning of scriptural imperatives. This means that traditional Judaism is not committed to a literal interpretation of biblical texts. In fact, sometimes a literalist interpretation constitutes heresy. The famous *lex talionis*, "An eye for an eye. . . . " (Exodus 21:23), over which there has been so much Christian polemic, illustrates this principle. The Talmud reasoned that the value of one person's eye is not always equal to the value of another person's eye, and that the pain suffered by one person in losing his eye is not necessarily equivalent to the pain suffered by another losing his eye. It would therefore, be a violation of justice if the court were to apply the verse literally. Instead, normative Jewish teaching demanded that monetary compensation equivalent to the value of the lost eye be paid by the aggressor to the victim.[3] Note that it is considerations of justice that guided the normative application of the verse, not the literal meaning.

Capital punishment is another case in point. The Bible stipulates 36 capital crimes, yet the intrinsic sanctity of each human person established a bias against taking any life. Hence, the talmudic rabbis established elaborate judicial procedures that for all practical purposes ruled out the actual legal implementation of execution.[4] One famous authority, Rabbi Akiva, even maintained that if he were the head of the Jewish court, he would rule out capital punishment in principle. One last example is the prohibition of charging interest. Biblically, this prohibition applies to all loans—whether business or personal. If applied literally, however, there would be little incentive to issue loans on property or for business purposes, causing all but the wealthy to be deprived of a livelihood. As a result, Jewish law found a way to permit charging interest indirectly on commercial loans, while retaining the prohibition on loans for personal reasons to the poor. In other words, biblical imperatives mean what authoritative rabbinic interpretation says they mean, not what the words literally connote. This is analogous to normative Catholic exegesis, which holds that Christian scriptures mean what the *Magisterium* says they mean. Both Catholicism and traditional Judaism are interpretive, not fundamentalist, traditions.

Overarching Values

There are a number of major guiding values that run through all Jewish ethical judgment. Most important is the doctrine that every human being is created in the image of God. This invests all human life with intrinsic sanctity and infinite value. A famous talmudic dictum (that later also found its way into the *Qur'an*) claims, "One who saves a single life is as if [i.e., is morally equivalent to] he saves the entire world; one who destroys a single life is as if he destroys the entire world."[5] Mathematically these equivalencies hold only if human life has no value or if it possesses infinite value. Obviously Judaism opted for the latter solution, and this means that all life/death ethical dilemmas cannot be solved by finite utilitarian calculations. Human life has intrinsic nonfinite value that is independent of any social or intellectual utility. Hence Jewish ethics insists that all human life is worth living, and that one may never destroy one innocent life to save another. The pervasive moral utilitarianism now found in academic circles and the apotheosis of the pleasure principle in general society is, from a Jewish point of view, little more than old paganism in new garb.

The intrinsic value of human life derived from the Hebrew doctrine of *Tzelem Elohim*—which later became known in Latin as *Imago Dei*—is the governing consideration in nearly all Jewish prescriptions for interpersonal relations,[6] and creates an absolute axiological dichotomy between physical objects and human beings. Well before Kant, Jewish ethics understood that the worst violation of ethics is to dehumanize a person and treat him as a finite object whose worth is measured by his usefulness to another.[7] Jewish rabbis and philosophers have interpreted *Tzelem Elohim* differently, including metaphysical freedom/moral sensibility, glory, conceptual powers, and creativity,[8] but all these interpretations converge on the principle that *Imago Dei* confers upon every human being sanctity and intrinsic dignity. In fact, arguably the foremost Orthodox theologian and legal authority in the 20th century, Rabbi Joseph B. Soloveitchik, maintained that the halakhic category of *kevod ha-beriyot* (dignity owed to all human beings) was nothing other than the rabbinic formulation of the biblical doctrine of *Tzelem Elohim*.[9] Thus, the sanctity of human life is the starting axiom of Jewish ethics.

There is another critical implication of the doctrine of *Tzelem Elohim*. Commenting on the Biblical prohibition against leaving the corpse of an executed criminal hanging overnight,[10] the rabbinic *Midrash* states:

> There were once twin brothers who were identical in appearance. One was appointed king, while the other became a brigand and was hanged. When people passed by and saw the brigand hanging, they exclaimed, "The King is hanging."[11]

This parable tells us that *Tzelem Elohim* constitutes an essential bridge between ethics and theology. To abuse a human being—even a human body that has lost its soul—is *ipso facto* to defame or blaspheme God. This means that God is present in all human relationships. In effect, there are no bilateral human relations because how one treats another human being necessarily reflects on God. One cannot be ethically impure and religiously pious. Thus, in Jewish terms, ethics always has theological consequences and cannot be isolated from one's relationship with God.

Although *Tzelem Elohim* confers infinite value on human life, Jewish ethics are not pacifist. Life—not suicide—is a religious *desideratum*, and Jewish ethics teaches that if someone attempts to kill you, you have the moral right to defend yourself by killing him first if necessary. Both Jewish values and Jewish history have taught Jews that while the abuse of power is sinful, so is powerlessness. There is no glory in martyrdom, and allowing evil to reign unopposed by physical force only promotes slaughter and greater evil, thus plunging the world back into primordial darkness. Jews today make no excuse for possessing sovereignty and defending their legitimate security interests with physical force. Neither unbridled power nor complete powerlessness is a virtue. The Jewish ideal is to have power and use it within moral limits.

A second foundational value of Jewish ethics is justice, or "*tzedeq*." This is articulated as a broad judicial and moral value by the Deuteronomic imperative, "*Tzedeq, tzedeq tirdof*"—You shall surely pursue justice.[12] More fundamentally, at the very beginning of the Jewish people, God establishes "teaching justice and righteousness" as an objective for Jewish covenantal identity.[13] Again there is a nexus here with Jewish theology. Pursuit of justice is not only a *sine qua non* of Jewish behavior, but as the continuation of that biblical passage indicates, Jews understand it as an essential attribute of God and His relationship with the world. When Abraham challenges God with the rhetorical question, "Shall not the Judge of all the world act justly,"[14] he indicates that the Jewish conception of divinity requires that God Himself abide by the demands of morality. An unjust God is no God at all, and certainly not the God of the covenant. As such, there can be no contradiction between morality and *mitzvah*, the divine command.

Jews never interpreted the story of the binding of Isaac as did Kierkegaard, namely a conflict between the demands of faith and ethics. Kierkegaard's entire dilemma is incomprehensible to people with a Jewish conception of God and what he wants of them. No matter how lovesick Jews are in their romance with God, Judaism insists that faith never transgress the boundaries of the moral.[15] Additionally, the majority of talmudic rabbis and medieval Jewish philosophers would have been equally perplexed by Tertullian's famous phrase, "*credo quia absurdum est*," which celebrates violating rationality to achieve religious goals. The classic Jewish understanding of the relation between faith and reason was best articulated by Sa'adia Gaon in the 10th century: Reason is a God-given gift and God would be a sadist if he required humans to deny this gift in order to attain faith.[16] Hence, Jewish ethical discussion typically contains a minimum of dogma and a maximum of practical reason.

A third fundamental guiding value of Jewish ethics is *Imitatio Dei*, imitating God. Here the Jewish concept differs essentially from the Greek philosophic idea of *Imitatio Dei* as contemplation, and the Christian understanding of *imitatio* as suffering or experiencing Jesus' passion.[17] Again, the Talmud supplies the key to the Jewish concept.[18] The discussion begins, "Who can walk after God? Is he not a consuming fire?" How can a mortal human being emulate the Perfect and Wholly Other? Philosophically, it is only because a person shares something with God, namely *Imago Dei*, that he is able to engage in *Imitatio Dei*. What religious obligations do the rabbis derive from the power of divine emulation within human grasp? The ethical imperatives to clothe the naked, feed the poor, visit the sick, comfort those in pain, extend mercy and compassion to those in need, and perform acts of voluntary *hesed* (loving-kindness)—because Jewish tradition understood God to have so acted in the Bible.[19] God as transcendent infinitude is beyond human understanding, but we can know God through his moral attributes and ethical behavior. God is immanent through his relations with others, and as such is the archetype for deepening existence by relating to "the other." This is the source of Emanuel Levinas' contemporary Jewish ethical philosophy of being. A corollary to this is that the Jewish concept of holiness is essentially social and moral, realized in community with others.[20] The monastic life is holy for some, but to Jews, leaving the community bespeaks of sin that is devoid of any trace of *kedushah* (holiness).

A corollary of *Imitatio Dei* is the notion of going beyond the requirements of law, and acting with loving-kindness out of voluntary motive.

Just as God is not constrained by outside forces, *imitatio* demands that Jews develop virtuous characters that impel natural love and giving. If legal imperatives are the floor for Jewish ethics, acts of *hesed* are the ceiling. From the virtue of hesed flow compassion and a general sense of moral goodness that cannot be legislated.[21]

The Guiding Vision

The global enterprise of Jewish ethical and religious life is messianic. That is, the vision of a messianic era is the endpoint of history that supplies direction and purpose to normative Jewish behavior. The messianic ideal is not a mere theoretical idea, but a practical goal to be worked toward. Unlike some Christian or mystical concepts, the Jewish messianic era occurs within empirical history. This means that taking the messianic vision seriously entails assuming moral responsibility for building a better future, indeed for repairing the world, which has become known by the popular Hebrew phrase, *tikun olam*. Jewish ethics therefore, is activist in nature and resists impulses to historical quietism or determinism. All acts—either ritual or interpersonal—are designed to produce the ultimate *telos*, that is, the vision of the Jewish Prophets:

> In the end of days the mountain of the Lord shall be established on top of all mountains and shall be exalted above the hills. And (many) peoples shall stream onto it. Many nations shall come, and say, "Come let us go up to the mountain of the Lord and to the house of the God of Jacob; and He will teach us His ways and walk in His Paths. For the Torah shall go forth from Zion, and the word of the Lord from Jerusalem." They shall beat their swords into plowshares and their spears into pruning hooks. Nation shall not lift up sword against nation, nor shall they learn war anymore. But every man shall sit under his vine and his fig tree; and none shall make him afraid. (Micah 4:2–4)

As the neo-Kantian, Herman Cohen, noticed in the early 20th century, postulating the messianic dream not only supplies vision and inspiration, it also provides practical motive for ethical commitment since it ensures ultimate efficacy of moral action.

The Processes, Methods and Future of Jewish Ethics

If the above schema of three dimensions of Jewish ethics is accurate, then Jewish ethics is a dialectic process balancing out law, values, and vision. Because of this balance, Jewish ethics tends to be casuistic—reasoning about a specific case in a detailed context—and therefore variable and pluralistic, leaving room for competing opinions. There are few absolutes ("categorical imperatives") in Jewish ethical discussion. In fact there are only three *mitzvot* that must be preserved, even at the cost of sacrificing one's life. These are the prohibitions against taking an innocent life, idolatry, and adultery/incest—and the Talmud makes clear that there are exceptions even to these seemingly ironclad imperatives.[22] Priorities, operative imperatives, and decisions are most often dependent upon the particulars at hand.

It is crucially important to understand Jewish ethics as developmental. Again, because of the balance of scriptural law with reason and human understanding of values, different applications of the same *mitzvah* can evolve and normative behavior can change over time. This is best demonstrated by the biblical command to destroy the nation of Amalek. According to the Bible, Jews are obligated to blot out all traces of the Amalekite people.[23] Taken literally, this means killing each and every Amalekite—not only adult male combatants, but also women and children. In other words, on a biblical level there is an imperative to commit genocide. Thus, Jewish authorities were faced with a morally dangerous, yet authoritative, text. This is the "dark side" that all revelatory religions need to honestly admit. Do religions follow the literal authority of the text and disregard the moral voice or do they acknowledge the darkness, face the problems, and somehow refashion new normative understandings consistent with moral consciousness?

There is no historical evidence that Jews in fact ever tried to fulfill this imperative literally, but even the potential and the theory are quite disturbing. Recognizing the morally problematic nature of the *mitzvah*, the talmudic rabbis ensured that the prescribed genocide never take place by announcing that the Assyrian king Sanheriv forced his conquered nations to intermarry as a way of subjugating them and undermining the threat of their own nationalisms.[24] Hence, concluded the rabbis, it is in principle impossible to know that any specific person is descended from Amalek and the imperative to annihilate Amalekites is *per force* inoperative.

One thousand years later, Maimonides was bothered by the conceptual or theoretical problem of how a moral God could command genocide, so he reinterpreted the imperative to apply only to those persons who do not accept the fundamental moral principles of civilization; i.e., the prohibitions against murder, theft, anarchy, and adultery/incest.[25] Maimonides achieved a conceptual revolution in the *mitzvah* by transforming the definition of Amalek from a genetic category to a behavioral one, consequently rendering the imperative consistent with our moral sensibilities and concept of justified self-defense. It is important to note that these developments were not done by unimportant Jewish voices in the wilderness, but by authorities who determined the normative understanding of Jewish law and the normative behavior of Jews.[26] The history of Jewish ethics indicates that similar conceptual and behavioral developments took place regarding polygamy, and the biblical institutions of servitude and monarchy, among others.[27] Here again we see a resistance to fundamentalism, and the thrust of progress dictated by the primacy of the ethical in Jewish tradition.

If, indeed, Jewish ethics is developmental, then there will be challenges for the future of that intellectual and spiritual discipline. Obviously, the rapid pace of technology, particularly in the biomedical sciences, changes our current existential reality and offers new possibilities for the future. These give rise to profound ethical questions around the subjects of cloning, extension of life, genetic engineering, disease prevention, and privacy. Jewish ethics will have to grapple with these new areas based on its traditional methodologies and guiding values, when scientific breakthroughs are thrown into the mix. Another area of required rethinking is feminism and women's rights. There is no gainsaying the fact that traditional Jewish ethics assumed a patriarchal dominance in domestic life, political and social roles, religious authority, scholarship, and many areas of ritual performance. Jewish ethics needs to find a way to honor tradition while taking into account a modern sensibility of justice and equality for women's rights and roles. This is a difficult—almost Solomonic—dilemma that will require pain, most probably both to tradition and to absolute egalitarian considerations.

Finally, the newfound status of Jews as full citizens in Western pluralistic societies, combined with the reality of a secure Jewish homeland, affords Jews the possibility to relate to gentiles as political and social equals. Today is perhaps the first opportunity to do this since the destruction of the Second Commonwealth in the first century and the subsequent Jewish exilic experience as a minority population in the Diaspora. Jews were often victimized but always vulnerable in this arrangement, and their condition of weakness tended to generate "an ethic of suspicion" toward the other. Today Jews can establish relations as equals with Christians (but not yet with Muslims in the Middle East), and assume that Christians are no longer their physical and spiritual enemies. In effect, modern tolerance and Jewish independence constitute an experiment in transforming Jewish culture: Can Israeli sovereignty liberate Jews from the image of being a victim? Can Jews generate an ethic of partnership and equality with the gentile world? Certainly the universal guiding values of Jewish religious teachings about the dignity and sanctity of all persons can be the foundation for this ethic, but psychological and intellectual transformations born of a new sense of security will also be required. Obviously, both Christianity and Islam will play essential roles in this experiment.

Conclusion: What We Should Teach About Jewish Ethics

What, then, should people teach regarding the essential characteristics of Jewish ethics? First and foremost, Jewish religion, ethics, and culture cannot be reduced to "Law," as past Christian polemics and current Christian Scriptures refer to them. Jewish ethics is a dialectic of law, values, and vision, all captured by the term that Jews themselves use, namely *"Torah."* Torah is best translated literally as "teaching," and not as "law" by way of the Greek, *"nomos."*

Second, Jewish ethics is interpretative and an ongoing process of bringing traditional values and imperatives into confrontation with evolving moral consciousness and sensibilities.

Third, redemption *within* history is the dream for which Jewish ethics—and hopefully Jews—work relentlessly. This will be achieved through concrete acts, some obligated and some out of voluntary motive, in the physical and social world, not a spiritual flight from the messiness of human affairs. Human bodies and biology, a particular people, and a particular homeland are all essential agents in this movement toward redemption and they become sanctified in the process. There is tension between the empirical present and the spiritual dream, but no Platonic motif of *"soma sema,"* of questing release from empirical reality and the problematics of history. Jewish holiness is the penetration of the spiritual into the physical.

Lastly, the doctrine that all human beings are created *b'Tzelem Elohim,* in God's image, necessitates that there is no cleavage between moral and religious duties, between Jewish ethics and theology. Kant strove to disentangle ethics from religion. He may have succeeded on philosophic or systematic grounds, but no faithful account of Jewish ethics can succeed in that enterprise. This is because the intrinsic value of human life as the beginning of Jewish ethics is fundamentally theological, and the messianic dream as the endpoint of Jewish ethics is a fusion of moral perfection and theological knowledge. Here is the way Maimonides formulates the prophetic vision:

> At that time (the Messianic Era) there will be no starvation; there will be no hunger, no war; nor will there be any jealousy, nor any strife. Blessings will be abundant, comforts within the reach of all. The single preoccupation of the entire world will be to know the Lord....Israel will attain an understanding of the Creator to the utmost capacity of the human mind, as it is written: "The earth will be filled with the knowledge of God, as waters cover the sea" (Isaiah 11:9).[28]

Note here how peace and social perfection are concomitants of "the full knowledge of God." Neither the prophets nor Maimonides were social workers. They were God-intoxicated personalities, passionate theocentric visionaries.[29] In their religious understanding, the knowledge of God necessarily leads to empirical ethical progress, because the ideal moral state of affairs is a world where every person fully recognizes the image of God of others, thereby making God felt with clarity and immediacy.

I mentioned earlier that there is no Hebrew word for "ethics." In fact, there is no indigenous Hebrew word for "religion" either. The term most often used is *"dat,"* whose more accurate connotation is "law" or "edict."[30]

This is because both Jewish ethics and religion are incomprehensible in isolation from each other. Jewish ethics and religion are inextricably intertwined—not only linguistically, but conceptually and experientially for all serious Jews.

The messianic dream is Jewish in origin, but all who have a vision and commitment to historical and ethical progress can play a role in this prophetic process. It obligates each of us to become moral agents, to take responsibility for our future and that of humankind by creating good and defeating evil. In the conceptualization of the ancient Jewish teaching, when we do this we not only imitate God, we become partners with the Holy One to help him perfect creation.

Notes

1. See *Essential Essays on Judaism by Eliezer Berkovits*, David Hazony editor, (Jerusalem: Shalem Press 2002) introduction.

2. Babylonian Talmud, *Baba Mezia* 59b

3. Babylonian Talmud, *Baba Kama* 83b–84a

4. Babylonian Talmud, *Sanhedrin* 81b

5. *Mishna Sanhedrin* 4:5

6. See Eugene Korn, "*Tzelem Elokim* and the Dialectic of Jewish Morality," Tradition, Spring 1997, pp. 5–30.

7. The nonfinite value of every human being is the origin of the popular Jewish custom of not counting persons. Counting presupposes both finitude and commensurability of that which is counted, thus implying that the countables are "objects." Hence the Jewish custom is to indirectly number persons by associating a word of a scriptural verse to assimilate the holiness of the person to the holiness of the Torah scripture.

8. Meir Simchah Ha-Kohen, *Meshek Hokhmah*, Genesis 1:26; Nachmanides, commentary on the Torah, Genesis 1:26; Maimonides, *Guide for the Perplexed*, 1:1–2; Joseph Soloveitchik, *Halakhic Man*, Part II respectively

9. *Days of Remembrance* (Hebrew), (Jerusalem, World Zionist Organization) pp. 9–11.

10. Deuteronomy 21:23

11. *Midrash Tanhuma*, ad loc.

12. Deuteronomy 16:20

13. Genesis 18:19

14. Genesis 18:25

15. Joseph B. Soloveitchik, "Lonely Man of Faith", *Tradition*, Vol. 7, No. 2 (Summer 1965), note pp. 61–62.

16. *Book of Beliefs and Opinions*, tr. By Samuel Rosenblatt (New Haven: Yale U., 1955) Treatise III

17. See David Shapiro, "The Doctrine of the Image of God and *Imitatio Dei*", *Judaism*, Vol. 13:1 1963

18. Babylonian Talmud, *Sotah* 14a

19. This is the message of perhaps the most philosophic text of the Pentateuch, Exodus 33:12–34:7. Moses' plea of "Show me Your Glory" (34:18) is refused on grounds that no living human can fathom the Divine Essence. Moses' request to understand God's behavior, "Teach me Your ways" (33:13) is granted by God revealing His 13 moral attributes of compassion, slowness to anger, abundant mercy and truth, etc. (34:7). See Maimonides, *Guide for the Perplexed* 1:54.

20. The clearest exposition of this is found in Lev. Chapter 19, which details holiness in terms of social relationships.

21. Nahmanides commentary on Deuteronomy 6:18. For an exposition for the extralegal character of *hesed* and the relationship of formal law to Jewish ethics, see Eugene Korn, "Legal Floors and Moral Ceilings: A Jewish Conception of Law and Ethics," *The Edah Journal, Tammuz* 7562 (2002) at www.edah.org.

22. Babylonian Talmud *Sanhedrin* 74a

23. Exodus 17:14–15 and I Samuel 15:2–3.

24. *Mishna Yada'im* 4:4, and Babylonian Talmud, *Berakhot* 28a, *Yebamot* 17b, *Yoma* 84b. For normative codification, see Maimonides, *Mishneh Torah* (MT), Laws of Kings 5:4.

25. MT, Laws of Kings 6:4 and commentary of *Kesef Mishnah* ad loc.

26. Nachmanides, for example, clearly followed Maimonides lead. See his commentary on Deuteronomy 20:10.

27. N. Rabinovitch, "The Way of Torah," *The Edah Journal, Tevet* 5763 (2002) at www.edah.org.

28. Laws of Kings, 12:5

29. See Abraham Heschel, *The Prophets*, (N.Y: Burning Bush Press, 1962) Introduction.

30. See Book of Esther 1:8,13,15.

B A R R Y   F R I E D M A N

A Reflection on Jewish Ethics

I f I were to stand on one foot and try to explain the Torah, my message would be that we can not make absolute "an eye for an eye and a tooth for a tooth." On the other hand, the opposite extreme of relativism whereby everything is contextual is also untenable for me. I do not want the fundamental principles, "Do not murder," or "Human beings are created in the image of God," to be considered contextual and therefore, meaningless. I think every person and religion has to come to grips with the foundations of his or her spirituality and ethics. I think this is a rational process and one has to dig very deep into what is really axiomatic in one's worldview and religious tradition.

Isaiah Berlin has a wonderful lesson where he teaches in one of his essays that people will disagree about morality, but we must be able to distinguish between fruitful and fruitless discussions. He concludes that if a person cannot see the fundamental moral difference between sticking a pin in a pin cushion and sticking a knife in someone's belly, then walk away. One will never come to any kind of moral agreement since that person's moral sensibility and spiritually are too different that one's own. However, if someone says that only Jews are created in the image of God, and non-Jews are not, then I can argue that he is wrong from Jewish tradition. Although scholarly discussions may not be enough to persuade him, our discussion will be able to take place in the context of shared experiences and vocabulary and may prove fruitful.

One's fundamental convictions do not come in a revelation overnight. Such insights come as the product of a long and arduous spiritual quest. I remember my teacher in Jerusalem once said, "If I only talked with people who agreed with me, I would only need to walk around with a mirror all day." I would hope that I could talk with people with whom I disagree because I believe there is a very rich common sense of morality among people of good will. For example, although he is a utilitarian, I can talk to Peter Singer at Princeton. I think he is morally bankrupt, but there are certain things we would agree on because we have certain common values such as freedom of speech and freedom of expression. On a fundamental level, there are some questions that we are never going to agree on since I do not think it is ever morally justified to kill a hemophiliac so one could properly care for a healthy child. My mother used to say, "Consider the source. If it is someone you respect, you listen to him and you talk to him. If not, it goes in one ear and out the other."

I can talk with a Christian, Muslim, and even a Buddhist because I think they also appreciate that there is value to truth and peace and justice. At certain points, the conversations would reach impasses, but I think that since their morality emanates from a spirituality grounded in the value of human beings, such a spiritual source would lead us to agree on many ethical propositions.

Judaism proposes an integral relationship between ethics and religion. The basis of religion for Jews is ethics and the basis of ethics is religion. There is righteous conduct because, in and of itself, it is righteous conduct. I cannot translate religion to mean only ritual observance while ignoring what is taught about the proper relationships between human beings. For example, a person who runs a nursing home and abuses the patients violates both social ethics and the Jewish religious tradition. Similarly, someone once asked why the Ten Commandments have two parts—in the Jewish numbering, the first five commandments are between humans and God, the second five between humans and humans—and why is the fifth commandment to honor one's father and mother? The response was that to a child, the father and mother is Godlike, making food and love available. The activity of parents and God in the world are intertwined and one cannot violate one part of the commandments without affecting the other.

One of the challenges of teaching about the Jewish ethical tradition is that, in order to understand where a Jew is coming from, one must understand the theological, sociological, and political factors that gave birth to many of what we call the ethical values, the ethical value stance, in this case, of the Jewish tradition. In short, the practice of Jewish ethics is both individual and communal, autobiographical and sociological.

I am the descendant of an eastern European maternal grandfather. He would not understand my presence here today among Christians and Muslims; nor could he have understood my traveling with Rabbi Joseph Ehrenkranz and people from the Center for Christian-Jewish Understanding to Poland to spend time with Cardinal Macharski or with Cardinal William Keeler. Nor would he have believed that I spoke at St. Patrick's Cathedral in New York City with Cardinal John O'Connor. In fact, I began my presentation that evening saying if my grandfather had ever seen me in St. Patrick's sitting on the dais with a prince of the Church, he would have had a heart attack and died on the spot. After my presentation, Cardinal O'Connor got up and said, "Rabbi Friedman, Barry, if my grandfather in west Philadelphia found out that I was the young man who had turned the lights on and off on the Sabbath for the Orthodox Jews, he would have laid down next to your grandfather and died." Similarly, my son who sits with me today cannot understand the mentality of his eastern European great-grandfather. This is a new America, this is a new age and the time is right for us to teach about each other. But when we discuss what I want the others to teach about my tradition, I want them to understand where I came from and some of the reasons that gave birth to my convictions.

The Jewish ethical tradition tells us that the seven Noahide laws are meant to apply to all people to unite us. The laws of Noah say that we are all human beings and we are meant to be religious people, people who worship God. But there is a difference between being religious in the ritual sense and ethical. For example, the person who went into the kosher butcher shop and ordered three quarters of a pound of chopped meat and received instead, a half a pound of meat and a quarter pound of thumb on the scale from a religious butcher is being robbed by a thief, regardless of how religious the butcher is. How do Jews decide on matters of legal significance, for example, whether or not one is a thief? One story recounts the rabbis answering that when the Law was in the heavens, it was for God to make the decisions. But, when God gave it at Sinai, it is now for us to make the decisions, and we have the responsibility for interpreting the Torah. The Jewish approach is not devoid of principles, but first reaches back to draw from our long tradition of learning and wrestling with simple and difficult questions. After such scrutiny takes place in a communal setting, then the appropriate principles are proposed and applied.

Therefore, we must understand each other, where we came from and what is important to us, as we make certain decisions. These decisions challenged us to be a strong community. Even the legal dictum that necessitated the presence of a quorum for prayer services and various rituals that would be performed, affirmed and strengthened a sense of community in daily and holiday observances. I would ask others who teach about me not to try to empathize with me, but to understand where I am coming from. I was always told that I needed to have ten men to hold a service. Therefore, I could not move somewhere to the top of the mountain and cut myself off from the community for better or for worse. My identity and ethical beliefs come from historical experiences living in a community, in a broad world, not in a cubbyhole.

When I grew up, *mitzvoth* was understood to be one's doing a good deed. And it was an imperative, a command. It is an interesting thing for me to note that each generation interprets these commands for themselves. When I was a young fellow, if I were to say to my parents, "What is the reason for the meat and dairy to be on separate dishes? " The answer was, "health reasons." And when I got to be a cynical teenager, I would say, "What do you mean?" And, my mother said, "In the old days, plates had pores and if you had meat, it got into the pores of the dishes and it soured there. And then, if you had dairy in that plate, you got sick." And, I said, "Ma, the Philadelphia Eagles are not Orthodox Jews. They are healthy as horses, and they eat milk and meat together." Later on, I realized that the reason was not as important as the answer. The answer was that faithful Jews listen to the word of God and this joins us together in community. This is the command and how one interprets it is up to the individual, as long as he or she understands where it originally came from.

God is the compassionate One and the interpretation of God changed from one generation to the next. For many, God is a judge. Abraham could engage God as a partner and say, "Shall the judge of all the world himself not act in a just manner?" We also are commanded to be people who work for justice for every human being. We are commanded to pursue, not watch, but to actively pursue justice. Justice in the

Jewish tradition—perhaps because we have always been the minority—is meant to have a universal application. Justice is not only for Jews, but when the Messiah comes he would be for all humanity. Some have suggested that Abraham was the original monotheist. I do not think so. But I do think that Abraham is the person we can look to who demanded that God play the game by the rules that He had set up. In the Jewish tradition, it is acceptable and important to confront God and demand that God play by the rules. Jews cannot agree with Kierkegaard's theological suspension of the ethical, which proposes that God suspended the laws of ethics to destroy Sodom and Gomorrah or for Abraham to sacrifice his son Isaac. We believe in the Jewish tradition that morality and ethical conduct are constant and binding for both God and humanity. Divine ethics are not contingent upon who is more powerful, who won the war, or whether or not you treat me decently today. Present in every human being is the divine image. And, to deny the existence of the divine image is to violate the tradition, the constant ethic as we know it. Our tradition demands a consistent mode of conduct between human beings—even in the marketplace—based upon the presence of God in every human being.

It was once noted at a Jewish Federation dinner that I attended that Jews have evolved from biblical times in many ways, but a foundational principle is that we cannot be observers of the human scene, we have to be active participants in the affairs of humanity. That is why there are so many Jewish attorneys, physicians, journalists, and researchers. It is important for Jews to be involved in *tikkun olam* and repair, heal and eradicate the ills that afflict the world. God created the world in a state of imperfection and it is our responsibility to move that world closer to perfection by observing this and other *mitzvah*. For example, those who worked to prevent polio or other diseases were acting in a partnership with God in the ongoing act of creation and the ongoing act of perfection of this rather imperfect world. The Rabbis also offer a similar perspective. We are born uncircumcised, and the commandment is to be circumcised. Circumcision is a divine command to perfect an act of imperfection. All of these factors have made me what I am today in terms of my position in the community and my ethical beliefs.

Jews ask God on the Sabbath before the new moon to grant to them a long life of good health, blessing, peace, abundance, harmony, and good conscience. The prayer continues by asking for God to implant within them a love of God's Torah and the wisdom to revere his name. And it goes on to ask that we would attain prosperity with honor and that our heart's desire be fulfilled for the good. Amen. Note in this prayer that the mundane is qualified by ethical conditions. We do not merely want a life of abundance, but it has to be abundance with harmony. We do not pray for prosperity alone, but it has to be prosperity with honor. And, what may seem to us to be superfluous—may our heart's desire be fulfilled for the good—we leave it to God to define what is for our ultimate good.

I remember back to a time when I was a young, 19-year-old Orthodox fellow living in Israel, and the love of my life had come to an end. I was despondent and wrote to my leader in the youth group saying that I had observed all the *mitzvah* and followed God's word, so why was I rewarded by my love affair being terminated? And, he wrote back to me reminding me of the Sabbath prayer before the new moon. "Who's going to pray for a bad month? We don't know what's for our ultimate good. Only the Creator of all knows what is for our earthly good.

As noted in an earlier paper, Jews are not pacifists, but there is a conduct that the tradition demands of us, even in situations where one has to be a combatant. A Jewish soldier should be governed by a law of purity or the responsibility of arms. There is not a tradition of war that is holy, but there are wars that ought to be fought because they are defensive or the lesser of the evil. Despite the biblical story of Sampson or the choices made by the Jews at Masada under Roman siege in the First Century CE, as a general rule, we do not promote notions of martyrdom and suicide. Jewish tradition says that humans are meant to praise God and they do such by staying alive, because dead people don't praise God. To stay alive is a religious act under almost all circumstances. Therefore, if someone comes to kill me, I have every moral right, and probably even a moral obligation, to kill that party first. By and large, Jews have been powerless for the last 2,000 years. They did not have an army or a country and they could not defend themselves, and we were slaughtered in the last century. Now, the great spiritual challenge for Israel is not only to have power, but to have power and to use it responsibly and to use it morally. And, that is a very difficult thing to do and a lesson that we have to learn. Perhaps we can learn with and from the experience of Christians who have struggled to maintain morality in the midst of secular power. We should remain hopeful and vigilant, but we, too, will probably have to learn from our mistakes with such power.

In conclusion, there is a commandment, which we all know; you shall love your neighbor as yourself. But, if one goes etymologically into the word "neighbor," every time it is used in the Bible, the word does not define neighbor in geographic terms. It means, in effect, that everyone in this room is my neighbor because we are neighbors intellectually and emotionally, and we are neighbors in our dreams for what we want humanity, this community, whatever that may be, to be. However, the Bible says also that one must love your peer or your neighbor as well as the stranger. We are commanded, "You shall not oppress the stranger because you know the heart of the stranger, having yourself been strangers in the land of Egypt" (Exodus 23:9). This occurs numerous times—36—so that if one does not get it right the first time, then get it right the second. Similarly, we cannot accomplish *tikkun olam* by ourselves or even by one nation.

These are some of the things that I would want others to know and teach about Jewish ethics, where I am coming from, and why I am part of this community in 2003—one that may not have been able to exist in 1929. It incumbent upon each of us to do God's commands, to pursue justice and righteousness and to accomplish good deeds so that the messianic era will be ushered in, not at the end of days, but at the time that people by their actions will welcome the redeemer of all humanity. I think that our coming together here at Sacred Heat University is an unending supply of food for thought, and nourishment for the heart that will bring the messiah closer to us. May we move from strength to strength in this most noble endeavor.

J O H N   L .   E L I A S

What Do We Want the Other to Teach About Christian Morality?

I have never taken on such an ambitious project as this. Who can presume to write a chapter essay on what other religious faiths should teach about Christian morality? I feel like Augustine of Hippo when he quipped that he knew what time was except when people ask him to explain it. Having lived as best I can the moral Christian life and having studied and taught Christian morality for many years at various levels does not give much help when I approach writing a chapter about a topic on which scholars write volumes.

Students of Christian morality know that there are disagreements on almost any question one might attempt to address, whether on the nature of Christian morality, approaches to Christian morality, the morality of particular issues or on the ways in which people should be formed in the principles and attitudes of Christian morality. Christians differ on the role of Scriptures, tradition, experience, reason, and authority in determining Christian morality. For some, Christian morality is a biblical morality; while for others it is a philosophical or natural law approach. Take an issue such as abortion and you will find a full range of Christian responses from condemnation as murder to a justifiable and perhaps laudable ethical choice. Methods of teaching range from authoritative teaching to open-ended discussions about ethical issues.

After much thought, prayer, and sleepless nights I have come upon an approach to the topic that is not totally unsatisfactory, at least to me. I have decided to present something that the three branches of

Christianity have to say about Christian morality: a distinctive approach or two within each of the three branches of Christian faith: Protestant, Catholic, and Orthodox. The approaches I present are representative and widely held, but they are not the only approaches. I begin with a Catholic approach, since the Catholic Church is my home and I am most familiar with it, and presumably we know our homes better than we know other places. Protestant approaches will follow; I have spent many years teaching Protestant Christian ethics. I will conclude with an approach that I am least familiar with, the Orthodox Christian tradition, which I more recently became acquainted with in researching a book on the history of Christian education. These three branches have different approaches since their moral focal points are somewhat different. Catholic morality is greatly influenced by the practice of confessing one's sins to a priest confessor. Protestant morality arises to a greater degree from the preaching pulpit. Orthodox morality is rooted in the worship and liturgy of the church.

What I have to say might be aptly summarized in an adaptation of an old story. A Catholic priest, an Orthodox clergyman, and a Protestant minister were asked to address a moral issue. The Catholic priest went first and began, "The Catholic Church teaches that according to the natural law. . . ." The Orthodox clergyman followed him and commenced "The ancient Orthodox tradition and worship teaches. . . ." The Protestant minister began his talk "I think that the Bible teaches. . . ." I may have already stated in essence all I will say, so you can all relax now with assurance that you have gotten the point of the talk. However, Rabbi Joe and Doctor David would not want me to stop now, so I will go on so there will be enough to be included as a chapter in this book.

What Does Christianity Add to Morality?

Perhaps this is the time to make a basic distinction between morality and ethics. Morality refers to the rightness or wrongness, the goodness and badness of human actions, attitudes, behaviors. Ethics, on the other hand, refers to the study of the justification of the morality of these actions, attitudes, and behaviors. Ethicians have devised many theories to explain and justify activity in the moral life of individuals and communities. It will not always be easy to maintain this distinction throughout this talk. Differences of opinion are more often in the ways that religious and secular ethicists make their cases for the morality of actions and attitudes than in their actual judgments.

All persons have some common agreements about what the good life is; what the moral virtues are, what attitudes and actions count as humanly responsible. These agreements in many areas are found among religious and nonreligious people. When one proposes to propose what to teach about Christian morality, much of what I say you should teach will be the same as Jewish morality, Muslim morality, or even secular or human morality. Of course there will be many areas where there are disagreements. But usually similar disagreements exist within religious and secular and nonreligious traditions. It is rarely, if ever, the case that religious people think one thing is right or wrong and secularists view it in an opposite manner. It is rarely, if ever, the case that all in a particular group view something as right, which all persons in another group view it in an opposite manner. When it comes to morality I believe that there is one human morality with regard to the content of morality. I realize that not all ethicists accept this position. But it does not invalidate my point that what we want you to teach about Christian morality is pretty much what you teach about your own morality.

The first question that must be addressed is what precisely does Christian add to morality or ethics. Christian morality is a normative ethic in that it provides the values or standards by which persons are to live their lives. To be Christian morality, the norms and standards must be related to the life and teachings of Jesus Christ. Jesus wrote nothing so we are dependent on what his followers recorded about his words and deeds. His followers presented him as a moral person worthy to be admired, a person who, like Socrates, was willing to die for what he believed. For followers of Jesus, Christian morality must take into account what God has done through Jesus. The ultimate moral questions for the Christian then should be: how should I live as a follower of Jesus? There is some truth in the question many Christians propose: what would Jesus do? It is a starting point, however, and not the only question to be asked.

The task of getting at the morality of Jesus is not an easy one. The materials that we have about Jesus combine a view of the Jesus of history and the Christ of faith. The Jesus of history is the Jewish rabbi. The

Christ of faith takes on the characteristics of the Christian communities of the early century in the Scriptures and the character of many communities throughout history. If the life and teaching of Jesus are the focal point of Christian morality, then we can say that "the quality of his life and the depth of his love revealed in the acceptance of the cross have been regarded by Christians as the decisive revelation of what goodness ultimately means" (Wogaman, 1989, 21).

Jesus, a Jewish teacher, preached about the moral life as the reign of God, the power of God acting in the world and in the life of individuals. God's reign entails an act of repentance, conversion or *metanoia* on the part of his followers, a turning away from sin and a turning to God. Jesus called people to discipleship, to be willing to learn from him as their teacher. This discipleship had a cost. Jesus said: Anyone who does not take up his cross and follow me cannot be my disciple (Gospel of Luke 14:26). Discipleship entails a life of faith, love, humility, and hope in the face of adversity. The morality of Jesus is connected with the law or Torah. It demands fidelity to the commandments of the Jewish law. Some Christian scholars consider that Jesus' moral demands were more demanding than those of the Mosaic covenant, for example, about marital fidelity. The ethic of Jesus was a morality of love. He called his followers to love even their enemies. The love of the Christian Scriptures is a call to a community or fellowship, to a service of others. Jesus declared certain people blessed in his beatitudes by proclaiming that the ordinary priorities of money, power, and comfort should not mark the life of his followers (O'Connell, 1990).

Christian theologians have debated over the past few decades whether there is a distinct Christian morality from what might be called human or secular morality. A Protestant theologian, James Gustafson (1975), even wrote a book *Can Ethics Be Christians?* Some Christians, aware of the failings of many Christians, rejoined with the question: Can Christians be ethical? Many have come to the conclusion that, when it comes to the content of morality—that is, the morality of particular actions—there is no distinctive Christian morality or ethics. Differences between approaches to morality lie more in the area of intentions, attitudes, dispositions, goals, ideals, and motivations of Christians. Christians as well as others who based their morality on religious grounds have specifically religious reasons for acting morally. Not all agree with this position, asserting that Christian morality adds something distinctive to secular or human morality. In general, Catholic moralists are more likely to reject the distinctiveness of Christian morality since most of them adhere to a natural law or philosophical approach to Christian morality (Curran and McCormick, 1980).

Catholic Morality: Natural Law Morality and the Teaching Church

In their approach to Christian morality, Catholic theologians and educators have for centuries utilized an approach called natural law morality, whose conclusions are buttressed by the authoritative voice of the church. While one can trace Catholic natural law morality back to Aristotle and the Stoic philosophers of Greece and Rome, including the great orator and philosopher, Marcus Tullius Cicero, a good place to begin explaining this tradition is to start with the moral theory of the medieval Catholic theologian, Thomas Aquinas (Porter, 1990; Hall, 1994). This Dominican saint contended that there exists in the world a moral law or order according to which certain actions are morally good and others morally bad. The rightness or wrongness of actions, therefore, lies in their very nature and not in any decision by God or humans; actions are intrinsically, or by their very nature, right or wrong. Of course there also exists actions which are morally neutral. Corresponding to this moral law or order there is present within each mature human being a capacity called conscience by which humans both know and judge the rightness or wrongness of their moral actions. Thus, when we contemplate or observe acts of benevolence and respect, we know them to be good. When we reflect upon or encounter acts of stealing and lying we know them to be bad.

This natural law approach rests on two basic concepts or analogies: nature and law. Human nature and human actions are conceived of in biological or physical terms. Every human action has its particular nature; it is what it is; it has its definition. The nature of a thing is something inherent in it and cannot be changed. Typing this paper is an action, which is at least morally neutral. Stealing a computer from a store is patently morally wrong; using a computer to advance a good cause is morally good.

The second concept or analogy in the concept of natural law is with human law. Just as human legislators make laws to govern people's lives according to what is permitted and what is prohibited, so God, the supreme legislator, promulgates laws to govern human life according to what is right and what is wrong. These laws are fashioned through a divine creative process and are there to be discovered when humans gradually reach a certain level of maturity.

The applications of the concepts of nature and law to Christian morality have become areas of controversy in Christian ethics. It is charged that it is simplistic to emphasize the physicality of human actions and misleading to view the complexity of the moral life from the perspective of human law. Focusing on the physical nature of actions may cause us to ignore what is distinctively human about these actions. Furthermore, the analogy with human law runs the risk of introducing an unwarranted and unwanted legalism into understanding and living the moral life.

One way in which proponents of natural law morality have dealt with the issue of the complexity of human actions is to distinguish various features of these actions. They recognize that the morality of human actions is greatly influenced by the intention of the person acting and the circumstances or situation in which one acts. Doing something accidentally is different from doing the same things with a clearly defined intention. Acting in the midst of a rage has a different moral quality than acting in a calculated manner. However, proponents of natural law theory contend that no intention, howsoever noble, nor any situation, howsoever extreme, can ever turn what is an objectively immoral action into a moral action. In their view, neither good ends nor noble intentions nor unique situations or circumstances can ever justify evil means or evil actions.

Proponents of natural law morality recognize that there are many factors that affect the responsibility or guilt to be ascribed to persons who commit actions that are objectively good or bad. Here is where dependence on law enters seriously into the discussion. Ignorance, fear, and coercion can greatly diminish, or in some cases even eliminate, the guilt of particular actions. But this does not change an objectively immoral action into an objectively moral action. What is at issue here is the distinction between subjective and objective morality and responsibility.

Thus the bedrock of the natural law approach to Christian morality is the essential nature or givenness of human moral actions.

This natural law approach to Christian morality infused the text-books or manuals which church educators used for centuries to train the clergy to be confessors and guides for their fellow clergy and laity (Curran, 1999). Through the work of Aquinas and the moral manualists, the principles of natural law morality extend to all spheres of moral life. It attempts to regulate personal conduct, the conduct of society, and even the conduct of nations. Its insights are applied to sexual relations, property rights, and issues of war and peace.

The origin of Catholic morality in confessional practice accounts for two further characteristics of the natural law approach: it is action-centered and sin-oriented. It is important to recognize how Catholic moral theory was shaped by its practical purpose of providing manuals to guide confessors in their work in administering the holy rite or sacrament of confession. The sacrament of penance or confession entails that priests accept the confessions of individuals, make a judgment of the morality of actions confessed, offer God's forgiveness and assign suitable penances. Consequently, this approach focuses primarily on the morality of particular actions.

The other feature of natural law morality is the development of casuistry. Since confessors deal with particular cases or moral problems in confessional practice, moralists provide moral cases that involve the application of moral principles to particular cases. The term casuistry has often had a pejorative connotation and is often associated with Jesuit priest-confessors, who were considered adept at finding loopholes or offering benign and even lax interpretations of natural and church law. While it is easy to caricature casuistry as excessive legalism, one has to admire the efforts made by casuists to deal with the complexity of peoples' moral problems. Whole systems of approach to dealing with moral problems arose over the years, ranging from rigorists' and perfectionists' interpretations to what are seemingly lax interpretations of laws and norms (Keenan and Shannon, 1995).

This natural law approach to Christian morality surprisingly did not make extensive appeals to the Christian or Jewish Scripture. To defend the whole notion of natural law, citations were made of statements of the Apostle Paul in his Letter to the Romans where he speaks of a law written in the hearts of all human beings. With regard to the moral quality of various actions, appeals were made for the Ten Commandments as indicating the principal moral and religious responsibilities, as well as particular actions deemed wrong and condemned. The teachings of Jesus, Paul, and the writers of the Christian Scriptures were used to praise and blame certain human actions. It would appear that the Scriptures were used more often to confirm the judgments of reason. Later proponents of natural law morality have attempted to remedy this lack by a more profound use of the Scriptures.

Adherents to the natural law approach recognize that, to be sure, there are levels of clarity when it comes to the dictates of the natural law. They distinguish three basic levels. At the first level of greatest generality and clarity the natural law obligates us to do good and to avoid evil. A slightly lesser level of clarity applies to principles at a second level embracing injunctions of the Decalogue concerning the immorality of such actions as stealing, adultery, lying, and killing. The least clarity exists in third level principles such as the morality of warfare, birth control, abortion, etc. It is particularly in this area that Catholics should seek the guidance of the Church and of respected moral theologians (Grisez, and Shaw, 1991).

The Catholic natural law tradition goes hand in hand with the role of the Church Magisterium or teaching authority in authoritatively making decisions on the morality of human actions. Recognizing the complexity of many moral issues and given the dangers of individuals making moral decisions out of unenlightened self-interest or proclivity to self-indulgence, and given the wide range of moral opinions in society, the Roman Catholic Church has traditionally made authoritative decisions on the morality of human actions both for its own members and for the broader society. While individual conscience is viewed as supreme in matters of moral choice, Catholic moralists contend that conscience needs to be properly formed by the authority and tradition of the church. The Church has not hesitated to take stands on many moral issues that are controversial in society. Of course, authoritative statements do not automatically command the assent and compliance that church authorities expect for their statements. To make matters more complicated, there are different levels of authoritativeness attached to authoritative statements. There are also documented instances where in time, changes have occurred in the Church's authoritative teachings; e.g., usury, slavery, and religious freedom.

The achievements of Catholic natural law morality have been considerable. Every moral area of human life has had extensive treatment. Some of its finest contributions lie in the area of social and political morality. John Courtney Murray (1960), the outstanding Jesuit theologian of the second half of the 20th century, applied natural law reasoning to such issues as church and state relations, religious freedom, and religious pluralism. His work, though viewed with suspicion in the 1950s, received strong validation from the Second Vatican Council in the 1960s, which issued documents on religious freedom and religious pluralism. For the past 100 years Popes and Councils have critiqued economic and political systems by utilizing principles of natural law morality. Beginning with the Encyclical Letter of Leo XIII in 1896, down to the social encyclicals of Pope John Paul II, natural law morality has informed judgments on such issues as the right of labor to organize, just wages, discrimination, just working conditions, distribution of wealth, the conditions for economic justice (Dorr, 1992). In the 1980s the American Bishops in their highly regarded and influential pastoral letter on the United States economy appealed in part to this tradition. Issues of peace and war have always been treated within this tradition of natural law morality, even down to the morality of the possession of nuclear arms for purposes of deterrence. Influential social and political theologies, including theologies of liberation, also draw on this moral stance for many of their principle positions, including the preferential option for the poor.

There is no doubt that, in recent social teachings of the Church, arguments for positions in the social, political, and economic sphere have increasingly appealed to teachings of the Christian and Jewish Scriptures. But all of these documents have made the decisions to speak in two languages, the particular language of the religious tradition and the universal language of natural law morality. One of the reasons for doing this is the pragmatic argument that the language of natural law morality is more conducive to influencing policy debates in the public forum.

Though there is controversy within the Catholic Church and outside the Church on positions that the Church has taken in the sphere of public life, even more controversy exists when it comes to the Church's teaching on sexual and life ethics (Cahill, 1996; Farley, 1987; Patrick, 1996). When Catholic leaders and moral theologians present their positions on such controversial issues as abortion, birth control, sexual expression before marriage, divorce, cloning, and many other issues they argue from what they believe are the universal principles of natural law and not the particular tenets of a particular religious faith. They contend that it is the very nature of these actions that render them immoral. Though Catholic moralists recognize that people in good faith arrive at different moral positions in these matters, they are insistent that an open and thorough examination of these actions in all their complexity will reveal them to be morally wrong. Most people recognize that the church's reasoning in these matters has not found acceptance outside the church and even within the church. Proponents of these positions point out that it took years and even centuries for societies to recognize the immorality of such actions as infanticide, slavery, and torture.

In Catholic schools, colleges, and seminaries the teaching of moral theology had a prominent place. I studied the subject for four years in a Catholic seminary. The strengths of Catholic moral theology must be seen along with its weaknesses and limitations. Catholic moral theology was taught as a subject separate from systematic theology and ascetical and mystical theology. Disconnected from these rich theological and spiritual sources, the subject tended to become legalistic and lacked inspiration for Christian living. More attention was given by its proponents to vice than it was to virtue, though the virtues were not ignored. Great novelists and playwrights have done the same, realizing that vice is more attractive than virtue. A distinction was made between the moral life and the spiritual life as if these two were disconnected (Billy and Orsutu, 1996).

For those of my generation, growing up Catholic meant being conscious of and keeping account of the sins one had to confess on Saturday afternoons. You did not usually go into the confessional to tell the priest about the good deeds you had performed during the previous week or fortnight. You were there to confess your sins of thought, word, and deed, telling how often each was done. We envied the Jews who we thought only had to do this one day a year and not in a dark confessional box. We knew that our Protestant friends were not obligated to perform this ritual. We were not aware of how Muslims handled their guilt.

Beginning in the middle of the last century, a number of developments took place that have significantly affected the Catholic approach to Christian morality and the natural law approach. There has been a significant decrease in the number of Catholics who approach priests to offer their confessions. Catholic life has witnessed an increased interest in spirituality. Within the field of Catholic moral theology, a more biblically centered approach, pioneered by Bernard Haring's (1978–1981) influential work has changed the way many moral theologians approach their discipline. Many Catholic theologians and philosophers no longer identify themselves with the theological approach of Thomas Aquinas and other classical moralists. Catholic moral theologians today draw on numerous philosophical traditions such as phenomenology, pragmatism, existentialism, analytic philosophy and even postmodernism (Callahan 1991; Maguire, 1978). Many Catholic theologians have pointed out the weaknesses and limitations of the traditional natural law approach to morality still enshrined in recent church documents as well as in the classical church documents (Fuchs, 1987). Furthermore, theologians are more in touch with and influenced by Protestant ethics and to a lesser degree by Jewish and Islamic ethics (Maguire, 1993).

One of the upshots of these developments is that there has emerged within the Catholic theological community a rather large group of theologians variously called progressive, liberal, or revisionists who have come to positions on moral issues at variance with the official teaching of the church. At times these theologians use the same natural law reasoning of the tradition to arrive at their viewpoints. If polls taken in this country as well as in other countries are to be believed, and I see no reason why not, a large number of Catholics seem to share the views of these dissenting theologians. Theologians and people dissent not only on issues of life ethics and sexual ethics but also on the morality of particular military actions and capital punishment.

All of this should not lead to the conclusion that the natural law approach to Christian morality is dead among Catholic leaders and theologians. Pope John Paul II offered a spirited and sophisticated defense of this approach in his encyclical letter *Veritatis Splendor* (1993). Appeals to the just war tradition are prominent in Catholic assessment of military actions. Natural law arguments are used to support traditional teachings in sexual and life ethics. Many theologians have come to realize that a

Christian morality and moral theology based on Scripture can go just so far. While the Scriptures may provide principles for living the moral life, they do not provide answers to the many concrete and complex moral issues that so frequently arise in our society. Asking "What would Jesus do?" provides a spiritual and religious orientation but it will provide concrete direction and solutions only if it is supplemented by a thorough investigation of relevant facts and moral principles.

In drawing this section to a close and in attempting to suggest what you should teach about Christian morality from a Catholic perspective, I get guidance from an experience in my life. While teaching a course in Christian ethics at Union Theological Seminary in Manhattan, an interdenominational Protestant seminary, a young student affiliated with a rather liberal Unitarian church volunteered that she was taking the course from a Catholic theologian because Catholics seem to have more fun theologically. From her vantage point, Catholics had so many interesting debates and arguments in comparison with her Unitarian congregation where people are generally expected to arrive at their own moral judgments and there is minimal debate. My advice to you is that you should teach the conflicts, the differences of opinion, the contrasting points of view. Very often, these are probably the same that occur within your own tradition. But what is more important, try to teach the arguments and reasons that are given for these points of view. It is a suggestion similar to Jacob Neusner's advice to not only teach what the great rabbis taught but also go deep into the reasons for their decisions (*Invitation to the Talmud.* Harper and Row, 1973).

Protestant Biblical Christian Morality

As I attempt to explain the Protestant ethical tradition, I realize that I am on much less firm ground. I have studied and taught the great Protestant ethicists, even teaching social ethics at Union Theological Seminary. But this is in no way comparable to growing up in an ethical tradition. But an attempt must be made to present all major elements of the Christian ethical tradition, even if parts are presented badly. I take consolation in the wise words of the English essayist, Gilbert Keith Chesterton: anything really worth doing is worth doing badly.

The sixteenth century reformers who protested against the abuses in the Roman Catholic Church based their reforms on the Christian Bible. They judged that the Catholic Church had departed in significant ways in faith, morals, and structures from the faith of the early church. Many reformers in Britain, Germany, Holland, Switzerland, and France began to develop a new approach to Christianity that corrected abuses and forged newer ways of being Christian in early modern societies and cultures that were emerging. The reforms had many prongs, some of which relate to a reformation of Christian morality. These include asserting the authority of the Scriptures in faith and morals, a questioning of the role of tradition upon which Catholics had depended for many of their beliefs, a rejection by some of the medieval scholastic theology upon which natural law morality was based, a rejection of the authority of the Roman Church in deciding issues relating to faith and morals, and a rejection of mandatory confession to a priest or at least removing confession from the sacraments or sacred rites of the church. In the place of these, the Protestant reformers put the authority of the Christian Scriptures and interpreters who they believed were faithful to the true meaning of these Scriptures.

The Protestant reform in Christian morality thus began with a return to fundamentals and that meant the Bible. Protestant morality in contrast to Catholic morality may be described as a biblical morality. Only those teachings that were firmly rooted in the Bible are to be matters of faith and morals. Decisions and practices of the Church that were not based on the Bible were to be rejected. Mandatory celibacy for priests and the monastic life were rejected not only because of widespread abuses in these institutions but because they did not have a sound basis in the Bible. Laws and canons of the church were overturned and doctrines were rejected. In their place, the reformers articulated a biblical faith based upon the reading and preaching of the scriptures and the celebration of only those rites or sacraments that had a firm foundation in the Bible. In the place of many pious devotions that had arisen over the centuries, the reformers privileged the prayerful reading of the Scriptures, to be interpreted not by any central authority but by individual believers. The Christian moral life would no longer be governed by Church ordinances but rather by faithful persons who piously read the Scriptures. In time, some reformers like the Swiss priest, John Calvin, introduced whole scale moral norms and laws in their churches. In the area of morality, their reforms led to a biblically based Christian morality. Calvin also espoused an approach to morality that is similar to natural law morality.

Protestant ethicists recognize both the strengths and the limitations of an ethic that is based on *sola scriptura*. The ethic is clearly Scriptural in its orientation and in its motivation. But many questions arise, as indicated by James Gustafson: "What is the authority of Scripture for ethics: How is Scripture relevant to, or applied to, practical moral matters?" (1978, p. 26). These questions obviously face all Christian ethicists, but they are less important for Catholic morality since natural law and church authority play such an important role in the Catholic approach to Christian morality. The doctrine of *sola scriptura* leads to other questions about discrepancies in the Bible, determining what are theological and ethical principles and what are not. Protestant ethicists are especially concerned with how principles of two thousand years ago are applicable to issues faced today and with how one applies principles enunciated in a powerless minority community to the cosmopolitan world of today (Gustafson, 1978, p. 29).

All Protestant reformers, to some degree, attacked the scholastic philosophy that then formed the basis for Christian doctrines and moral teachings. Aristotle became the whipping boy for many of the reformers. Faith and morals expressed in his language and concepts were viewed as a corruption of the fundamental and pristine Christian faith, which was to be found only in the Scriptures. The natural law tradition encoded in the medieval legal system of the church was in the eyes of many reformers a corruption of the pure moral teaching of Jesus and the Apostles. Christians were not to be saved through philosophy. The reformers severely criticized the school of theology at the University of Paris where Aristotle and scholastic philosophy and theology ruled supreme. This school was considered the intellectual center of a corrupt faith, with its monkish Dominican and Franciscan teachers. Corrupt Renaissance Popes in Rome had long been unduly influenced by their explanations of Christian faith and morality. A later target of the reformers was the fast growing Society of Jesus or Jesuit priests who took up the task of combating what they considered the errors of the reformers through preaching and the establishment of schools and colleges throughout Europe and into new worlds. Early Jesuits were educated at the University of Paris and became strong advocates of its highly rational approach to Christian faith and morality.

For many centuries the chief moral authority in the Western Church had been the Roman papacy. Final judgments on all moral issues came ultimately from this source. In rejecting the moral authority of the papacy, the reformers indirectly rejected its approach to Christian morality, which depended most often on legal and canonical norms. The strongest blow that the reformers struck at this moral authority was its attack on the practice of mandatory private confession of sins to a priest. This practice was viewed as a corruption of the Gospel since it required an unnecessary human mediator to be interposed between the believer and God. Through this practice, consciences were unduly burdened and there crept into widespread practice the biblically unfounded and corrupt teaching on indulgences, a practice by which the papacy did away with punishment incurred by sins.

The Protestant approach to Christian morality has certain characteristics that distinguish it from Catholic and Orthodox morality. While Catholics emphasize sins to be confessed to a priest, Protestants place stress on sin or the state of sinfulness. Sinfulness in Protestant theology is more a religious state than the moral state of Catholic sins. At liturgical services, it is this state of sinfulness, that is confessed rather than individual sins. This Protestant moral teaching is more pedagogical than it is moral. In focusing on sin or sinfulness, there is a strong desire to reject any form of legalism. Good actions are a result of our justification before God and not ways to achieve salvation and justification, as proposed in Catholic moral theology.

When one looks at the range of ethical approaches among Protestants, one finds it very wide. I can only give a representative sampling of Protestant approaches to Christian ethics. Since the Protestant ethical tradition did not develop as a separate branch of theology until recent years, the tradition includes some of the most prominent theologians of the twentieth century. At one end of the spectrum one finds a historicist or sectarian ethic, one that is termed Biblical Realism. In this view the Scriptures are the sole basis for this morality. Its proponents find no reason to enunciate a universal ethic since Christian ethics are only for Christians. In their view, Christianity is a particular historical community that is called to be faithful to the Scriptures. Members of this community are called to a radical obedience to the teachings of Jesus. The reformers rejected natural law or philosophical approaches to Christian morality. There is no need for a philosophical basis to Christian morality.

This ethic plays out especially in those theologians like John Yoder (1972; 1985) and Stanley Hauerwas (1975; 1983; 1996) who take a pacifist position on matters of war and peace. For them, the Scriptures provide the norm and the content for Christian morality. Christians are called to be a faithful witnessing minority. Very often, these theologians are in the radical Anabaptist tradition which was in tension with both church and state. For them, fidelity to Jesus, which entails nonresistance to evil, is the fundamental norm for Christians. It is the task of Christian morality not to accommodate the teachings of the Scriptures to the particular historical situations of the time. In their view, the Christian Church went into error when it adapted its teachings to the Constantinian era. It is this tradition of biblical realism that supports the strong pacifist ethics that is prevalent in many Protestant church like the Amish, Mennonites, and Quakers. It is this viewpoint that undergirds the rising movement of Radical Orthodoxy in Christian theology.

Another approach to a Protestant biblical morality is termed Historical Realism, which proposes an ethics of God acting in history. The Bible recounts how God acts in history. God still acts in history; biblical history helps us determine what God wants of us in present situations. God reveals moral ordinances through the medium of revelation. The task of Christian morality is to determine what should be our response to God's present acts in history. Ethics in the mode is more one of command and response, action and responsibility This is the ethic of such prominent Protestant ethicists as Karl Barth, H. Richard Niebuhr (1963), and Paul Lehmann (1963). It also seems to be the ethic underlying the ethics of liberation theology, which is espoused by both Catholic and Protestant theologians.

There is an implied historical relativism in this view of Christian ethics since it is clear that Christians have come to different historical conclusions about slavery, usury, abortion, or divorce by reading the same Bible. Were the teachings of the past in moral error or is God gently instructing us through history about what we are to do? Basic principles appear within the Scriptures but it seems that other considerations must enter into our decision-making before a final judgment can be made. Just what help does the Bible provide in concrete moral situations? Catholics and some Protestants appeal to a natural law. Questions about this approach abound: how do we account for historical changes? Is the past always a good guide to the present?

Historical realism may have been at the heart of the Social Gospel Movement at the beginning of the twentieth century, which attempted to apply Christian moral teachings to moral problems arising from increased industrialization and the ills associated with it. Such prominent Protestant preachers as William Gladden and Walter Rauschenbusch (1912) drew their inspiration from the social teachings of Jesus and the Hebrew prophets. The Social Gospel maintained that Jesus could be a reliable guide for both individual and social life. It stressed the immanence of God, the goodness of humankind, and the coming Kingdom of God on earth. Social Gospelers held the utopian view that the Kingdom of God could be achieved through the social efforts of humans. The ethics of the movement stressed Christ's way of love that would enable humankind to work for the good of all.

A third approach to Protestant biblical ethics is found in those theologians who have utilized the philosophy of existentialism to interpret the Christian Scriptures. In this approach what is emphasized is humans' radical freedom and their need to subjectively confirm their moral choices. Each moral situation is a unique occasion calling us to make a choice. Rudolph Bultmann, the theologian and biblical scholar, adopted this approach, which he believed was based on the reading of the New Testament. Each moral situation presents us with a crisis of decision in which we stand before God. This approach is similar to that of Protestant situation ethics of Joseph Fletcher (1963) who placed love at the center of Christian morality.

In the twentieth century, the most prominent ethicist in Protestant Christianity was no doubt Reinhold Niebuhr (1932; 1935; 1953), who developed an approach to Christian theology and ethics that has been called Christian Realism. As his biographer noted:

> The twentieth century Christian Church was shaken to its foundations by his piercing voice. So were the secular organizations of often agnostic liberals who flocked to him for inspiration. No one else could

speak with such authority to Christian, Jew, and unbeliever. (Richard Fox, *Reinhold Niebuhr: A Biography*. New York: Pantheon, 1985, p. 293)

Niebuhr's *Moral Man in Immoral Society* written in 1932 remains the most important exposition of his Christian realism and is influential to this day. Both theologians and political leaders have turned to this work in developing realistic moral positions for public life. The work asserts the inevitability of social conflict and the evil behavior of human collectivities. It also treats the resources Christians have for engaging in political action. This work contains the controversial moral principle that there is a different morality for individuals and for collectivities.

Niebuhr's ethics is primarily a social ethics; his theology is in service to ethics. Niebuhr was interested in the traditional Christian doctrines only to the degree to which they related to the ethical and moral life of individuals, communities, and nations. His Christian realism stated that though we live in a sinful world, there are reasons both for pessimism as well as optimism. Both elements are needed for a balanced theology of the world. While he contended on the one hand that the ideals of freedom and equality could not be achieved, on the other hand he held that we should not accept the inequalities of capitalism or other economic systems. For him the principles of love and justice can be achieved in the real world only in their approximations, or what he termed rough justice.

Niebuhr's ethical system is particularly relevant in times of armed conflict among nations as we experience today. His social ethics was shaped by his abandonment of pacifism and development of Christian realism to argue for United States entrance into the Second World War. He did not believe that the Gospel could be reduced to a law of love. He recognized that, at times, forms of coercion were needed to counter institutionalized violence. He admitted that pacifism was an alternative of Christians but rejected the Christian perfectionism of Christian sectarians and liberal Protestants. In his view, the absolute ethic of Jesus could not always be realized in the course of history. His was a theologically based relativism with an emphasis on the limitations of human nature. He argued that in our finitude we cannot grasp all the truth and that our sinfulness permanently distorts the truth that we do grasp and the good that we do express. Robert Bellah (1991) explained that:

He argued with great public effect that because of the tragic limitations of human nature, human beings could not help doing some evil in the course of doing good; yet, he continued, God commanded sinful men and women to bring justice to bear on human efforts, despite the ironic consequences that often meet such attempts. (Robert Bellah et al., *The Good Society.* New York: Knopf, pp. 33–34)

For Niebuhr moral judgment is the sorting out of the most realistic means to attain the most defensible proximate ends, without precommitment to some means as inherently more moral than others. For example, the decision for or against a war, for Niebuhr, is based on a cost benefit analysis in which war is seriously considered alongside other alternative means of attaining a desirable end. He argued for the agonized participation of Christians in particular wars.

As might be expected, Niebuhr's Christian realism has received its share of criticism over the years. He is charged with lacking prophetic insights and actually sponsoring policies that have brought human destruction. He leaves unclear the relationship between morality and politics. He is charged with an undue Christian pessimism. *Time* magazine's cover story on him in 1948 was captioned "Man's Story is not a Success Story." The heart of his pessimism lay in his facing up to extensive self-interest and abuses of power in individuals and especially in nations. The heart of his optimism lay in the biblical warrants of God's fidelity and love and redemption. At a tribute to Niebuhr after his death the following passage from his writings was read to encapsulate his interweaving of human activity with trust in God:

> The world community, toward which all historical forces seem to be driving us, is mankind's final possibility and impossibility. The task of achieving it must be interpreted from the standpoint of a faith which understands the fragmentary and broken character of all historical achievements and yet has confidence in their meaning because it knows their completion to be in the hands of a Divine Power, whose resources are greater than those of men, and whose suffering love can overcome the corruptions of man's achievements, without negating the significance of our striving. (In C. Brown, *Niebuhr and His Age.* Phila.: Trinity Press International, 1992, p. 4)

Orthodox Christian Ethics

Eastern Orthodox Christianity is the least known but the oldest tradition among the three major branches of Christianity. Christianity had its origins in the Eastern part of the Roman Empire. The Orthodox Churches originated in the Middle East and spread to countries of Eastern Europe and are now found in the West, including North and South America. The Orthodox Church takes it doctrinal lead from the Christian Scriptures, the Fathers of the early church, especially the Greek Fathers, and the first seven ecumenical or worldwide councils of the Christian Church. Orthodox Christians share many beliefs with Roman Catholics, differing mainly over the papal role and clerical celibacy. While there are many branches among Orthodox Christians the main Orthodox traditions are Greek and Russian.

The Orthodox Church has a profound theological or religious tradition. But when one looks specifically for Christian morality or Christian ethics one does not find a predominance of writings utilizing this terminology. Bishop Timothy Ware's popular and well regarded introduction *The Orthodox Church* does not include any references in the index to morality or ethics. One would not find such a phenomenon in examining standard Catholic and Protestant treatments. To find what Christian morality or ethics is for Orthodox Christians one must look to such terms as theology, spirituality, mysticism, and deification. In recent years a branch of theology called Christian ethics has emerged. For sure there are identifiable scholars such as Stanley Samuel Harakas, Vigen Guroian, and Chrestos Yannaras who write on Orthodox ethics, like Catholic and Protestant scholars, but they are few in number and not as influential as the theological and spiritual writers.

What the Orthodox approach to Christian ethics provides to Christian morality is an approach where ethics and moral laws are closely connected with theology, mysticism, spirituality, worship, and art. In Western Christianity there is a tendency to separate these elements of life and to study them as distinct elements, although all scholars make protestations of a basic unity among the various dimensions of Christian faith and theology. Moral formation comes about chiefly through participation in the liturgical services of the church. An Orthodox theologian has expressed this close connection between liturgy and Orthodox moral formation explaining that:

The Orthodox faith has its most adequate expression in worship and that truly Christian life is the fulfillment of the grace, vision, teaching, inspiration and power that we receive in worship. Therefore it is in the organic connection between the liturgical life of the Church and their educational effort that we find the uniquely Orthodox principle of religious education. (Schmemann, 1983, p. 5)

For this theologian, the Orthodox moral life takes its heed from the words of the Psalms, "O taste and see that the Lord is good!" (Psalm 34.8). Experience comes before understanding and participation before explanation. While this is the ideal and exists in potential, one reads Orthodox leaders who complain that people neither understand nor even sing the beautiful liturgies of the Church.

Another way of expressing the Orthodox moral life is through "the *phronema* of the Orthodox tradition: an attitude, a position and/or posture which reflects a particular spirit, a theological sentiment or frame of mind. . . . It postulates a scriptural, traditional, doctrinal spirit, a sentiment and frame of mind which is reflected and existentialized in the liturgical life of the individual both within and without the Church." (Nicozisin in Vrame, 1999, p. 6) The *phronema* is the living tradition of practices and customs which are passed down from one generation to the next by examples and personal instruction. It includes not only the vestments, icons, candles, incense, etc., but especially the inner spirit, its way of thinking, its way of living. It is the Orthodox heritage. It gives life, vitality, and meaning to each Orthodox Christian (In Vrame, p, 7).

Orthodox Christian morality has profound theological roots. A classic text *Toward Transfigured Life: The Theoria of Eastern Orthodox Ethics* (1983) by Stanley Samuel Harakas offers a rich scholarly approach. He emphasizes the close connection between belief and the Christian life. He wrote this book to balance what he considers the overemphasis on mysticism and liturgy as partly responsible for a weak ethical dimension of Orthodox moral theory. Still he admits that icons and hymns have their moral effect. In his well-organized study he deals with both theological and philosophical ethics. Recognizing that Orthodox ethics as a field of study has lagged behind Protestant and Catholic ethics, he attempts to supplement the more pastorally oriented approaches to Orthodox Christian morality.

Orthodox theologians develop an extensive theological and historical background before attending to particular moral issues. In the Orthodox approach to moral theology one finds lengthy quotations from the Bible, the Holy Tradition of the Orthodox Church, its Theology, and a real and powerful "Spirit of Orthodoxy." Moral issues are addressed according to the faith, beliefs, and traditions of the Orthodox Church. For Harakas, though, the Orthodox Church has a documented history of ethical teaching; its spirit is not dominated by rules and rigid sanctions. The strict rules and standards of the Orthodox are set within a perspective that is dominated by compassion and love (1990, p. 18).

The Orthodox approach to Christian morality is rooted in tradition; it is rooted in history and its sense of continuity with the past. For the Orthodox, the past is always connected with the present. Harakas explains that "most Orthodox people understand the past to contain within it the seeds of the future and the future to be grounded in the present and the past" (Harakas 1990, p. 4). The past provides the standing place to make judgments about the present. For Harakas, Church Fathers like St. Basil of Caesarea and St. John Chrystostom are contemporaries. He explains:

> I view the biblical personages and the church fathers as alive and vividly present to my personal experience of the Christian faith, the Old Testament saints, the apostles, the martyrs, and the Christian saints of every kind throughout history. Above all, through the sacramental life and the mystical tradition of Orthodoxy Christ is also a living contemporary. Nearly every feast in the church celebrating an event in the life of Christ is observed with hymns which begin: Today. . . ." (1990, p. 6)

A distinctively Orthodox approach to Christian morality is found in the work of Vigen Guroian, a contemporary lay professor of theology and ethics. The sources of his theological ethics are the Christian Scriptures, the early church fathers, the liturgical rites of the Church, the classic novels of Dostoevsky and Tolstoi, the religious philosophy of Nicholas Berdyaev, contemporary novelists such as Walter Percy, John Updike, C. S. Lewis, John Cheever, and modern films. In his ethical treatise on living and dying, he utilizes all these sources to present a vision of life and death that is informed by biblical faith and is Church-centered. He also draws on the Christian teachings of creation and redemption. This ethic is closely connected with Christian catechetical instruction, preaching, and the rites of the Church. He concludes that caring for the sick and dying begins with caring for the healthy and living. Guroian explains:

> The resources that the Christian faith holds for living toward dying in freedom and with hope and courage cannot be instantaneously trans-mitted to the sick person waiting for death whose flesh is already ravaged and mind tormented with disease. Nor are those resources of faith likely to be helpful to the sick and bereaved who have not been nurtured throughout their lives in that faith. The meaning for living and dying that faith provides must be owned over a lifetime. (1996, p. 194)

The ultimate goal of the moral and spiritual life of Orthodox Christians is *theosis*, a participation or union with God through Jesus. In the strongest language possible, it is a divinization or deification of the human being, becoming like God. It is a term used to describe the inti-mate union, communion, and fellowship of the human with the divine (Vrame, 1999, p. 92). The process is a holistic one that includes the entire person. It is, in Vrame's words, living, acting, and knowing with the totality of one's being (p. 15).

One concrete way that Orthodox Christians strive for *theosis* is through their veneration of icons. Icons present a vision of lives lived in union with God. Understanding icons is a valuable way to get a feel for a distinct Orthodox approach to the moral and spiritual life and explore the theology and the use of icons in Orthodox life and theology. Icons serve to socialize and initiate Orthodox Christians into the beliefs and moral values of their church. An early Orthodox writer, John of Damascus, called these icons "the books of the illiterate, the never silent heralds of the honor due the saints, teaching without use of words those who gaze upon them" (Vrame, 1999, p. 1). Icons lead both to the ortho-doxy (right belief) and orthopraxis (right practice) of Orthodox moral life. Icons are sacred images of Jesus, Mary, or one of the saints of the Orthodox Church. Icons are religious art that comes from a spiritual vision and spiritual understanding. They are pervasive in Orthodox life, not only in Churches but also in homes, classrooms, and automobiles. The meaning and use of icons was debated for centuries in the Orthodox

Church between iconoclasts (destroyers of icons) and iconophiles (lovers of icons). The Mosaic prohibition against graven images was at the heart of the controversy.

In Orthodox theology and spirituality the moral value of the icon is that it produces an emotion and understanding that will inspire the worshipper to imitate the virtues of the persons depicted in the icons. In the Orthodox view, iconic art has the power to shape one's moral behavior. The Seventh Ecumenical Council of the Church made this case for the moral and educational value of icons:

> These holy persons of all times who pleased God, whose biographies have remained in writing for our benefit and for the purpose of our salvation, have also left the catholic church their deeds explained in paintings, so that our mind may remember them, and so that we may be lifted up to the level of their conduct. (Vrame, 1999, p. 54)

It is of interest that many contemporary moral educators have emphasized the power of examples and stories of virtuous persons as having moral formative value. For Orthodox Christians the teachings of Jesus and the lives of the saints of the past as depicted in icons, as well as in words, present the ultimate moral norms for living the moral life. These depict the qualities of love, gentleness, kindness, mercy, and forgiveness that are to characterize the life of believers. Orthodox ethicists do not leave the matter there since they also want to give practical guidance to their congregants. These ethicists also propose rules, commandments, duties and responsibilities that are proper to persons who want to establish the presence of God in their lives. They point out, however, that rules are only guidelines for Christian living and recognize that there are exceptions to many of the rules. But they emphasize that no one can live the Christian moral life without the grace of God and participation in the rites of the Church.

Conclusion

The overriding moral issue for our time and, indeed, for all times is the issue of the morality of war and resorting to violence to settle conflicts.

No issue is more important than that which affects the lives of millions of people, especially those who live in nations that have had a long history of conflict and warfare. The Christian tradition on the morality of warfare has been a diverse one in different times and places. A brief look at how the three branches of Christianity look at the morality of warfare may highlight to some degree the differences I have tried to draw among the three traditions.

The Catholic tradition is well known. For fifteen hundred years it has adhered to the teaching of the possibility of a just war. The tradition began in the West with Augustine of Hippo who developed a set of ethical prescriptions and proscriptions concerning the entrance into war (*jus ad bellum*) and behavior during war (*jus in bello*). These principles were ultimately derived from the Roman orator Cicero. The foundation for this theory is natural law morality. This tradition has been enriched by many theologians, notably Thomas Aquinas, and has been utilized by popes and theologians down to the present day. Some attempts have been made to root this theory in the Jewish and Christian Scriptures. Pope John Paul II has enunciated this teaching in a number of his addresses and pronouncements. Within the Catholic tradition has also been found a justification for a holy war or crusade, but not since medieval times. St. Bernard of Clairvaux preached a medieval crusade.

In our day, beginning with the encyclical *Pacem in Terris* of Pope John XXIII, the Second Vatican Council, the Catholic response to the Vietnam war, and the 1986 statement of the American Bishops on peace and war, there has emerged an ever-increasing pacifist voice and movement. This theory is more dependent on the Christian Scriptures, which largely endorse a pacifist approach to violence. The development of nuclear arms has also given added impetus to this growing movement. Many pacifists argue that in this nuclear age it is increasingly impossible to meet the conditions for a just war.

The Protestant tradition on the morality of warfare is a wide one. Within Protestantism, with its scriptural based morality, pacifism has had a long history. For centuries there have been peace churches such as the Amish, Mennonites, and Quakers. Pacifism had strong support in many Protestant Churches before the Second World War. However, a just war approach entered into Protestant morality as well as Niebuhr's agonized participation in war as an inevitable evil. Since it is difficult to make the case for a moral or good war from the Christian Scriptures, many Protestant ethicists developed theories similar to those of Catholic ethicists.

If one examines the statements of the World Council of Churches (WCC), a basically Protestant organization, one sees that it has not been an essentially pacifist organization. However, in 1975 the Council raised the question: how can Christians, children of God's love and followers of Jesus Christ, live and work in a world where the use of force and violence against the countless forms of human sin seems unavoidable (Muelder 1980, p. 154). Within the WCC there has been a growing movement toward pacifism in this nuclear age, which includes a struggle against militarism and recognition of the ambiguities of wars for national liberation.

The Orthodox tradition on warfare is both "broad and rich. It honors not only princes who gave up their lives rather than resist evil, but also warrior-saints whose icons were carried into battle by soldiers chanting, 'Grant victory to Orthodox Christians over their enemies'" (Harakas, 1992, 1). The evolution of Harakas's views may give some insight to the wide range of attitudes and worship celebrating victories in war, even while it also affirms the values of peace. His evolution also shows how Orthodox ethicists arrive at their conclusions. At first he maintained that the Orthodox position was that of the just war. He then pondered the significance of the position that Orthodox clergy were forbidden to engage in military activity, although laity could engage in it. Clergy were to maintain a pacifist witness. At a later stage he came to the conclusion that the just war tradition of Augustine could not be found in the Greek fathers or in the canonical tradition of the Orthodox Church. Using patristic sources, Byzantine military manuals and contemporary statements about war, he concluded in 1986 that the Orthodox position had an amazing "consistency in the almost totally negative moral assessment of war coupled with an admission that war may be necessary under certain circumstances to protect the innocent and to limit even greater evils" (1992, p. 2). For him, in the Orthodox tradition, war cannot be just or good but can be seen only as a necessary evil. While war may be necessary, pacifist strains are retained in liturgy and clerical standards. In the Orthodox view of war, the peace ideal remains normative and no theoretical efforts were made to make conduct of war into a positive form.

References and Bibliography

Roman Catholic

Billy, Dennis J. & Orsutu, eds. (1996). *Spirituality and Morality: Integrating Prayer and Action*. New York: Paulist.

Cahill, Lisa Sowle. (1996). *Sex, Gender, and Christian Ethics*. New York: Cambridge University Press.

Callahan, Sidney. (1991). *In Good Conscience: Reason and Emotion in Moral Decision Making*. San Francisco: Harper.

Curran, Charles E. (1999). *The Catholic Moral Tradition Today*. Washington, DC: Georgetown University Press.

Curran, Charles E. & McCormick, Richard. *Readings in Moral Theology No. 2: The Distinctiveness of Christian Morality*. New York: Paulist Press.

Dorr, Donald. (1992). *Option for the Poor: A Hundred Years of Vatican Social Teaching*. rev. ed. Maryknoll, NY: Orbis.

Farley, Margaret. (1987). *Personal Commitments*. New York: Harper and Row.

Fuchs, Joseph (1987). *Christian Morality: The Word Becomes Flesh*. Washington, DC: Georgetown University Press.

Grisez, Germain & Shaw, Russell. (1991). *Fulfillment in Christ: A Summary of Christian Moral Principles*. Notre Dame, IN: University of Notre Dame Press.

Gula, Richard. M. (1989). *Reason Informed by Faith: Foundations of Catholic Morality*. New York: Paulist.

Hall, Pamela M. (1994). *Narrative and the Natural Law: An Interpretation of Thomistic Ethics*. Notre Dame, IN: University of Notre Dame Press.

Haring, Bernard. (1978–1981). *Free and Faithful in Christ. Moral Theology for Clergy and Laity*, 2 vols. New York: Seabury Press.

Keenan, James & Shannon, Thomas A., Eds. (1995). *The Context of Casuistry*. Washington, DC: Georgetown University Press.

Maguire, Daniel C. (1978). *The Moral Choice*. Garden City, NY: Doubleday.

Maguire, Daniel C. (1993). *The Moral Core of Judaism and Christianity: Reclaiming the Revolution*. Minneapolis, MN: Fortress.

Murray, John Courtney. (1960). *We Hold These Truths*. New York: Sheed and Ward.

O'Connell, Timothy E. (1990). *Principles for a Catholic Morality*. Rev. Ed. San Francisco: Harper.

Patrick, Anne. P. (1996). *Liberating Conscience: Feminist Explorations in Catholic Moral Theology*. New York: Continuum Press.

Pope John Paul. (1993). *Veritatis Splendor*. Origins 23.

Porter, Jean. (1990). *The Recovery of Virtue: The Relevance of Aquinas for Christian Ethics*. Louisville, KY: Westminster/John Knox.

Protestant

Bennett, John C. (1945). *Christian Ethics and Social Policy*. New York: Scribner.

Bonhoeffer, Dietrich. (1955). *Ethics*. New York: Macmillan.

Bonhoeffer, Dietrich. (1963 [1937]). *The Cost of Discipleship*. New York: Macmillan.

Boulton, Wayne G., Kennedy, Thomas D. & Verhey, eds. (1994). *From Christ to the World: Introductory Readings in Christian Ethics*. Grand Rapids, MI: Eerdsmans.

Fletcher, Joseph. (1963). *Situation Ethics: The New Morality*. Philadelphia: Westminster.

Harrison, Beverly. (1985). *Making the Connections*. Boston: Beacon Press.

Gustafson, James M. (1968). *Christ and the Moral Life*. New York: Harper and Row.

Gustafson, James M. (1975). *Can Ethics be Christian?* Chicago: University of Chicago Press.

Gustafson, James M. (1978). *Protestant and Roman Catholic Ethics*. Chicago: University of Chicago Press.

Gustafson, James M. (1981). *Ethics from a Theocentric Perspective*. Chicago: University of Chicago Press.

Hauerwas, Stanley. (1975). *Character and the Christian Life: A Study in Theological Ethics*. San Antonio, TX: Trinity University Press.

Hauerwas, Stanley. (1983). *The Peaceable Kingdom: A Primer in Christian Ethics*. Notre Dame, IN: University of Notre Dame Press.

Hauerwas, Stanley. (1996). *Where Resident Aliens Live: Exercises for Christian Practice*. Nashville, TN: Abingdon.

Lehman, Paul L. (1963). *Ethics in a Christian Context*. New York: Harper and Row.

Lovin, Robin W. (1995). *Reinhold Niebuhr and Christian Realism*. New York: Cambridge University Press.

McClendon, James W. (1975). *Ethics: Systematic Theology*. Nashville, TN: Abingdon.

Muelder, Walter G. (1980). Pacifism and the World Council of Churches. In Thomas A. Shannon, ed. *War or Peace? The Search for New Answers*. Maryknoll, NY: Orbis Books.

Meilander, Gilbert. (1981). *Friendship*. Notre Dame, IN: University of Notre Dame Press.

Meilander, Gilbert. (1984). *The Theory and Practice of Virtue*. Notre Dame, IN: University of Notre Dame Press.

Niebuhr, H. Richard. (1963). *The Responsible Self: An Essay in Christian Moral Philosophy*. New York: Harper and Row.

Niebuhr, Reinhold. (1932). *Moral Man in Immoral Society*. New York: Scribner.

Niebuhr, Reinhold. (1935). *An Interpretation of Christian Ethics*. New York: Harper and Row.

Niebuhr, Reinhold. (1953). *Christian Realism and Political Problems*. New York: Scribner.

Ramsey, Paul. (1950). *Basic Christian Ethics*. New York: Scribner.

Ramsey, Paul. (1967). *Deeds and Rules in Christian Ethics*. New York: Scribner.

Ramsey, Paul. (1961). *War and the Christian Conscience: How Shall Modern War be Conducted Justly?* Durham, NC: Duke University Press.

Rauschenbusch, Walter. (1912). *Christianizing the Social Order*. New York: Macmillan.

Tillich, Paul. (1954). *Love, Power, and Justice*. New York: Oxford University Press.

Wogaman, J. Philip. (1989). *Christian Moral Judgment*. Nashville, TN: Westminster/John Knox.

Yoder, John Howard. (1972). *The Politics of Jesus*. Grand Rapids, MI: Eerdsmans.

Yoder, John Howard. (1985). *The Priestly Kingdom: Social Ethics and the Bible*. Notre Dame, IN: University of Notre Dame Press.

Eastern Orthodox

Breck, John (1999). *The Sacred Gift of Love: Orthodox Christianity and Bioethics*. Crestwood, NY: St. Vladimir's Press.

Guroian, Vigen. (1987), *Incarnate Love: Essays in Orthodox Ethics*. Notre Dame, IN: University of Notre Dame Press.

Guroian, Vigen. (1994). *Ethics after Christendom: Toward an Eastern Christian Ethics*. Grand Rapids, MI: Eerdsmans.

Guroian, Vigen. (1996). *Life's Living toward Dying: A Theological and Medical-Ethical Study.* Grand Rapids, MI: Eerdsmans.

Harakas, Stanley Samuel. (1983). *Toward Transfigured life: Theoria of Eastern Orthodox Ethics.* Minneapolis, MN: Light and Life.

Harakas, Stanley Samuel. (1985). *Let Mercy Abound: Social Concern in the Greek Orthodox Church.* Brookline, MA: Holy Cross Orthodox Press.

Harakas, Stanley Samuel. (1990). *Health and medicine in the Eastern Orthodox Tradition.* New York: Crossroad.

Harakas, Stanley Samuel. (1990). Icon and ethics. *Orthodoxes Forum* 4:2, 195–214.

Harakas, Stanley Samuel. (1992), *Living the faith: The praxis of Eastern Orthodox ethics.* Minneapolis, MN: Light and Life Publishing Co.

Harakas, Stanley Samuel. (1999). *Wholeness and faith. Orthodox Christian ethics.* Brookline, MA: Holy Cross Orthodox Press.

Schmemann, Alexander. (1974). *Liturgy and Life: Christian Education through Liturgical Experience.* Synosset, NY: Orthodox Church in America, Department of Religious Education.

Vrame, Anton. (1999). *The Educating Icon.* Brookline, MA: Holy Cross Press.

Woodill, Joseph. *The Fellowship of Life: Virtue Ethics and Orthodox Christianity.* Washington, DC: Georgetown University Press.

Webster, Alexander. (1998). *The Pacifist Option: The Moral Argument Against War in Eastern Orthodox Moral Theology.* International Scholars Publications.

Yannaras, Christos. (1984). *The Freedom of Morality.* Trans. Elizabeth Briere. Crestwood, N Y: St. Vladimir's Press.

B R I A N   S T I L T N E R

Teaching About the Others' Ethics: A Response to Professor John Elias

This conference is titled, "What Do We Want the Other to Teach about Our Ethical Traditions?" Professor Elias admirably approached his task by stressing the *what* question, that is, the content of the Christian tradition. I approach my task by commenting on the context and challenges of the what question, then asking some related questions: why teach about the other, where and how to teach about the other, and who is teaching about the other? This topic is hard to write about, as Professor Elias said, because it is hard to condense accurately "the Christian tradition" or any of its sub-traditions. In addition, it seems presumptuous to tell Jews and Muslims what they should teach about us. But we can all take comfort in being in the same boat on these matters. The ideal way to approach the matter would be as Rabbi David Fox Sandmel described to an earlier CCJU conference in this series: "In an ideal situation, "we" would not teach about the other at all. Rather, when we want to learn about the other we should invite the other into our classroom or onto our pulpit to teach. The presence of the living, breathing other is itself a lesson that we can never duplicate. I recognize that there are many situations where this is either impossible or impractical, but I say it nonetheless to underscore the delicacy, the challenge of teaching about the other as the other would want us to teach about them." His point is well-taken. What can we do to make such opportunities more common and more practical? And when we can not hear from the other directly, what are some of the beneficial methods and forums for presenting the other's tradition? Those are questions I will touch on in my response.

It is hardly necessary for me to expand on what Professor Elias wrote. My emendations or interpretations would turn the conversation into an intramural one. He took on this massive task with aplomb. His 30-some pages summarizing the basic methods and paramount concerns of Christian ethics in its three main branches are as good a summary of the field for a nonspecialist as any single article I know. In addressing the *what* question, Professor Elias started with the big picture: "Christian morality is a normative ethics in that it provides the norms or standards by which persons are to live their lives. To be Christian morality, the norms must be related to the life and teachings of Jesus Christ. . . . For Christians, Christian morality must take into account what God has done through Jesus. The ultimate moral question for the Christian should be: How should I live as a follower of Jesus?" Christian ethics occurs when the community that confesses Jesus Christ reflects on values and principles to guide individual and communal actions. Christians seek to pattern themselves after deeds and teachings of Jesus, not so much because he was a great teacher as because he offered a liberating experience of the Divine under the paradigms of freedom and grace. Christian ethics is a thankful response to God.

Christian ethics, similar to Jewish and Muslim ethics, draws upon the sources of Scripture, Tradition, reason, and experience to derive its values and principles. Professor Elias rightly noted that many of our judgments will be the same as yours. This is because we draw upon certain common Scriptures, guard overlapping and parallel traditions, lived through common historical contexts, and especially, because we see our overarching goal as faithfulness to the one God who is the Creator of the universe and who offered a covenant to Abraham.

Professor Elias also rightly noted that there is great variety in the particular judgments arrived at in the Christian community, both as a whole and in the particular denominations. That the sources of Scripture, Tradition, reason, and experience can interact in numerous ways is one of the main reasons for the different patterns found in the three Christian branches. Professor Elias's differentiation of the Catholic, Protestant, and Orthodox traditions was adept and helpful in explaining these variations. I want to take a different tack and look at how the ethical variations that occur within Christianity are parallel to variety of particular judgments found in Judaism and Islam. Thus, we find some Christians agreeing with some Jews and Muslims on a given issue while they disagree with fellow Christians.

Take the example of family life. Jews, Christians, and Muslims have always respected the family as the basic building block of society, the primary vehicle for teaching faith, and the locus of good and holy vocations. None of the traditions have condoned infidelity, rape, incest, or abandonment of spouse and children; none have seen divorce or having children out of wedlock as a preferred path. Yet the traditions work out the acceptable variations differently. So, for example, Catholic and Orthodox Christians have seen celibate life as a worthy alternative to family life; Muslims could historically accept polygamy as a form of faithful marriage; and Jews could build the possibility of divorce into the laws governing marriage. In addition to these tradition-dependent tendencies, we have the phenomenon James Davison Hunter described as the "culture wars": that progressives have more in common with progressives in other religions than with conservatives in their own religion (and vice versa). For instance, many Catholics, evangelical Protestants, Orthodox Jews, and Muslims agree that homosexual relationships fall outside the scope of acceptable family structures and should not be honored with the status of marriage, especially within the religious community. By contrast, many Christians and Jews, and perhaps some Muslims, regard homosexual relations as morally neutral or morally good and want to see greater acceptance for the legitimacy of these relationships in their religious communities. Some congregations have conferred such legitimacy by blessing gay unions.

There are many reasons for this interesting phenomenon, owing to religious traditions and cultural influences. The point here is not how to frame or resolve the debate as to note that the *what* question raises consideration of the contexts that shape the teaching and the challenges and opportunities that arise from these crosscutting patterns. The examples of family and sexual ethics I have just described present challenges such as how to talk to others in our communities across differences, how to portray the other traditions fairly, and how to avoid the attitude that it is all politics—that what is most important about religion is our ethical policies and the strategic alliances we make around them. The crosscutting pattern also leads to opportunities such as interreligious dialogue leading to a nuanced understanding of the other and finding common cause with believers against cultural and other external threats to faith. The culture wars thesis is in many ways overstated, but even to the extent that it holds, it is not the last word. Religious traditions themselves do much to support and teach cross-cultural principles such as love, justice, and the Golden Rule.

Why teach about the Other? This question was addressed by Rabbi Tsvi Blanchard in his keynote, but each person who addresses the *what* topic has a *why* in mind; it is helpful to keep attending to it. The overarching reason is that it has to do with the will of God. Believing in God as Creator and Lord of all, we must have respect for every one of God's human creations. Respect is not possible without some understanding, so we teach about the others in order to understand them better and respect them more authentically. Christians should consider themselves as part of a family of Abrahamic faith; they are called to respect, understand, and indeed facilitate the faith of the Abrahamic others. It would be naïve and misleading if I suggested this was a long-standing concern. For instance, until the 1960s, the Catholic Church prayed on Good Friday for the conversion of the Jews, but now we rightly pray that they remain faithful to their covenant.

I believe there is a threefold purpose in any interreligious dialogue and teaching about the other. We teach about the other's ethics in order that our community might better understand the *other*, better understand *ourselves*, and create a context for improved *cooperation* for common causes. Let me try to illustrate how these three goals are carried out, using the example of debates about human cloning and stem cell research.

When Dolly the sheep was cloned in 1997, all religious traditions felt at sea in trying to address this act that had moved abruptly from science fiction to science fact. The first move of most religious bodies was to affirm rather similar principles—that God is the ultimate creator of human life, that each human being deserves respect and the opportunity to develop as a unique individual, that any individual human, however born, will have an individual soul, and that we should take care not to master the creation of life for selfish ends. In the ensuring years, these traditions worked out particular responses under their respective methods of reasoning. Though there is now some debate over the propriety of therapeutic cloning, major religious traditions maintain a fairly united front against reproductive cloning and they keep a number of issues on the public agenda that might not otherwise be there.

Religious traditions can also benefit from their disagreements. For example, the Catholic Church's positions on cloning, stem cell research, and reproductive technologies are driven by its basic teachings of full respect for the human embryo as an individual human life from the earliest moments, and its natural law teaching about the unity of procreation and sexual expression in marriage. It is hardly right or fair to say that the Catholic Church takes these positions because it is against medical progress or wants to oppress women. When the other learns about the Catholic tradition and vice versa, they find some broad shared concerns, and both sides benefit. Liberal Protestants and Reform Jews, for instance, may find that they share with Catholic teaching a concern about commodifying reproduction and instrumentalizing human life. Though not all members of the Western faiths believe early abortion is morally impermissible, many have found a shared concern that creating embryos for research erodes respect for human life and the reproductive responsibility. Likewise, Catholics need to learn that most arguments in favor of stem cell research are generated not by a desire for technical mastery over the human condition (though some of the biotech pioneers give this impression) but by real concern for mollifying horrendous genetic diseases and helping childless couples achieve their goals of family life. Many American Catholics, if not the Church, have been influenced by arguments differentiating reproductive cloning from therapeutic cloning and the use of spare embryos from the use of embryos created for research. The outcome of such learning is still unclear, but Catholics are no doubt helped by hearing thoughtful arguments from fellow Christians, Muslims, and Jews.

My example still relies mostly on the paradigm of religious communities offering their own views to an interreligious or public dialogue. *Where* does teaching about the other take place? *How* is such teaching carried out, and *how* could it be done better? A list of the contexts includes: the pulpit, the liturgy, adult education, religious education for youth, official religious documents, institutional religious literature, media communications, universities, and centers and programs affiliated with religious bodies. In all these contexts, in a variety of ways and to a variety of audiences, a religious community communicates its own views and sometimes presents its understanding of the views of the other. Let me comment on a few of the settings. First, religious education is a formative influence. Religious organizations take it seriously but rely upon families to bring their children to the settings where it can happen and to reinforce it at home. Second, the university. My experience is that it is a daunting task teaching about our own and the others' traditions, when the students have only a rudimentary knowledge of both. Catholic universities are wrestling today with the balance of helping students learn more about the tradition they represent along with the multiple traditions of culture and religion. How do we go deep, especially when the students may not have much or any religious background, but also present other religious traditions with enough nuance and detail? Third, adult religious education is a valuable setting for members of a synagogue, mosque, or church to continue growing in their faith as well as learning about the other. Although the opportunities are usually punctual, the learning for an individual can go on over many years. But capitalizing on such opportunities varies widely. My experience and impression is that many Protestant churches do a good job at adult education while Catholic churches find it an uphill battle—if they even try. I do not know what it is like among Jews and Muslims, but I would be interested to learn about it from you.

The last area I want to address is *who*—who is the other in relation to our faith and our ethical traditions? This is not an easy question owning in part to the historical and ongoing inequalities of the relationships. Christians should see Jews as brothers and sisters, in Pope John Paul II's words, "elder brothers in faith." Jews are those who gave a patrimony to Christians—the Scriptures, the laws of Moses, the vision of the prophets, the call to justice, the hope of a messiah. Christians celebrate this deposit of faith, but their celebration has also generated overt claims or subtle suggestions that Christians represent the proper fulfillment of Jewish teaching and are the only heirs of the covenant. Christians should eschew this teaching, known as supersessionism, or even an attitude of it. They should remember that they stand in a similar position vis-à-vis Muslims, who claim to have the fuller and complete revelation.

Christians should view both Jews and Muslims as the others who are not so other, who share overlapping and parallel doctrinal foundations that therefore, lead to overlapping and parallel teachings and methods regarding ethics. They are ones we want to learn more about and with whom we want to cooperate in more constructive ways. They are ones toward whom we owe respect. They are ones from whom we desire respect, knowing that, in many ways, we still have to earn it. Our intersecting histories are fraught. In most societies, Christians have had the greatest numbers and most or all of the political power; too we often used it to the harm of Jews and Muslims. Aware of this, Christians today should feel awkward trying to shape how our tradition is presented in the fellow communities. But we can move toward a more constructive situation by frankly acknowledging and atoning for wrongs we've committed and by teaching more fully and fairly about the other in our communities.

As we suggest to the other how they might teach about us, Christians will have some concerns about how the teaching is presented. Perhaps the major concern is simply about accuracy; they will want such teaching to present, as Professor Elias did, some of the nuance of the overall Christian approach and its subsidiary traditions. Catholics will want such teaching not to reduce its ethics to a rule-based approach, not to focus only on sins and vices, but on its rich preoccupation with virtue and moral/spiritual development; and they will want such presentations not to misstate how the authoritative process works in Catholicism, not to overstate the role of the hierarchy. Protestants will want such teaching by the other not to overstate the role of the individual, as if every Protestant simply makes up his or her own mind after reading the Bible. The Orthodox, I would surmise, will want such teaching, including that by other Christians, to take more account of their contributions. Christians together will want such teaching not to neglect that the deepest foundation of its ethics lie in a belief that the compassion of God was communicated incarnately in Jesus Christ. Though this claim carries us into a realm of profound theological disagreement, it also reminds us that the ethics of all three traditions are unabashedly theocentric.

ASAD HUSAIN
MOHAMMAD A. SIDDIQI

What Do We Want the Other to Teach About the Islamic Ethical Traditions?

Prayer

(Moses) Said: My Lord! Open for me my chest (grant me self-confidence, contentment, and boldness). And ease my task for me. And loose a knot (the defect) from my tongue.
That they may understand my speech. (*Al-Qur'an*, 20:25–28)

Introduction

The word "ethics" is derived from the Greek word *"ethos"* which means habit or customs. The word "morals" is derived from the Latin word *"moralis"* which means mores or customs (Zaroug, 1999). Ethics, according to *The Oxford American Desk Dictionary* (2001) means a system of morals. In secular worldviews ethics is separated from morals and linked to professional standards. Textbooks in most social science disciplines include a chapter on ethics emphasizing upon professional standard of conduct agreed upon by professionals themselves and approved by a professional body representing a particular profession. For example, in journalism or public relations, ethical standards are established by the Society of Professional Journalists or the Public Relations Society of America. In contrast to the above, different religious traditions link ethics with morality based on divine guidance derived in many cases from scriptures. Islamic ethical traditions are deeply rooted in

Qur'an and the *Sunnah* or the traditions of Prophet Muhammad. Islamic spirituality and morality are the foundations of human action and thoughts. The enduring ethical principles of Islam are at the heart of all human endeavors.

Ethics in Islam: Values and Principles
Guiding the Human Conduct Pertaining to all Walks of Life
and Carried Out in Full Consciousness of God

In this discourse we will discuss the following themes/concepts to illustrate various aspects of Islamic ethical traditions.
   a. Sources of inspiration or authority for Islamic ethical traditions.
   b. Salient features of Islamic ethics.
   c. Prophet Muhammad's exemplary life as the ideal for promoting and practicing Islamic ethics.
   d. The importance, meanings, and understanding of ethics for individual Muslim and the Islamic community.
   e. The primary ways Muslims have taught and communicated about Islamic ethics.
   f. Ethics and interreligious relations.
The first three topics will be dealt with in somewhat detailed manner and the later three will be discussed more briefly for these are topics that require detailed treatment in a separate paper.

Sources of inspiration or authority for Islamic ethical traditions

The two primary sources for understanding Islamic ethical traditions are indeed the *Qur'an* and the *Sunnah* because both attach great importance to ethics. The *Qur'an* and the *Sunnah* contain the broad principles needed to negotiate the problems that arise in human societies in different ages (Al-Kayasi, 1992). The *Qur'an* emphasizes the ethical dimensions of sending Prophet Muhammad by declaring: "And we have sent you (0, Muhammad) not but as a mercy to all creatures" (21:107). The *Qur'an* also states: "And the Word of your Lord has been fulfilled in truth and in Justice." (6:115).

In the *Qur'an*, as Ansari (1989) points out, God and the hereafter are not merely postulates of morality as Kant had thought; they determine very much the meaning and content of ethical concepts and values. The famous tradition narrated by the Prophet Muhammad's wife, Ayesha, is a strong testimonial that Islamic ethical traditions are first and foremost rooted in the *Qur'an*. When asked about the morals and manners of the Prophet, Ayesha replied, "His morals are nothing but *Qur'an*." The Prophet Muhammad himself described the purpose of his prophethood in these words, "I have been sent so that I can perfect the morals." In chapter 91, verses 9 and 10, the *Qur'an* clearly points out that "Indeed one who purifies himself/herself (by following God's command) is the one who is successful and the one who corrupts it (his or her soul by disobeying God) is the one who miserably fails." (91:9–10)

The roots of Islamic ethics, as Esposito (1988) has observed, is in the implementation of God's will as ordained in *Qur'an*: "It is God who has made you (His) agents, inheritors of the earth. . . ." (6:165) Thus, as representatives of God, one can not but fulfill the mission for which God has created human beings; and this can be realized by adopting to the moral and ethical worldview and system that the *Qur'an* offers and that the Prophet Muhammad fulfilled and exemplified in his life. In numerous verses the *Qur'an* provides definitive status to Prophet Muhammad as the route through which one can attain God's love and mercy. For example, the *Qur'an* clearly says, "Say (0, Muhammad) if you really love Allah then follow me" (3:31); and "But no, by your Lord, they can have no faith until they make you (Muhammad) judge in all disputes that they have. . . ." (4:65); and "He who obeys the messenger (Muhammad) has indeed obeyed God" (4:80). Thus, it is clear that the two primary sources of formulating Islamic ethical codes are the *Qur'an* and the *Sunnah*. However, many Islamic scholars have pointed out that in order to understand the full scope of the Islamic ethical traditions one has to look into some of the secondary sources as well.

Among the other sources of Islamic ethical traditions are the lives and examples set by the companions of the Prophet, especially the first four caliphs known as the rightly guided caliphs, namely, Abu Bakr, Omer, Othman, and Ali. These companions were the purest, after the Prophet, and they made sincere efforts to excel in the Islamic ethical traditions. They, as Ansari (1989, p.82) points out, "were trained by the prophet himself, and their lives as individuals and as a society are the best embodiment of Islamic ethical traditions."

Last, but not the least, two other sources of inspiration and directions to formulate Islamic ethics are the sources of Islamic *Shariah* or the Islamic law. These two sources are *Ijma*, or the consensus of the scholars on issues that have no direct mention in the *Qur'an*, and the *Sunnah* and *Qiyas*, or analogical reasoning done by a process known as *ijtihad*, which means an effort made by a qualified scholar or body of scholars to formulate a guideline to deal with a new issue or situation. These sources of authority and inspiration provide a dynamic process for both the formulation as well as the preservation of Islamic ethical traditions in all the areas of ethical discourse: descriptive, normative, and metaethics.

Salient Features of Islamic Ethics

1.Islamic ethics is universal, divine and permanent

The basic elements of Islamic ethics are neither a product of a particular culture, nor they are limited to a particular time and space. As mentioned in verse 107, Chapter 21 (quoted above), the Prophet Muhammad was sent as mercy to all creatures, and not to Arabs of his time or to Muslims alone. God of Muslims is the same God who created all human beings regardless of their religion, race, or nationality (*Qur'an*, 1:1, 3:1, 6:159, 6:165, 7:158, 13:16–18, 49:13, 57:25, among other numerous verses). The ethical conduct that Islam considers good for Muslims is in fact, good for all human beings. Truth, honesty, equality (spiritual as well as social), freedom, dignity and sanctity of human life, love, humility, sharing and giving, patience, fairness, balance, commitment and integrity, cleanliness and purity (both physical and spiritual) are some of the core values that are essential components of Islamic ethical traditions. The Prophet Muhammad once said that, "Those who were good human beings before coming to Islam are the one who are good after becoming Muslim." This saying of the Prophet recognizes the basic values of goodness among human beings.

In a beautiful verse (24:35) God describes himself as the "Light of the heavens and the earth," from whom originates all the goodness that enlightens and inspires the entire world. One of the unique features of the Islamic values is that it is based on eternal inspirations from God. These values, enshrined in the Islamic ethical traditions, guide and beautify human conduct and social structures, rather than being influenced by the changes in cultures and civilizations. The concept of monotheism brings a universal vision and encourages people to look at humanity as one human race and treat people with love and respect.

2. Islamic ethics is comprehensive

The ethical traditions of Islam aim at both individual as well as societal transformation. It covers personal virtues and also guides on how to establish good societies and better families. Family occupies a central place in the Islamic ethical traditions. Family is considered as the strongest component of a healthy and stable society. The Prophet Muhammad emphasized the significance of marriage by saying, "Marriage is my *Sunnah.*" The *Qur'an* describes the relationship between husband and wife as the two garments that protect each other and provide comfort and peace to both (2:187). A number of *Qur'anic* verses ordain rules and regulations concerning family life and family relations including marriage, divorce, inheritance, roles, obligations, and the duties and rights of each other in the institution of family. In the life of the Prophet Muhammad, says Yahya Emenck (2002, p.234), "Ample opportunity existed for people to see how a prophet coexisted with his family."

The comprehensive nature of Islamic ethics is also evident from the strong foundations of ethics in the Islamic faith. Strong commitment and reaffirmation to faith is a binding force that enriches the Islamic ethical traditions. Obligatory prayer and laziness in prayers is directly linked with being heartless, being unkind, and being uncharitable. The *Qur'an* aptly illustrates this in Chapter 107:

> Have you seen the one who denies the Recompense?
> That is the one who repulses the orphan.
> And urges not on the feeding of the poor.
> So woe unto those performers of prayers.
> Those who delay their prayers from its stated times.
> Those who do good deeds only to show to people.
> And prevent even the small acts of kindness.

Amartya Sen, a leading scholar of economics, has strongly argued, among numerous others, in favor of an ethics-based economic system. Zaroug (1999, p.49), while analyzing Sen's arguments, notes that, "Economics, as it has emerged, can be made more productive by paying greater and more explicit attention to the ethical considerations that shape human behavior and judgment." Islam encourages charity and helping the needy and the poor. One of the basic principles guiding the ethical conduct of wealthy people, as Qutb (1972) has noted, is that "wealth should not remain confined in only fewer and fewer hands, instead it should flow from rich to the poor as *Qur'an* clearly instructs: It (wealth) may not become a fortune confined among the wealthiest among you" (59:7). As such, there is no compartmentalization of ethics in Islam. Human behavior in every walk of life is governed by it.

3. Positive and practical nature of Islamic ethics

As creator, God has enjoined upon us to fully enjoy the richness and comfort of this life. God says in the Qur'an, "But seek, with that (wealth) which God has bestowed on you, the home of the hereafter, and do not forget your portion of lawful enjoyment in this world" (28:77). Islamic ethical traditions, observes Siddiqi (1997), "are not ascetic, monastic, morbid, or moribund in nature." It wants people to be free, happy, optimistic and forward-looking.

Another major characteristic of Islamic ethical traditions is its practicality. It is neither difficult nor beyond the reach of people. The *Qur'an* emphasizes the practicality of Islamic ethical traditions by pointing that "God does not burden a person beyond his/her capacity" (2:286). The Prophet Muhammad repeatedly reminded his companions that God has made Islam easy for people; so do not make it difficult for them.

4. Islamic ethical traditions are free of double standards

Islamic ethical norms are the same for all class of people. Rich and poor, rulers and the ruled, and men and women are all governed by the same standards of moral and conduct. What is forbidden is forbidden for all and what is permissible is permissible for all. Islam, for example, while emphasizing the notion of "justice for all" reminds Muslims:

O believers! Stand out firmly for God as just witness;
And let not the enmity and hatred of others make you avoid justice;
Be just: That is nearer to piety; And fear God.
Verily, God is well acquainted with what you do. (*Qur'an*, 5:8)

The *Qur'an* makes it very clear that God does not like people who pretend to say what they do not practice (61: 2–3). Hypocrisy is the most sinful act after polytheism in Islam. Also, Islam is against force and coercion in religion (2:256; 10:99). Human freedom is granted by God and is one of the most valuable assets of an individual. However, once a person discovers Islam or realizes his/her faith to be Islam, Islam invites him/her to become fully committed (2: 208).

5. Islamic ethical traditions are progressive and dynamic

Islamic ethical conduct is, first and foremost, based on God consciousness or *Taqwa*. According to the *Qur'an* and *Sunnah*, there are four stages of Islamic ethical conduct: Faith (*Ima'n*); Submission (*Islam*); God consciousness (*Taqwa*); and the exalted goodness (*Ehsan*). As a person enters the faith, he/she consciously starts a journey toward excellence in ethical conduct. This journey progress through these four steps that are built upon one another in the above sequence. Without faith, there is no question of belief and submission, and without submission there can be no conscious realization of the will of God and hence no piety; and without piety there is no attainment of the excellence in ethical conduct. In order to fully understand the dynamism of the Islamic ethical traditions, one has to understand that faith is the first step, which begins with a simple declaration that "There is no God but one God, and Muhammad is his messenger." With this declaration the legal requirements of faith are fulfilled but the moral obligations of faith are beginning to provoke a truer understanding of and greater commitment to Islam. The five pillars of Islam, namely, 1) *Shahadah* or witness that God is one and Muhammad is God's messenger, 2) five daily obligatory prayers, 3) fasting during Ramadan, 4) giving to the poor, and 5) pilgrimage to the House of God in Makkah at least once in a lifetime, provide a vast area of Islamic practices that become less and less ritualistic and more and more an act of life enrichment as one progresses through these four stages.

During the first stage, a person undergoes a conscious mental transformation and becomes a true servant of God, whereas in the second
stage his or her understanding of faith manifests through his/her actions.
The relationship between the two stages, as Moudoodi (1968) has noted,
is that of the seed and the tree. Faith is the seed and Islam is its practical
manifestation. The third stage, *Taqwa*, in fact, brings an order, a system
and enrichment to a Muslim's conduct. The fourth stage is the most qual-
itative attainment of the Islamic ethical traditions, which is guided purely by a true love of God, his messenger, his divine book, his angels, and
everything that he has created including his best creation, human beings.
Thus, a true believer cannot have hatred or animosity to any of God's creation, thereby attaining the most pure and enriched state of Islamic
ethics.

The Prophet Muhammad's Exemplary Life as the Ideal
for Promoting and Practicing Islamic Ethics

The actions, sayings, and teachings of Prophet Muhammad show that
Islam came to illuminate peoples' lives by elevating their conduct
through the practical guidance that the life of the Prophet provided
them. God testifies to this in *Qur'an* by saying: "Indeed! in the Messenger
of God you have the best example to follow; for every person who hopes
(for the meeting with) God, and the Last day and remembers God much."
(33:2 1) The life of the Prophet is the most perfect and vibrant aspect of
the Islamic ethical traditions. The Prophet is the utmost embodiment of
Islam's moral and ethical teachings as noted by the testimony of his wife,
Ayesha, above. Numerous sayings of Prophet Muhammad further clarify
his own emphasis on a high ethical and moral conduct: "The best thing
given to people are excellent moral character" (Tirmizi); "A Muslim with
the best moral character has the perfect faith" (Mishkatul Masabih); and
"On the day of Judgment there will be nothing weightier in the balance
of a Muslim than his/her goodness of character" (Muslim).

The Prophet Muhammad's life as a messenger of God, as a husband,
as a spiritual, political, and military leader, as a head of state, and as an
individual person is glorified by his excellent ethical traditions. It is surprising that in a short span of just 23 years, the Prophet Muhammad was

successful in establishing not only the religion of Islam and an Islamic state in Medina, but he fulfilled the excellence of human conduct in every aspect of human activity. To this, the *Qur'an* testifies in these words, "This day I have perfected your religion for you, completed my favors upon you and have chosen for you Islam as your religion." (5:3) In 23 years, the Prophet Muhammad provided the excellence of human conduct in family life, in worshiping God through prescribed acts of worship as well as through voluntary acts of worship, in establishing the rights and duties of neighbors, in detailing the ethics of war and conflict, in outlining the relationship with non-Muslims, in establishing the rules for conflict resolution, in presenting the best qualities of a leader, in providing guidelines for economic and business transactions, political discourse and statehood, and in developing an ethics not only for Muslims but perhaps a charter of human rights when he delivered his speech during his last farewell pilgrimage to Makkah.

It is impossible to even briefly discuss the various aspect of his life in such a short paper, however, a brief portrait of his life is presented here based on numerous authentic traditions narrated by his close companions, his wives, and some of his archenemies.

The Prophet Muhammad was most excellent-mannered, most humble, most soft-spoken, and most philanthropic person. He was the Prophet and the leader; yet he was the first to serve people. He was a commander in chief often found in the front rows of the battlefield. He used to carry the loads of weak people. He was most forgiving even to his staunchest enemies. This was evident on the day he entered victorious in Makkah. He was humble and softhearted. He exchanged ideas with his companions, mixed with them freely and listened and acted upon their suggestions in many instances. He never took personal revenge from any one in his life, never spoke a lie, never accused any one, never uttered an obscene or indecent word, and never humiliated a person in his life. Whenever possible he chose the easy way of doing things and tried to make life easier for others around him. He played with children, took his wives to watch game shows, and always had a smiling face. He never talked without necessity. The world was presented to him with all its allurement and amusements but he was indifferent to extravaganzas and luxurious life. Even when he died, his chosen conditions were humbling and his armor was pledged to a Jew.

Thus, in the life of the Prophet, indeed, is the best manifestation of Islamic ethical traditions. It is worthy of serious attention and study by scholars and common folks alike. The authenticity of the *Sunnah* has been a focus of scrutiny by many in the West as well as in the East; however no serious reader of Prophet's life has ever contradicted the *Qur'anic* assertion that "Indeed in Prophet's life is the best example to follow."

The Importance, Meanings and Understanding of Ethics for Individual Muslims and the Islamic Community

Islamic ethics is at the core of individual growth and development. It is also central for the development and continued progress of an Islamic community. As the saying of the Prophet, quoted earlier, emphasizes that "the better in faith among you is the one who is better in morals," all movements that attempted for Islamic revival gave ethical learning and attainment of higher moral conduct a central place in their agendas and plans. Also, in books of *Hadith*, ethics occupies a central place. Many chapters are devoted to ethics of cleanliness, ethics of neighborly relations, ethics of engagement with non-Muslims, ethics of family discourse, and ethics of economics and politics.

However, given the state of Muslim communities, it seems that the dynamic nature of Islamic ethical traditions and its dynamic relationship with Islamic faith are being lost or ignored. More emphasis is placed on prescriptive and control ethics than on normative and inspirational ethics. Morality at individual level is being emphasized while morality at public and collective level is being ignored. The primary cause of this is the emergence and later prevalence of kingships and elimination of true caliphatehood from earlier Muslim societies to the current kingdoms. Vested interests dictated Islamic discourses and legitimacy was sought by monarchs and kings by ignoring and hiding the true nature of Islamic ethical traditions. Colonialism brought alien thoughts that dominated Muslim minds for centuries. As a result, realism dissipated from Muslim scholars and intellectuals and fantasization of the Islamic glorious past overshadowed any real progress in many walks of Islamic understanding, including that of the ethics and morality. Muslim's understanding of Islam was frozen in history (Sardar, 1985) and Muslim intellectuals and scholars lost confidence about Islam's ability to stand in the marketplace of ideas.

Thus, the Islamic ethical traditions became confined to the Individual and lost its relationship with public and collective spheres. Consequently, the ethical traditions at individual level too became diluted and weak.

The Primary Ways Muslims Have Taught and Communicated About Islamic Ethics

During the days of the Prophet, ethics was not taught through books; it was presented as examples in the real lives of the Prophet and his companions. However, later when the sayings and life of the Prophet were compiled by historians and scholars of Islam, ethical traditions was compiled in the books of *Hadith* and the biographies of the Prophet and his companions. In early literature of Islam, Muslim jurists and scholars did not discuss ethics separately, instead they discussed it under various subtitles such as the chapter of cleanliness, the chapter of family, the chapter of marriage, etc. In these chapters they discussed the standard of conduct as prescribed by the *Qur'an* and the *Sunnah* pertaining to these specific areas. Most earlier works on ethics by Farabi (d. 950 CE), Tusi (d. 1273 CE), and Dawwani (d. 1502 CE) seem to be influenced by the Greek Philosophical scheme of ethics. Explaining the drawbacks of these works, Ansari (1989, p.85) points out that "The real reason why Greek scheme of virtue could not express the entire gamut of Islamic virtues lay deeper in its concept of man. According to it, man was only a rational and moral being. Religion was not a part of his essence, and hence religious virtues could not be treated as a separate class. Muslim philosophers were not able to discern that fact."

Ansari (1989) has critically analyzed various other schools of thought including Sufi writings and notes that only a few scholars such as Shah Waliuallh Dehlawi (d. 1762 CE) have included the religious dimensions as an independent factor primarily influencing the realm of Islamic ethics. Zaroug (1999, p.56) has introduced many contemporary scholars who have published important works on Islamic ethical traditions. These, among others, include Abdullah Draz (1982), Toshihko Izutsu (1966),

Fazlur Rahman (1985), Hourani (1985), Majid Fakhry (1991), Danniel H. Frank (1996), Hossein Nasr (1996), and Rafiq Beekun (1997). These books, as Zaroug (1999) observes, are important in understanding the contemporary Muslims understanding of the ethical traditions of Islam. Some of these discourses are philosophical, some historical and some limited to a specific concern of the author in a particular area of study.

Ethics and Interreligious Relations

The basis for interreligious discourse is founded both in *Qur'an* and in the *Sunnah* of the Prophet. The *Qur'an* advises Muslims in these words: "And do not indulge in disputation with the People of the Book except in a refined way. . . ." (29:46) The *Qur'an* commands Muslims to show respect and reverence to all prophets of God: "Say, we believe in God, and in what has been revealed to Abraham, Ishmael, Isaac, Jacob, and the Tribes, and in what was given to Moses, Jesus, and the prophets from their Lord. We make no distinction between any of them." (3:84) Sayeed (2003, p. ix) notes that the *Qur'an* "commands Muslims to invite the followers of Moses and Jesus to help them identify common grounds and promote cooperation for doing good and preventing harm." Chapter 3:64 makes this explicit point: "Say, O People of the Book! Come to common terms between you and us, that we will worship none but God, that we will not associate partners with Him, that we erect not from ourselves patrons other than God."

It is obvious that beside commonalities, there are differences too. Both the *Qur'an* and the *Sunnah* provide fundamental guidelines to deal with differences. In fact, there is an entire set of ethical guidelines that can be termed as "ethics of disagreement." Faith communities have a moral obligation to actively engage in interreligious discourses on issues such as religious freedom, human dignity, and the disintegration of families, human rights concerns worldwide, poverty, and hunger. To begin with, Muslims, Jews, and Christians can go back to their respective scriptures and find out common ethical grounds to deal with the issues of love, wisdom, God, faith, charity, sin, and the hereafter.

The most common Islamic ethical principles that guide active interreligious relations are love, respect, tolerance, mutual cooperation, freedom, and understanding. These same ethical principles are part of the Christian and the Jewish ethical traditions. Whereas Muslims themselves must strengthen their ethical conduct, and as Nasr (2003, p. 315) has noted, "We must draw ever more from these inner springs of Wisdom." Nasr finds it important to mention that the essence of human worth is in the basic goodness enshrined in all religious traditions. He continues, ". . . the West must seek to understand Islam in the light of these central truths, which are also to be found in Judaism and Christianity, and other religions. . . The heart of Islam is none other than the witnessing to the oneness of the Divine Reality, the universality of truth, the necessity of submission to His Will, the fulfilling of human responsibilities, and respect for the rights of all beings."

Thus, the Islamic ethics of interfaith relations, it can be said, is based on a true love of God, a real concern for the betterment of all people, mutual love and respect, tolerance, a commitment to strive for what is universally good for all people and a struggle against what is essentially bad for every one. This, by no means, is an easy task. It is a challenge to come out of hypocrisy, arrogance, racism, hatred, and to accept the truth that all human beings are in fact, one community and one nation in the service of God. It is not rhetoric. It is, if we may use the term, a real *jihad* to which you all are invited.

References

Abdullah, Aslam. *Morals and manners: An Islamic Perspective* (Adopted and compiled from Muhammad Al-Ghazali's Khuluq al Muslim. Plainfield, Indiana: ISNA, 1997.

Al-Kayasi, Marwan Ibrahim. *Morals and manners in Islam*. New Delhi: Qazi Publications, 1992.

Ansari, Abdul Haq. "Islamic Ethics," *The American Journal of Islamic Social Sciences*, v. 6, Number 1, September, 1989: 81–92.

Beekun, Rafiq. *Islamic Business Ethics*. Herndon, Virginia: International Institute of Islamic Thought, 1997.

Draz, Abdullah. *Dastural-akhlaq II al Qur'an* (translated by al-Sabur Shahyn) Beirut: Muassast al-Risalah, 1982.

Emerick, Yahya. *The Complete Idiot's Guide to Understanding Islam*. Indianapolis, Indiana: Alpha Books, 2002.

Esposito, John L. *Islam: The Straight Path*. New York: Oxford University Press, 1988.

Fakhry, Majid. *Ethical theories in Islam*. Leiden: F. J. Brill, 1991

Frank, Danniel H. "Ethics," in Hossein Nasr and Oliver Leaman (eds.). *History of Islamic Ethics*, part II. New York: Routledge, 1996.

Hourani, George F. *Reason and Tradition in Islamic Ethics*. Cambridge: Cambridge University Press, 1985.

Izutsu, Toshihiko. *Ethico Religious Concepts in the Qur'an*. Montreal: McGill University Press, 1966.

Moudoodi, Abul Ala. *Ethical Foundations of Islamic Movement* (11th reprint, Urdu). Lahore, Pakistan: Islamic Publications, 1968

Nasr, Seyyed Hossein. *The Heart of Islam: Enduring Values for Humanity*. San Francisco: Harper Collins, 2002.

Noble Quran (All translation of *Qur'anic* verses) translated in English by Taqiuddin Al-Hilali and Mohsin Khan. Madinah, Saudi Arabia: King Fahad Complex for Printing of the Holy *Qur'an*, 2001.

Oxford American Desk Dictionary and Thesaurus (2nd ed.). New York: Berkley Books, 2001.

Qutb, Syed. *Social Justice in Islam*. Urdu language translation by Mohammad Nejatullah Siddiqi, Delhi: Markazi Maktaba Islami, 1972.

Rahman, Fazlur. "Law and Ethics in Islam," in Richard G. Hovannisian (ed.). *Ethics in Islam*. Malibu, California: Undena Publications, 1985.

Sardar, Ziauddin. *Islamic Futures: The Shape of Ideas to Come*. London and New York: Mansell, 1985.

Sayeed, Sayyid M. "Foreword," in Joey Green (ed.). *Jesus and Muhammad: The Parallel Sayings*. Berkeley, California: Seastone, 2003.

Sen, Amartya. *On Ethics and Economics*. Oxford: Basil Blackwell, 1990: ix.

Siddiqi, Muzammil. "Introduction," in Aslam Abdullah, op. cit.

Zaroug, Abdullahi Hassan. "Ethics from an Islamic Perspective: Basic Issues," *The American Journal of Islamic Social Sciences*, V. 16, number 3, Fall 1999: 45–63.

PART V ~ WHAT DO WE WANT THE OTHER TO TEACH ABOUT
OUR ETHICAL TRADITIONS?

For Further Discussion and Study

Does each tradition have a notion of conscience or that divine values or virtues are imprinted on the human being as part of being God's creation? If so, what are such values? Are these normative for all people?

What is the function of law in fostering the identity of each religion? Is there a hierarchy of laws or a scale on which laws are based? Is there a propensity in the Abrahamic faiths toward becoming too legalistic and is this tendency related to their being religions that place an emphasis on the study of sacred texts?

Is there a methodology for ethical decision-making that is grounded in the experience of the contemporary world? To what extent have advances in science and medicine influenced ethics and moral behavior for Jews, Christians, and Muslims? How has each religion refashioned new ethical understandings consistent with traditional ethical insights?

What is the proper place and priority for each tradition of action, contemplation, mystical prayer and union with God, or right intention in ethics?

Are there absolute ethical prohibitions in each tradition? If so, what are they?

How does each religious tradition understand legal imperatives found in sacred texts and their relationship (if any) to natural law or contemporary theological study? How do Judaism, Christianity and Islam remain faithful to the literal authority of their scriptures when confronting problem texts that have nefarious ethical implications?

What does each tradition teach about witnessing by one's life to the love of God, thus being a light to the nations? What is the ultimate goal of the moral life of a Jew, Christian, or Muslim?

What are the sources of inspiration or authority for each tradition's ethics? Does the balance and application of sources of ethical decision-making vary between religions? What help and how much weight are the sacred texts given in concrete moral decision-making? Similarly, what is the weight given to tradition, natural law, authority, holy people, and present historical contexts? Is there a general overarching principle for ethical decision-making or is each situation unique and stands on its own merits?

Who has the final authority in each tradition in deciding and disseminating conclusions on the morality of human actions such as personal conduct, the conduct of society/nations, sexual relations, laws, and issues of peace and justice?

How does focused study, contemplation of art, singing, dancing, meditation, teaching, worship, and/or prayer have the power to shape one's moral convictions and behavior?

How does one formally learn about ethics as a child other than from one's parents? What are the ways the values of right and wrong are taught—memorized principles, stories, liturgical experiences, lives of holy people, scriptural texts, others? Is it possible or even desirable to separate the autobiographical and communal religious experiences of a person from his or her ethical decision-making?

For Action in the Community

How does each religion describe the good society? What can believers do to help bring about a just society? Can the language of natural law morality be more effective in influencing public policy debates than religious language?

What are the challenges to traditional religious values posed by contemporary society and how can local efforts on the part of Jews, Christians, and Muslims respond to such threats against religious values? What are the emerging future challenges in collaborative Jewish, Christian, and/or Islamic ethical decision-making?

What justifications do some so-called religious leaders give when they teach tyranny, terrorism, discrimination, or violence? How can such teaching be appropriately confronted and overcome?

Do faith communities have a moral obligation to pursue interreligious dialogue on issues such as religious freedom, human dignity, justice, peace, and human rights? Why, and what can local communities do to promote such conversations?

Is it the right and responsibility of religious leaders to make authoritative decisions on the morality of human actions both for its own members and for the broader society? If so, what are the positive contributions of such efforts toward promoting the common good as well as for the rights and freedoms of individuals? What are possible negative results of such political engagements? How can religious voices appropriately work together with each other and civil leaders to promote the common good?

How does each tradition understand sin or failures of individuals? What are the ways that each tradition facilitates (privately or publicly) reflection, repentance, and reconciliation? Are there opportunities for Jews, Christians, and Muslims to pray together for reconciliation? When and where?

How are religious leaders trained to assist individuals and families making difficult ethical choices? How can synagogues, parishes, and mosques assist their members in promoting religious values and principles of ethical decision-making?

What are the ways that Jews, Christians, and Muslims can organize communal learning around ethical issues and topics? What are some resources, curricula, bibliographies, commentaries and study guides for individuals or groups to use when wrestling with contemporary ethical issues?

Can members from each religious tradition sponsor lectures and educational programs in the community on important ethical issues? Can the results of these lectures or educational programs be published and distributed through a local newspaper or other means?

APPENDIX A

Suggestions for Further Reading
What Do We Want the Other to Teach About Us?

Happily, there is a wealth of resources on Judaism, Christianity, and Islam, both in print and on the World Wide Web. To the students and teachers who wish to continue learning about the Abrahamic faiths in dialogue, these sources will be helpful but certainly not exhaustive. They were chosen because of their continued interest to both university students and religious educators. See also Appendix B for web resources on interreligious issues.

Allen, R., & Williamson, C. (1989). *Interpreting Difficult Texts: Anti-Judaism and Christian Preaching*. Philadelphia: Trinity Press International.

Baker, B. (1998). *More in Common Than You Think: The Bridge Between Islam and Christianity*. New York: Defenders Publications.

Bewley, A. (1998). *A Glossary of Islamic Terms*. London: Ta-Ha Publishers.

Bickerman, E. (1988). *The Jews in the Greek Age*. Cambridge: Harvard University Press.

Bishops' Committee for Ecumenical and Interreligious Affairs, United States Conference of Catholic Bishops. (2004). *The Bible, the Jews, and the Death of Jesus: A Collection of Catholic Documents*. Washington, DC: USCCB Press.

Bogle, E. (1998). *Islam: Origin and Belief*. Austin, TX: University of Texas Press.

Boys, M. C. (2000). *Has God Only One Blessing?* Mahwah, NJ: Paulist.

Braybrooke, M. (1990). *Time to Meet: Towards a Deeper Relationship Between Jews and Christians*. Philadelphia: Trinity Press International.

Braybrooke, M. (2000). *Christian-Jewish Dialogue: The Next Steps.* London: SCM Press.

Burrell, D. (1986). *Knowing the Unknowable God: Ibn-Sina, Maimonides, Aquinas.* Notre Dame, IN: University of Notre Dame Press.

Cernera, A. J. (1995). *Toward Greater Understanding.* Fairfield, CT: Sacred Heart University Press.

Charlesworth, J. (Ed.). (1992). *Overcoming Fear Between Jews and Christians.* New York: Crossroad.

Cohn, S. (1991). *A Dictionary of Judaism and Christianity.* Philadelphia: Trinity Press International.

Cook, M. (2003). *Justice, Jesus and the Jews: A Proposal for Jewish-Christian Relations.* Collegeville, MN: Liturgical Press.

Coppola, D. (Ed.). (1999). *With My Last Breath: Let Me See Jerusalem.* Fairfield, CT: Sacred Heart University Press.

Coppola, D. (Ed.). (2004). *Religion, Violence and Peace: Continuing Conversations and Study Guide.* Fairfield, CT: Sacred Heart University Press.

Cunningham, P. (2001). *A Story of Shalom: The Calling of Christians and Jews by a Covenanting God.* Mahway, NJ: Paulist Press.

Dirks, J. F. (2001). *The Cross and the Crescent.* Beltsville, MD: Amana Publications.

Dirks, J. F. (2002). *Abraham: The Friend of God.* Beltsville, MD: Amana Publications.

Dirks, J. F. (2004). *The Abrahamic Faiths: Judaism, Christianity and Islam, Similarities and Contrasts.* Beltsville, MD: Amana Publications.

Dunn, J. (Ed.). (1999). *Jews and Christians: The Parting of the Ways: A.D. 70 to 135.* Grand Rapids, MI: Eerdmans Publishing.

Duran, K., & Hechiche, A. (2001). *Children of Abraham: An Introduction to Islam for Jews.* Hoboken, NJ: Ktav Publishing.

Egan, E. (1999). *Peace Be With You: Justified Warfare or the Way of Nonviolence.* Maryknoll: Orbis.

Ehrenkranz, J., & Coppola, D. (Eds.). (2000). *Religion and Violence, Religion and Peace.* Fairfield, CT: Sacred Heart University Press.

Ellis, M. (1997). *Unholy Alliance: Religion and Atrocity in Our Time.* Minneapolis: Fortress.

Feiler, B. (2004). *Abraham: A Journey to the Heart of Three Faiths.* New York: Perennial.

Firestone, F. (2001). *Children of Abraham: An Introduction to Judaism for Muslims.* Hoboken, NJ: Ktav Publishing.

Fisher, E. J. (Ed.). (1993). *Interwoven Destinies: Jews and Christians Throughout the Ages.* New York: Paulist Press.

Fisher, E. J., & Klenicki, L. (Eds.). (1995). *Spiritual Pilgrimage: Texts on Jews and Judaism 1979-1995.* New York: Crossroad.

Frymer-Kensky, T., Novak, D., Ochs, P. Sandmel, D., & Singer, M. (2000). *Christianity in Jewish Terms.* Boulder, CO: Westview Press.

Girard, R. (1979). *Violence and the Sacred.* Trans. P. Gregory. Baltimore, MD: Johns Hopkins University Press.

Girard, R. (1986). *The Scapegoat.* Trans. Y. Freccero. Baltimore, MD: Johns Hopkins University Press.

Gopin, M. (2002). *Holy War, Holy Peace: How Religion Can Bring Peace to the Middle East.* New York: Oxford University Press.

Green, J. (2003). *Jesus and Muhammad: The Parallel Sayings.* Berkeley, CA: Seastone Press.

Greenberg, I. (2004). *For the Sake of Heaven and Earth: The New Encounter Between Judaism and Christianity.* Philadelphia: Jewish Publication Society.

Hill, C. (1992). Hellenists and Hebrews: *Reappraising Division Within the Early Church.* Minneapolis: Fortress Press.

Hughes, T. (1994). *Dictionary of Islam.* Chicago, IL: Kazi Publications.

John XXIII. (1963). *Pacem in terris.* [Peace on earth]. 11 April 1963. Acta Apostolica Sedis.

Kessler, E. (2005). *Dictionary of Jewish-Christian Relations.* Cambridge: Cambridge University Press

Kuschel, K. (1995). *Abraham: Sign of Hope for Jews, Christians and Muslims.* New York: Continuum.

Laistner, M. L. (1951). *Christianity and Pagan Culture in the Later Roman Empire.* Ithaca, NY: Cornell University Press.

Marty, M., & Appleby, R. S. (1991). *Fundamentalisms Observed.* Chicago: University of Chicago Press.

Mendes-Flohr, Paul. (Ed.). (1983). *A Land of Two Peoples, Martin Buber on Jews and Arabs.* Oxford: Oxford University Press.

Meyers, E. M., & Strange, J. (1981). *Archaeology, Rabbis and Early Christianity.* Nashville, TN: Abingdon Press.

Miller, R., & Bernstein, L. (2006). *Healing the Jewish-Christian Rift: Growing Beyond our Wounded History.* Woodstock, VT: Skylight Paths Publishing.

Momigliano, A. (1987). *On Pagans, Jews, and Christians.* Middletown, CT: Wesleyan University Press.

Neusner, J. (1991). *Judaism in the Matrix of Christianity*. Atlanta, GA: Scholars Press.

Neusner, J., Chilton, B., & Graham, W. (2002). *Three Faiths, One God: The Formative Faith and Practice of Judaism, Christianity, and Islam*. Boston: Brill Academic Publishers.

Neusner, J., & Sonn, T. (2000). *Comparing Religions Through Law*. London: Routledge.

Novak, D. (1983). *The Image of the Non-Jew in Judaism: An Historical and Constructive Study of the Noahide Laws*. Lewiston: Mellen.

Pawlikowski, J. (1989). *Jesus and the Theology of Israel*. Wilmington, DE: Michael Glazier.

Peters, F. E. (1982). *Children of Abraham: Judaism, Christianity, Islam*. Princeton, New Jersey: Princeton University Press.

Polner, M., & Goodman, N. (Eds.). (1994). *The Challenge of Shalom: The Jewish Tradition of Peace and Justice*. New York: New Society Publishers and Jewish Peace Fellowship.

Rahner, K., & Lapide, P. (1987). *Encountering Jesus—Encountering Judaism: A Dialogue*. New York: Crossroad.

Randall, A. (1998). *Theologies of War and Peace Among Jews, Christians and Muslims*. New York: Edwin Mellen Press.

Sanders, E. P. (1985). *Paul and Palestinian Judaism and Jesus and Judaism*. London: SCM Press.

Sandmel, D., Catalano, R., & Leighton, C. (2001). *Irreconcilable Differences? A Learning Resource for Jews and Christians*. Boulder, CO: Westview Press.

Sandmel, S. (2004). *A Jewish Understanding of the New Testament*. Woodstock, VT: Skylight Paths Publishing.

Schiffman, L. (1994). *Reclaiming the Dead Sea Scrolls: The History of Judaism, the Background of Christianity, the Lost Library of Qumran*. Philadelphia: Jewish Publication Society.

Segal, A. F. (1986). *Rebecca's Children: Judaism and Christianity in the Roman World*. Cambridge: Harvard University Press.

Shanks, H. (Ed.). (1992). *Christianity and Rabbinic Judaism: A Parallel History of Their Origins and Early Development*. Washington, D.C.: Biblical Archaeology Society.

Steffen, L. (2003). *The Demonic Turn: The Power of Religion to Inspire or Restrain Violence*. Cleveland: Pilgrim.

Swidler, L. (Ed.). (1992). *Muslims in Dialogue: The Evolution of a Dialogue*. Lewiston, NY: Edwin Mellen Press.

Swidler, L. (1999). *For All Life: Toward a Universal Declaration of a Global Ethic, An Interreligious Dialogue*. Ashland, OR: White Cloud Press.

Swidler, L., Eron, L. J., Sloyan, G., & Dean, L. (1990). *Bursting the Bonds? A Jewish–Christian Dialogue on Jesus and Paul*. Maryknoll, NY: Orbis.

Telushkin, J. (1991). *Jewish Literacy: The Most Important Things to Know about the Jewish Religion, Its People, and Its History*. New York: William Morrow and Co.

Ucko, H. (Ed.). (1997). *The Jubilee Challenge: Utopia or Possibility? Jewish and Christian Insights*. Geneva: World Council of Churches Publications.

United States Conference of Catholic Bishops. (1983). *The Challenge of Peace: God's Promise and Our Response*. Washington, DC: USCCB Press.

United States Conference of Catholic Bishops. (1998). *Catholics Remember the Holocaust*. Washington, DC: USCCB Press.

Urbach, E. E. (1979). *The Sages: Their Concepts and Beliefs*. 2 vols. Jerusalem: Magnes. van Beeck, F. J. (1989). Loving the Torah More Than God?— Toward a Catholic Appreciation of Judaism. Chicago: Loyola University Press.

Weiss, H. D. (1986). *Midrash, Mishnah, and Gemara: The Jewish Predilection for Justified Law*. Cambridge: Harvard University Press.

Wilcock, E. (1994). *Pacifism and the Jews*. New York: Hawthorn.

Wilson, M. R. (1989). *Our Father Abraham: Jewish Roots of the Christian Faith*. Grand Rapids, MI: William B. Eerdmans Publishing Company.

Yoder, J. (1984). *When War is Unjust: Being Honest in Just-War Thinking*. Minneapolis, MN: Augsburg Publishing House.

Websites Concerned with Interreligious Understanding and Dialogue

Center for Christian-Jewish Understanding of Sacred Heart University
www.ccju.org

Common Ground Global Initiative Interreligious Engagement Project
http://cg.org/cgis.asp

Council of Centers on Christian-Jewish Relations
www.ccjr.us

The Elijah Interfaith Institute
http://www.elijah.org.il/

Global Ethic Foundation
www.global-ethic.org

Islamic Studies: Internet Curricular Resources (Academic Organizations)
http://www.unc.edu/depts/islamweb/organizations.html

JCRelations: Insights and Issues in the Ongoing Jewish-Christian Dialogue
www.jcrelations.net

The Macdonald Center for the Study of Islam and Christian-Muslim Relations
http://macdonald.hartsem.edu/

Marywood University: Tools for Prophets in the Information Age
http://ac.marywood.edu/skb/prophets/resource2.html

The Near East Collection at Yale University
http://www.library.yale.edu/Internet/neareastern.html

PBS Religion and Ethics
http://www.pbs.org/wnet/religionandethics/

Religion and Intellectual Life Association (ARIL)
http://www.aril.org/World.html

SIDIC: International Jewish and Christian Documentation Service
www.sidic.org

Yad Vashem: The Holocaust Martyrs' and Heroes' Remembrance Authority
www.yad-vashem.org

INDEX

Index ✥ *419*

Neusner, Jacob, 65, 161, 364
Niebuhr, H. Richard, 368, 369
Niebuhr, Reinhold, 369–371, 377
Noachide Precepts, 154
normativity, 65–68
Nostra Aetate, xiii–xiv, 4–5, 10, 33, 93
Nuri, Abu'l Hassan, 310

O'Connor, John, 347
Okumenischer Taschenbuchkommentar
    series, 206
The Orthodox Church, 372
Orthodox Jews, 146, 333
Otto-Friedrich University, 126
Ottoman Empire, 141

Pacem in Terris, 39–40, 41, 377
Paisley, Ian, 181
Palazzi, Abdul Hadi, 249
Palestine, 37, 60, 135, 146–147, 153, 331
Palliser, Margaret, 285
Passover Haggada, 67
Paul VI, 169, 176, 181
peace, 36–41
Pentateuchal narrative, 134
Percy, Walter, 374
Peter the Venerable, 92
phronema, 373
pilgrimage, 256–257
Pius XII, 185
pluralism, 198–199, 237–240, 361
Pontifical Council for Interreligious
    Dialogue, 35–36
pope, authority of, 196–197
prayer and liturgy, 253–258
    Catholic perspective, 279–284
    Christian perspective, 285–295
    Jewish perspective, 259–278
    Islamic perspective, 297–315
Protestant-Jewish dialogue, 209–226
Psalms, 90, 257, 265, 282

Qiyas, 394
Qumran sectarians, 65
Qur'an, 84, 85, 86, 92, 232–234, 237–240, 298, 314, 392–394, 397–400, 401, 402
Qushayri, Iman, 309

Rabbinic Judaism, 130–131, 136, 144–145, 266
Rabin, Leah, 48
Rabin, Yitzhak, 48, 181
Rahman, Fazlur, 402
Rahner, Karl, 93–94, 185, 190
Rakospalota, Budapest, 153
RaMBa'M. *See* Maimonides, Moses
Ratisbonne Papal Institute, 47, 57
Rauschenbusch, Walter, 369
redemption, 268–269
Reformation, 184, 190
Reform Jews, 145
Reform Judaism/Reform Synagogues of
    Great Britain, 10
Religion and Violence, Religion and Peace, 329
*Religion, Violence, and Peace: Continuing
    Conversations and Study Guide*, 329
Rescuer from Error (Ghazzali), 309
Revelation, pastoral process of, 183–201
Roche, Douglas, 114
Rosenzweig, Franz, 267
Rossing, Daniel, 6, 47
Ruether, Rosemary, 218
Rumi, 310, 313

Sa'adia Gaon, 337
Sabbatean movement, 66
Sacks, Jonathan, 7, 8–9
sacraments, 291
Sacred Heart University, xiii, 5, 10, 38, 47, 114, 117, 151, 249, 323, 347, 351
sacred space of dialogue, 3–12
St. Augustine, 87, 91, 190, 290, 353, 377–378
St. Basil, 374
St. Bernard, 377
St. John, 83–84, 90, 172
St. Matthew, 89
St. Paul, 34, 82, 89, 172, 189, 192, 219–222, 223, 359–360
St. Peter, 203
Sambi, Pietro, 47, 48
Sander, Hans-Joachim, 183
Sandmel, David Fox, 383
Sanheriv, King, 339
Sarsur, Ibrahim, 47
Scholasticism, 185, 190
Scholem, Gerschom, 74